THE WVU COED
MURDERS

THE WVU COED
MURDERS

WHO KILLED MARED AND KAREN?

GEOFFREY C. FULLER
& S. JAMES McLAUGHLIN

THE
History
PRESS

Published by The History Press
Charleston, SC
www.historypress.com

Copyright © 2021 by Hawk Mulch, LLC
All rights reserved

First published 2021

Manufactured in the United States

ISBN 9781467146166

Library of Congress Control Number 2021943434

Notice: The information in this book is true and complete to the best of our knowledge. It is offered without guarantee on the part of the authors or The History Press. The authors and The History Press disclaim all liability in connection with the use of this book.

GEOFF

To my father, Winston Fuller, my first and best writing teacher, and my stepmother Louise Lamar-Fuller, whose recent passing left the world a darker place. I love and thank you both.

SARAH

To my husband, Eric: Thank you for the encouragement, the emotional and mental support and never getting sick of the same topic.

To J. Kendall Perkinson: The work that you've put into this story helped us reach more people who wanted a voice in it. Your contribution to this project is invaluable, thank you.

And also to Greg Carte and Sydney Pringle, for their never-ending support and obsessive promotion: Thank you both for everything.

Lastly, to my coauthor, Geoff: Your kind guidance, patience and unwavering determination have been the backbone of this book. Thank you.

AUTHORS' NOTE

The full story of the coed murders is reconstructed from newspaper coverage, police reports, court records, WVU records and extensive interviews with reporters, police, WVU personnel and students and other people who were there. The story that unfolds covers fifty years, from 1970 to the present. Much of the information was corroborated by multiple sources. When only a single source was available—a single police report, one newspaper article or an author interview with a single person—the story is told in present tense, as a scene. The settings, circumstances and topics discussed in these scenes mirror the source material, although some of the details and all of the specific quotations are author invention.

If you have information that clarifies, expands or contradicts our research, please let us know. We have tried to present the most authoritative case possible, but a fifty-year-old tragedy presents its difficulties. We may have inadvertently included erroneous information. Help us correct that.

You can reach us 24/7 at coedmurders.com. There, you can also sign up for our bonus newsletters, which keep you up to date on new developments in the case and offer you glimpses of investigative dead ends and scenes we had to cut from the book due to lack of space.

CONTENTS

Acknowledgements   13
Reader Guide   15
Introduction: Mared and Karen   23

I. WHAT REMAINS
  Preface: *West Virginia is rough country.*   33
  1. "I like to rub furry things."   38
  2. "It's just unbelievable that this could happen
     in Morgantown."   42
  3. "Don't leave me in this room by myself."   46
  4. "We're thumbing."   52
  5. "No evidence of abduction."   57
  6. "Apparently disappearance was run away type."   63
  7. "The heart of a woman aches for the things she loves."   66
  8. "Hey, I found something!"   70
  9. "Girls shouldn't hitchhike."   74
  10. "Some considered alcohol."   79
  11. "Heard you were looking for me."   86
  12. "Something's been dead for too long."   92
  13. "Down the holler there."   99

II. THE PARADE OF HORRIBLES

Preface: "Very strange, very violent, very nasty people."   109
1. "Maybe a hatchet?"   110
2. "I want a fucking press conference!"   117
3. "A white male, 6', blue eyes, brown hair, 197 lbs."   119
4. "More heads will roll!"   124
5. "There is no need to cover news."   128
6. "He was a crusading journalist."   132
7. "Aren't you afraid of getting into a stranger's car?"   136
8. "Why did Rowe see a green car?"   142
9. "Someone emotionally disturbed wrote the letters."   148
10. "Ridicule could trigger further violent reactions."   154
11. "I have seen him lose his temper to a very strong degree."   158
12. "I think he's a good suspect."   164
13. "Put him down."   168
14. "We are religious people here."   173
15. "Kill the pigs!"   178
16. "Former Fairmont man quizzed in decapitation."   182
17. "Whatever happened to the probe of the coed case?"   187

III. SO MUCH SMOKE

1. "The confession itself should be punished."   197
2. "I met one Eugene Paul Clawson."   206
3. "Clawson really, really tried hard to convince people he did it."   212
4. "Take your trash."   218
5. "He cannot stand up to pushy, authoritative or powerful people."   224
6. "It was in some woods, remote."   233
7. "It seemed like a ritualistic murder."   237

IV. HUNTING

Preface: "Remember that house."   247
1. "We called it the Shade Effect."   250
2. "I still think Costanes did it."   256
3. "He set some fires."   264
4. "May be."   270
5. "Skull's the hardest part."   277
6. "One of America's first serial killers."   280

CONTENTS

7. "Getting their drink on."   285
8. "Bill was as crazy as they get."   291
9. *Whoever Fights Monsters*   296
10. "The investigation's over."   299
11. *The Vampire Next Door*   304
12. "Someone was writing *my* book."   310
13. "Broken dolls."   314
14. "Women in Morgantown were still vulnerable."   318
15. "These guys were violent and abusive."   324
16. "Some kind of forest coven?"   329
17. "They should know."   334
18. "Protection from anything."   338
19. "The Ferrell girl probably would have froze."   343
20. "I can't believe it leads to someone."   347
21. "Danny ran the jackets for DNA."   350
22. "She reached up and she grabbed John by the throat."   355
23. "Very sinister and very dark."   360
24. "The murders looked ritualistic, scripted."   365
25. "He either killed someone or robbed a bank."   370
26. "A white car and a boot."   376
27. "I was convinced."   382
Epilogue: "It's never too late to uncover the truth."   388

Interviewees   401
Index   405
About the Authors   411

ACKNOWLEDGEMENTS

We are thankful to many people who helped over the years. Without their invaluable assistance, the stories in this book would be far less complete.

Valena Beety
Alexis Berry
Nancy Burkhammer
Patrick Buzzini
George Castelle
Russell Clawges
Mark Crabtree
Jim Elkins
Ray Evans
Kathie Forman
Karin Fuller
Maureen Glass
Candace Jordan
Carl Kimble
John Kimble

Ressie Kimble
Eric McLaughlin
Lawrence C. Messina
Margie Miller
Mary Mullett
Holly Naylor
Dimas "Ponch" Reyes
Ron Rittenhouse
Brad Stalnaker
Stephanie Thompson
Celeste Vingle
Jacque Weiss
Jim Wilt
Barb Yingling

Thank you all for everything.

And we want to call attention to the people whose assistance was far beyond what we expected or deserved. Thank you for making yourselves available when there was no reason for you to be, for pitching in where there was no expectation that you would, for not hanging up or cutting us off when there was every fear that you might and for acting as sounding boards to keep us focused and on track. To you, we shout out our great appreciation.

Kelly Ayers
Chris Berry
Nick DeMedici
R. Korshi Dosoo
Bob Leatherow

Freda Moore
J. Kendall Perkinson
Evelyn Ryan
Tyrone Trujillo

READER GUIDE

This complex story involves many people over fifty years. To help the reader keep track of who's who, we list here people who are mentioned more than once and whose identity might not be immediately obvious. In some cases, we had to rely on the spelling of the name given in West Virginia State Police (WVSP) or FBI reports, and in the 1970 reports names were sometimes spelled in more than one way. Lastly, in some cases in *The WVU Coed Murders*, the names have been changed to protect the innocent.

Amma*
Anonymous source convinced that Dale and Jimmy Daft killed Mared and Karen and burned the evidence in a barrel.

Aucremanne, Stephanie
WVU student who said she was interviewed by the FBI.

Bailes, Candace "Candy"
One of two WVU students kidnapped in March 1970.

Berry, Chris
WVSP corporal who helped with the authors' investigations.

Best, Nancy Elizabeth
WVU student and resident of Westchester Hall. Witnessed Karen's illness and her fears.

Blankenship, Maxine
Had unsettling encounter with a young blond man around Thanksgiving 1969.

Bonar, R.L.
Colonel Robert L. Bonar, superintendent of the West Virginia Department of Public Safety (WVSP). Accused of malfeasance on April 23, 1970, by Trooper Gooden.

Bowers, William A.
Monongalia County justice of the peace and county coroner. Speculated to the press about the killer being a madman on LSD.

Burns, Paulette "Itsy"
WVU student and resident of Westchester Hall who was walking with Clarence "Skip" Lewis when they saw Mared and Karen hitchhiking a ride.

Cain, Glen Franklin
WVU student photographed on April 16, 1970, pointing to Mared's and Karen's remains.

Carter, Donald
Psychiatrist with WVU, one of the "profilers" of the author of the Triangle Letters, heavily involved with psychological assessments of Clawson.

Casazza, Lawrence "Larry"
Mared's high school boyfriend. Said by other Westchester residents to have violent tendencies.

Castelle, George
Law clerk who examined all the evidence from Eugene Clawson's 1976 trial for Justice Thomas B. Miller of the West Virginia Supreme Court of Appeals.

Claro, Jeanne
Reported lewd conduct and, according to Stephanie Aucremanne, was interviewed by the FBI.

Clawson, Eugene Paul
Convicted twice for the abduction and decapitations of Mared Malarik and Karen Ferrell.

Cobun, Herbert
Victim of William Bernard Hacker whose headless body was found on the Kimble farm.

Cole, Kenneth "Kenny" Franklin
Resident of the Weirton Mine Section and thought by some to be a Peeping Tom.

Costianes, Elias
Mared's dentist in Morgantown. Briefly suspected by WVSP in 1970 investigation and looked at in more depth by Richard Hall.

Crutchley, John Brennan
Convicted in 1985 of kidnapping and sexual battery of a hitchhiker whom he held captive while he drained and drank her blood and raped her. Investigated for the deaths of as many as thirty other women. Geoff's leading suspect.

Crutchley, Carolynn Adele
Younger sister of John Brennan Crutchley and freshman at WVU in 1970 while she was having an affair with her brother.

Cunningham, R.L.
Trooper Richard L. Cunningham, first WVSP on scene for discovery of Mared and Karen's remains.

Daft, Dale Ralph
Lived in the Weirton Mine Section, often in trouble with the law. Known to pick up hitchhikers with his cousin Jimmy.

Daft, Ivan Russell
Lived in the Weirton Mine Section. Incarcerated at time of the murders.

Daft, Kenneth "Jimmy" James
Lived in the Weirton Mine Section, often in trouble with the law. Known to pick up hitchhikers with his cousin Dale.

DeMedici, Nick
Monongalia County deputy sheriff for nine years and WVSP for three. Assisted authors with their investigations.

DeYoung, Donna
Mared's roommate at Westchester Hall. Contacted FBI and led petition drive that got Governor Moore's attention.

Dosoo, Korshi
Junior team leader of the project "The Coptic Magical Papyri: Vernacular Religion in Late Roman and Early Islamic Egypt" at the Julius Maximilian University of Würzburg. Decoded the copper plate.

Evans, Ray
City desk editor at the *Dominion-News*. Provided authors with newspaper files from 1970.

Ferrell, Richard and Bess
Karen's adoptive parents, who lived in Quinwood, West Virginia.

Friend, Edward
Eugene Paul Clawson defense attorney, 1976 and 1981.

Gerkin, William Ray, III
WVSP suspect due to his odd behavior, violent tendencies, attitude toward women, multiple weapons and a story witnesses said he wrote involving death and dismemberment.

Glass, David L.
Shared cellblock with Clawson. Alleged by Clawson to be one of the authors of his confession.

Gooden, P.B.
Trooper Preston Gooden was one of the early leaders of the WVSP investigation. Fired on April 24, 1971, for whistleblower speech about the coed case.

Hacker, William Bernard, Sr.
Convicted of shooting two people to death at Wright Tavern in 1952 and, after release, of murdering and decapitating Herb Cobun in 1971. Suspected in the 1927 disappearance of his first wife, Opal Anna Toothman.

Hall, R.M.
Lieutenant Colonel Richard Mansfield Hall of the WVSP was convinced Clawson was not guilty and continued to investigate the case until his death.

Harpe, Felton
Jailhouse lawyer who shared cellblock with Clawson. Alleged by Clawson to be one of the authors of his confession.

Hayes, Steve
Karen's navy boyfriend.

Heis, John
Sergeant Detective John Heis, MPD's lead investigator of coed case.

Herald, L.L.
Sergeant Larry Lee Herald of the WVSP, who was one of the early leaders of the investigation.

Herron, Charles "Charlie"
Lived in the Weirton Mine Section but moved away in the summer of 1970. Charlie was the uncle of suspect Eddie Thrasher, and together they later became Nick's chief suspects.

Hoover, Richard Warren
Self-proclaimed doctor and reverend of the Psychic Science Church, author of the Triangle Letters, the handwriting of which was used to rule out suspects early in the investigation.

Hypes, Betty Jo
Instructor in WVU's English Department who complained to WVSP about being followed by a "goofy-looking" young man.

Johnson, Richard
Indicted for kidnapping of Smith and Bailes.

Kimble, Carl
Hunting and fishing friend of William Hacker whose brother found headless victim at the family farm.

Kroll, John Leroy
Convicted child rapist and suspect in coed murders. Drove a white 1963 Chevy.

Lantz, Thomas "Tom" Wesley
Violent felon and serial sexual harasser of hitchhikers.

Laurita, Joseph "Joe" A., Jr.
Monongalia County prosecuting attorney in 1970. Nearly assassinated two weeks before Mared and Karen disappeared.

Leatherow, Robert "Bob"
Brevard County, Florida, deputy sheriff and lead investigator in the Crutchley case. Trained in criminal profiling by the FBI and Robert Ressler.

Lewis, Clarence "Skip"
WVU student who was walking with Itsy Burns when they saw Mared and Karen hitchhiking a ride.

Malarik, Edward and Margaret
Mared Malarik's parents.

McClure, Gwen
Resident assistant at Westchester.

Mitchell, W.H.
Sergeant William H. Mitchell of the WVSP, key investigator in the coed case.

Mongiello, John A. "Munch" or "Munchy"
Boyfriend of Mared Malarik.

Moore, Arch, Jr.
Governor of West Virginia.

Mozingo, R.L.
Sergeant Robert "Bob" Leslie Mozingo of the WVSP, key investigator in the coed case.

Palmer, Bennie F.
Chief of the Morgantown Police Department.

Ressler, Robert
Cofounder of FBI's Behavioral Analysis Unit, mentor of Bob Leatherow and author of *Whoever Fights Monsters*.

Ringer, Dan
Clawson's lead defense attorney in the 1981 trial. No relation to Dwayne.

Ringer, Dwane Randell "Randy"
Fraternity brother of William Gerkin. No relation to Dan.

Rittenhouse, Ron
Photographer for the *Morgantown Post* and, later, the *Dominion Post*.

Rogers, J.R.
WVSP trooper James "Jim" R. Rogers, who went undercover in Kroll's jail cell as "Landis."

Shade, D.M.
WVSP trooper Donald M. Shade.

Smith, Cindi
One of two WVU students kidnapped in March 1970.

Solomon, David
Prosecuting attorney in the 1976 trial of Eugene P. Clawson.

Sparks, W.Z.
Corporal William "Bill" Zane Sparks, first WVSP to take report of Mared and Karen missing.

Spitznogle, Mary Kathryn "Kathy"
Assistant to the dean of Westchester Hall.

Swiger, Daniel "Danny"
WVSP lieutenant. Cold case investigator at time of Hall's investigation and later connected the authors with Bob Leatherow.

Thrasher, Charles Edward "Eddie"
Original suspect of WVSP in 1970, who lived in Weirton Mine Section. Moved to Ohio in April 1970. Eddie was the nephew of Charlie Herron, and together they became Nick's chief suspects.

Townes, William
General manager of the *Dominion-News* and the *Morgantown Post*.

Tritchler, Gene Edward
Indicted for kidnapping of Smith and Bailes.

Trujillo, Tyrone
Karen Ferrell's biological brother.

Werner, Richard "Dick" and Margo Ann
Brother-in-law and older sister of Mared Malarik.

West, Charles "Charlie"
WVSP lieutenant, worked WVCIB as a handwriting analyst and discovered identity of author of the Triangle Letters.

Wilt, James
Retired Fairfax County, Virginia police detective turned private investigator who determined that John Crutchley was the last person to see Debbie Fitzjohn alive. Helped authors with their investigation.

Yost, Norman
Governor Moore's chief of staff.

Young, Annabel
Devoted follower of Reverend Hoover.

Zinn, John
Informant to the WVSP in 1970 and to Richard Hall in 2008.

MARED AND KAREN

*Some day soon, perhaps in forty years, there will be no one alive who has ever
known me. That's when I will be truly dead—when I exist in no one's memory.*
—*Irvin D. Yalom*

This book is about injustice, unresolved questions and violence, but it's
also about loss, the tragic loss of two young women that's still felt by
their families and friends. The loss of a loved one to violence is awful to
endure, an emptiness made worse by the loss of full knowledge of what
happened, how and why. Both women's parents died never knowing how or
why their daughters were murdered. Mared Ellen Malarik and Karen Lynn
Ferrell were laid to rest, friends and family left with only closed caskets and
their own memories to salve their feelings of grief, anger and horror.

Those who weathered that pain for fifty years were mostly reluctant to talk
about it, understandably, but a handful agreed to keep their lost loved ones
alive a little longer. It is from their statements and passed-on personal effects
that we were able to learn more about Mared and Karen, not as victims, but
as individuals, vibrant women with plans for the future. In the 1970s, news
coverage of an event like this did not focus on the victims so much as the
crime, but we felt that was not enough.

"[Karen] was a sweet person, bubbly, laughing all the time," reported
Freda Moore, a friend of Karen's from childhood and through high school.
"Her laugh was a pleasant one—a giggle—like girls do during girl talk."
She liked the things little Karen liked: dressing up, wearing makeup, playing

make-believe, acting like "high class movie stars" with cups of Kool-Aid, juice or tea at the play table. They made up silly songs about each other as they sat in the porch swing. "My little sister would try to butt in, and I'd tell her to go away, but Karen would say, 'Let her sing with us!' As girls, we were always skipping. Not walking. Just girls being girls." Karen liked leather and favored wearing short heels to make herself look taller.

In many ways, Mared and Karen were opposites: Mared came to Morgantown from a gated community called Smoke Rise in the New Jersey borough of Kinnelon, just under forty miles from New York City. Karen, on the other hand, hailed from Quinwood, West Virginia—five hundred miles

MARED MALARIK

KAREN FERRELL

Top: Mared Ellen Malarik.

Bottom: Karen Lynn Ferrell. *West Virginia Newspaper Publishing Company*.

southwest of Smoke Rise—a coal town so small most people said they lived in the larger, more recognizable town of Rainelle. Mared's father was a successful dentist, while Karen's adoptive father was a coal miner.

But the two shared similarities: Karen wanted to become a psychologist because she wanted to help people, the same reason Mared was drawn to major in sociology. Both favored the color blue. Former classmates described both women as "gentle," "kind," "quiet," "warm," "intelligent" and "two nice, normal people." Both cared deeply for their friends and family and kept in touch while in college—however briefly.

Dr. and Mrs. Malarik welcomed their new baby girl, Mared, at 8:15 p.m. on New Year's Eve 1950 in the Ackerson Maternity House in Passaic General Hospital. It was a Sunday. She became the youngest of four, with one brother, Edward Jr., and two sisters, Margo and Ann. The name Mared was a portmanteau of her parents' names, Margaret and Edward. Mared was especially close to her father, and over Christmas break in 1969, they had a conversation about life until after three o'clock in the morning.

Karen's delivery took place under Dr. Lee B. Todd's supervision on April 4, 1951, on a Wednesday. Her birth mother signed over parental rights to Bess and Richard Ferrell, who took her home as a newborn and raised her in Quinwood. If anyone asked, Bess and Richard told people they were actually Karen's grandparents, though records showed they never had biological children of their own.

———◆———

Mared swam competitively as a child, often taking first place in the twenty-five-yard freestyle and breaststroke. She attended St. Anthony's School in Butler and served as a bridesmaid for the wedding of her sister Margo to Richard Werner.

As for Karen, she "got to do what Karen wanted to do," Freda Moore told me one of the first times we talked. "Karen was [Bess and Richard's] life, their baby girl." Freda grew up a few houses down from Karen in Quinwood, and the two became inseparable at the age of nine.

"Karen would tell me, 'I wish you were my sister,' or 'I wish I had a big family.'" Freda was one of nine children, and Karen often dropped in. "If I wasn't at her house, she was at my house!" The two were so close, they called each other's parents Mom and Dad.

Because Karen was adopted, she planned to wait to have children of her own so they were 100 percent wanted, according to Freda. "She didn't want to have babies until she was out of college with a job and a house."

When Freda was seventeen, she got pregnant. She planned to give up her daughter for adoption and told Karen, who looked at her, concerned. "Do you love her?"

"Yes."

"Well, if you think it's right, do what you know is right in your heart."

Karen remained supportive of her friend and never looked badly on her decision.

———◆———

Former high school classmates described both Mared and Karen as popular and well-liked. Karen stood four feet, eleven inches tall, but rounded up to five if asked. Her chin-length blond hair sported lighter streaks, and some said of her gait that "she walked like a man." Karen excelled in school. She went to Crichton High through her junior year and then was a senior at Greenbrier West the first year after school consolidation in Greenbrier County. There, she was named a Homemaker of Tomorrow in 1969 and received a charm and certificate from General Mills.

Karen was inducted into the National Honor Society in high school. Her litany of extracurricular activities was that of a successful small-town girl in the 1960s: She was on the yearbook staff, served as an attendant to both the Snow Queen and the Homecoming Queen, was elected vice president of student council her junior year, participated in the Crichton Coed Hi-Y and served as a member of the Montana Senior Club and the C-14 club for two years before she graduated. She attended Quinwood Baptist Church and played piano for the Junior Quinwood Baptist Youth Fellowship. She took part in a Masonic youth group, Order of Rainbow for Girls, as a "worthy advisor." Initially, she planned to attend Marshall University close to home but enrolled at West Virginia University, far away in the northern part of the state.

Mared stood tall and slender, with dark brown shoulder-length hair. In her senior yearbook, above the photo police and newspapers later used, a fellow classmate designated her personality as "The Provocative Puzzler" and summed her up as "tranquil and turbulent…'but like'…Spanish class cut-up…'power rests in opinion'…demure but dynamic…warm-hearted and generous nature."

For four years, Mared attended a private prep school, DePaul Catholic High, in Wayne, New Jersey, and worked during the summer. Sundays she rang up customers shopping at the bakery in the Meadtown Shopping Center in Kinnelon. In high school, she dated one of the football team's co-captains, Larry Casazza. Her family did not approve of Larry, and her mother in particular encouraged Mared to date other boys and not keep him as a steady boyfriend. They broke up often, usually because she saw other boys, even though she did it to keep her parents from separating them. They never stayed broken up for more than a couple weeks.

Mared planned to major in sociology while Karen set her sights on psychology. Mared never got the chance to take a sociology course, but Karen penned, "I'd like to go to grad school and be a clinical psychologist," on the back of one of her college papers. Karen sometimes passed her spiral-bound notebook back and forth with her friends so they could scribble quick messages in class. In one exchange, she cited Sigmund Freud as her hero. She drew silly doodles, like a cartoonish grinning boy with a propeller hat or a fluffy bunny. She seemed to daydream often when not taking notes.

Those who knew Mared described her as "fun," "people-oriented," "sweet" and a "nice person" who loved to dance. She liked Karen for her dry sense of humor and told a friend in New Jersey, "Dry people appeal

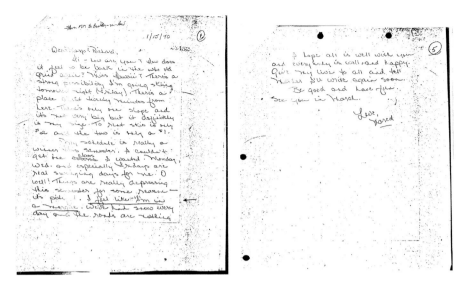

The first (*left*) and last (*right*) pages of Mared's final letter home (underline not in original), from Monongalia County Circuit Court records. *S. James McLaughlin.*

to me." She described Karen as a "cute little blonde kid." Mared thought Karen came off as funny without knowing it, even when she said something serious. She told her best friend in New Jersey that Karen stood in as her Morgantown replacement.

Meanwhile, most people described Karen as shy, perhaps less assertive than Mared. She normally acted cheerful and friendly in person and in her letters, but underneath her outwardly effervescent exterior, Karen struggled with intrusive thoughts and personal doubts.

Sometimes a darker side emerged when intoxication allowed Karen to speak freely. She told dormmates that she hated her biological mother, and others believed she was disturbed as a consequence of her birth mother giving her away. But as we learned from exploring this entire story, the truth was more complex than people thought. This work reveals secrets about the crime and its effects, including the one secret that Karen never let slip out, whether she was sober or drunk. Something she never shared with even her best friend in Quinwood. A truth her whole family kept in confidence.

Everybody has secrets. The secrets we keep and why we choose to keep them define us as individuals. We don't have the ability to tap into Mared's and Karen's thoughts, memories or dreams—no journals or diaries exist—but we know their killer didn't care about those details. They didn't recognize Mared or Karen as a person at all. We've done

Above: The first (*left*) and last (*right*) pages of Karen's final letter home, from Monongalia County Circuit Court records. *S. James McLaughlin.*

Left: Karen upon her graduation from high school. *Holly Naylor.*

our best to comb through the vestiges of Mared and Karen to remember them as real people. But we cannot portray those two young women as they deserve to be portrayed, because someone stole their potential. Their futures. We can't measure what could have been, but the savagery enacted on Mared and Karen, and all of those who they touched in a short time, will not be forgiven or forgotten if we pass on their story and refuse to give up on the truth.

Sarah James McLaughlin
June 2020

I

WHAT REMAINS

WEST VIRGINIA IS ROUGH COUNTRY.

The story you may have heard, the story most often told about Morgantown's 1970 coed murders, is full of terror, rape, decapitation, cannibalism, necrophilia and incompetent policing. That story is based on lies.
The story we tell is not.

Mared Malarik and Karen Ferrell, both college freshmen, disappeared while hitchhiking. Both were good students, smart and popular and pretty. They had no enemies. Their dormmates were clueless about what might have happened. Two friends of theirs saw them hitchhiking home after a movie, which was common at the time; they got into a small, off-white car and were never seen alive again.

If two pretty, white freshmen vanished from West Virginia University in 2021, there would be blanket coverage on every news channel, 24/7. Intensive investigation would begin within hours. Standard protocol in most of the country calls for investigators to assume the missing are in immediate danger. Time estimates vary, but missing persons not found within the first couple of days are usually not found alive.

If progress in the investigation weren't made immediately, no clues concerning their whereabouts, we would hear all about both of them, every detail of their lives. "Experts" would opine constantly about what could have happened to them, about their chances of being found alive, about who might be responsible. After finding the coeds in the woods, headless, the

West Virginia State Police (WVSP) would use twenty-first-century methods to catalogue the scene and examine the remains. Profilers from the FBI's Behavioral Analysis Unit would offer their assistance.

None of that happened in 1970. An overmatched Morgantown Police Department (MPD) was on its own and not saying much. Reporters learned only bits and pieces. Three months of near-total silence ensued. In the small mountain community, relatively isolated back then by rough terrain and a lack of interstates, fear and rumors spread, as did frustration with what appeared to be a lack of effort on the part of authorities.

Some people said investigators were covering something up, that maybe the son of a rich and politically connected family murdered the coeds. Others said the cops were in over their heads, so incompetent that they couldn't even develop a single solid suspect. Rumors spread about drug-addled hippies, insane sex killers and ritualistic sacrifices. Whispers of a police coverup of the coed murders, as they came to be called, are still heard today, fifty-one years later.

West Virginia is rough country. Ancient mountains—among the oldest in the world, gentle in the north and much steeper toward the south—the hills and valleys are masked with trees and pockmarked with coal mines. Streams and rivers run everywhere. People who work here are hard and do tough jobs, often for little money. Everyone knows everyone. Fights are common but murders few.

The murders that do happen are usually solved easily. A man dies in a fight at that bar (*That was like to happen sooner or later—some serious drinkers in there, you know?*), or a woman kills her husband (*Everyone expected that shit—she shoulda taken that trash out years ago*). Violence is always near—whether from a mine explosion or an aggrieved neighbor—especially in the country, away from town. With too few police, people in West Virginia handle things themselves.

The state never had any large cities—it still doesn't. The dozen or so urban areas were built around such things as coal and timber; tiny communities and scattered homesteads compose the balance of the state's population. Few interstates existed in 1970, and the difficult conditions presented by mountains, rivers and poor roads kept travel to a minimum. Despite its proximity to many large urban areas, West Virginia was arguably the most isolated state in the lower forty-eight.

Welcome sign on Beechhurst Avenue leading into Morgantown, 1974. In the background is the PRT. *West Virginia Newspaper Publishing Company*.

One of the state's dozen or so urban areas, Morgantown was first settled by Europeans in 1772 along Decker's Creek, which is named after a family slaughtered on its banks. Decker's Creek flows into the much larger Monongahela River, which rambles north to meet the Ohio in Pittsburgh. With river access to Pittsburgh in the north and Fairmont and Clarksburg to the southwest, Morgantown became a growing hub of commerce. The plentiful coal, oil and natural gas reserves, as well as massive amounts of available timber, anchored trade.

West Virginia University's founding in the last half of the 1800s created a fundamental social division in Morgantown: As WVU grew, a rift developed between *town*—the people of the area's prosperous working-class industries—and *gown*—the university's students, faculty and staff.

As of this writing, much of the county is totally dominated by WVU and related knowledge industries, but in 1970, town and gown were roughly equal in size. The university is revered as an endless fountain of revenue, but few townies are ever enthusiastic about the biannual invasion of students. A local population of fifteen thousand swells to almost thirty thousand, lines grow in theaters and banks, and traffic becomes unbearable.

In the 1960s and 1970s, WVU was growing rapidly, with most construction occurring on the Evansdale Campus, a mile away from the downtown Morgantown WVU campus. Students were often compelled to navigate between campuses, which considerably increased bus and car traffic. The coliseum, shown here during construction and after completion, quickly became one of WVU's iconic facilities. *West Virginia Regional History Collection (WVRHC); completed coliseum inset courtesy of Mark Crabtree.*

In 1970, some felt Morgantown was collapsing like a house of cards. The town seemed suddenly to reel from rampant crime and even experienced a few murders and a couple of bombings. Gambling was everywhere—cards, slots, sports—all of it simply ignored by police. Concerned citizens of Monongalia County were fed up and elected a vigorous young prosecutor who promised to go to war with the "gangland forces" that had a stranglehold on the county.

Morgantown citizens were increasingly on edge as the national news became even more dramatic and frightening. The Kennedys and Martin Luther King Jr. were assassinated. In December 1969, explosions destroyed offices in five states; the bombings were blamed on the Weather Underground, a radical splinter group of the Students for a Democratic Society. A four-hour shootout shredded the Black Panther headquarters in Los Angeles. By December, the mayhem and blood of the Altamont Speedway Free Festival had eclipsed the muddy free love of Woodstock.

Traffic light on Walnut Street stops cars on High Street, the heart of downtown Morgantown, at dusk. *Mark Crabtree.*

And an ongoing series of United Press International articles, beginning in December 1969, hinted at a new kind of murder in America. The murders were not for profit or revenge or jealousy but bloody and apparently random, perpetrated by hippies and fueled by mysticism and psychedelic drugs:

> LOS ANGELES (UPI) At least nine members of a pseudo-religious cult, including the leader known as "Jesus," were in custody today as suspects in the bloody slayings of actress Sharon Tate and at least six other persons....
>
> Police chief Edward Davis told a news conference Monday that the suspects were members of "The Family," a hippie band that roved through Death Valley 150 miles north of here.
>
> The leader, Charles Manson, 34, has a lengthy record that includes assault, theft and arson.

The Tate-LaBianca murders dominated broadcast and print journalism nationwide when Mared Malarik and Karen Ferrell disappeared on January 18, 1970.

"I LIKE TO RUB FURRY THINGS."

THE EDGE OF GRAFTON, TWENTY-FIVE MILES SOUTH OF MORGANTOWN

Late November 1969, two months before Mared and Karen disappear

Maxine Blankenship tightens the neck of her brown faux-fur jacket against the cold and presses down on her father's Cossack cap. Damn, it's cold! She didn't plan on this. The day before, the temperature peaked near seventy degrees, but tonight feels down around freezing. She should've brought a scarf at least.

Back and forth on North Pike Street she paces, trying to get the blood going. She glances over her shoulder at the Sunoco and the attendant inside, no doubt nice and toasty. She considers waiting there but decides against it. Her ride's due, and she's afraid they won't check good and leave her stranded.

She's been selling encyclopedias door to door in the Grafton neighborhood just down from where she now stands. She works on commission and didn't sell much that night. The sample bag is heavy, and her feet hurt. The job stinks, really, but it's something. She could work someplace like Biggie's, the burger place across the street from the Sunoco, but can't stand the thought of that grease stink every day. This job she works evenings. She'll give it a few more days, maybe look for something daytime in Fairmont.

Not much traffic, but an old sedan driving a little too fast pulls into the gas station from the east. She stamps her feet and glances over at the car. Two-tone, the body lighter than the roof and hood, maybe white and pale yellow or pale tan, hard to tell at night under the lights. The car doesn't pull up to the pumps but stops between the road and her. The driver's window rolls down.

Biggie's is still open in 2021. *S. James McLaughlin.*

The driver, a baby-faced kid about eighteen, smiles at her. She hears incoherent goading from other guys in the car, and he says, "Like your coat."

"Thank you." She turns her back and steps away from him, but not too fast. Can't show fear to guys like this.

"Hey, wait up, wait up," he says, the car idling forward to keep up. "Where you going? We can give you a ride."

"Thanks, but my friends are picking me up."

"Where you going?"

"Fairmont," she says. "The station's open til ten. They'll be here."

"If you say so. Tell you what, I'll come back by ten, and if your friends aren't here, I'll give you a ride."

"Suit yourself."

He pulls past her, and she watches his taillights recede as he drives away. Going too fast.

———— ◆ ————

Minutes before ten o'clock, still waiting for her ride, Maxine sees headlights coming toward her, from the west this time. She can't see anything but headlights. Still, she knows it's him, and when the car rolls past her, angling into the Sunoco lot, she sees the same two-tone. No one but the driver inside this time. The car eases beside the station and stops, the engine ticking as it cools.

The driver's door creaks open, and the boy steps out. He's taller than she expected, maybe six foot, and about 180–85 pounds. He smiles as he approaches.

"I don't see your friends." He makes a point of looking around as if he might find them lurking nearby. His words tumble over each other, in a rush to be heard. "I can give you a ride not a problem I give rides to hitchhikers all the time."

It takes her a second to understand what he said, and as he closes on her, she sees him fixate on her coat. Strange.

"Don't you have anything better to do?" she asks.

"Me? Nah." He stops beside her. "Well that depends I might could go work down at Sterling Faucet up by Morgantown, but now I'm a janitor up there at Westchester Hall." He rolls his eyes. "That's a girls' dormitory."

"Bet you like that." Maxine never thought about work up in Morgantown. It's twenty-five miles straight north of Grafton and twenty miles northeast of Fairmont, where she lives. But maybe that's where she should look. More jobs up there for sure. She just doesn't know how she'd get up from Fairmont every day.

"Lots of pretty girls," he says. "But I never get to talk to 'em they don't want to talk to me anyway."

"Why not?" Maxine isn't thinking about her question so much as watching the road.

"Boy, is it cold!" He looks over his shoulder at the station; the attendant is just locking up. "Tell you what let's wait in my car where it's warm." He claps his hands together. "If your friends don't show I'll give you a ride."

The offer is tempting. With the station closed… "How 'bout if you pull up under those lights there? Let me sit on the driver's side, and I'll wait in the car with you. They'll be here any minute, though."

"Just a sec," he says and jogs to his car. It fires up, and he revs a couple of times. The engine roars like an animal, and when he puts it in gear the car creeps toward the light, gravel popping under the tires. The car stops but keeps idling. The door cracks open and he jumps out, hustles over to the passenger side. The promise of heat urges Maxine to the car. She gets in.

"That's a pretty coat," he says before she's all the way in.

"You said that." The heat does feel good. She rubs her hands together.

"I just think fur looks really nice."

She scans out the windshield, hoping her ride will show soon. This should be okay for now, and if he gets all handsy, she'll just get out. The fingers of her left hand worry the black and gold bracelet on her thin right wrist.

"You get that job, the janitor job? At WVU?"

"Kind of, my parents got it. Or a friend told them about it, and they said I should try to get it. Not my parents, more like my grandparents."

"You live with your grandparents?"

"They're like my parents for…I don't know, a long time. They're nice. Sometimes he drinks too much, but it's not that bad. He doesn't do anything to me or nothing." He pauses before saying, "I like you. I hope you need a ride home. I mean, I don't hope your friends forget about—"

"I know what you mean." The warmer Maxine gets, the less she remembers why she's in this guy's car in the first place. "How come you don't live with your parents?"

"My mom run me off," he says, then as if realizing that what he said was depressing, he quickly adds, "I like fur coats that's a nice one. I like to rub furry things."

That's it, thinks Maxine and snaps her door open. *Too much, too weird*. She glances at him, one foot on the concrete. He reaches out.

2

"IT'S JUST UNBELIEVABLE
THAT THIS COULD HAPPEN IN MORGANTOWN."

On January 2, 1970, Monongalia prosecuting attorney Joseph "Joe" Laurita Jr. walked out of his house in Sabraton, the working-class east end of Morgantown, home of Sterling Faucet, and crossed the street to his small Datsun. Friday, 7:30 a.m., and Laurita was running later than usual. He slid into the driver's seat and turned the key.

A bomb under the driver's side demolished the front end of his vehicle and blew out the rear window of the blue Rambler parked ahead of him. Broken glass and twisted metal flew. People up and down Listravia Avenue heard the blast as windows in many houses cracked and shattered. Doors opened, the curious peering into the cold morning. Laurita was grievously wounded, blood everywhere.

As emergency vehicles wailed toward the explosion, *Dominion-News* photographer Ron Rittenhouse heard them, irresistible lures for a photojournalist, especially in this apparently quiet town. When he got closer, he saw a police car rush by and a column of smoke rising over eastern Sabraton. On the job less than a year, Rittenhouse had never encountered the like. He arrived on the scene and exited his car, lugging his bulky camera equipment. All he could see was the wreck of a small compact car, smoke pouring from its front end.

A police officer, William Hughes, stood across the road from the car, his six-foot-seven or -eight, 350-pound frame towering over Rittenhouse, who was under six feet tall.

"What's going on, Bill?"

Hughes looked in Rittenhouse's direction. "Oh, uh, Ron, can't really say much. You can't go over there."

As if he hadn't heard Hughes, Rittenhouse walked on and began snapping pictures. From inside the car came a man's voice, its source shrouded by smoke: "Ron, if you take any pictures of me and this car, I'll sue you and the newspaper!" The photographer managed to keep shooting, but he was surprised anyone survived the blast. A small crowd of neighbors gathered amid the debris and glass, and an emergency vehicle arrived. When the EMS driver got out to survey the shocking scene, his first thought was someone had dropped "a ten-ton safe on the front of the car."

Young Rittenhouse did not learn the identity of the victim until he got back to the nearby newsroom. The thirty-two-year-old prosecutor had been on the job only a little longer than Rittenhouse had been a working photographer—one year and one day—having won the election in his first year after graduation from law school. With a campaign platform of law enforcement planks, Laurita led a surprising upset of the incumbent. During the campaign, Laurita's platform stated, "Perhaps the greatest frustration in America today, aside from the issue of Vietnam, is the apparent inability of those concerned to maintain law and order." The citizens of Monongalia County agreed and elected him.

That Friday, Laurita had been headed to his office to prepare a number of gambling and marijuana-possession cases for the grand jury to convene the following Thursday, which also happened to be the first day of classes for WVU. Despite Laurita's threat, photographs of the car ended up in Morgantown's *Dominion-News* the very next day. Ray Evans, the city desk editor at the *Dominion-News*, later described the photographs this way: "One shot showed the driver's seat in the interior of Laurita's bomb-blasted car with a cutline pointing out the prosecutor's blood spattered on the inside of the door; another shot showed the blast was powerful enough to damage the motor block. Such gory details were and are rarely printed in newspapers."

More than a dozen city, county and state police rushed to the scene. State police experts flew in from the state capital, Charleston. FBI agents traveled to Morgantown to aid in the investigation. West Virginia governor Arch A. Moore Jr. called Laurita a "very close" personal friend and told reporters the state police lacked proper investigative resources. He said he would ask the legislature to fund twenty-five new full-time criminal investigators.

An editorial published in the *Dominion-News* the day after the Laurita bombing revealed fissures among the "ruling elite" in Morgantown political and civic life:

Mr. Laurita had precious little help in his efforts against the rackets....
More than four years ago the Dominion-News *started a concerted and*
continuous exposé of unmolested gambling operations in Morgantown.

In City Council, the Chamber of Commerce, the County Court and other
groups interested in the public welfare, there was sustained silence. The
Chamber welcomed a gambling club as a dues-paying member.

Shortly before the 1968 fall election, a Grand Jury was called to
investigate this newspaper's editorial allegations and wound up criticizing
the newspapers for failing "to provide this jury with any evidence to
support" its allegations and "felt that in reporting of this type mere
opinion is not sufficient."

Years later, Editor Evans said the editorial was probably written by
William Townes, the general manager of both the *Dominion-News* and the
Morgantown Post. The *Dominion-News,* especially, had been speaking out for law
and order and hadn't been getting much cooperation from government or
civics groups. Townes began his campaign against gambling and corruption
a few years after he arrived from Baltimore. During his four decades as a
newspaperman, Townes had become known as a "fixer" for the Hearst
chain of newspapers, often dispatched to newspapers in trouble in order to
raise circulation and revenue. But in 1965, nearing retirement, he left the
Hearst organization to accept the job in Morgantown.

On January 4, 1970, he announced a $5,000 reward for information
"leading to the arrest and conviction of the perpetrator or perpetrators
of the attempt to assassinate Prosecuting Attorney Joseph A. Laurita Jr."
In other *Dominion-News* stories that day, the mayor expressed sympathy for
Laurita's family, as well as the hope that "we can quickly apprehend whoever
is responsible." A Morgantown businessman and former Pennsylvania law
officer called the bombing a "crime against the community." He firmly
believed the crime was instigated by someone threatened by Laurita's pursuit
of crime in Monongalia County.

Laurita's serious injuries brought shock from all quarters. The secretary of
Circuit Court Judge Marvin R. Kiger, the judge who would later preside over
the first trial in the coed case, said what was on many people's minds: "Isn't
it horrible? It's just unbelievable that this could happen in Morgantown."

Evans later recalled, "Some people reacted [with] fear, asserting that 'we
are not safe in our own homes.' Many reacted in anger as event piled on top
of event. Others reacted with some suggestion of mass guilt" that assumed
everyone played a role in things becoming as bad as they had.

Morgantown's attention to the assassination attempt continued through the first half of January. Both papers, the *Dominion-News* and the *Morgantown Post*, constantly ran headlines like "Murder Attempt Made on Laurita" and "Prosecutor 'Fair' after Bomb Rips Car" on the front page. Many people were convinced it was a professional hit, often calling it a "gangland-style" attempted murder. By January 9, the reward fund had reached $12,500, over $80,000 in today's dollars.

The Morgantown rumor mill cited the stranglehold of organized crime and the corrupt incompetence of Morgantown's good-old-boy police force as reasons the crime had not been solved. Townes saw himself as a crusader for the people. However, many people who had grown up in Morgantown, no small number of them businessmen, considered Townes a meddlesome outsider.

With authorities scrambling for answers in the wake of the bombing and townies speculating about how such a thing could have happened in their quiet mountain home, few people noticed two weeks later when three WVU freshmen women disappeared.

3

"DON'T LEAVE ME IN THIS ROOM BY MYSELF."

Insulated in their own bubbles, college students are notoriously ignorant of events outside academe, but even those who escaped specific knowledge of Morgantown's gambling issues or the Laurita bombing felt the effects of the crackdown on local establishments. According to the *Post-Herald* of Beckley, West Virginia, "Night life appeared on the verge of nonexistence."

Morgantown winters are somber, the skies a perpetual white or gray. The region is one of the least sunny places in the United States, and the winter sky brings frequent rain and snow. Immediately after a snow, especially a deep one, a blanket of white shrouds trees, yards, houses and cars. But as people dig out, begin to drive and maybe temperatures rise a little, the whole tableau turns into a slushy, blackening mess. Dark, bare branches claw white skies. Mared, in a letter written in early January to her sister and brother-in-law, described how there was nothing to do in Morgantown and spoke of the place as "a morgue."

Mared Malarik and Karen Ferrell met in 1969, the first day of their freshman year at WVU. Their backgrounds differed, Mared from the rapidly growing Kinnelon, New Jersey, and Karen from the tiny southeastern West Virginia town of Quinwood, with a 1970 population of 370. But the two hit it off immediately. Mared loved Karen's droll humor, and Karen was drawn to what she saw as Mared's worldliness, sophistication. They quickly became good friends and by the end of the first semester planned to room together their sophomore year.

Looking west down Willey Street, the dividing line between downtown Morgantown (*left*) and the downtown campus of WVU (*right*), 1969. *West Virginia Department of Transportation (WVDOT).*

In the first days of the new semester, January 8 and 9, Mared was settling in and adjusting her class schedule, but a pain in her tooth was bothering her. Her father, a dentist, had done some work over Christmas, but now the pain was back. He told her to go see someone in Morgantown. Karen also had her hands full adjusting to the new semester, and she had had a visit from her main boyfriend, Steve Hayes. Steve was in the navy and visited on Saturday the tenth.

On Monday, Mared and her boyfriend John Mongiello—Mared called him "Munchy," but everyone else called him Munch—had gone to see the rock 'n' roll group Ezra, a New Jersey band she'd seen a couple of times. Karen and another one of her boyfriends, Kenneth Eye, had gone with them to the show. Kenneth didn't really fit in, mostly because he was still in high school, but he wasn't Karen's "real" boyfriend anyway. The foursome went to the Castle, one of the coolest clubs in Morgantown—the drinking age was eighteen at the time—a place that had become a favorite of Mared and Karen's. Ezra rocked the joint, and everyone was talking about maybe going to see them when they played a second gig the next week, on Monday, January 19.

SUNDAY AFTERNOON, JANUARY 18, 1970, THE DAY MARED AND KAREN GO MISSING

Mared and Munch hold hands as they walk across the Stadium Bridge toward the main campus and Woodburn Circle, thought by many to be the prettiest spot on the WVU campus. Three sides of the "circle" are formed by the ivied brick walls of classical Victorian buildings. The open side of the U faces University Avenue and the Mountainlair, WVU's new student union, in many ways the heart of the downtown campus. One of the busiest streets of Morgantown, University Avenue slices right between Woodburn Circle and the Mountainlair. The temperature around forty degrees, spotty clouds drift in the late afternoon winter sun.

Mared met Munch the previous fall, her first day at WVU, the same day she first met Karen Ferrell. During the fall semester, their relationship grew so serious that Munch visited the Malariks in New Jersey over Thanksgiving break. Her family liked him. Mared and Munch had begun to talk about marriage—unfortunately, her high school boyfriend, Larry Casazza, still didn't know about their relationship.

"So, we're copasetic?" Mared says. They had a fight the previous night, but it wasn't serious. Larry had visited her that week, the first full week of the

Woodburn Circle on the WVU's downtown campus. *Mark Crabtree.*

The Mountainlair, WVU's student union, stands across the street from Woodburn Circle. *Mark Crabtree.*

new semester, and he pressured her into going out on a date. She'd planned to tell him about Munch but hadn't been able to go through with it. Larry had other ideas. When Mared told Munch about "the date," they had words. "We didn't do anything. Really."

Now, Munch just shrugs. He isn't too surprised she hasn't been able to finally, officially, break up with Larry, but he's still not happy about it. He keeps looking at his shoes, the way they schlick along the sidewalk. "Tooth okay?"

As soon as he says it, her tongue worries at the rough spot. "I'm going back tomorrow. Eleven o'clock. Dr. Costianes still has more to do."

Munch stops; they both stop. "What's bothering you, then?"

"I guess I'm still thinking about what Karen and I saw at the Red Cellar last night."

"You don't even know what that girl took. She drank way too much, that's for sure."

Munch starts to walk again, but Mared holds his hand, stops him. "That's what Karen said, but Munchy, the girl went to the hospital."

He sighs.

Mared starts walking again, swinging the link of their hands. "Let's change the subject. Tonight's your big night."

"Yeah, well…."

"But you're getting your pin." Mared knows that's why he wants Larry out of the way, even if he doesn't know that. Once Munch is awarded his fraternity pin, he'll pin her. She will belong to Munchy. When he first proposed the idea, she thought getting pinned would make her feel secure enough to make the final break with Larry. But maybe she's been thinking wrong. Maybe it's really security for *him*.

"Yeah, yeah," Munch says, looking around. "Hey, you want to get high?"

"Somebody will see." She steers him up the steps to stroll the sidewalk loop of Woodburn Circle. "Once around then we'll go over to the 'Lair for some hot chocolate."

———◆———

Nancy Best lives in room 242 at Carlyle Hall, the companion dorm of Westchester Hall; together, the two dorms are referred to as Beverly Manor. That Sunday afternoon, she is visiting Karen Ferrell in room 423 on the Westchester side. Karen's roommate, Sandra Fitch, is not around. Karen sits on her own bed, her legs drawn up to her chest, her chin on her knees. She rocks in place, front to back.

In a small, straight-backed chair just off the foot of the bed, Nancy Best watches her friend, concerned. Karen isn't a sickly person, but lately seems extremely uncomfortable.

"You sure I can't get you something?" Nancy asks. "You think it's a kidney infection again?"

Karen shakes her head. "I *don't know*." Her voice has an edge to it. "I've been coughing bad, and nothing helps."

Nancy stands and paces the little area at the foot of both beds. The small dorm room is of cheap construction and has little in it. Much of the space is taken by two parallel beds, each bolted to opposing walls, the door from the hall between them. On the wall opposite the door is a window with a small desk underneath. At the foot of each bed is a small dresser beside a free-standing wardrobe. Every piece of furniture in the room is bolted to a wall; apparently, someone thinks it would be a bad idea to allow freshmen to arrange their own furniture.

"You should see a doctor, Karen. The school clinic won't cost you anything."

"That's what Gwen wants," Karen says, referring to the floor's resident assistant. "But Mom gave me a note. I don't have to."

Nancy stops walking. "That's crazy."

"I got my own doctor back home. I don't—" She looks down at her bare feet. "I don't like to be touched by strangers. Strange men. Or even seen, really."

"But he's a doctor!" Nancy doesn't understand her friend's reluctance. Over the past four months, since the beginning of the fall semester, she learned Karen had a number of unusual worries, a number of fears. Most of the time Karen seems very friendly, and she could be the life of the party when she drank beer, but darker thoughts lurk underneath. Karen can be cynical or pleasant and warm, by turns.

"I'm very…" Karen hesitates. Starts over. "I have this fear of…someone putting their hands on me. You know." She shrugs.

"Seriously?" Nancy senses her friend's darkness drawing near again. Maybe they shouldn't have stayed so late the night before. Maybe that was it, a little hangover. "Tell you what. I've got to run down to my room and get some homework done so Sandy and I can go do something toni—"

"Don't leave me in this room by myself!" Karen's eyes are wide, her voice tremulous. Nancy doesn't know the first thing about how to comfort her friend. Karen doesn't talk about it unless she's drunk, but Nancy and several other girls on the floor know Karen believes she will be raped and killed before she turns twenty.

4

"WE'RE THUMBING."

On their way down University Avenue into town, Mared and Karen stop at the Sunnyside Superette, a small grocery store for students in Sunnyside. Considered WVU's student ghetto, Sunnyside is a collection of old houses cut into apartments, small shops and the bars where students drink too much, too fast. At the Superette, Mared cashes a ten-dollar check, enough for a movie and a pack of cigs.

At the bottom of the hill is a four-way section where Campus Drive comes up the hill from the right, Stewart Street down from the left and University Avenue continues; they head across University Avenue's Stadium Bridge. Mared's knee-high boots make the old iron grating resound metallically with each step.

At five-foot-six, Mared is more than half a foot taller than her friend, who tells everyone she is five feet tall, although she isn't quite. Karen weighs barely ninety pounds. Mared looks more sophisticated, her dark hair frosted with highlights, wearing her lime green Lady Manhattan blouse, blue hip-hugger bell bottoms with white stripes and tall fur-lined boots. Beside Mared, Karen feels frumpy, almost invisible in her dark brown sweater, cuffed brown and white bell bottoms and brown loafers. Her black imitation fur coat highlights her shoulder-length sandy hair, which she is wearing up that night. Still, as they walk, she self-consciously fingers the Greenbrier High class ring dangling from the chain around her throat.

"Far out!" Mared exclaims. "Look down. I love how you can see right through as you walk. Look how small the roof down there is." The university building below has a steep roof and holds a small swimming pool and some athletic department offices. To their right is the bridge on which cars cross the tiny valley. On the other side of the road is a ten-foot white concrete wall, the top of the east end of the football stadium. Mared glances into the open air to their left.

"Maureen canceled about six, but no one else wanted to see the movie?"

Karen shrugs. "You know, Ruth had a thing. Jessie said she still had homework for tomorrow. Like that. You didn't ask Donna?"

At the end of the bridge they veer right into the heart of West Virginia University's downtown campus and pass Woodburn Circle, where Mared and Munch had taken their walk earlier.

"She's going out with that B.C."

"You didn't say anything to her yet, did you?"

"No way Jose!" Mared declaims, her finger in the air. A light rain comes and goes, the air getting nippy. "This will turn into snow." Hovering around freezing, the evening feels colder. Mared suddenly spins around breathlessly. "You tell Sandy?"

"No." Neither girl much likes her roommate lately, and they decided to room together in the fall semester. It would be harder for Mared, of course, because she and Donna DeYoung were friends in high school. Karen and Sandy met only a few months earlier. Donna claimed she and Mared were best friends, but Karen—and about a million other girls at the dorm—knows better.

As the two of them walk along University Avenue, a few students thumb from a small strip of land dividing the two lanes of University Avenue in front of the new Mountainlair, the student union. Students walk into town from their dorms, but it's less appealing to walk back up the mile-long hill. After Sunnyside, going up the hill, there are no sidewalks, just the road and a steep wooded hill. Buses are few and don't run late, so students hitchhike; when a car stops, as many pile in as will fit.

Mared's boyfriend is at a fraternity party, one he's required to attend to get his fraternity pin. Mared and Karen both know he's going to pin Mared, and Karen is pleased for her friend. Mared and Munch will probably marry, and Karen knows the talk around Westchester about Mared and her old high school boyfriend is empty gab, no matter what Donna says. Donna says a lot of things.

The two friends hurry down High Street toward the Metropolitan Theater. Local rumor has it Stravinski and Maria Callas performed there, and the Metropolitan Pool Hall underneath was once on the professional pool circuit.

Willey Street approaching intersection with High Street, where a left turns into the WVU campus and a right leads into downtown Morgantown, 1969. *WVDOT.*

View of downtown Morgantown from southern end of WVU campus, where Willey Street crosses High Street. *WVDOT.*

The historic Metropolitan Theater, on High Street between Fayette and Walnut, downtown Morgantown, where Mared and Karen saw *Oliver! United States Library of Congress, Carol M. Highsmith Archive.*

They buy their tickets and sit on the ground floor rather than going up to the balcony. The show is well attended but not too crowded. As they walk down an aisle, Mared spots another girl from Westchester and her date. She pulls Karen into the row behind them. "Itsy!"

The two turn in their seats. Itsy smiles broadly.

"Mared, Karen. Cool. Oh, uh, this is Skip. Mared, Karen," she says, indicating each with her upturned palm.

———◆———

As they left *Oliver!* around 10:30 p.m., Mared and Karen and Itsy and Skip burst out of the double doors into the night air. Their mood wasn't dampened by the light rain.

"I thought you said it would be snowing," Mared said.

Karen laughed. "That was you!"

Mared said the four of them should skip, like in the movie, and they locked arms, Karen then Mared then Itsy then Skip, and together they bounced up the street.

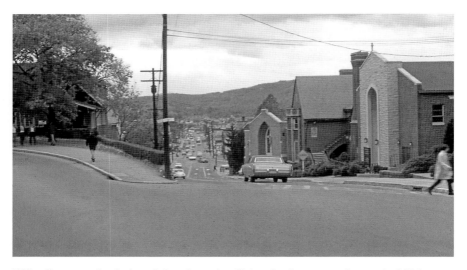

Willey Street coming in from left and meeting University Avenue coming up the hill from Beechhurst Avenue, which runs along the Monongahela River. Mared and Karen were picked up by a small white car here on January 18, 1970. *WVDOT*.

"Consider yourself AT HOME!" they sang, lost in the movie's version of nineteenth-century England. "Consider yourself part of the family. We've taken to you SO STRONG! It's clear! We're! Going to get along!"

A block up High Street, they began to slow, and Itsy said to Mared, "Come with us. We're going to catch the bus."

"The bus doesn't go to Westchester," Mared said. "We're thumbing."

At the top of High, Mared and Karen let Skip and Itsy pull ahead.

Skip looked back to see Mared and Karen at the curve near where Willey met University Avenue by the Mineral Industries building. A light-colored sedan stopped, and both girls climbed in the front seat, Mared first and then Karen. The car started again, rolled about fifteen feet and stopped at the stop sign. Skip saw a male driver. Short, dark hair. Well groomed. The car started again, moving toward Skip and Itsy, who both waved. Skip thought it strange neither girl acknowledged their presence as they passed, Mared talking to Karen.

5

"NO EVIDENCE OF ABDUCTION."

When the girls don't make it back for curfew, a resident assistant at Westchester, Gwen McClure, follows standard protocol. She traces their activities and canvasses the entire dorm to make sure Mared and Karen aren't in someone else's room, having lost track of time. No luck. Mared and Karen are probably at someone's house partying, but if she can't find them, she's going to have to notify the campus police. First, she should talk to the roommates again, Sandy Fitch and Donna DeYoung, in case something has turned up.

She finds Sandy and Donna, along with three others who were close—Jessie Chuey, Ruth Pellegrino and Andrea Ward—the five of them sitting on couches and chairs in the fourth-floor lounge. Gwen watches from the doorway.

"I just know something terrible has happened," Donna says to no one in particular. "They left a little before seven, right? Something like that. A little before or a little after. I don't think the movie started until, like, eight or something." She looks at Andrea. "Don't you think something bad happened?"

"I have no idea. Neither do you."

"What movie were they going to see?" Sandy Fitch asks.

"I guess I'm not sure," Donna says. "They asked me to go with them, but I had plans with B.C. Does anyone know?"

"They said they were going to see *Alice's Restaurant*," Ruth says. "I think."

Donna shakes her head solemnly. "I don't think they would have gone to a movie about marijuana. Neither one of them is a hippie, and there's *no way* they smoke reefer. Karen might, but I *know* Mared doesn't." She looks from one to another, and then speaks as if she is pleading the case. "They *barely* even drink. I *should know*. I'm Mared's best friend."

"Oh, come on, Donna," Ruth says. "They both drink, especially Karen."

"Just socially." Donna is digging in her heels.

"I heard," Sandy says in an effort to turn the conversation, "that Miss Spitznogle is gathering information for the police. She's probably going to tell them about Munch. Larry, too. Mared's having a hard time deciding."

Just then, Itsy Burns comes out a door, scratching her head, half asleep. "You all are *loud*."

"You didn't hear?" Donna says. "Mared and Karen are missing! They're probably dead…or *worse*."

"Really?" Itsy flops on the Naugahyde couch next to Donna and mumbles, "Skip and I just…We were at the movie with them. They were right behind us. We talked during intermission."

"*Some* people are saying they ran away," Donna says, glaring at Ruth.

Ruth counters, "I said it was too soon to say whether they—"

"They were both in a good mood." Itsy's eyebrows knit together. "Neither one said any— Running away? Not likely."

None of the girls says anything. Andrea looks toward her room, and Sandy is pacing. Ruth and Jessie sit back down.

"I didn't think it was worth it," Itsy says at last.

"What wasn't worth it?" Donna says, leaning against Itsy like she's Donna's new best friend.

"They hitchhiked. After the movie. Got a ride almost instantly." Itsy looks at Sandy, Karen's roommate. "I could have gotten the license number. I didn't think of it."

"There, there." Donna taps Itsy's knee and sits back. "Let me ask you this, Itsy. Do you think Mared or Karen ever smoked marijuana?"

Itsy looks thoughtful. "Karen definitely drinks a lot, but I don't really know her. I don't know if she smoked—smokes—reefer. Mared does. Probably."

"My thoughts exactly," Donna says. "Sort of. I—" She stops mid-sentence as Gwen steps into the lobby. She's heard enough.

"If you all wait up, you're in for a long night. Time to break this up, girls." Her job is to keep the peace. "Off to bed. Shoo. They'll turn up."

———◆———

Morgantown chief of police Bennie Palmer places a public service call to the Morgantown Detachment of the West Virginia State Police. Around one o'clock in the morning, the department received a call from a Gwen McClure. A couple of her girls didn't come home that night. College students are pretty damned crazy these days, especially the girls. Seems anymore like the girls think they're boys, and the boys think they're girls.

At the West Virginia State Police, William Z. Sparks answers. "Corporal Sparks."

"This is Chief Palmer in Morgantown. We got a report of two girls missing from Westchester Hall. Yeah, at the top of the hill there." Benny switches the phone to his other ear. "No, no, Corporal. Not the same."

The second missing student report tonight. The first was a girl last seen at her dorm, Arnold Hall, on North High Street. Palmer has only been chief for a year, but he doesn't remember a night with this much action.

"Okay," Palmer says. "You ready?"

He begins to read the descriptions to Corporal Sparks. With this information, WVSP will be able to issue the same notices he's already sent out: a missing persons complaint and an APB. Policemen around the state and throughout the region will be on the lookout for the missing girls.

"Okay, here goes. First one. Mared Ellen Malarik, age nineteen. DOB: 12-31-50. 5'6", 105 pounds. Fair complexion. Frosted, short, brown hair. Wearing brown imitation fur coat and carrying a brown leather handbag. Second one. No, wait. The first one was from Kinnelon, New Jersey." He pauses, then, "K-I-N-N-E-L-O-N. Now, the second. Karen Lynn Ferrell, age 19. DOB: 4-4-51. Wait. No. Not 19. 18. Five feet tall, 90 pounds. Fair complexion. Frosted medium-length hair. Home address Box 74, Quinwood, West Virginia. Wearing a black fur coat, brown slacks, and carrying a brown, shoulder-length strap purse."

He pauses, switches ears again. "Yeah, Corporal Sparks. APB and all, the usual. They're just stoned somewhere. Couple days, they'll turn up. Okay, thanks."

Chief Bennie Palmer hangs up and stands. *Oh, jeez.* Hard to tell which is worse, his back or his knees. He walks over to his office doorway and pokes his head out.

"Heis!"

Shit, *now* where is that guy?

———◆———

Subterranean police garage beneath the Morgantown Public Safety Building on Spruce Street, which housed the Morgantown Police Department. *Mark Crabtree.*

Overnight and into the morning, Chief Palmer and his staff notified county, state and federal authorities, who followed protocol. The state police sent out all-points bulletins, also called BOLOs—be on the lookout—on the teletype, which was the fax machine of the day. The APBs were distributed across thirteen states around West Virginia, as per the state police's standard procedure. The FBI was alerted about the missing coeds on January 19 and immediately began to track the status of the case. Little else was done by authorities in those crucial first few days to actively locate the missing coeds.

———————◆———————

That Monday morning, Mary Kathryn Spitznogle, assistant to the dean in charge of Westchester Hall, stepped in, speaking for the university. She dutifully made the phone calls to Mared's and Karen's parents but could tell them nothing except their daughters had not returned to their dorm the night before. According to a report she later gave to both the local and state police, Mrs. Malarik was "understanding, but obviously upset" while Mrs. Ferrell "displayed no emotion at all." Later that morning, when requested to do so by a superior, she called both women back to assure them WVU was doing everything they could. Mrs. Ferrell was "once again unemotional," but Mrs. Malarik, while still emotional, asked a few questions she hadn't thought to ask earlier.

Spitznogle also told Gwen McClure to impress upon the girls at the dorm the need to refrain from spreading rumors. Residents were not to talk about Mared and Karen to anyone outside the dorm. Anyone asking about the disappearance should be referred to the Morgantown police. This advice was later seconded by the police themselves.

With the help of Donna DeYoung, Mared's roommate, and Sandra Fitch, Karen's roommate, a list of the clothing worn by each coed was assembled. Quoting from Spitznogle's report:

> Mared Malarik
> Small chocolate brown purse with a zipper on the side
> Blue bell bottom slacks with thin white stripes—small cuffs—
> hip huggers
> Lady Manhattan lime green blouse—satin—size 32
> Tall brown boots with a flap
> Black leather wrist length gloves
>
> Karen Ferrell
> Brown suede purse with long strap and top zipper (light green
> wallet)
> Brown and white stripe bell bottom slacks with small cuffs
> Dark brown pullover sweater
> Dark brown loafer type shoes
> Black gloves

———◆———

FBI WASH DC
FBI PITTSBURGH
7:31PM   URGENT 1/19/69 [*sic*] PVC
TO   DIRECTOR
FROM   PITTSBURGH (79-NEW)

MARED MALARIK; KAREN FERRELL; MISSING PERSONS.

ON JANUARY NINETEEN INSTANT, COP BERNIE PALMER, MORGANTOWN, W.VA., PD ADVISED THAT MALARIK AND FERRELL, BOTH WHITE FEMALES, NINETEEN YEARS OLD, STUDENTS AT WEST VIRGINIA UNIVERSITY, MORGANTOWN, ON NIGHT OF JANUARY EIGHTEEN, LAST, ATTENDED MOVIE AND WERE RETURNING TO THEIR DORMITORY WHEN THIRD GIRL, AN ACQUAINTANCE OF BOTH SUBJECTS, OBSERVED THEM HITCHHIKING IN DOWNTOWN MORGANTOWN. AT APPROXIMATELY TEN-FIFTY PM, JANUARY EIGHTEEN, LAST, LONE WHITE MALE DRIVING WHITE OR CREAM COLORED CAR, POSSIBLY SIXTY FIVE CHEVROLET, STOPPED AND BOTH GIRLS VOLUNTARILY ENTERED CAR. THIRD GIRL DID NOT KNOW THE DRIVER AND DOES NOT KNOW IF SUBJECTS WERE ACQUAINTED WITH DRIVER. SUBJECTS HAVE NOT BEEN SEEN SINCE AND WERE REPORTED MISSING AT ONE FIFTEEN AM, JANUARY NINETEEN, INSTANT TO MORGANTOWN PD.

PALMER ADVISED THAT HE HAD BEEN TELEPHONICALLY CONTACTED BY MALARIK'S FATHER AND MALARIK INDICATED HE WOULD CONTACT FBI IN NEW JERSEY RE THIS MATTER.

NO EVIDENCE OF ABDUCTION EXISTS AT THIS TIME BUT PITTSBURGH IS MAINTAINING CLOSE LIAISON WITH MORGANTOWN PD IN EVENT EVIDENCE OF FEDERAL VIOLATION DEVELOPS.

6

"APPARENTLY DISAPPEARANCE WAS RUN AWAY TYPE."

The first published report of Mared and Karen's disappearance came Monday afternoon, January 19, in the *Morgantown Post*:

> 3 missing
> "U" coeds
> are sought
>
> City Police today are searching for three missing West Virginia University coeds missing since last night.
> Two of the girls were last seen together, hitchhiking on Willey Street near…

In addition to Mared and Karen, a third "girl" was reported missing, but police learned within hours she had returned to her dorm, Arnold Hall. (A present-day newspaper report would refer to missing "women," but in 1970 the age of majority was twenty-one—plus, adult women were often referred to as "girls.")

The next day, all three newspapers in Morgantown—the *Dominion-News* in the morning and the *Morgantown Post* in the afternoon and WVU's student paper, the *Daily Athenaeum*—covered the disappearance. With the exception of the student newspaper, which printed the story at the top of the front page, the coverage was not prominent. All three papers contained essentially the same information—what little there was.

———◆———

The same Monday, the payphone on the fourth floor of Westchester Hall rings twice before a breathless DeYoung bursts from the room she shares with Mared. She's skipped classes for the day in case something comes up about Mared.

"Hello!" she says, practically before the phone is to her mouth.

"I'm trying to reach Mared Malarik." A man's voice. Hesitant. Donna's mind turns over and over. Someone with information?

"She's—umm…" Donna thinks this can't be the police, because they'd know Mared was missing. Oh! Unless they think Mared and Karen aren't really missing, maybe hiding or something, and want to secretly question someone at Westchester. "She's not in right now. May I help you?"

"I don't think so. This is Dr. Costianes, her dentist. She had an appointment at 11:15."

"You haven't heard? She and Karen didn't come home last night. Everyone was up waiting all night. We don't know what's happened. My name's Donna DeYoung. I'm Mared's roommate and her best friend."

———◆———

Dr. Edward Malarik couldn't just sit at home in New Jersey with the news of his daughter's disappearance. As Richard Werner, who was married to Mared's older sister Margo, prepared to travel to Morgantown for a few days, Dr. Malarik called the Morgantown police department and learned they had opened an investigation. He contacted the Newark office of the FBI to alert them to events and furnished a detailed description of Mared and the details of the disappearance. He was told "missing persons notices" had been posted on their behalf, and he promised to send a photograph of Mared. The Newark office told him that unless they received indication of forced kidnapping, foul play or any other violation of federal law, the FBI could not get involved. Besides getting the word out, there was little an investigative agency, or a worried parent, could do but wait.

A memo by the special agent in charge of the FBI's Pittsburgh field office, Charles F. McKinnon, to FBI director J. Edgar Hoover, refers to a January 19 phone call from the Morgantown chief of police:

On this date Chief of Police BENNIE PALMER, Morgantown, West Virginia Police Department, advised that MALARIK mailed a letter to a boyfriend on 1/18/70, prior to her disappearance. BETTY BOYD, Dean of Women, West Virginia University, telephonically contacted boyfriend and he acknowledged receipt of letter and advised letter from MALARIK indicated that she was tired of school, but she did not want to return home. MALARIK also indicated in letter she desired a change of scenery. Boyfriend promised to notify West Virginia University officers if MALARIK contacted him.

PALMER advises from letter apparently disappearance was run away type.

In addition to being the first civilians to contact the FBI, Dr. and Mrs. Malarik were the first to announce a reward for information about their daughter's disappearance. Replies to the alerts circulated by law enforcement began to come in almost immediately. At 9:00 p.m., Chief Palmer was contacted by police in Ripley, West Virginia, a few hours southwest of Morgantown. Girls matching the coeds' description were seen at J&J Truck Stop. According to witnesses, they told some customers they were headed to Ashland, Kentucky, and were last seen in a tractor trailer with "Parsons" printed on the side.

According to FBI documents, "Ripley PD showed captioned photographs to people at truck stop and they identified girls at truck stop as resembling subjects." Not only that, but on the back of the hitchhikers' check from McClure's Restaurant in Ashland was written, "Very nice waitress." The Morgantown police department sent the check, along with one of Mared's theme books from school, to the FBI for a handwriting comparison.

Less than twenty-four hours after Mared and Karen's disappearance, all the evidence considered by the police pointed to their having run away, and Morgantown police appeared to have settled on this conclusion. All over the country, young people were "dropping out," "going hippie," heading toward San Francisco with flowers in their hair. America's youth had gone mad, and Mared and Karen had run away, MPD decided. Little was done except follow up on reports of various sightings until the West Virginia State Police began to investigate. That wouldn't happen for nearly three months.

7

"THE HEART OF A WOMAN ACHES
FOR THE THINGS SHE LOVES."

Within two days of Mared and Karen's disappearance, residents of Westchester Hall began circulating a petition calling for better bus service between campuses. Concern about hitchhiking was also part of the local conversation immediately, and not for the first time. According to the *Morgantown Post*, the previous February, "Councilman Harold Wildman complained to City Council about hitchhiking coeds along University Avenue at Grumbein's Island. He called the practice, 'A disgrace to the city, the university, and the state.'" When the coeds went missing, the paper again contacted Councilman Wildman, who reiterated his concerns about hitchhiking and his belief that women were especially in danger: "I brought the matter up before council because I didn't like to see young women hitchhiking. I wouldn't want my daughter doing it, and I think it is the University's obligation to provide transportation."

The lives of the Malariks and the Ferrells were upended by Mared and Karen's disappearance. In addition to Dr. Malarik's contact with the FBI and his announcement of a reward for information, he and Mared's brother-in-law, Richard Werner, traveled to Morgantown for a few days to assess the situation. That first week was also rough for Karen's parents, Richard and Bess: Richard suffered a heart attack. He survived and was put on bed rest for weeks, but his condition served stark notice that Mared and Karen were not the only victims.

The state police remained focused on the Laurita bombing. Reports vary, but the WVSP had between two and six officers investigating what they now referred to as an assassination attempt. They received a degree of cooperation from federal authorities, but the Alcohol, Tobacco and Firearms Division was still an arm of the IRS and would not have the autonomy it needed to truly dive deeply into investigations until 1972. Still, ATF and the FBI were available for laboratory analysis and limited on-site investigation.

Newspaper coverage and public perception insisted the bombing was retaliation against the prosecutor's office—and Joe Laurita specifically—for the stepped-up pursuit of gambling in Monongalia County. Townes continued to use his editorial and story-assignment powers to pressure both law enforcement and political forces to bring the bomber(s) to justice, but little public attention—outside the world of the university—focused on Mared and Karen through the end of January and into February.

———◆———

The handwriting analysis of the café receipt came back from the FBI on February 5: "Because of…the lack of sufficient comparable known handwriting, it could not be determined whether the handwritten notation on [the back of the restaurant check] was or was not prepared by MARED MALARIK."

Gwen McClure had been in touch with Steve Hayes, navy man and Karen's most serious boyfriend, as had the FBI. A Telex sent to Hoover in D.C. and to the special agents in charge in Pittsburgh, Miami and Norfolk referred to this contact while he was stationed on a ship at sea. It says, in part, that Hayes

> ADVISED HE LAST SAW KAREN FERRELL, HIS GIRL FRIEND, DURING THE WEEKEND OF ONE ZERO, LAST, AT HER HOME.…HE LAST HEARD FROM HER BY AN UNPOSTMARKED LETTER DATED JANUARY ONE THREE.…HE HAS KNOWN FERRELL SINCE ONE NINE SIX SIX HAVING MET HER IN WEST VIRGINIA THROUGH A SCHOOL ASSOCIATION. HE KNOWS OF NO PROBLEMS BETWEEN FERRELL AND HER FAMILY. HE STATED THEY RECENTLY STARTED TALKING OF MARRIAGE.…DURING THEIR MOST RECENT CONTACTS SHE HAS INDICATED "HIPPIE" TENDENCIES, ALTHOUGH HE CLAIMED SHE DOES NOT USE NARCOTICS IN ANY FORM.

To people today the term *narcotics* conjures up heroin, cocaine and opiates, but federal law placed marijuana in the same category. It's possible that Karen and Steve—and Mared, for that matter—smoked pot, at least occasionally, but there's no definitive evidence about whether they did or didn't. Nevertheless, Steve would likely deny it when questioned by the FBI.

Consideration of drug use and flourishing hippie culture in 1970 requires modern readers to realize that back then both were completely foreign to the general public. Everyone had heard of both, of course, but they had zero experience with drug culture and didn't personally know any hippies. Common opinion was based on media caricature. And like the law of the land, few people distinguished between smoking an occasional joint and mainlining heroin. To most people in West Virginia, hippies were as alien as drugs.

Police were no different. Reports from 1970—WVSP reports, MPD investigations—often referred to the subculture with quotes: "hippies." They were interviewed warily, as if at any second they could say or do something bizarre, unpredictable, even dangerous. One early WVSP report repeatedly refers to a "hippie cabin" in the Weirton Mine Section that had weekend residents; WVSP investigated them as potential murder suspects. What they were actually doing, according to two people who used to visit there, was getting away from town on the weekends to get high and play guitars and bongo drums.

The Dafts, the family that moved in when the hippies left, however, were not so harmless.

One of the most touching appeals for the FBI's help came from Donna DeYoung, certainly the most indefatigable of Mared and Karen's classmates. In a note written with large, looped letters and dated February 9, she appealed to J. Edgar Hoover:

> I'm writing to you concerning two missing girls from West Virginia University. I can more honestly speak for one, Mared Malarik, for I've been a close friend of hers for over four years....
>
> There is no reason whatsoever why Mared would leave school. She was very happy with W.V.U., and looked at her education as important....

Her letter continued, making the case that her two friends did not run away:

> Sir, Mared's personality is very unique. If you, your self, knew her I'm sure that you would not believe that this girl would go on a "joy trip."...

I'd like to ask you a few questions: What are these two girls living on? How can they afford to eat, sleep, and clothe themselves? Why, if they were planning to leave school, did they invite me to go to the movies with them?

No one seems capable of answering these questions for me. But I, myself, can answer them all in one sentence: There is definitely something WRONG, and it was <u>not</u> premeditated....

Mared could never leave a vicinity, especially over a lapse of three weeks, without contacting her parents, myself, or one of her close friends. Could you see your daughter or wife do it? The heart of a woman aches for the things she loves, and those that love her...

Sir, I speak now as one of Mared's closest friends. We both knew each other inside-out. I knew when something was bothering her, without her saying a word. With this, I'm asking you to give us immediate action—and also your prayers. I wish not to speak in the past tense much longer.

Thank you for your time.

Sincerely,
Donna DeYoung

Director Hoover replied promptly.

On February 12, 1970, I received your letter and enclosures regarding Mared Ellen Malarik and Karen Lynn Ferrell.

I can certainly understand your concern for your friends and I am pleased to inform you that missing person notices have been placed in our Identification Division files....We do not have the authority to conduct an active investigation in the absence of a violation of a Federal law within our jurisdiction.

At the bottom of the letter is an addition clearly not sent to Donna:

Correspondent would ordinarily not be entitled to information from our files, however, in view of plea in letter for assistance in locating two schoolmates and apparent wide-spread local interest it was felt information regarding missing persons notices could be given.

The FBI was not looking into the case, but with an instinct that had kept him in power for decades, Hoover seized an opportunity for beneficial public relations.

8

"HEY, I FOUND SOMETHING!"

Published in the *Dominion-News* on February 10: "IT IS NOW 40 days since the attempt to assassinate Prosecuting Attorney Joseph A. Laurita Jr. It is 40 days in which Governor Moore has failed to formally call for the full participation of the U.S. Department of Justice."

The *Dominion-News* had begun a countdown box on the front page to track the number of days since the bombing, the number of days without a suspect. Townes, in keeping with his view of newspapers as a force for public good, was holding authorities' feet to the fire. The assassination attempt had made his anti-gambling, anti-corruption message more urgent, but the bombing investigation was taking too long to produce results. As he put it, "State Police have been diligent and are applying their skills and the equipment they possess," but it was time to call for help from federal authorities and empanel a grand jury, which he believed could "be the real conscience of a community." He also viewed the residents of Morgantown as largely apathetic; he wanted to rouse a sense of justice long lulled to sleep by the dark forces of vice.

One week later, a man with a gun entered the swimming pool area in the old Mountainlair, beneath the stadium bridge. He surprised two coeds dressing in the women's locker room after a swim and told them to lie down. When neither cooperated, he tried to pull the clothes off one and attempted to drag the other toward the door. She screamed and screamed, and the man lost his nerve and fled. Neither woman was harmed physically, but the WVU community was again traumatized, especially the female students. Despite the fact two female students had disappeared a month earlier, authorities treated the incident almost casually. The MPD didn't dust for fingerprints but did retrieve a single unfired bullet that had apparently been dropped by the perpetrator; the university responded only by adding a bolt to the side door.

But the incident raised public concern and marked the beginning of increased coverage. On February 22, in the Sunday *Dominion-Post*, a combined effort of the *Dominion-News* and the *Morgantown Post*, a poignant story opened with a quote from Bess Ferrell, Karen's adoptive mother: "I can't understand it. Everything is just as quiet as if—well, as if they'd gone to the moon or something. We haven't heard a thing."

The article said MPD sergeant John Heis was investigating the disappearance and quoted him as saying, "We're going to turn over the girls' photographs to the FBI." When Heis said this, either he didn't know the FBI had had their photographs for a month or he was lying. He refused to say much about the case: "There's a lot of speculation, but not too many facts to build on," he said.

Neither Margaret Malarik nor Bess Ferrell believed their daughters had run away. Bess told the newspaper, "They didn't run away, they were taken away. It's like believing the lesser of two evils, that she ran away and is alive rather than that…she…" Her sentence trailed off.

The investigation seemed to have stalled, and even the subsequent discovery of the first real clue did not kick it into gear.

————•————

It's March 1 and thirteen-year-old Steven Trickett is walking with his sister in a field just off Route 119, called the Grafton Road by locals. They're collecting glass pop bottles people have thrown away so they can turn them in for the five-cent deposit. Lots of people do that in 1970, especially kids.

As they walk, twenty-five feet or so off the highway, Trickett uses his stick to swish and swat the weeds for bottles. As does his sister. They've both done this, like, a million times, but they haven't done it since before Halloween because of all the nasty rain and snow. They're raking in the bottles, and he has a full poke, as does his sister. They're going to be rich!

Swish-SWAT! Not a lot of traffic on Sundays, but the Grafton Road runs between Grafton and the big city, Morgantown. Swish-SWAT! Even though Morgantown is only twenty-five miles away, most people don't get up there much, unless they work at Sterling Faucet or the hospital or the power plant.

Swish-SWAT! His left arm is getting tired. He can't wait to get home to count his loot. Maybe Papop can take them down to the store to cash them in. Swish-SWAT! *What the shit?*

"Hey, I found something!" he calls out. His sister comes running, the bottles in her bag clink-clinking with her every step. Trickett is peering down, moving the thing cautiously with his stick. It looks like a small purse. He nudges it with his stick again. Nothing happens. He crouches down, peers at it. Black. He flips it over with his finger; it's waterlogged and heavy. His sister crouches down beside Steven, who cautiously unzips the purse. The zipper sticks, like it's been out in the weather a while.

He sees a dime and three pennies. He sees a soggy piece of paper with some handwritten numbers and the letters *pd* circled under the printed name *Dr. Elias Costianes*. An address on Willey Street in Morgantown. He sees a West Virginia University ID with Mared Malarik's name on it. News of the find is not released to the public for over six weeks.

———•———

By March, Laurita was healing, both his hand and his legs. The reward for information about the bombing had grown to $12,905, about $85,000 in today's dollars, but law enforcement had still not made any visible progress. Public interest in the unsolved bombing seemed to be waning.

In contrast, the repercussions of Mared and Karen's disappearance were beginning to reverberate. In city council meetings, more people addressed the problem of hitchhiking, which was illegal within city limits. But the council stopped short of demanding the law be enforced or even publicized. Enforcing the law was discussed, but there was surprisingly little talk about providing more transportation for students. Ultimately, the city felt that hitchhiking was a symptom of WVU's split campus, leaving the university to find and pay for a solution. Concurrently, the university didn't want too much attention paid to transportation problems created by the burgeoning two-campus layout and couldn't afford to alienate students' parents by jailing or slapping fines on hitchhiking students. Stalemate.

But people on campus were passionate about the fates of Mared and Karen. Right in Westchester Hall, starting two days after the disappearance, Donna DeYoung circulated petitions demanding the police call in the FBI. Mared's boyfriend Munch was immediately on board with the effort, and he likely enlisted the assistance of his fraternity brothers. The petition drive spread from there.

City workers protesting in front of the city building that housed the police department, city council and other city offices. Around the corner to the left was the entrance to the police garage. *Mark Crabtree.*

Both the *Dominion-News* and the *Morgantown Post* used the slightest of pretexts to keep the missing coeds' story alive. Each time the reward grew, no matter how little, it was reported. (The Laurita reward fund was more than three and a half times larger, but no one was making such comparisons.) On Sunday, March 5, the *Dominion-Post* ran an article by reporter Jim Stacy: "A growing dispute now revolves around what is being done, what hasn't been done and what can be done."

9

"GIRLS SHOULDN'T HITCHHIKE."

Neither the Malariks nor the Ferrells believed Mared and Karen ran away, which still seemed to be MPD's prevailing theory. The families pointed to several factors police seemed to be ignoring:

- no clothing missing from either girl's room;
- no missing makeup;
- Mared and Karen had invited other girls to go with them to the movies;
- neither girl had much money (Mared had not drawn on her bank account, which she easily could have done);
- both girls did well in school, and there was no trouble in either home;
- letters from Mared to her sister Margo and to a girlfriend in New Jersey indicated no thoughts of running away.

Detective Heis somehow sounded both defensive and smug when he said, "We have followed up every lead. We have listened to every practical idea. We have traced tips all the way from New York to Miami to Ohio. Of course, the longer you go in a case like this the dimmer things look, but I have a hunch that the girls are safe some place."

The rest of the article took a more activist stance, insisting the early "sightings" of Mared and Karen in Ripley were *actual* sightings. The police had neither located the truck drivers nor interviewed witnesses in the J&J

Truck Stop or at McClure's Restaurant in Ashland, the article claimed, though records show the latter not to be true. Authorities hadn't even looked, the article said, apparently unaware of the FBI check of the handwriting on the café ticket. In frustration, both Richard Werner and reporter Jim Stacy had done what they could to track down the reports, talking with witnesses at both restaurants and the Parsons Trucking Company.

Stacy's reporting often hinted at a lack of effort on the part of Sergeant Heis to check into any theory other than the runaway theory. For instance, in a March 17 article: "Sgt. Heis said this weekend that he is awaiting a report from the FBI about the drivers." Stacy checked into Sergeant Heis's statement and found the "FBI office in Pittsburgh said it was not aware of any request to check out the drivers' identities." Stacy didn't say it, but it looked to him like Heis lied in an effort to conceal the fact he wasn't interested in looking for the drivers.

At the same time, the petition circulated by Donna DeYoung, Munch Mongiello, Jessie Chuey, Rick Franzblau of the Mountaineer Freedom Party and other students began to pay off. The students met WVU president James G. Harlow in mid-March with 1,200 names. Jessie said they had another 1,500 names on other petitions, nearly 1 in 5 WVU students calling for better campus transportation and FBI involvement in the case.

The small intercampus bus system in Morgantown was so overburdened even minor accidents had major repercussions. *Mark Crabtree*.

During a nearly two-and-a-half-hour meeting, President Harlow was attentive and, according to Jessie, tried to help. President Harlow praised them for their concern "about their missing fellow students" and suggested they personally hand their petitions to Governor Moore because he would be better positioned to pressure the FBI. Harlow said he'd help set up the appointment, and together they decided to aim for the following week.

Momentum was beginning to shift in the two biggest cases Morgantown had experienced in years. The investigation into the Laurita bombing hit a wall, despite the massive local, county, state and federal resources brought to bear and the fact such a brazen attack on an officer of the state could not be allowed to go unpunished. At the same time, all the various pressures on the coed investigation were coming together—public fear and anger, media attention and family efforts. Soon, yet another incident would show how dangerous it was to hitchhike in Morgantown.

———— ◆ ————

On March 16, roommates Cindi Smith and Candace "Candy" Bailes are standing on Grumbein's Island, outside the Mountainlair, after their evening biology lab let out at 8:45 p.m. They are about to start thumbing when a red GTO stops beside them with two men inside. The driver is blond. The passenger has dark hair and is drunk. Both men are wearing uniform shirts from a local plant, Hire's Bottling Company. Neither man is very large, and the girls aren't particularly alarmed by them.

Both girls are fighters, known for being as tough as they are pretty. Candy's grandfather is Ed Buck, a naturalist famed statewide for picking up rattlesnakes with his bare hands, and she lives up to his reputation. They both think the passenger just looks "goofy." So, despite the fact the coupe has only two doors and the only way out is through the front seat, they get in. They sit tightly together in the back because half the seat is taken up with a case of Royal Crown Cola.

The blond driver turns on the radio as the car begins to move, and the drunk passenger slurs, "Pleased to meetcha." He half turns toward the back and gestures as if shaking hands.

"We're going up to Carlyle," says one of the girls, and the car rolls around the stadium loop to the stop light.

"Your driver tonight will be Gene," the dark-haired passenger says, and the driver turns the radio louder and heads up University Avenue toward Westchester Hall. The passenger doesn't say anything as the car travels up

Students hitchhiking on WVU campus, 1969. *West Virginia Regional History Collection (WVRHC).*

Sunnyside Hill, and near the top, one of the girls says, "This is good. You can let us out here," but the car keeps moving. The girls look at each other but say nothing.

The car continues over the top of the hill and down three-quarters of a mile to where University Avenue crosses Patteson Drive. Still silent, Gene the driver runs the red light and pulls into a gas station. Cindi thinks maybe he's turning to take them back, but instead he heads up Patteson toward the newly constructed Coliseum.

Cindi says, "My boyfriend is expecting me back at the dorm around nine."

The passenger laughs and says, "Then we have plenty of time."

Just then "Suspicious Minds" comes on the radio, and a little unnerved but eager to keep up the patter to prove the girls aren't afraid, Candy says, "I love this song!"

"Elvis is the best," the passenger says. "He's amazing! I've liked him since 'Now or Never.' And 'Little Sister'—that was amazing. I mean, damn! All the old people even like him now. 'Can't Help Falling in Love,' 'Blue Hawaii,' Can't forget 'Crying in the Chapel' and…" The man keeps on about Elvis like he's the be-all and end-all as the car turns right at the Coliseum and continues down the hill toward Star City. By the time they're passing Hills

Department Store to cross the river toward less developed, more forested land, both girls are getting nervous. The blond driver won't say a word and the passenger won't shut up.

"Really, we got to get back to the dorm," Cindi says, and when neither man says anything, the girls look at each other. The car turns left toward Osage, a small mining town. Gene hangs a right down a very bumpy dirt road. No one's on the streets. Once they get past the buildings, moving once again toward a wooded area, the passenger speaks abruptly: "I don't mean to be vulgar, but I gotta take a piss."

The driver still doesn't speak, but he pulls over and stops. The passenger hops out to relieve himself. The driver jams the car in gear and turns it around, the tires spitting gravel. Cindi tries to make small talk with the driver as he stops the car, and at first he won't acknowledge her, then he turns in the seat and stares at both girls angrily.

Just then, "Hey, Gene! Hey!" comes the voice of the pissing passenger from outside. "Get out here! I got an idea."

The driver turns off the engine and yanks out the keys. He glares at the girls and gets out. As he does, Candy rips at the case of soda and both girls grab a bottle to hide inside their coats. Cindi pushes the seat forward to open the door. They start to run, but the passenger appears from behind the car and grabs at Candy. His hand wraps around her throat.

"Let me go!" she screams, but he laughs and rasps, "You ain't going nowhere!"

Cindi tugs at his arm to try to free her friend, and Candy crashes a bottle against his head. The bottle breaks, root beer and broken glass flying, the bottle slicing Candy's hand. The drunken passenger is stunned and swaying, soda dripping down his hair and face.

Both girls take off toward Osage about fifty yards away. Once there, they hide behind cars parked along the road until they are sure the men in the GTO are not after them. But they are a good four miles from their dorm and have no ride, and it isn't long before they again stick out their thumbs. After a few minutes, two men in a pickup stop to give them a ride back to their dorm.

Worried she'd killed Gene, Candy calls the state police to report the incident. A trooper takes their names and numbers and tells them, "You girls shouldn't hitchhike."

10

"SOME CONSIDERED ALCOHOL."

On Monday, March 23, Richard Werner and the Malarik family attorney visited Morgantown. They first went to see Munch, who Richard had met back at the Malarik home over Thanksgiving break. Munch told him Mared had dental work on January 10, done by Dr. Elias Costianes at his office on Willey Street—less than two blocks from where Mared and Karen had been picked up.

Richard wanted to see if Dr. Costianes could tell them about his sister-in-law's visit or the dental work provided—*anything*. The *Morgantown Post* caught wind of the meeting, and a long story appeared in the next day's edition. Although they did not name Dr. Costianes, they did print his thoughts: "He explained that he had put in a temporary treatment filling with several layers of insulation in an effort to save the tooth. The nerve of the tooth was exposed and possibly dying."

Costianes also told the *MP* that Mared almost certainly would have seen another dentist by now and that could possibly be a lead to the coeds' whereabouts. "A dentist probably would remember doing work on a new patient. And very likely he would not have gotten paid since the parents indicate she had no money with her." Werner asked, via the article, that "any dentist who remembers doing such work contact the Morgantown City Police."

The same day the article appeared, DeYoung, Chuey and Franzblau held a press conference. The students feared foul play, and DeYoung was quoted as saying, "Many coeds assume it will not happen to them, but it could....It is definitely a kidnapping."

Spruce Street, with Dr. Costianes's office on the left, at the corner of Spruce and Willey. A left turn onto Willey Street crosses High Street one block down. *Mark Crabtree.*

They wanted to stay focused on the disappearance by further increasing the reward fund and again pressuring the FBI to enter the case. Local and state authorities were outmatched, according to Donna. "Morgantown police have never had such a case.... [T]hey just don't know how to handle it. State police don't know where to start." If the local and state police wouldn't do their jobs, the students said at the press conference, maybe it was time to bring in a private investigator.

Meanwhile, women's frightening experiences of harassment and threat continued, reports stacking up on desks at the Morgantown Police Department. Incidents of violence against women were downplayed in the newspapers; traumatic encounters were whitewashed with casual wording, referring to an extended series of crimes against women as a *rash* rather than an *epidemic*. In the newspapers, women were "accosted" instead of the more accurate—and distressing—"assaulted at gunpoint." The attacks were seen as isolated incidents, not crimes that either exposed a growing danger or were possibly connected to the coed murders. In the sixty days after Mared and Karen disappeared, there were *thirty-eight* reports of attempted abductions, indecent exposures, obscene phone calls and "molesting attempts."

——— • ———

Betty Jo Hypes taught in the English Department at WVU in 1970. One day over spring break, she was walking downtown to a movie. Near the plaza behind the Mountainlair, she saw what she called a "junky-looking" white car with a young man driving. He was twenty-four or twenty-five years old, with dark hair and glasses. He smiled at her. She thought he looked "goofy," but something about him also scared her for reasons she couldn't put her finger on.

The streets were deserted because of spring break, so she noticed when he rolled past her again. More certain he was a threat, she walked off North High and onto Prospect, a one-way street. Since she was walking the "wrong way," she couldn't be followed in a car. She was convinced he was trying to, though, so for good measure, she turned down Spruce Street's slight hill; Spruce is also one-way—headed *up* the hill.

She didn't see him again and cut over to duck into Flora Dora, a boutique dress shop. She waited to make certain he was gone before she walked the half block down to the Met Theater. Nearly fifty years later, she still remembered clearly how he was simultaneously goofy and creepy.

In fact, she recalled the details well enough to dispute a WVSP report that said she had seen the man on Easter: "It couldn't have been Easter," she said. "Flora Dora was closed on Sundays."

———————◆———————

In late March, Westchester Hall got a surprise visit from Sergeant William H. Mitchell and Trooper Preston B. Gooden of the West Virginia State Police. Mitchell was the senior officer, but Gooden was a man on the move, literally. He was known for his constant energy, hands and feet always restless, even when seated. His physical energy was mirrored by his constant efforts to improve what he was already good at: policework. Becoming a state trooper was the epitome of success for him.

Before joining WVSP, Gooden was a police officer for four and a half years in Martinsburg, West Virginia. After he graduated the West Virginia State Police Academy, Gooden had narcotics enforcement training with the New Jersey State Police and then trained with the FBI and the U.S. Justice Department. He taught other troopers criminal evidence and criminal investigation. He would become the most significant investigator on the coed murders case.

Both Gooden and Mitchell had been working the Laurita case. They had exhausted their leads and wanted to check the rumors they'd been hearing for weeks, that the assassination attempt and the disappearance of the coeds were somehow connected. To that end, they met with "roommates and associates of the two missing girls."

The two investigators didn't hear anything they could connect to the Laurita bombing, but what they did hear surprised them. The "students, certain members of the faculty and other people" were unanimous in their discontent with the MPD investigation. Gooden wanted to look deeper into the case. In the process, perhaps they would find a missed connection to the Laurita case, but at the very least they could determine if the case was being handled properly by the MPD.

One of the first people they talked with was DeYoung. She said there was definitely foul play involved or she would have heard from Mared. She insisted she had been asked to go to the movies and she didn't "because of a previous engagement." The April 9 summary report, written by Gooden, stated caution was called for:

Several statements made by Miss DeYoung to Sergeant Mitchell and [Trooper Gooden], *as well as statements to the Morgantown Police*

Department, have since been found to be erroneous, if not completely false. It is the opinion of several of Miss DeYoung's associates that the main reason she is getting involved is to gain personal attention.

At Westchester, Mitchell and Gooden also talked with Paulette "Itsy" Burns. Burns—once again—told what she and Skip had witnessed. Gooden had read her story many times, but he wanted to hear it from her. The only new information was that Karen did drink heavily and may or may not have been using drugs.

RA Gwen McClure told them Mared was "very outspoken with a typical New Jersey attitude." She was very emotional: "If she got mad everyone knew and if she was happy everyone knew." In McClure's estimation, Mared was fairly high strung and "gradually going 'hippie.'" McClure also suggested Karen "would come in drinking and sometimes very disturbed. Karen knew she was an adopted child and acted very depressed over it. There would be times Karen seemed to have a bad illness and she would seem to be in great pain and would have to sit up in bed with her knees drawn up to her body."

Mitchell and Gooden continued talking to residents of Westchester and, for the first time, ran into this: "The word around the floor was that Larry [Casazza, Mared's high school boyfriend] was very violent and that may have worried Mared." They heard the same claim several more times that day.

The most fruitful conversation Mitchell and Gooden had in that three-day investigation was with Mary Kathryn Spitznogle, the assistant to the Westchester dean. She had compiled some information back when the girls first disappeared. She interviewed a few of the other girls—Fitch, DeYoung, Chuey and Pellegrino—on her own and gave her findings to Sergeant Heis. She was glad Mitchell and Gooden were looking into the case because she'd become completely dissatisfied with the MPD's investigation. She felt Sergeant Heis wasn't really committed to finding out what happened.

Spitznogle's statement was full of information, but Gooden didn't know where it might lead. She mentioned Karen had kidney problems before and had been ill recently but didn't want to see a doctor. Spitznogle had spoken with her mother, who backed her daughter. She was also "curious as to why the Ferrells have not been in closer contact" after Karen's disappearance. The Malariks remained in constant contact, but the Ferrells called only once, as far as she knew. She understood Mr. Ferrell had had a heart attack, and that could be why.

Of the girls Spitznogle interviewed, she pointed out two whose statements were likely the most reliable. She believed McClure's was as well, because as an RA—a few years older than the girls—McClure saw everyone more objectively. All the girls she talked to "vetoed the idea of drugs but some considered alcohol."

Gooden noted one girl said she'd been in the room on Sunday when Donna asked Mared and Karen where they were going that night. Spitznogle said the girl told her that "they looked sideways at each other and indicated they were going to Sunnyside then a movie." After Donna left, they asked the girl if she would like to go, but they turned them down "because the sideways glance to her meant they wanted to be alone." In addition, she was certain "that Donna had NOT been invited."

The last day of their three-day investigation, Trooper Gooden checked around both WVU campuses and noted "any and all cars" matching the description of a cream-colored or white Cadillac or Chevy, possibly with fins on the back, seen picking the girls up. He found a number of cars that fit the description and took their license plate numbers so he could run checks on them.

Later the same day, Trooper Gooden went back to Westchester. He tasked Spitznogle with compiling a list of all the things she could find in both rooms, but first he wanted permission to examine the belongings of both girls. Spitznogle escorted Gooden to their rooms. Everything seemed to be there, according to Spitznogle, except the clothes they had worn to the movie.

One of the first things Gooden found in Mared's room was a card from Fairmont General Hospital with Mared's blood type. When he later asked Mongiello about it, Mongiello stated Mared often sold blood there because they paid more than the university hospital in Morgantown. Gooden found a note in Karen's room, signed by her mother, Bess Ferrell: "My daughter, Karen Ferrell, has my permission to sell blood to the University Hospital."

He also found a Panasonic Tape Recorder with one cassette tape. The tape contained a discussion between Donna and a few other girls, apparently other friends of Mared's and Karen's. From what Gooden could determine, they were discussing a party: "[T]hey were mentioning among them sex, dope, and apparent scheming to make their parents give them permission to sign out of school to spend the entire night at this party. The conduct on this tape could be described as having much profanity."

In Karen's room, Gooden found "different letters to Karen Ferrell from different boys in the Armed Forces." Each letter indicated the men thought she was "in love with them." In Mared's room, he also found some letters: "Most of those letters were from girl friends and these two carried very strange conversations. These letters were from females and indicated a great love for each other."

As an experienced investigator, Gooden was not surprised Mared and Karen were not as innocent as they had been portrayed, but they sounded like normal college freshmen. The girls were starting to experiment with things like drugs and sex. People didn't talk about these things much, but there was nothing too unusual here. Normal, but risky. Such things could get them into trouble in ways they couldn't anticipate.

Efforts over those few days convinced Gooden there were severe problems with the coed investigation. Available records do not reveal when, precisely, Gooden and the WVSP were officially detailed to the coed disappearance, but Gooden maintained it was a result of his March 25 notification of Colonel Bonar about what he and Mitchell were finding. As soon as they began to focus full time on the coeds' disappearance, the case broke wide open.

11

"HEARD YOU WERE LOOKING FOR ME."

Corporal Neely, CIB," the trooper says, identifying his office, the Criminal Investigations Bureau of the WVSP in Charleston.

"Yeah, I'm calling from Morgantown." A man's voice. "I thought I should call because of…what's going on and all. I have some information about a man here driving around and picking up hitchhikers, female hitchhikers."

"Yes, sir." Corporal Oscar S. Neely doesn't usually field calls from civilians, but in just the last week, that coed thing is affecting everyone statewide. "You've seen this man pick up female hitchhikers?"

"Yes. Does it all the time. I think he's the one picked up them girls. He's, um… He drives a white Chevrolet. I think he's about forty."

"Do you know this man's—"

"I mean, I don't know he did it, but I think he might have."

"Do you know how to find him?"

"What do you want first, his name or address? I can give you his license number, too."

"Whatever order you want, sir. Go ahead, please."

———— • ————

Trooper Gooden sighs and rocks in his desk chair. He's been calling around for forty-five minutes, trying to locate Sergeant Heis, when he sees the detective walk into the large main room of the Morgantown Detachment of the state police. Holding a small cardboard box, Heis scans the room.

"Sergeant Heis," Gooden's voice loud but not shouting.

Heis looks in his direction and nods. "Heard you were looking for me, Trooper."

"I've been trying to reach you for several days." Gooden doesn't try to hide his irritation. He'd learned the MPD investigation was every bit as disorganized as he'd heard—and by all accounts, this was the man responsible. Maybe Heis wasn't doing his job, Gooden suspected, although he hoped he was wrong.

"You know, Sergeant Heis," Gooden says when the officer draws near, "when I came to MPD in compliance with *Colonel Bonar's express order*, do you know what I found?"

"Nope." Heis shrugs; he isn't concerned. He even seems to find Gooden's anger amusing. "I didn't even know you were in town until last Thursday."

"Of course you didn't. I've been here since your prosecutor was bombed. Now I'm detailed to the coed case. First thing at the MPD, I see a purse sitting on a filing cabinet. Someone says, 'Oh, that's the purse belonged to one of them girls that ran away.' Is that any way to treat evidence, Sergeant Heis?"

"Girls got a wild hair and played rabbit. Probably run off to wherever it is hippies go. California, I s'pose. Like to go there myself. I hear the chicks don't wear bras." Heis flicks something from the lapel of his suit jacket. "But I heard you were looking for it. Here it is." He hands a shoebox to Trooper Gooden. "You'll have to sign for it."

"Thank you, Sergeant Heis." Gooden accepts the package. Inside, according to Heis, is the handbag found on March 1 by one Steven Trickett. "Anything else I should know?"

"That how it is? Staties are in charge, and we're supposed to jump?"

Gooden hates the way police officers turn everything into a pissing contest. "*I'm* not in charge of anything, Sergeant Heis. This is a team effort. We're the good guys. You've *been* in charge for almost three months. What else have you developed that might be of assistance to the *team effort?*"

Heis looks away. "Nothing's turned up because there's nothing *to* turn up. If there was, I'd have found it. Nothing. Nada. Goose eggs, Trooper."

Gooden takes a deep breath to calm himself.

"Do you have any documents to verify the inquiries made of the whereabouts of the boyfriends of the two girls on the night of January 18?"

Heis throws Gooden a hard look. "The Federal Bureau of Investigation—you've heard of them, I assume—advised me that Steve Hayes, the Ferrell girl's navy boyfriend, was at sea that night."

"Do you have any correspondence from the FBI to that effect?" It doesn't escape Gooden's notice he had asked about the boyfriends of both girls, but Heis had only spoken of Hayes.

"It was a public service call, Trooper. What, you don't believe me?"

"There's a lot about this investigation that's unbelievable." Gooden sets the box down on his desk. "Never mind. Do you have anything further to add by way of background from your two-month investigation?"

"Let's see." Heis takes out a notepad and flips through it. "A John Frisco of Westover told me he'd seen two girls hitchhiking 119 north. Getting into a car, English green in color. This was in the late evening of January 19. Two men in the car, one in front and one in back. The driver had reddish hair, thinning. About forty, like the guy those two colored kids saw pick up the coeds. It's in my report."

"That's something. We'll check it out."

"I already did. There's nothing to it."

"We'll check it out." Motionless for once, Gooden glares steadily at Heis.

———— ◆ ————

That first week of April was a pivot in the coed case because of more than WVSP's growing role. Earlier in the week, Bess Ferrell had driven to Morgantown to collect her daughter's things from Westchester. She had given up hope.

Sergeant Larry Herald took Mitchell's place as the other primary investigator in the coed case, along with Gooden. On April 4, Herald requested and received permission to conduct an air search of the area around where Steven Trickett found Mared's purse a month earlier. A National Guardsman flew a helicopter up from Huntington to the Morgantown Detachment, and together with the guardsman, Herald and Gooden flew south.

The search lasted a few hours and "covered all side roads, wooded areas and fields" of the hills around Route 119 almost twelve miles south of Morgantown. For good measure, they flew over the "strip mines and water holes" and went south along 119 "all the way to Grafton and back." As Trooper Gooden's report says in its understated way, "This search was conducted with negative results." The failure to find anything was not much of a surprise. Most of West Virginia is heavily forested, and the chances of an air search revealing much are slim.

Gooden and Herald also began to search WVSP files for anything from the previous few months that might help them jumpstart their overdue investigation. They found a report filed by a Maxine Blankenship of Fairmont. She claimed that in November, just before Thanksgiving, she had a strange encounter with a young blond man. She thought little of it at the time, but two days after the coeds disappeared, she decided she'd better tell the state police.

She made the report on January 20, two days after the coeds went missing. At the time, the Morgantown Detachment had been notified, but because the state police were not investigating the disappearance of the coeds, the report was not followed up. Gooden and Herald decided to interview Blankenship.

But before they did, they went to talk with Joe Shelton, owner-operator of Joe's Sunoco. Shelton said he remembered seeing a woman at the station about 10:00 p.m. on the Friday before Thanksgiving. She was on foot, and he didn't remember seeing any cars approach her. But, he said, he wasn't paying too close attention.

———•———

"My father's asleep in the back," Maxine Blankenship says after checking their IDs. "Do you need to talk to him?"

"No, ma'am. Just you," Herald says in his deep, gravelly voice. She steps back from the door, and they enter the living room.

"Do you want coffee? I can make some." Maxine motions them to the couch.

"Thank you, no." Trooper Gooden shifts his weight and touches the round brim of his service hat. He's uncomfortable with wearing it indoors; he's heard too many rumors of the awkward headgear being used against troopers during indoor confrontations. Still, regulations are regulations. "We won't take up too much of your time."

She laughs and sits down across from them, patting her hair. "Can you tell me what this is about?"

"You filed a report last January?" Gooden says. Herald, the ranking officer, had said Gooden should take the lead.

She nods. "Is this about the coeds?"

Neither man answers her, but tapping his right foot, Trooper Gooden says, "You were at Joe's Sunoco in Grafton on November 21 of last year? Is that right?"

"Something like that." She nods again.

"Please tell us what happened there, Miss Blankenship," Trooper Gooden says.

"It's been six months. I'll try." She closes her eyes briefly. "I was working this shitty door-to-door job, excuse my French. Around Grafton. They'd drop us off in a neighborhood, and we'd go knock and ring bells and stuff. Take orders, if we got any."

"Do you mind if I ask what you were selling?" Gooden asks.

"Encyclopedias. They call it cold calling. Like you're calling on people cold, like without an intro, but I call it that because people are cold to the idea. Anyway, we'd do that for a few hours of an evening. The idea was Christmas presents." She sighs. "I doubt I'll do it again this fall. Depends on maybe if I find something else."

"So they would pick you up after your shift?" Gooden prompts.

"To give us rides home. Let's see." She closes her eyes again, and Gooden realizes she remembers by visualizing. "I was over at the Sunoco there, by Biggie's, and this guy pulls up. His friends were in the car the first time but not now. He wants to give me a ride."

She falls silent, and Gooden taps his pad with his pen to prompt her: "He thought you were hitchhiking?"

"I don't know about that, but, yeah, he must have. Or he just wanted to pick me up to, you know, 'give me a ride.'" She pauses and smirks. "Yeah, right, *give me a ride.* Anyway, he pulled in and when he saw me standing there—looking cold as shit 'cause I was—he came over."

"What kind of car was he driving?" Herald asks.

"Older. Two-tone, but really close, like yellow and white or pale tan and white. Cars look different at night, but something like that. He just came over and started talking. He really liked my fur coat. He said he was a janitor at Westchester Hall. Wasn't that where the girls lived?"

———◆———

Trooper C.N. Cook of the Ripley State Police Detachment was dispatched with new photographs of Mared and Karen to the J&J Truck Stop, the place where the waitress and others believed they saw Mared and Karen. Law enforcement was fairly satisfied, based on interviews back in January, that these girls were not Mared and Karen, but Mared's brother-in-law had joined the public outcries for more follow-up.

Cook arrived at the truck stop about 8:45 a.m. He located two other people who identified the girls from the new photos he had. He also learned something new: The girls had gotten out of a Parson's truck with two men, and the truck was heading south on Interstate 77, one of the few interstates in West Virginia in 1970.

Cook called in the information he'd found, and at 11:15 p.m., Mitchell, now back in Charleston, reached the dispatcher at Parson's Trucking in Wilkesboro, North Carolina. The dispatcher told him the trucker he wanted to talk to was Richard Walker and would be at the Orangeburg Manufacturing Company in Ravenna, Ohio, the next morning at 8:00. Mitchell left South Charleston at 1:30 a.m., arrived in Ravenna before 8:00 a.m. and conducted the interview with Walker at 9:00 a.m.

One of the most notable aspects of police investigation, especially statewide investigations conducted by an understaffed force, was the remarkable amount of driving WVSP troopers engaged in. As often as possible, investigative follow-up was carried out by whoever was stationed nearest, but sometimes a task simply had to be done by someone already familiar with the case. Primary investigators often had to drive five, six, seven hours, spend six or eight hours investigating and then drive home.

In the interview in Ravenna, Richard Walker told Mitchell about seeing a man in a Parson's truck pull into J&J Truck Stop with two girls, one with a short mini skirt and nice legs. Mitchell showed him Mared's picture first, and Walker said, yes, she was definitely the one with the mini skirt and long legs. Shown Karen's picture, Walker said he wasn't sure, but he remembered she'd been short and skinny but well built. He declined to give a signed statement about the incident but said he'd swear under oath Mared was one of the two girls.

After the interview, Mitchell drove back to South Charleston. By phone, he managed to reach the Parson's driver Walker had seen. He learned one girl was a stewardess and the other was from Holland or "some foreign country." She didn't speak any English. All that driving for nothing. That pattern, time-consuming work that led to a dead end, was to repeat itself over and over in the coed investigation.

12

"SOMETHING'S BEEN DEAD FOR TOO LONG."

Kenny Cole has lived on Route 119 on the edge of the Weirton Mine Section for thirteen years. He knows everybody, and everybody knows him. He often wanders the hills, sometimes by himself, sometimes with friends. He never knows what he'll find.

Most of the time, it's just junk, weird trash. Why would anyone toss an ashtray out the window of a moving car? Or a doormat? Once in a while he finds something useful, like a tire iron or some copper wire he can sell. Mainly, it's just nice to walk around in the woods, especially in the spring. Several times that spring, he noticed a white Chevy parked along the little roads. He knows all the cars that belong around there, but he'd not seen this one before.

———————◆———————

By this time, the state police were casting a wider net. They requested information from the IRS. They reached out to the Los Angeles Police Department, although it's unclear what they were looking for three thousand miles from Morgantown. They even asked the FBI to check their files on unidentified bodies.

None of these efforts yielded anything. Gooden was a great believer in the power of positive thinking, but that was getting more difficult in this case. The story they'd heard from Maxine Blankenship was the closest thing they had to a lead. They'd been on the case for barely two weeks, but so far it felt like they were running in place.

On April 8, the *Dominion-News* and the *Morgantown Post* published stories revealing that Mared's purse had been found five and a half weeks earlier. The purse was described as being "very wet, because it had been in weather for quite some time." Inside the purse, according to the governor's chief of staff, Norman Yost, authorities found a mirror, a comb, thirteen cents and a WVU student ID card and a dental receipt, both bearing Mared Malarik's name. (Other articles and WVSP records do not mention the mirror or comb, so either Yost was mistaken or the reporter misheard.)

Both the Malarik and the Ferrell families already knew about the purse. Dr. Malarik would only say, "We did not get any direct information from the police, and the discovery of the purse was not learned through any official source." Bess Ferrell said she couldn't remember how she found out about the purse, but she had known for some time, adding, "I now feel encouraged that the girls will be found."

Yost denied the governor's office had kept the purse secret. "The Morgantown Police Department received this purse," he said. "It was their prerogative to make or not to make it public, and they did make it public in about two weeks." The recovery of the purse was previously published in the Morgantown newspapers, he claimed, but Mickey Furfari, the *Dominion-News* managing editor, denied it. "If it was in any of the local three papers," he said, "I would like Mr. Yost or anyone else to come up here and show us where." Sergeant Herald seemed to concur with Furfari. When asked for more information, he referred all questions to the governor's office: "Apparently, they are the only ones who have released any information on the pocketbook."

The public didn't know what to believe, but they were increasingly focused on the case. West Virginia's national representative Harley Staggers and Senators Robert Byrd and Jennings Randolph had eyes on it. Governor Moore couldn't tell if MPD's Chief Palmer and Sergeant Heis had botched the investigation or simply hadn't yet produced results. But he knew that the students' primary demand, that he use the weight of his office to push the FBI to get into the case, was not going to be met. No way the feds were going to get involved—jurisdictional grounds, supposedly.

Meanwhile, the girls had been missing for eighty days, and still, investigators knew next to nothing. Reports of women being harassed, frightened and even kidnapped continued to pour in without prompting much action from the MPD.

———◆———

April Morgan is hitchhiking from Oglebay Hall, near the stoplight and across from Grumbein's Island. She stands a little back from a small knot of students. She's only out there a few minutes before a dirty beige car passes the other hitchhikers and stops next to her. She opens the door to see a filthy red interior. The driver looks over at her and smiles. A white guy, early twenties, greasy black hair and bad teeth.

"I'm going to Westchester," she says as she gets in.

"Lucky you. I'm fixing to go all the way."

She can't tell if his words are some kind of weird come-on and looks closer at him. He's wearing a long-sleeved blue shirt with his sleeves rolled up to his elbows. Still, she thinks, he's skinny. She can get out fast if she needs to. She decides to get in.

The car rolls around the dip that loops the stadium and heads up University through Sunnyside. April's still nervous, but he doesn't make any moves. She relaxes a little.

"I pick up hitchhikers all the time. I been there, no car and all that, so I pick 'em up. No guys, though. Just pretty girls. Like you." He leers at her. Her stomach lurches.

"I can spot you don't like that," he says. "Who you think I am, Jack the Ripper?"

"No?" she says in a small voice.

He laughs and doesn't say anything until they get up the hill to Westchester. He's not going to let her out, she thinks, but he does. Right there. She walks across the parking lot to the front door. Even without looking back she can tell he just sits there, watching her.

———•———

When the letter came to the *Morgantown Dispatch* on April 9, Trooper James R. Rogers barely looked at it. He assumed it was normal police business. When he finally read it, he exhaled a low whistle. He reread it twice, slowly, and looked at the envelope: Postmarked Cumberland, Maryland, about seventy-five miles east of Morgantown, it had been mailed that morning. The letter was handwritten, not unusual at the time, and the script was neat, precise. Trooper James Rogers knew it might be the first big break in the case.

April 8–70
Gentlemen,

I have information on the whereabouts of the bodies of the two missing West Virginia University co-eds, Mared Malarik and Karen Ferrell.
Follow directions very carefully—to the nth degree and you cannot fail to find them.
Proceed 25 miles directly south from the southern line of Morgantown. This will bring you to a wooded forest land. Enter into the forest exactly one mile—There are the bodies.
25 + 1 = 26 miles total.
Will reveal myself when the bodies are located.

Sincerely,
Δ

Wednesday afternoon was bright and sunny, a good day for a drive. The rainy and chill Morgantown spring was mellowing, ambling toward summer, although still cold at night. Rogers brought the letter immediately up to the common area, and an impromptu road trip was planned. Trooper Gooden, along with Sergeants Herald and Mitchell and Trooper Jerry DeQuasie were going to follow the letter's directions to see if they were accurate or complete nonsense. The letter writer claimed to know where the bodies were, which was both bad and good. Bad because it meant Mared and Karen might be dead, but good because the letter could lead them to the killer. But the letter *seemed* clear without actually *being* clear:

"Twenty-five miles <u>directly south</u> from the southern line of Morgantown"? Where exactly was "the southern line"? Air miles or road miles?

"Enter into the forest exactly one mile"? So was that telling them to drive south on 119 for twenty-five miles and park? Then go a mile into the woods—east into the woods or west into the woods?

The letter sounded like maybe the author was trying to be helpful. Was the lack of clarity unintentional? Was the letter writer trying to help and failing or simply pretentious and taunting?

There is a long history of criminals writing letters to the police, either to taunt or to try to convince them of something. Jack the Ripper sent letters, and as recently as December 1969, the Zodiac Killer mailed one in the San Francisco Bay area, and his next letter would be mailed that same April.

The four WVSP troopers decided to follow the directions the best they could and see where they ended up. Twenty-five miles south of the Morgantown city limits, the troopers found themselves in downtown Grafton, a fading town that had once been a river and railroad hub of north-central West Virginia. Sitting beside the railroad tracks, near the Tygart Valley River, which was one of the tributaries for the Monongahela River, the troopers looked around at the cars and cement, the grand brick buildings. The note said the girls would be found in a "wooded area," and clearly, this wasn't it.

They decided to drive more. One mile farther, at the southern edge of Grafton—twenty-five miles plus one from Morgantown—they came to a wooded area west of Route 119. They stopped the car.

A search turned up nothing.

———— ◆ ————

Kenny Cole and Willis Summers are walking west along Owl Creek Road, about to cut left toward Owl Creek. The space between the road and the creek is flat, a small floodplain for the tiny creek. Flat land is rare in this area, and over time the spot had become an informal dump, a site where people discard junk. Cole and Summers want to check out the rubbish to see if there's anything new since they last looked.

Kenny and Willis both work as contractors, carpentry and labor, mostly, but the work is unreliable. They could both use more cash; they'll find something soon enough.

"I don't know if I want to get in there," Willis says. "Rain's been high. Looks wet as shit."

Kenny smacks the taller man's shoulder with the back of his hand. Kenny's only about five foot six, a stout fireplug of a man.

"Baby don't want to get his feet wet," Kenny mocks.

"I don't want to walk around in wet shoes." Still, Willis is about to step from the gravel road to the swampy undergrowth when he stops mid-step. "You smell that?"

"Kinda rank."

"Smells like something's been dead too long."

"That's not it," Kenny says. "Somebody's dumped some kitchen shit. Like food and stuff."

"Maybe." Willis looks perplexed. "Now I really don't want to go in there."

"Here's what we're gonna do." Kenny looks down Owl Creek Road the way they'd been headed. Less than a mile away there's the Goshen Road, the 4-H camp on the other side. "We're about to run out of road. Let's go back and cut up Ridgedale. We'll find stuff up there. We can work our way over the hill and hook up with the Grafton Road near my house."

"Whatever. Let's just get away from this shit. We'll come back when it don't smell no more."

————◆————

Back in the Morgantown Detachment after 10:00 p.m., Gooden fielded a phone call from Spitznogle at Westchester. She told him Donna DeYoung had received a typewritten letter signed with only the words "A University Supporter." Despite the long day he and Herald had already put in, they went immediately to Westchester. Maybe *this* lead would be the one that broke the case.

DeYoung gave them the letter in the first-floor lobby. Each man read through the detailed recommendations for how to conduct the investigation. The girls had been the victims of foul play, the letter asserted, and were most likely dead. The bodies would be found within a twenty-five-mile radius of Morgantown—two letters the same day that cited the twenty-five-mile radius. Residents were urged to check outbuildings and abandoned mine openings on their land. Boat owners were told to search the lakes and rivers, and citizens and students in Morgantown should check side roads, dumps and "secret parking places." The letter said all this "must be done this weekend as the foliage will be out within the next two weeks."

DeYoung also told an interesting story. According to her, Mared had come back to their room after a date with Munch. She said Mared was acting oddly and finally admitted that Mongiello had given her a shot of heroin. Mongiello was, according to DeYoung, a heroin addict who had the needle marks on his arm to prove it. DeYoung said Mongiello got the heroin from his home in Chelsea, Massachusetts; she didn't think he was dealing but couldn't be sure. It's worth quoting from the WVSP report here:

> *Donna DeYoung proceeded to say a few things that the undersigned [Gooden] knew was not the truth, and she was told these statements were not true, at which time she proceeded to tell Sergeant Herald…[that] she and Mared had had arguments and that Mared was angered because*

Donna was dating a B.C. Williams, a colored subject. Donna also said Mared had been changing and appeared to be getting closer to Karen Ferrell and farther away from her. Donna DeYoung further stated she felt there was foul play involved; however, she had been thinking about narcotics, particularly the heroin, and feels this could possibly be involved in their disappearance.

After hearing Donna out, Herald and Gooden left, but the next day about noon Gooden called Spitznogle to arrange a time for him and Herald to reinterview the fourth-floor girls. This was necessary because of inconsistencies between the stories WVSP had been hearing from students and university authorities and the way these stories had changed over time. That part of the report, written by Gooden, ends with the words, "The undersigned further feels that the use of the polygraph may be in order."

13

"DOWN THE HOLLER THERE."

The next day, DeYoung's letter was the primary focus of a story headlined, "Public Urged to Search for Missing Girls." The article also reported that the reward for information had risen to $3,569.50 (which for some reason was $55 less than had been reported previously) and hinted at the existence of an unknown tipster WVSP seemed to believe was credible. The handwritten letter addressed to WVSP had not been leaked, but word of its existence was getting out.

The article quoted Sergeant Heis as saying, "I still think the girls are alive, because what was found in the purse doesn't indicate anything suspicious." Heis added, "I personally think this is a wild goose chase, but we've got to start somewhere."

Of course, while there was nothing *inside* the purse that was "suspicious," many people believed a rain-soaked purse found twenty-five feet off the road seemed suspicious all by itself.

———◆———

Activity by troopers was picking up. The Huntington Detachment, located in the southwestern part of the state, received a report of a student at Marshall University who claimed to have received a letter from Karen Ferrell. A trooper in Huntington learned that was not the case. WVSP received tip after dead-end tip—and every one had to be checked out, stretching resources even further.

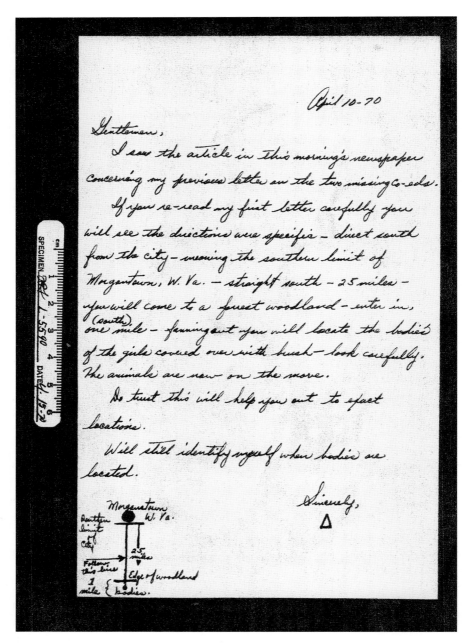

April 10-70

Gentlemen,

I saw the article in this morning's newspaper concerning my previous letter on the two missing co-eds.

If you re-read my first letter carefully you will see the directions were specific – direct south from the city – meaning the southern limit of Morgantown, W. Va. – straight south – 25 miles – you will come to a forest woodland – enter in, (south) one mile – fanning out you will locate the bodies of the girls covered over with brush – look carefully. The animals are now on the move.

Do trust this will help you out to exact location.

Will still identify myself when bodies are located.

Sincerely,

Δ

Morgantown
W. Va.
Southern limit City
25 miles
Follow this line
1 mile { Edge of woodland
bodies.

The second anonymous letter received by WVSP. *WVSP.*

Herald and Gooden spent most of the day reinterviewing Westchester residents, hoping to find something that had been missed. They talked again with DeYoung, Fitch, Burns and Ruth Pellegrino. Nothing much developed, but Herald and Gooden collected samples of everyone's handwriting. In the wake of the anonymous letter, investigators had begun to gather handwriting samples from everyone.

The next day and the day after that, Herald and Gooden again checked the roads south of Morgantown, a copy of the anonymous letter in hand. They checked Route 119 between Morgantown and Grafton and the roads branching off that highway. The Grafton Road was becoming central to the case. As they drove, they scanned the roads and driveways and yards for a small white car that might fit the description given by Skip and Itsy. Again, nothing.

The next day, April 11, they received a call from dispatch: A second anonymous letter had arrived. Once again, the postmark was Cumberland, Maryland.

———◆———

Gooden sits on the edge of his hotel bed, his hand on his bouncing knee. A table lamp is the only light on in the room. The investigation is not going well. All the bulletins to law enforcement in other states; all the checks with local, state and national agencies; all the tips people have provided; all the hours searching the roads—almost three weeks and they have next to nothing. One report of a man Maxine Blankenship felt was odd, but that wasn't really even a lead. Gooden's days have been getting progressively longer, and he's trying to stay positive, but still, he has nothing.

He runs his hands over his face and back through his hair. He stamps his feet and shakes his head to clear it. The Westchester girls insisted from the beginning, as did both families, what he now believes: Mared and Karen were taken. He is sure of that. He knows he's thinking like a civilian—his opinion based on nothing concrete—but he doubts they'll be seen alive again.

If they are alive, they are being held captive—terrified, needing his help. If they are dead—if anyone can find who killed them, he can. As a man coming into the prime years of his career, as a student of Zig Ziglar's lessons, Gooden has confidence in his abilities as police. He is a good father, strict but loving, but policework is where he excels.

He looks at his watch and stands, steps to the television. He turns the channel until he finds WBOY, the station out of nearby Clarksburg. He runs his hands over his face again and sits on the bed to watch the eleven o'clock news. First thing, he sees footage of men searching a field. The Monongalia County Rescue Team has found a pair of eyeglasses and an eyeglass case off Route 119 about two miles north of where Mared's purse was found. The information on the newscast had come from "one of the rescue team members and Sergeant Heis."

Shit!

Gooden reaches for the phone to call the detachment, where he learns that the glasses were tortoise, demi-amber, with "Seymour of Paterson, New Jersey" written along the inside of the left arm.

He's glad the glasses have been found but wonders why, as a lead investigator for the state police, he had to learn about it from the TV news.

———— ◆ ————

Still more people joined the search the next day. The National Guard's 201st Field Artillery, one of the oldest military units in the country, was called out, and it along with volunteers were strung out down Route 119, on Halleck Road, on Goshen Road and along the spiderweb of connecting minor roads. By 9:45 a.m. on April 13, the search of the Halleck Road had recovered a pill bottle with Mared's name on it, a ballpoint pen and a pink compact broken in two. All were believed to belong to Mared and Karen. Karen's purse was found at 4:00 p.m. and the search was terminated at 5:00 p.m., to continue the next day.

The search continued on the fourteenth, primarily in areas near the Halleck Road. Nothing was recovered that day, and the search was again terminated at 5:00 p.m. The search resumed the next day, the most fruitful day yet. By 3:10 p.m., the group searching Secondary 76 from the Halleck Road to the entrance to Weirton Mine had found one ballpoint pen, two tubes of lipstick, one eyeshadow pencil, one mascara, a Ronson gas lighter identified as belonging to Mared and a vial with Karen Ferrell's name on it that contained three capsules. By 3:30 p.m., the group searching Route 76 between the Halleck Road and Route 119 had found a black clothes brush and one green headscarf.

About noon, Gooden and Herald were in the Halleck Road area. After briefing them on the search's progress, a WVSP corporal mentioned a personal encounter a couple of days earlier. At a farm owned by Lloyd and Velma Herron, less than a quarter of a mile away, the corporal met a young blond man named Eddie Thrasher, who was there to visit his grandparents.

National guardsmen and volunteers comb the woods of the Weirton Mine Section, south of Morgantown. *West Virginia Publishing Company.*

Thrasher said he used to work at Westchester Hall as a janitor, and in fact, the corporal had just seen Thrasher passing on Halleck about an hour earlier. Gooden recalled seeing Thrasher's name, Charles Edward Thrasher, on a list of Westchester employees.

Lloyd and Velma seemed happy to talk with the troopers. They said Eddie had just left for the University Hospital in Morgantown, where he was receiving treatment for a burn on his arm. Herald and Gooden learned Lloyd and Velma had raised Thrasher, who Mrs. Herron said was "run off from the home by his mother when he was young." Thrasher had attended Morgantown High School, currently worked at Sterling Faucet in Sabraton and now lived in a trailer in Masontown, about twenty miles southeast of Morgantown. When asked, they produced a two-year-old picture of the blond, long-haired Thrasher and three of his school notebooks for handwriting samples.

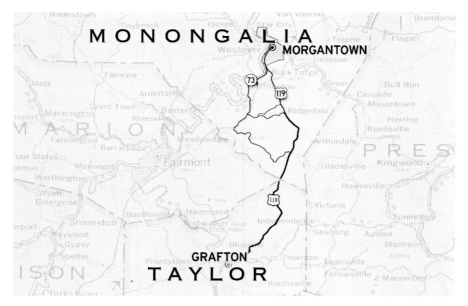

Map showing area between Morgantown and Grafton. Most of the searches covered the darkened area in Monongalia County. *S. James McLaughlin.*

Herald calls Maxine Blankenship to see if she is free for another interview. He wants to see if she'll recognize the picture of Thrasher, who might be the man who liked to "rub furry things." That evening, Gooden and Herald again find themselves at Blankenship's Fairmont home.

"Come on in," Blankenship says, opening the door for the two state policemen.

"Thank you for seeing us again, ma'am." Gooden's fingers drum the coffee table on which a folder sits.

"You guys have a picture? That was fast."

"We're still looking into it, ma'am." Gooden opens the folder. "We'd like you to take a look, see if anyone looks familiar to you."

Inside the folder are eight photographs, including the one from Lloyd and Velma Herron. She peers at them all and then picks Thrasher.

"This looks like the guy who was after me. I don't think it's him, though. This guy looks different. Younger, maybe."

"Thank you, Miss Blankenship," Gooden says, closing the folder.

As they leave, the two men look at each other, silently acknowledging what they both know: Thrasher is the only real person of interest they have, much better than the two they'd developed earlier that day when they checked the handwriting in the dorm sign-out logs. One person's writing looked similar to the handwriting of the letters mailed from Cumberland: Spitznogle. Not only that, but Sandra Fitch, Karen's roommate, had traveled to see her husband in Baltimore a week earlier, passing through Cumberland the same day the first anonymous letter was mailed from there. But Thrasher looks better than either woman, Spitznogle or Fitch.

———◆———

The next day, on April 16, Steve Slavensky and another guardsman were walking with Trooper Richard L. Cunningham on Route 76/2, called by locals both Owl Creek Road and Old Sawmill Road. They stopped right where a narrow dirt road branched up a small hill and ran along a ridge at the base of a larger hill. On the other side of that hill lay the Goshen Road and Camp Muffly, the local 4-H camp.

"Why don't you two go on ahead," Slavensky said to Trooper Cunningham and the other guardsman. "I'll check out this little valley. We'll meet down the holler there."

Slavensky ambled over the little valley's uneven ground, careful to step around tire tracks—looked like a bus turned around here regularly—looking for anything that might be of interest. He'd been one of the early searchers and had walked the single-file row of searchers off and on for ten days. The valley stretched more than one hundred yards from the road and about seventy-five feet to the right of the creek. He didn't feel like going up the hill, and besides, this seemed like a perfect time for a smoke.

A tree stood toward the back of the holler, about fifteen feet from the creek. In the middle of the trunk, four or five feet off the ground, a large knothole. As he drew closer, Slavensky realized the hole was a good place to stash something. He bent and swept up a solid stick.

He stopped beside the tree. Recalling his training, he used the stick to explore the unseen insides of the dark hole in the tree. Nothing. Shifting his gaze, he looked to the right, about ten feet past the tree. A mound of rocks and leaves and…

He shook his head to clear his thoughts. Looked back. Sticking out from the rocks and leaves was a tangle of dark bone, tattered flesh.

II

THE PARADE OF HORRIBLES

"VERY STRANGE, VERY VIOLENT,
VERY NASTY PEOPLE."

Gooden and Herald were called to the scene and wild speculation began: The murderer couldn't have been someone from Morgantown. The killer was the wealthy son of a prominent Morgantown family. The girls were victims of a madman and LSD was involved. Mared and Karen were sacrificed by a Satanic cult. The rumors took on lives of their own, and some still thrive fifty years later.

Criminal investigation is a group activity, and its tedium doesn't translate well to paper or screen. Investigators do not develop suspects one by one, in a linear fashion, but piece together bits of information, looking for a coherent story, often developing many persons of interest at once. They grow frustrated by dead ends while resource constraints and political interference further inhibit progress. In a long investigation, suspects aren't ruled out, like they are on TV, so much as never again mentioned in the reports.

With any given investigation, the public often believes the police aren't doing enough. But the scary truth is that in 1970 investigators didn't have too few suspects, they found far too many: the Westchester janitor with a fur fetish, the "harmless" delivery man who beat a woman nearly to death, the nursing home orderly with the bloody broomstick, the bouncer with the "girlish" laugh who threatened to cut off people's heads. The actual investigation looked into between forty and one hundred persons of interest over the next eight months in 1970. The parade went on and on.

There are a lot of very strange, very violent, very nasty people out there running around. And every time we would find one, we would say, Maybe this is the guy that did it. It's one of the things that kept the police going in twenty-four different directions.
—Attorney Dan Ringer

1

"MAYBE A HATCHET?"

On the morning the bodies are found, lead investigators Gooden and Herald are at the Morgantown Detachment going over what they have. They both like the subject Eddie Thrasher, who Maxine Blankenship tentatively chose from a photo lineup. She said the man in the photo looked too young, but they know the photo is two years old.

They also want to look closely at Kathryn Spitznogle, the assistant to the dean of Westchester, and Sandra Fitch, Karen's roommate. The handwriting of both women looks similar to that in the anonymous letters. Fitch frequently travels back and forth from Baltimore and could easily mail letters from Cumberland, which is right on the way.

And the subject Donna DeYoung continues to be of interest, if only because she has proven herself fairly loose with the truth. Police are used to hearing lies, every day, from everybody, so constant skepticism is a job hazard. Gooden and Herald were told a number of times that Donna craves attention and believe that to be the root of her gossip. Probably, she has nothing to do with her friends' disappearance, but investigators' antennae are up.

It's almost noon when radio traffic picks up, flat voices that talk quickly, without affect. Herald and Gooden look at each other, both suspecting the same thing.

Gooden and Herald arrive at the section of Owl Creek and Goshen, where roadblocks are up. The men are waved through to the scene, where they park. Immediately, Corporal Sparks approaches their car.

"Trooper Cunningham was the first on the scene," he tells them, indicating a man looking up the woodsy incline that surrounds the dumpsite.

Abruptly, Cunningham yells loudly, "Ron! We know you're up there! Come on down!"

Silence falls as everyone freezes. After a couple of seconds comes a crashing, branches breaking as someone stumbles down the hill. A man twists his way to where the trees thin out, awkwardly carrying camera equipment. It's Ron Rittenhouse, the newspaper photographer. He looks toward the little knot of men on the road as Gooden and Herald get out of the car. He heads straight for them, his eyebrows raised. He has a leaf in his hair, and tiny branches are caught under his camera strap.

"How'd you know I was up there?" Rittenhouse smiles, but it's tentative and forced. A small man in casual clothes and bristling with camera

National Guard and WVSP gathering on road in Weirton Mine Area, April 16, 1970. *West Virginia Publishing Company.*

equipment, Rittenhouse doesn't fit in with the paramilitary officers of the MPD, the WVSP and the National Guard. He's a border collie among wolves.

"You have to leave," Cunningham says. "You have to leave right now."

"That sounds like good thinking, Trooper Cunningham," Rittenhouse says and turns to go back up the hill.

"Take any pictures?" Cunningham asks before Rittenhouse has a chance to go.

"You didn't give me time." Rittenhouse still looks nervous. He's new to the job and not used to dealing with police.

"Gimme your film."

"Umm...okay." Rittenhouse hesitates, but only for a second. He winds the film to remove it from his camera.

"Don't come back," Cunningham says. He pockets the film pack. "We'll call you when we're ready. You all will have ample time. Maybe around five or six. Still be plenty of light for pictures."

———————◆———————

Gooden and Herald were put in charge of the recovery scene. The small valley was shaped roughly like a horseshoe, open end to the road. Over the next several hours, the National Guard conducted a massive ground search, the line of men parting only around the grave itself. Then they proceeded up the hills into the woods on all three sides going back a few hundred feet. Gooden was to coordinate, mark and chart the evidence they found; two other troopers were ordered to bag and initial everything.

The troopers were not looking to solve the crime, but to learn as best they could what had happened there, on that spot. The site where a body is found may or may not be where a murder took place. Police refer to such a site as the *disposal site*, or *dump site*, the latter term accurately capturing the murderer's casual dismissiveness. Often, victims are simply discarded, like refuse, as if their bodies have no more meaning than rotting vegetables.

Gooden and Herald's first task was simply to stand back and look—really *look*—at the scene. The pile of stones and branches and leaves on the remains appeared to be forest debris. The leaves could have fallen there or been swept there by wind.

Across the pile lay a large, forked tree limb one WVSP report said took "four (4) or five (5) men to remove." The large branch was not precisely on top of the grave and may have been placed there, but it was also possible the bodies had been left *under* the arching branch. Or the limb might have come down in the eighty-eight days *after* the bodies were left.

Some of the stones on the grave were large and flat and might have been brought from the nearby creek. A couple were the size of tombstones and looked as if they had been carried by two men or one strong individual. However, the rocks, like the tree limb, could have simply been tumbled onto the grave. The whole flat area was littered with stones of various sizes, probably having been scattered about by flooding over decades.

The way the material mounded up from the flat valley looked as if the bodies had been placed on top of the ground and covered with stones and smaller branches. The lower leg of one victim was exposed, probably due to weather and animal action.

Once Gooden and Herald finished their observations, other troopers began carefully removing the material, piece by piece. Slowly, two bodies were uncovered, one on top of the other, both belly down. The one on top was angled slightly, not aligned with the bottom body as if carefully placed, and her legs were partially drawn up as if tossed there. The one on top might have been tugged off-kilter by whatever had taken the foot. The disposal had been casual and didn't look posed or staged.

West Virginia State Police around the "tomb" that held Mared and Karen. *WVSP.*

Gooden brushed the top leaves away to get a better look at the body on top, to see if he could identify it as either Mared or Karen—and found himself looking right down into the cavity of the body. Her head was gone. He paused, took a deep breath. Brushed away more leaves. The second body was missing her head as well. Despite his horror, he pressed on, assessing the scene.

Both bodies were fully clothed. Shocked as he was by the decapitations, he also was struck by how undisturbed the bodies looked, despite the ravages of weather and time. The top one, the smaller one, had protected the one underneath; her clothes had worn to shreds. The clothes on the bottom body were much less deteriorated. To Gooden, the bottom one appeared almost neatly clothed. As if they had been beheaded and simply fallen over.

Gooden and Herald believed the one on top to be Karen, the other one, Mared. Both men leaned closer to observe the bodies, as they had with the undisturbed mound of rocks and sticks. The only articles of clothing missing from Karen's body were one shoe and her black faux-fur coat. Gooden thought of Maxine Blankenship and Eddie Thrasher.

"There," Gooden indicated with his pen. The dark brown turtleneck sweater on the top body had a couple of identical three- or four-inch slits with ragged edges and a small amount of what appeared to be blood. He glanced at Herald, who was staring at the slits. Gooden mumbled, "Maybe a hatchet?"

"Maybe." Herald indicated the bottom body's bare feet. "Her boots are missing."

Gooden nodded. "Her fur-lined boots."

—— ◆ ——

Uncovering the bodies was slow, methodical work. Members of the press and other concerned locals waited at the police barricade most of the afternoon. For the most part, WVSP did not inform the press of anything, but when the bodies were found to be headless, word got out. By five o'clock, both had been marked for identification, put in the coroner's containers and removed.

That afternoon, Karen Ferrell's driver's license was found down in Taylor County, the county south of Monongalia County. The dingy paper license had been reported by a woman whose three-year-old grandson discovered it in the driveway, a couple of miles north of Grafton, about two hundred feet from Route 119. The license was farther south than anything found so far.

Monongalia County coroner William Bowers, standing at the police barricade, found himself slammed with reporters who hammered him with questions about the new discovery. He spoke freely, hoping to take the edge off the tense situation, and neither he nor the press differentiated between case facts and uninhibited speculation.

Some of his statements were on point—he said the decapitation "couldn't have been done by animals because the tomb served as a sort of protection for most of the body"—but others were misleading. For instance, the *Dominion-News* reported Bowers said the top body was unclothed and the two bodies were placed side by side. Both "facts" were remembered and reported by many, but weren't true.

Sometimes, Bowers simply speculated. He painted a lurid picture: "[T]he girls, finding themselves in the hands of 'a maniac' threw the items out of the car to mark their path." Perhaps under the influence of Dr. Malarik's statement a week before that Mared had thrown her purse out "as a marker," Bowers told the crowd the girls had thrown out their personal effects to leave a trail: "They were saying, 'Here I am. Follow me.' They were scared."

Bowers went on to opine about the kind of man who must have killed them, saying he "must have been a madman or 'someone taking drugs.'" But his imagination didn't stop there, plastering yet another half-cocked theory for the media: "LSD sends you on this trip and you can't quit whatever crosses your mind."

His guesses played into public fears of drug-addled hippies and were vivid and memorable. The image of a killer driven mad by drugs fit the chaotic, unpredictable nature of this crime, like the Manson Family murders.

The remains of Mared and Karen being removed. *West Virginia Publishing Company.*

But the idea Mared and Karen intentionally left a trail of debris, tossing items randomly from their purses to serve as breadcrumbs for searchers, was nonsense. Mared's glasses were found 144 feet off the road, too far to have been tossed out the window of a moving car. That was true of other items found 50, 75, 100 feet off the road. The items had been distributed intentionally, presumably by the killer.

2

"I WANT A FUCKING PRESS CONFERENCE!"

Herald stands in the dark outside the small Morgantown Airport terminal while Gooden fiddles with his keys to unlock the police cruiser's trunk. Richard Werner, Mared's brother-in-law, only recently having taken over as family spokesman, charges out of the front double doors, electric with grief and anger. Lagging only slightly behind him is Dr. Edward Malarik, his wheelchair pushed by John J. Byrne III, the family attorney.

Werner spots the troopers right away, zones in on Herald. "I want to see Mared." Dark circles hang below his glassy, bloodshot eyes. His voice loud, it wavers between tight and gravelly. "When can I see her?"

Gooden pops the trunk while Herald answers in a hushed voice: "You don't want to see her that way. We don't need you to ID her." Herald can just hear the lashing Superintendent Bonar will dole out if the victim's brother-in-law were to barge into the pathologist's office.

Werner steps closer to Herald. His face inches from the trooper's, he shouts, "You can't keep me away! This whole investigation is bullshit!" He pivots toward Gooden, still shouting, "Right from the beginning! We've been lied to, ignored, and now you're telling me I can't see her—my own family!" He looks at Byrne. "I want a fucking press conference! Right now! I want to see some goddamn results!"

Dr. Malarik flinches at his son-in-law's profanity. For the first time, he speaks. "Getting angry won't bring her back, Dick." His knuckles are white as his hands grip the chair's wheels. A folded plaid blanket hides his lap, the edge curving slightly and tucked under the seat of the chair. Dr. Malarik navigates closer to Werner and turns toward the troopers before stopping. Gooden realizes Dr. Malarik is a double amputee.

Byrne slides closer to Werner and gingerly rests a hand on his shoulder. "Let me talk to the troopers, Dick." The last thing he wants is his client spending a night in jail.

Werner looks angrily at the officers but says nothing. He balls his trembling hands into fists before bending and grabbing the handles of two suitcases. He turns sharply, trudges to the back of the cruiser. Under the bright light of a streetlamp, he mechanically wedges the luggage into the open trunk.

"We need an update here," Byrne prods, his voice low. "Dick's beside himself, and I can't blame him. I'm hoping your arrival means we won't be dealing with the Morgantown police any longer. The entire family—and I can't stress this enough—is disgusted with the progress—the *lack* of progress—we've seen from the beginning." His voice is getting louder with each sentence, until he catches himself. He pushes his glasses up the bridge of his nose. "We need answers to take back home. And we need honesty."

Gooden glances back to see Werner's eyes glistening at the rims. He heads toward the distraught man.

"I think we've gotten off to a bad start. Let me try again, Mr. Werner." Gooden extends his hand. "Trooper Preston Gooden." Werner begrudgingly accepts his hand. "I agree that you all and the Ferrell family have been done wrong. I pledge to you my full attention to this case, Mr. Werner."

Anger crosses Werner's face again. He lifts his gaze to meet Gooden's eyes. "I need someone I can trust, Mr. Gooden. I need you to promise me that if at any time this investigation is stalled or stopped, you'll let me know."

"The Morgantown police aren't in charge of this investigation anymore, Mr. Werner. The state police have taken over and there are at least eight men I know of working full time on this." Gooden's arm comes up, his open palm next to his ear as though he is taking an oath. "If the investigation is corrupted in any way or abandoned by the state, not only will you know, but I'll make it public myself."

This time it's Werner's hand that extends, and Gooden shakes it firmly.

3

"A WHITE MALE, 6', BLUE EYES, BROWN HAIR, 197 LBS."

The next morning, Gooden and Herald are waiting with several other troopers for a briefing to start. However grim the previous day's discoveries had been, finally there is something concrete to dig into. Yes, the lower half of Karen's body is severely deteriorated, as Gooden and Herald had noted, and Mared's body was neatly dressed, her stocking seams straight, a cigarette packet with two remaining cigarettes tucked neatly into her waistband. But the initial check also yielded new information: Mared had a small contusion of her wrist and one single short hair was found on her shoulder. Both clues are of limited use. The wrist bruise means nothing unless they can find how it got there, and in 1970, the only way to compare hair samples is visual. The hair might have been a pubic hair, but there was no telling if it was Mared's, Karen's or the hair of some unidentified third person. Perhaps evidence, perhaps simply trace.

Sergeant Robert L. Mozingo begins the meeting by slapping down a copy of the April 17 *Charleston Gazette* with an article on the front page titled "Wooded 'Lovers Lane' Yields Headless Coeds." In the accompanying photo, a bearded man in a light button-down shirt, blue jeans and boots stiffly points at the forked tree that arched over the coeds' bodies.

"Who the hell is this?" demands the exhausted Mozingo.

Gooden and Herald exchange glances.

"A Glen Cain, according to the paper," snaps Mozingo. "They don't usually get that shit wrong. It says he, uh—" He peers at the paper, squinting.

Glen Franklin Cain, from *Morgantown Post. West Virginia Publishing Company*.

"A WVU student and U.S. Forest Service officer. Says he was one hundred feet away when the Guard found the bodies."

He slides the paper over to Gooden and Herald. "I want you to find out *everything* about this subject. Who is he? What does he know? Why is he in this picture, and for the love of God, does he have a record?"

"We need to run down a few things on the Thrasher subject," says Gooden.

"Find out about this man first," Mozingo orders.

A new person of interest has crowded into the investigation.

———•———

Gooden and Herald head for the university to check out Glen Franklin Cain. It's about 11:00 a.m., and the day is passing quickly so they split up to save time. They have a lot to do. Gooden stops in to interview someone in the offices on the first floor, and Herald goes downstairs to Dean Joseph Gluck's basement office. Dean Gluck's assistant greets Herald.

"I'm Gordon Thorn. Mr. Gluck is dealing with another pantry raid, unfortunately, but I'll help you any way I can." At WVU in 1970, pantry raids are common, with students stealing anything from plastic cups to quantities of food from dorm kitchens, fraternity houses or the Mountainlair.

"Thank you, Mr. Thorn. I'm here about Cain's records."

"I went to the registrar's office to pick those up for you. Miss Jones works there, and she knows Mr. Cain, actually." His voice lowers as he resumes. "She said the girls in the office heard him tell a strange story, Officer."

Herald says nothing, just looks at Thorn, deadpan. After a long pause, Thorn clears his throat. "He told those women his dog pulled a blanket off the dead girls and dragged the bloody thing through the woods."

Herald feels a resigned sigh coming on, but stifles it. He never knew a dog that would play with a blanket when there was dead meat to investigate.

Thorn doesn't pause this time. "Cain is from Winfield—down by Charleston—but he lives in a trailer park here in Morgantown now."

"Were you able to determine if he has class today?"

"Let me make a call. It will take me a moment."

Herald lets himself out of the office and walks over to one of the large windows of Martin Hall to wait. Two dead birds lie in the concrete well of the window. They must have been trapped by the leaves and debris in the deep, narrow well. Herald stares silently.

Thorn steps into the hall, looking for Herald. Finding him looking at the dead birds, he casually mentions, "Oh, this happens all the time. I'll have to call the Physical Plant. We usually find them still alive, but things have been so hectic around here."

Herald slowly turns his gaze from the birds to Thorn. "Any luck?"

"Sorry, no. None of the professors took roll today. Professor John Scherlacher probably knows Cain the best. You should talk to him. If you can't find Scherlacher, try Cain's advisor at the Forestry School, Dr. Mount."

"Thank you, Mr. Thorn. Could you direct me to the registrar's office, please?"

As Herald walks toward the registrar's suite of offices, Gooden comes down the hallway.

"Hey, Pres, did they drain that pond yet?" asks Herald as they bustle through the hallway. He thinks there's a chance the skulls are at the bottom of a pond across Owl Creek Road from where the remains were found.

"Fifty thousand gallons. Might take most of the day."

The troopers together go on to interview Ruth Ann Foe, a neighbor of Cain's whose desk in the registrar's suite is just down the hall. Foe tells them Cain met his wife in Arizona and returned to Maple Drive in August of '69. Foe describes her as about five foot, six inches, with long, dark hair. Very pretty. "I think her name is Marsha or something. She looked about eight months pregnant." She glances around as if to hide a secret. "I heard she's a race car driver."

"Tell us about Cain. What's he like outside school?" Herald pulls a chair closer to her desk and sits.

"Well, I think he's in a band with Bill Curry and Larry Matheny. I'm not sure what they see in Glen." Her nose wrinkles. "He's a big liar, that boy."

The troopers' eyes meet for a quick second. They wait for her to elaborate, but she doesn't. She does tell them a variation of the blanket story but has nothing to add. She sends them to Louise Robinson, another staffer in the office, for more details. Unfortunately, Robinson adds little, just the blanket story again, and the two troopers thank her and leave. They both have the feeling the blanket story is just baseless gossip, probably started by Cain.

They walk to Professor Scherlacher's office, where he tells the officers he figures Cain will be withdrawing from school soon if he hasn't already: "Cain once told me he was in the state police in Logan County. He tends to…exaggerate a bit." He shrugs. "You should know."

———— ◆ ————

Gooden and Herald proceeded to Dr. Mount's office, where they gathered Cain's prior addresses from January 1966 to January 1969. They also obtained a record of Cain's absences. Mount described Cain to the best of his ability: "He was drawn to authority—liked to dress in uniform. He's usually a pretty easy-going guy. He has some latent tendencies toward violence, but I can't see him using malicious or unjustified violence."

Back at the Morgantown Detachment, Mozingo listened to the summary of Cain's background. He in turn called Captain Bowley at the Shinnston office to arrange to deliver the handwriting samples to CIB in Charleston.

Police rarely explicitly rule anyone out, but a subject can be moved from the active to the inactive list. By the end of April, Gooden and Herald had learned enough about Cain to consider him an inactive suspect. And when they received word from CIB's look at Cain's handwriting, they were even more sure Cain wasn't their guy. As would happen so much in the summer and fall of 1970, the troopers spent hours of their time investigating a dead end.

Opposite: When the ponds were finally drained and dredged, authorities found only a baby doll's head. *West Virginia Publishing Company*.

4

"MORE HEADS WILL ROLL!"

That April 17 was a momentous day for the nation and for Morgantown. The first warm day of spring, a crowd of about fifty people gathered on the Monongalia County Courthouse Square in downtown Morgantown. They were waiting for the 1:00 p.m. splashdown of Apollo 13, America's seventh manned Apollo mission.

The flight had a WVU tie-in, a fact that made Morgantown residents proud. Apollo 13 had relied on the computing work of Katherine Johnson, a WVU alumna, for trajectory calculations. She was what NASA then referred to as a "computer." But the mission was a mixed success. One of its primary goals, landing on the moon, was scrubbed.

The crowd engaged in pensive small talk, some standing and others leaning against poles along the sidewalk, uncertain whether the astronauts would return alive. The crowd murmured in low tones about the terrible discovery in the woods south of Morgantown the day before.

A completed pathology report wouldn't be available for weeks, but the press published information as it came piecemeal from the governor's office, including that no bullet wounds or stab marks were found on the bodies during the initial observation. The governor's assistance proved double-edged, as always; his involvement propelled the investigation, but he'd clamped down on the transparency of the case, including firmly prohibiting photographers at the crime scene and the hospital.

Left on top, unprotected without her coat, Karen's body was the most damaged. Her body had lain sprawled on Mared's for three months, almost a shield over her friend, keeping her from the worst of the elements. That was why William Bowers, the county coroner, mistakenly told the press Karen had been nude from the waist down. Closer to the truth: Karen's clothes had simply fallen away from her bare bones.

Two fire trucks stood by on the square, prepared to declare the safe South Pacific Ocean splashdown of the spacecraft. Suddenly, the sirens sounded, and a wailing cacophony bounced off buildings and pavement while some bystanders covered their ears.

———◆———

By April 20, Mared Malarik's body had been positively identified by her fingerprints. State, county and city police searched an eight-mile radius for the missing heads, and troopers canvassed the houses in the Weirton Mine area again. The same day, Spitznogle's handwriting samples came back from CIB in Charleston: None matched the handwriting in the letters.

On Tuesday, April 21, a brief memorial service for the coeds was held at St. John's Chapel on campus; 150 students attended, mostly women from Westchester. They listened as one fellow coed spoke with tears running down her face. She quoted Kahlil Gibran's *The Prophet*: "When you part from your friend, you grieve not; For that which you love most in him may be clearer in his absence, as the mountain to the climber is clearer from the plain."

The thin, dark-haired Father Richard Marold led the service with scripture readings and pleaded with the students to not let fear keep them locked inside their dorms. Some students wept while others somberly looked on, listening intently to the Catholic campus minister.

When the service let out, students cascaded down the steps, a few with red, tear-weary eyes hidden behind dark sunglasses. If anything, the memorial service reinforced for students the need to take charge and help each other.

———◆———

Cathy Montgomery, student body vice president, met with about fifty fellow students to discuss university security and proactive solutions to the transportation issues faced by students. Bus service was limited on campus, and concerned students strongly felt the need for a better alternative. One proposed solution was the creation of a campus-based motor pool that only operated when no buses were scheduled. The system would be temporary, in place until better options could be developed.

The motor pool was tightly run: Riders looking to use the pool could identify the cars by the phosphorescent placards in the upper right-hand side of the windshield. The Line-O-Scribe (a type of small printing press) signs could not be counterfeited, and drivers could check them out for their shifts. Directly below the sign, a driver's identification allowed riders to match ID to driver before entering the vehicle. The university allocated the cars a spot in front of the Mountainlair, and the rules permitted only university students to operate the fleet.

The motor pool began shuttling passengers from downtown to Beverly Manor and Towers and had a total of twenty-one riders the first day. Fourteen previously screened male drivers escorted fellow coeds, with a required second male presence occupying the vehicle at all times.

Students at the meeting also discussed the implementation of dormitory floor meetings to help dispel rumors. Most importantly, students planned to hold a press conference on the twenty-eighth before a rally and then a peaceful walk to present the committee's safety proposals to the city council. Ironically, buses were provided from Towers and Westchester for interested students.

Student sitting near front of Mountainlair, where motor pool cars picked up students. The mast of the USS *West Virginia*, sunk at Pearl Harbor, is visible on the left. *Mark Crabtree.*

The bodies of Mared and Karen were officially released from the custody of Mon County the same day as the memorial service. The Associated Press called the Ferrells to see what would become of the reward money and inquire about their daughter's funeral arrangements. Bess refused to respond to their questions. Margaret Malarik also refused press questions: "I don't have anything to say."

Karen was laid to rest in Clintonville's Wallace Memorial Cemetery nineteen days past what would have been her nineteenth birthday, her most vivid fear come true. The Malariks made sure Mared's arrangements remained private, shunning the city that had failed to protect their vulnerable teenage daughter and further failed to find her killer. From then on, the Malariks communicated with Morgantown's police or press only through the family lawyer.

———◆———

Life at West Virginia University in 1970 didn't look much like campus life today. Today, twenty-four-hour news channels and social media announce "breaking news" on cable, smartphones and trending hashtags. In 1970, most students living on campus did not have access to televised news. Aside from local printed media and AM radio, most information came word of mouth.

Unfortunately, with little access to a way to check facts, people's "knowledge" was fueled by gossip and wild rumors. One rumor spoke of yet another missing coed who'd possibly been murdered, while a second described packages of body parts arriving in the mail. Female students began fielding what might be called *fright calls* that promised things like "You're next" and "More heads will roll!" Women in dorms felt increasingly susceptible to a skilled and vicious roving killer, and worse yet, they felt their fates relied too heavily on inept and uncaring law enforcement.

The girls of Westchester Hall felt especially vulnerable. Several phoned the DA to ask about rumors of a master key with which a killer could gain entry to every dorm room. Students from Towers, a new complex of dormitories, phoned President Harlow at 2:30 a.m. to ask if there was any truth to the talk of the governor receiving another letter promising four more coeds would die.

The hysteria reached such proportions that the campus posted guards outside the dorms every night from 9:00 p.m. to 6:00 a.m.

5

"THERE IS NO NEED TO COVER NEWS."

A t the same time Gooden and Herald were gathering information about Cain, they were also looking into Eddie Thrasher. They first went to Sterling Faucet, the tin plate mill on the southeast side of Morgantown, near where Laurita was bombed. Eddie's grandparents, Lloyd and Velma Herron, said he worked there, but Gooden and Herald learned from Sterling's personnel manager he was no longer employed at Sterling. The troopers were allowed to search his personnel files and learned one telling detail: Thrasher was scheduled to work on January 18 and 19 but did not show.

The two troopers then returned to question Thrasher's grandparents, who mentioned that Thrasher's car had burned in the parking lot of Sterling Faucet while he was at work. Sterling's personnel manager failed to mention this fact. Suspecting the car might have been burned to conceal evidence, Gooden and Herald headed to a nearby firehouse. The station had no record of the fire.

———◆———

A murder investigation in real life bears little resemblance to a fictional one. Real investigations don't unspool like TV narratives, where the facts are clear and present a linear narrative. Instead, progress happens piecemeal: Investigators come across dribs and drabs of information and often don't know what is significant and what is not. Investigations involve many officers, each checking a tip here, a hunch there. As information begins to stack up, sometimes a story starts to form that lends meaning to the facts, but the meaning often changes according to the story investigators construct.

The information on Thrasher was beginning to pile up, but no story had yet formed: Maybe Thrasher missed work because he killed the coeds, but maybe he just had the flu. Maybe he burned his car to hide evidence, but maybe—considering Sterling never said anything and the firehouse had no record—he simply lied to his grandparents because he wrecked the car. What Gooden and Herald had seen so far *looked* incriminating, but they needed more. Gooden wanted to find telling facts about Thrasher that were *only* illuminated by the story of the coed murders.

To many people the troopers talked with, including his employers, twenty-year-old Eddie Thrasher was a nice, ambitious young man. His neighbors, on the other hand, said he was untrustworthy and *at least* a thief. Investigators heard both reports multiple times. For instance, a neighbor of the Herrons said Thrasher and another boy were at his place in a blue pickup. He believed they were looking for something to steal. He'd had a .25 pistol stolen a while earlier and believed Thrasher was responsible.

Thrasher recently had a series of injuries. In September 1969, he was temporarily hospitalized, complaining of dizzy spells. In February 1970, he received treatment for a puncture wound between the fingers on his left hand. On April 11, he came to the hospital for muscle strain in his left arm. Three days later, he received treatment for first-degree burns to his right arm. On April 20, he was treated for "a fragment in the eye." Investigators didn't know if these injuries were meaningful or simply the job hazards of a young man doing hard physical labor.

However, on the same day Thrasher had the eye injury, Gooden and Herald learned that his handwriting did not match the handwriting in the Triangle Letters. They appear to have lost interest in him at that point.

In 2007, Lieutenant Colonel Richard Hall, ret., learned something that WVSP did not know at the time: Living with Thrasher and his grandparents was another, much scarier man.

———————◆———————

"We seldom criticize police work," said an editorial in the *Huntington Herald-Dispatch*, "but the apparent indifference and ineptness of police and school authorities in the case...defies rational explanation. The kindest thing that can be said about the loose investigational work of police…is they believed the girls had taken off on a spree." The *Herald-Dispatch* wasn't alone in its sentiments—newspapers all over the state were printing commentaries lambasting the police and the governor.

Ron Rittenhouse had his film confiscated, and WVSP troopers on the scene also compelled a reporter from Charleston's WSAZ-TV to hand over his film. But the WSAZ reporter was older and craftier. He handed over a blank roll. His instincts proved right: After the *Dominion-News* complained to the Governor's Office about the confiscation of Rittenhouse's film, the roll was returned—only it had been exposed to light and ruined.

Because of the executive interference, the only published photos of the disposal site were all taken discreetly by determined reporters and completely unauthorized by law enforcement—some taken from a distance with a telephoto lens. The *Fairmont Times* added, "We were shocked by the actions reported by the Associated Press that State Police confiscated a news photographers' film.…We thought those 'bully' tactics had gone out years ago."

The press was angry they'd been forced into subterfuge just to do their jobs. The *Fairmont Times* wrote that the Governor's Office made a point of saying the state police were instructed to treat the case as a murder. Sarcastically, the editorial commented, "Come now, Governor, Col. Bonar and his state police…would probably have surmised this without such an order from your office."

Morgantown papers found themselves stuck with making long-distance calls to the Governor's Office to request story developments. Reporter Charles Ryan of Beckley's *Post Herald* published his opinion of the situation: "When reporters must get all information from one source, then there is no need to cover news."

A still-stung *Dominion-News* attacked the credibility and efficiency of the Morgantown Police Department. In an editorial, the paper claimed police bungled the case by deciding to keep private the discovery of Mared's purse, and after the state police stepped in, the girls were found within eight days. The article went on to goad Governor Moore—yet again—into reaching out to get FBI participation.

Authorities made statements to the press that were convoluted, conflicting or—sometimes—retracted. Coroner Bowers's statement on Karen's state of dress was refuted by Captain W.F. Bowley of the WVSP: "I saw clothes." Bowley was echoed by Mozingo when he stated that their clothes helped identify them. Superintendent Bonar was quoted as saying the police "had

Newsroom of *Dominion-News*, with reporters (*left to right*) Evelyn Ryan, George Samsell and C. Zoe Smith. *Mark Crabtree*.

someone in mind" as a possible suspect, but Mozingo stepped in once again to say that at this stage, the letter writer was only a person of interest rather than a suspect. WVSP now suspected the letter writer was not the killer but a gimmick conceived by a WVU student to engage the FBI by using the federal postal service.

The public's curiosity about the mysterious letters was growing.

6

"HE WAS A CRUSADING JOURNALIST."

Kathy Spitznogle is sitting at her desk with the phone to her ear and a pencil in her hand. "Uh huh…Okay, slow down…What color again, two-tone?"

She records notes on her clipboard, looks up when Betty Boyd, WVU's dean of women, appears in her doorway.

"Okay, thanks. I'll make sure the police check into it. Thank you for calling." She looks up at Betty. "Those girls are in real danger out there, and the police aren't—"

"Tell me about it." Betty slumps in a chair by the door with a labored sigh. "Did you know one of the girls called the newspaper this morning at 1:30 a.m.? They put it in the paper. I guess she was huddled with a bunch of girls, scared out of their minds."

"Oh my goodness, those poor things. What did they want?"

"Apparently, they heard another body was found in Cumberland. They just don't trust us when we say these things aren't remotely true."

"Add those to the ever-growing list." She props her elbow on the desk and cradles her head in her palm. "I heard the girls talking yesterday that the second body wasn't Karen's. One asked me if it was a fifty-year-old woman's. I guess since they found out Mared was ID'd, they assumed Karen would have been by now, too."

"They're terrified, Kathy. The prank calls don't help." She pulls a piece of paper out of her purse. "Lots of scary men picking up hitchhikers. I have more notes to give to the police. License numbers, mostly." She hands it to Kathy.

"Thanks, I'll put it in with the others. I'm about to call these in anyway." She lifts her clipboard to show Betty when the phone rings.

"Hello?" Kathy puts her hand over the mouthpiece and whispers to Betty, "Speak of the devil," before returning to the call. "Hello, officer."

———•———

Nearly a week after the bodies were found, the *Dominion-News* stretched a headline at the top of the second front page across all six columns: "Coeds Tell of Hitchhiking Ordeal." The news broke more than five weeks after Cindi Smith and Candy Bailes were terrified by Gene and his passenger. *Dominion-News* reporter Shelby Young snapped a picture as Smith and Bailes headed into the office of Justice of the Peace and County Coroner William Bowers.

Smith and Bailes lived at Carlyle Hall, Westchester Hall's companion. They'd been telling others on campus about their abduction, and the DA published an account of their kidnapping experience. The article caught the attention of *Dominion-News* general manager William A. Townes.

Recalling the incident decades later, Ray Evans, the *DN* city editor at the time, said in 2017 that Townes was "a stern kind of a guy that believed in community journalism and in justice and represented the people—he was a crusading journalist."

Townes wanted to hear the whole story from the girls, and more importantly, he wanted to print it, but there was no story if legal actions were not pursued. His motives were questioned—while some colleagues lauded him as a crusader, his critics called him a sensationalist.

In 2017, Evans said of the editorial stance of the *Dominion-News* in the days of Townes, "We were representing the people. Our job was to get to the bottom of things and tell the truth. [Townes] would hammer a story."

Critics who slammed Townes for sensationalizing the Smith and Bailes story also had to admit a disturbing reality: Two hitchhiking coeds, one brunette and one blond, were driven against their will far from Morgantown. The parallels to Mared and Karen's disappearance were unnerving.

"We found out which dormitory the girls lived in and sent a reporter," Ray Evans recounted. Yes, it was true that the sensational story would sell newspapers, but what if those men had something to do with the deaths of Mared and Karen? "[Smith and Bailes] weren't all that interested in pressing it—I think they even said they were a little bit embarrassed about it, but their friends in the dormitory thought they had a civic duty."

Remarkably, Smith and Bailes were the ones responsible for tracking down their kidnappers. After police offered no further assistance a second time, the girls decided to do some investigating of their own. Their abductors wore Hire's Brewing Company uniforms, so Smith called the company and asked for Gene. Gene wasn't working that day, but someone gave them another piece of the puzzle, Gene's last name: Tritchler.

Armed with this new information, they went to the phonebook. There were four Gene Tritchlers listed. After a few false starts, Smith and Bailes finally got confirmation of his number and address.

Not long after, Smith saw Tritchler in a pickup, and she and Bailes decided to follow him. She said he noticed them and "seemed rather shook" about being pursued. A week later, his red car was spotted driving by the dorms, and Smith and Bailes went to the WVSP barracks in person to relay the information they sleuthed.

Townes decided police had been handed the details of a crime and still weren't doing enough. He contacted the prosecuting attorney and asked whether charges could be filed against Tritchler and his sidekick, now identified as Richard Johnson.

According to Evans, Townes told him to take a reporter and a photographer to the dorms and give the coeds a ride to the Magistrate's Office. Evans protested: "I told him that we were more or less crossing a line in the journalism business to be escorting people to get warrants filled out. He didn't object to my position, he just turned around and did it [himself]." Evans still didn't think Townes was in the wrong. "He was doing it as a citizen. I never regarded myself as a citizen—I saw myself as a journalist."

Both Smith and Bailes seemed reluctant to press charges and cause trouble, so Townes told them it was misdemeanor abduction and the boys would only be fined. Both girls agreed, and JP Bowers opened his office at 9:00 p.m. to accommodate the urgency of the request. The warrants, though, were not for abduction but for kidnapping. The sentence for kidnapping was more than a fine—it ranged from ten years to life in prison. Smith asked if the charges could be reduced to abduction but was told by Bowers that Townes had insisted on kidnapping charges.

A week later, Smith and Bailes tried to cancel the charges, according to Evans. "The girls came in and recanted, based on..." He took a long pause. "What?" He chuckled. "Based on what? Based on the fact that their parents were with them."

Smith defended their position on retracting their charges: "Our parents didn't want us to be dragged any further into this thing and felt that there was sufficient evidence for the State to take up the case." Both girls insisted the newspaper played no part in their decision not to press charges.

Tritchler and Johnson later took West Virginia Newspaper Publishing Company and Townes to court in a million-dollar malicious prosecution civil suit. They claimed Towne's irresponsible push for their arrest led to their embarrassment, loss of wages and damage to their reputations. Tritchler and Johnson won their suit, and shortly thereafter, Townes retired.

There is no record that Tritchler or Johnson was ever a suspect in the deaths of Mared and Karen. Nor were they ever tried for kidnapping, assaulting and terrorizing Smith and Bailes.

7

"AREN'T YOU AFRAID
OF GETTING INTO A STRANGER'S CAR?"

In late April, Kathy Spitznogle contacts the WVSP to turn over notes about all the harassment and abuse reported to her by her Westchester girls. One student, Mary Talley, has particularly vivid recollections of an odd hitchhiking experience she had before Christmas. Spitznogle suspects that whoever killed Mared and Karen might be on campus again, looking for his next victim, and convinces Herald to come talk with Talley and some of the others.

"He had a faded Rambler station wagon," Mary says once she and Herald are sitting in Spitznogle's office. "I was walking to Westchester when he offered me a ride. He was white, maybe twenty-five, medium dark hair and a protruding nose. First thing I noticed was that his gear shift was on the floor."

"Tell me about him, please, ma'am. What made you report this?"

She crosses her arms over her chest and hugs herself, leans back in her chair.

"He sounded nasally. He kept saying things like we'd have to get out and push, but then he got really weird and said, 'Aren't you afraid of getting into a stranger's car and getting raped?'"

She pauses. When Herald stops writing, she speaks again.

"He laughed like it was a funny joke, put his hand on my shoulder and said, 'Don't worry, I'm not going to rape you—I just like to eat it,' like it was absurd to worry about dying yet it was totally okay for him to talk to me that way. I didn't say anything, so he repeated himself like maybe I didn't hear him right the first time."

She shakes her head. "I stayed silent, and he drove me the rest of the way up to Carlyle and let me out. But you know what? I'm not the only one he's picked up."

She waits for Herald to finish his notes again.

"Mary, can you give me names of any of the others?"

"Sure, Sharon Katusa. K-A-T-U-S-A. She saw him in a green and white Kelly cab. Oh, and a white Valiant, too."

"He drives three cars?" Herald lists the cars in his notebook, with a check beside the white Valiant.

"Yep," Mary says, rocking as much as nodding. "He's picked up other girls, too."

Herald pauses. When it's clear she has nothing to add, he asks, "Any idea when these incidents occurred?"

"I think it was her first semester. Sharon's. There are probably about ten other girls. It's hard to forget being trapped in a car with a guy who says disgusting things like that." She lets her arms drop, laces her fingers and twiddles her thumbs. "I've heard other girls talk about him. None of the others take him seriously, but after, you know, what happened to Mared and Karen, I'm not so sure. Same three cars, too."

Herald clears his throat uncomfortably. "Mary, did he ever try to physically force himself on you or the others that you know of?"

"No, he just acted creepy. He always let us out whenever we asked."

"When's the last time you saw this man?" Herald barely takes his eyes off his notepad between questions.

"Um…he's still around. He's got a white van now. Big letters on it—RCA. Barb and Jeanne got a ride with him a couple days ago. Today's the twenty-fifth? So I guess the twenty-third."

"Thanks, Mary, this is very helpful." Herald writes down the new names as Mary recites them. "Do you think you would recognize him if you saw him again?"

"No question." For the first time in the conversation, she smiles. "You don't forget a beak like that."

———•———

Herald tracked down another girl Mary mentioned, Barbara Nab. She said Monday, around 9:00 p.m., she was walking with a friend when the white RCA van stopped. The driver leaned out and asked if they needed a ride. They declined, so he turned around and left.

Stephanie Aucremanne was next on the list. She also reported a white RCA van and described the man as about five feet, nine inches, with glasses and dark, slicked-back hair. She specifically noted he had bad teeth and might have had a speech impediment. She was with her friend, Jeanne, and said he exposed himself. He said they didn't need to worry because he'd rather eat them than rape them.

Nancy Miller was another.

"I lived above Mared," Nancy told the authors in 2016. "I was in 528, and she was in 428."

Nancy had been hitchhiking "at Oglebay Plaza, where everybody hitchhiked. A white car drove up to pick me up. I'm thinking an Impala because I recall pointed bumpers in the back. A gentleman [got out of the car and] stood up on the street and opened the door to allow me to get in on the driver's side. I thought it was weird. I glanced in and noticed the passenger door was wired shut."

Nancy remembered the next moment very clearly: "The hair on my neck stood up. I refused to climb in and motioned for him to go on. His car peeled out, his tires leaving a whiff of rubber." She thought he was very, very angry.

"I was among the people that were called into the [director's] office to speak to a state trooper that apparently was investigating the case....As I entered her office, I noticed maybe eight fellow residents sitting quietly in a half circle. The trooper stood in front of them. An artist was to his left. I think the director [of Beverly Manor] told him something like 'This is the last one' before she closed the door....

"As women described their incidents to the trooper, it became apparent that we were describing two different men. Three or so students identified a blond male. The rest of us described a male with dark hair....We tended to agree on most characteristics—the jawline, the hair length, the eye color—as the police artist drew our descriptions. I don't remember too many specifics now. I think the man's hair was intentionally greasy, like he used Brylcreem. He was wearing a white T-shirt, and he looked like a local worker rather than a student."

———◆———

Later, Gooden looks at the sketches of the two persons of interest that Nancy and other coeds had identified. He shakes his head. One of the two men might be the sicko who had killed Mared and Karen. Maybe after three months of silence, not even a hint of who the killer was, maybe he is confident enough, or compulsive enough, to try again. Or maybe the investigation is just finding out that hitchhiking coeds and other women in Morgantown are—and always have been—in far more danger than anyone cared to admit.

Gooden doesn't like the way this case is going.

———◆———

Within days, WVSP found one of the men, the dark-haired person of interest: Thomas Wesley Lantz. He was definitely no joke.

On a chilly October evening in 1962, eight years before Mared and Karen were murdered, twenty-five-year-old Betty Hart Murray found herself in a predicament with a car she'd borrowed from a neighbor. A faulty door latch forced her to stop on an access road near the Morgantown airport. She got out and, as she was fiddling with the door, heard a car come up behind her and stop. A man with dark hair approached, asking if she needed his help. She said no. He didn't say anything and walked back to his car. She assumed that was that.

But seconds later a metal pipe slammed into the back of her skull with enough force to split her scalp. Hitting her over and over, he knocked her into the car, blood splattering.

When someone finally found Murray's car, still sitting in the middle of the road, her unconscious body inside, the six deep gashes in the back of her battered head were leaking blood. Rushed to the hospital, she regained consciousness momentarily to gurgle incoherently, but police heard her say, "He had a gun," before she sank back into oblivion. She remained unconscious for several weeks.

Two months passed before a twenty-three-year-old Lantz sat in the MPD's interrogation room. He'd been arrested for loitering just hours before, but really they wanted him on four state-issued warrants. Bennie Palmer, then just a detective, grilled Lantz on three local robberies and the attack on Murray. After two hours, Lantz finally broke down and confessed to the thefts and the felonious assault of Murray. He claimed he didn't know Murray and, unable to explain the attack, said only that he "lost [his] head and beat her."

Lantz's conviction for the robberies carried a sentence of two to ten years in the West Virginia State Penitentiary. The judge recommended, as part of Lantz's rehabilitation, that he be admitted to Weston State Hospital for psychiatric testing. Doctors there diagnosed him with passive-aggressive behavior and a personality disorder. During his incarceration, Lantz escaped but surrendered a week later. In 1967, he walked out of the penitentiary a free man after serving four years.

In 1969, Kelly Cab hired Lantz as a driver. He now had access to a taxicab, his father's light-colored '64 Oldsmobile and his mother's black Falcon station wagon to covertly prey on the women of Morgantown. He cruised the campus looking for hitchhiking coeds.

Lantz again attracted the attention of MPD in November 1969, when Beth Hayes, then head resident of Westchester, filed a report stating a suspicious cab was trying to pick up college girls on campus. Nevertheless, he remained a free man, loose and on the prowl. And he didn't target only college coeds; several reports from women passengers detailed physical assault and sexual harassment, leading to his eventual dismissal from Kelly Cab. When he again turned up on WVSP's radar in 1970, they tracked him down through his current employer, the House of Audio, where he drove the delivery van. Herald and Rogers spoke to a former coworker, James Hydzik, who seemed unaware of Lantz's criminal record. He was aware Lantz had spent time in Weston State Hospital because, as Lantz himself said, he was "crazy."

Lantz was looking like a viable suspect in the coed murders. But somehow, despite those hints in the summer of 1970, Lantz was taken off the active list. This happened several times in the coed murders case: People who maybe looked good for the murders were never followed up on. Starting with Eddie Thrasher, the fur lover, the very first person of interest in the case, the records simply never speak of the person again. (Presumably, WVSP had solid reasons to move people to the inactive list, but after fifty years, the records could not be found.)

Whatever the reason, Lantz was able to continue his "career." He eluded arrest until December 1971, when once again, he unleashed violence toward another WVU coed. Part of the problem, according to Assistant Prosecuting Attorney David L. Nixon, lay in the lack of laws in West Virginia concerning molestation. In an attempt to compensate, officers linked offenders to additional misdemeanor charges, but that didn't always work. Women and children were being accosted with greater frequency, and more than *a dozen* cases of child molestation and attempted abductions occurred on Morgantown's streets in 1970 and 1971. The situation grew so severe that off-duty officers patrolled the streets in their own cars to keep up.

Offenses against women, whether violent or "only" abusive, just weren't taken seriously. Not only did many men commit similar crimes, the judicial system meted out little punishment. The career of Justice of the Peace Ruth Shale was typical. Over and over, she let offenders off with short or nonexistent sentences. In one case, she fined a man fifty dollars for molesting a coed.

As a letter to the Combined Civic Clubs Committee from Trooper Gooden read, "I only wish more people were concerned with the deplorable conditions that exist in West Virginia in relation to law and order in the criminal circles. There exists too much talk and not enough action."

Morgantown largely did not see itself as having a crime problem, or more precisely, the citizens and the powers that be were of two minds: On one hand, citizens were concerned enough about crime that in 1969 they had elected Joseph Laurita as Monongalia County prosecutor on his law-and-order platform; on the other, the crime rate in Morgantown was—and still is—one of the lowest in the country.

But violence against women in all its forms was epidemic. Betrayed by a culture that considered women second-class citizens and unprotected from daily abuses large and small by a weak legal framework, women in Morgantown and around the country in 1970 faced a lot of predators waiting for the chance to intimidate, harass, molest and rape—and most of the time the men received little punishment.

Whatever the reason, Morgantown citizens in 1970—and today, truth be told—largely preferred to feel like they were living in a small and sleepy and *safe* town than to address the constant menace women faced.

8

"WHY DID ROWE SEE A GREEN CAR?"

Despite the campus memorial service for Mared and Karen, Karen's remains were not definitively identified by her fingerprints until April 24. Other investigative findings also trickled in about the same time. Menus from the Westchester cafeteria on January 18 listed foods that matched the autopsy results to the contents of the deceased girls' stomachs. The report from the FBI indicated they had eaten two or three hours before they were killed. Although digestion times vary according to such factors as temperature and victim stress, unless the bodies were immediately frozen, the coeds were killed the night they disappeared.

More significantly, WVSP finally eliminated Mared's boyfriend Munch Mongiello as a suspect, only to temporarily replace him with another: the dentist, Elias Costianes. On March 24, he wrote a letter to the *Dominion-News* that purported to be from a concerned citizen simply being helpful. However, in early April a woman called to insist that ten years earlier she was molested in a dental chair by Dr. Costianes. Even though she never pursued charges, she said the trauma he inflicted caused her to drop out of WVU. Herald was dispatched to talk with Costianes to see if he could determine the truth of her accusation. After that talk, WVSP dropped Costianes as a suspect, but in 2006, retired Lieutenant Colonel Hall found more to be suspicious about.

Throughout, tensions between law enforcement and the press continued to increase. When a Camp Muffly caretaker called a local newspaper with a tip, the Associated Press ran it without reporting it to authorities. The caller said he spoke with a cop after the bodies were found, but the "disinterested" officer didn't even take his name.

The caretaker lived a little over a mile from the Owl Creek disposal site, and a man had knocked on his door two to four days after the girls disappeared. The visitor, who said he lived in Fairmont, asked for tools to dig out a stuck car from the icy Weirton Mine Road. In 1970, the West Virginia Department of Transportation left piles of cinders alongside the road to assist stranded drivers, and the man wanted a shovel to spread cinders for better traction. The caretaker lent him a shovel and mattock, and the stranger never returned the tools.

As soon as the story hit the stands, the press badgered law enforcement about the new lead and published another article about the lack of follow-up. Places as far away as Shreveport, Louisiana, published the anecdote with emphasis on the shovel's sharp point, implying it could be used in a beheading. Public pressure forced WVSP to track the man to his Fairmont home and question him. They cleared him, finding him guilty only of irresponsibly leaving the tools at a cinder pile. After publishing dramatic information that pressured the police, the AP barely covered the low-key follow-up.

Running down another tip, Gooden and Herald interviewed John Zinn at his farm near Grafton. Zinn and one of his farmhands told troopers they had seen a suspicious car near where the bodies were left. The car, a white 1963 Chevy Impala, was in bad shape—upholstered in red with an aerial on the right rear fender, its body "eaten out." They'd seen it two separate times and thought it might be the white car seen abducting Mared and Karen.

Zinn also remembered noticing tracks in the snow the previous winter that looked as though something heavy had been dragged through. At the time, he chalked it off to a deer carcass. Hunting season had ended, but 1970 West Virginia viewed such regulations as suggestions rather than firm rules. Curious, Zinn returned to the area to see what he could find and discovered a pair of fur-lined leather gloves. Unfortunately, Zinn left the gloves where he found them, assuming whoever lost them would come back for them. He told Gooden and Herald exactly where the spot was, and the troopers went to look for themselves. They found nothing.

———◆———

Later that evening, FBI agent Steve Thompson calls Herald back at the Morgantown Detachment: "Look, I'm not vouching for the authenticity of the tip. I'm just passing it on to you. For whatever it's worth."

"We're getting a lot of that. We appreciate the help."

"Sure. Anyway, got a message here the man says he came by third-hand."

Herald hears papers shuffling on the other end. "A Bob Accosta, lives on Maplewood Avenue here. White male, about twenty-seven to thirty years of age. He's been telling people that he's got those girls' heads in the deep freeze. Said he ate part of the one."

"Heads in a freezer?" Herald says and looks at Gooden. "That's a new one. What's the informant's name?"

"He didn't leave it. Rumor is this guy's into narcotics and runs the JJ Club on Adams. Accosta, not the informant. We're giving this lead low priority."

"Thanks, Thompson." Herald sighs, hangs up the phone and jots down the information.

Gooden plops down in front of his desk with a steaming cup of coffee. "What was that all about?"

"You don't want to know, kid," Herald says. "Shit just gets weirder and weirder." He stretches his arms over his head and yawns, pushing back against his chair until the front legs lift off the ground, briefly, then slam back to the floor. "Pres, I'm thinking about going out to the 4-H again, seeing if anyone knows anything."

Gooden checks the clock on the wall. "It's after eight now, Pappy. But let's squeeze that in and, after, we should check traffic again." The men have been surveying every day, sometimes two or three times a day, hoping to see cars that match the description of the car that picked up the coeds. Gooden had begun to think of Mared and Karen almost as his own children, or as "everybody's children," as his eldest daughter, Terri Nehari, put it later.

One "tip" took the form of a copper plate WVSP acquired around the time the bodies were recovered. The rectangular copper plate, $4\frac{3}{8}$ inches by $5\frac{3}{4}$ inches, was believed to be connected to the murders.

The plate was inscribed with Greek letters and astrological and alchemical symbols. Referred to as "specimen Q1," the plate was shipped to the FBI for cryptanalysis and came back in June packaged with an examination report:

> Inasmuch as the Greek letters were not formed in a consistent manner and variations of upper and lower case letters are mixed with symbols which may or may not represent Greek

One side of the copper plate. The three vertical rectangles in the upper third of the plate have been redacted to maintain the anonymity of the person for whom the plate was made. *WVSP*.

letters, no precise interpretation could be developed for all of the word length units.

The vertical word on the left of the top portion appears to be the Greek word for "coptic" and the center vertical word appears to be the Greek word for "logic." Two of the three five-letter groups in the matrix appear to be the Greek word for "opera" and a Greek word which could refer to initiations into mysteries.

The foreign text and pictographs appeared ritualistic. Some observers characterized the "eyes and eyebrows" on the plate as sinister eyes and *horns*. Troopers speculated about a witch coven or Satanic cult in the area. The victims, found fully dressed and headless, suddenly appeared to have been sacrificed in some pagan ritual.

The copper plate remained a mysterious element of the files in the coed case until 2019.

———◆———

"Police May Have Suspect in the Coed Case" blared the headline across the top of the *DA*'s front page on April 29. Reporters learned from a confidential source in New Jersey that the WVSP were investigating "a suspect or suspects" in the coed case. The source also said someone spotted Mared and Karen at the Morgantown Motel with members of Ezra, a band that played in Morgantown back in January. The manager of the Castle, a popular club in Morgantown, confirmed Ezra "was performing at the nightspot at the time of the coeds' disappearance."

MPD's Sergeant Heis said, "I've no reason to check into any musical groups," but WVSP's Sergeant Mozingo confirmed they were looking into Ezra, who hailed from New Jersey. A year before, two nineteen-year-old women were stabbed to death near where Ezra had a gig. Police theorized someone following the band committed those murders and later killed Mared and Karen. In the long run, the Ezra lead went nowhere, but years later, the prevailing theory ties the New Jersey murders to Ted Bundy.

———◆———

John Rowe calls the WVSP to tell them he was in the Mineral Industries Building on January 18 between 9:00 p.m. and 11:00 p.m. While taking a study break, staring out a window, Rowe saw some girls get into a "small compact" car, medium green in color. Rowe also said he saw *three* girls, not just two.

Gooden relayed this information to Herald.

"Could be," says Herald. "We thought it might take two men. To restrain both girls, to lift those rocks, that tree. Just never thought the other man was a girl."

"What if it wasn't? A guy with long blond hair from behind, it looks like a girl."

"Not to me."

"Long coat," Gooden says. He's thinking the coat hides the hips.

"Okay, but Clarence and Paulette both said they were sure no one else was in the car. Young guy, clean cut, dark hair."

"Maybe leaning down so as not to be seen?"

"That's possible. But why did Rowe see a green car?"

Gooden pauses, thinks. "I was looking at a tree the other day. Out back, off the balcony. The branches, the bark on top of them, looked green. I know the bark's brownish, grayish, but it looked green."

Herald's eyes narrow. "So what are you saying?"

Gooden shrugs. "White car next to that big expanse of green lawn. Maybe the streetlight reflects green."

Herald scoffs, but doesn't say anything.

9

"SOMEONE EMOTIONALLY DISTURBED WROTE THE LETTERS."

Throughout the spring of 1970, WVU students continued to feel vulnerable. The unsolved murders became symbols of just how expendable Morgantown and WVU believed them to be. Disgruntled student sentiment manifested across campus. At Towers, two girls put on a skit in which they were hitchhikers and said, "I sure hope we don't get kidnapped. No one would bother looking for us around here." Other students prepared to take matters into their own hands.

The students' newly formed Committee of Evaluation of Student Safety and Welfare proposed six improvements, ranging from better lighting and more sidewalks to agreement of responsibility between city and university administrations. Armed with this new proposal, between 250 and 300 students, an equal mixture of men and women, rallied at Oglebay Plaza near the mast of the decommissioned battleship USS *West Virginia*, which sank at Pearl Harbor. The event was led by Alan Woodford, newly elected student body president, and Al Pritchard, a member of the committee that adopted the proposal. The last to speak was a dark-haired Alpha Xi Delta sorority sister named Joann Alger. Alger hailed from Kinnelon, New Jersey, just like Mared. After reading a *Dominion-News* editorial citing recent upswings in local violent crime, she pleaded with the crowd, "Do not hitchhike—it is not worth your life!"

After the speeches, the participants headed to city council. Some held handmade signs with stenciled or handwritten slogans like, "BETTER POLICE PROTECTION," and "LET'S END POOR LIGHTING" and

WVU students protesting for better lighting and safer transportation between campuses. *WVRHC.*

chanted, "Now safety! Safety now!" as they made their way to city hall. Fraternity brothers of Alpha Phi Omega served as marshals, guiding the assembly in rows of two and three that stretched a full block.

Woodford and Pritchard presented the committee's proposals to the council. The rest of the group remained outside, chanting loud enough to be heard inside the building. Woodford expressed his apprehensions: "The murderer could still be in Morgantown, and even if he is not, there could be other emotionally disturbed people here." He expected copycat crimes unless combined efforts from the city and the university could clean up the risks.

City council voted unanimously to accept the committee's proposals, though they conceded it was only a start. Morgantown and WVU were looking to a new mass transit system to save public transportation. Dr. E.C. "Samy" Elias, WVU professor and respected authority on transportation, headed an examination of mass transit system feasibility, cost, safety and community impact, which settled on one that would entail electric, emission-free pod cars on an elevated, computerized track between campuses. The system would be known as the Personal Rapid Transit, or PRT.

Downtown PRT station, across the alley from the back of the city jail. *Mark Crabtree.*

Locally, many people were convinced the murders played a role in Boeing's decision to test the PRT in Morgantown, but no clear evidence of that has been found. Boeing said Morgantown was chosen based on a variety of factors, from its traffic congestion and hilly terrain to its high precipitation and extreme weather variations. The PRT was to be Boeing's proof-of-concept project and, if successful, would advertise the system to cities across the nation.

As of this writing, Morgantown's PRT is still the only one in the country.

———◆———

Meanwhile, WVSP investigators finally track down Kenny Cole, a ubiquitous figure who has been encountered repeatedly in their canvas of the Weirton Mine Section. Trooper Cunningham is tasked with the initial interview and locates the address on Route 119, a couple of miles south of Morgantown. He checks his watch and writes down the time: 4:45 p.m. Good chance he's interrupting supper. He notes the three cars in the yard—a wrecked white four-door '63 Chevy, an old green Jeep and a white four-door '63 Chevy with red interior. The trooper takes his time before walking up to the door.

He wants Cole to be able to see him, give Cole enough time to get nervous if he has anything to hide.

Cole answers the door with a vigorous greeting. If he is nervous, he sure doesn't show it. "How are ya, officer? You mind if we talk out on the porch? If the young'ens get wind of a badge in the house, we'll never get to eat tonight." He lets out a big guffaw. He's short, has a potbelly and light-brown hair pokes out from under the rim of a welder hat.

Cunningham stands while Cole sits on one of two cushioned chairs, side by side with a small table between them.

"I've only got a few questions, Mr. Cole. Won't take up much of your time."

"Call me Kenny—everyone does." He folds his hands on his lap and rocks back and forth.

"All right, Kenny. I'm sure you've heard about the recent events out this way."

"Oh my yes. Terrible. Those poor girls."

All told, Cunningham's conversation with Cole takes less than ten minutes. He starts out by pointing to the car with the red interior and a radio antenna mounted on the rear fender. It's similar to the one tipster John Zinn reported seeing. Cole claims to have wrecked it the Christmas before: "Hasn't moved from that spot since. Got a near identical one to replace it."

"Do you remember where you were the eighteenth of January this year?"

"The night them girls went missing?" Cole scrunches his eyes to indicate he's deep in thought. "Bert!"

Alberta, Kenny's wife, was in the house getting dinner ready. She had a clearer head for details than Kenny and, after realizing January 18 was a Sunday, announced that they were home, with the family: "Sundays we normally spend together. If something unusual had happened, I'd've remembered it."

Cunningham then turned the conversation toward the April day the remains were discovered. Kenny remembered the day: "I heard the National Guard was over to the mine, searching for those girls, so I headed out that way to see if they found anything."

"You find yourself out in that area often, Kenny?"

"Oh, sure." Cole scratches at the top of his balding head, his hat bobbing up and down, and wipes his mouth with the back of his hand. "You know, funny you mention it—about a week before they found them bodies, I'm up there with Willis Summers. I didn't think nothing of it at the time, but when we're out at the dump, we both smell something."

Cunningham scribbles something quickly on his notepad. "The dump? How far is that from the site?"

"Quarter mile? Maybe half? You know, I didn't really put it together 'til now, but I bet we smelt them bodies." He shakes his head. "There's always something going on out that way. I think it was a week before the girls was found I seen some kid hangin' out up there. He was sitting on the ground, all slumped over, and I asked him what he was doing and he said he was shooting crows. He had some homemade camo made out of burlap. I didn't get a good look at him, but I think he was driving a white Volkswagen."

"Would you mind writing down that last part for me? Try to remember as many details as you can." Cunningham turns his notepad to a fresh page and hands it and a pen to Cole. He doesn't think Cole is involved after all, just a nosy busybody most likely, but a handwriting sample won't hurt.

———◆———

No one knows anymore why Sergeant Heis did what he did. One of the reasons the coed case is still linked to triangles by the public is because Heis said it was. Publicly. On April 30, Heis told an audience of WVU students he observed a triangle mark "carved" in the ground at the grave site the day after the bodies were removed. Rumors swirled of a "warlock's sign" near the bodies. The *Dominion-News* attempted to track Heis down to get confirmation of such a symbol, but Heis remained unavailable. The police withheld the letters' triangle signature from the public as best they could, but readers remembered earlier reports in the *Dominion-News* that mentioned a V or a Δ sign-off. People in Morgantown still remember rumors that the killer arranged branches in a triangle on the graves, a rumor that was entirely untrue. If an investigator ever mentioned the copper plate or the stone circle with the burlap pouch full of stones, no record exists.

Attempting to confirm Heis's bombshell, the press began to dog other officials: Captain Bowley, Justice of the Peace/Coroner Bowers and even Colonel Bonar. Bowley asserted the letters contributed nothing but extra work for his department; in his opinion, Mared's eyeglasses catalyzed the intensive search. Coroner Bowers chimed in that an exposed foot, not a triangle, indicated the grave site to searchers. However, Colonel Bonar fueled the growing speculation about madness: "We haven't ruled out the potential that someone emotionally disturbed wrote the letters."

On the last day before 1970's spring break, the *DA*, perhaps angered by the disappointing answers, issued an exposé on the problems plaguing the MPD. "Morgantown's police department is an example of getting what one pays for," the paper wrote, citing inadequate funding toward training police to solve murders, bombings, robberies and other complex cases.

Furthermore, the *DA* cited educational deficiencies: "243 policemen [in West Virginia] have below a 12th grade education. Five are serving with less than a sixth-grade education." In 1970, the state did not require a college education for any of its departments, nor were monetary incentives offered to employees for furthering their education with college courses. West Virginia and twenty-four other states had no recruitment or training standards. Only three MPD officers had attended courses beyond the firearm safety program offered by the State Police Academy. In closing, the article emphasized that "no person, regardless of his individual qualifications, is able to perform police work on his native abilities alone."

"RIDICULE COULD TRIGGER
FURTHER VIOLENT REACTIONS."

Mozingo looks around the table of the Morgantown Detachment's conference room and clicks on the tape recorder in front of him. "Sergeant R.L. Mozingo here with Trooper P. B. Gooden, Morgantown assistant prosecuting attorney Edgar Heiskell III and psychiatrists and psychologists from West Virginia University, the WVU medical school and the Kennedy Youth Center. The date is April 23, and the time is…" He glances at the black-and-white industrial clock on the wall opposite. "Eight minutes after seven in the evening. Thank you all for coming tonight."

He nods to Pres Gooden, who sits forward on his chair, his right knee bouncing as he speaks.

"The purpose of this meeting is to allow these doctors to evaluate the case," Gooden says, glancing around at the eight men at the table, "the letters, et cetera, and to give us some idea of the type of individual we are looking for. I assume you gentlemen have had time to look over the materials we provided."

The five doctors mutter assent, and two of them toy with their coffee cups. APA Heiskell doesn't look up from his notes.

"Okay," Gooden says and taps the report. "Any thoughts?"

Formal personality profiling doesn't yet exist, but ad hoc psychological discussions are common in 1970. By 1972, the FBI inaugurated the Behavioral Sciences Unit to systemize efforts to "get in the heads" of suspects in order to grapple with a growing number of bizarre, apparently motiveless murders and other crimes. At first, the unit develops almost as many approaches as there are agents. But a belief in the general usefulness of profiling is in the air.

"These letters were written by a younger person, probably under thirty years of age," comments Dr. Donald Carter, a psychiatrist from WVU. Most everyone seems to agree with him. Several of them also feel that he—for everyone speaks of a nameless *he* committing the crime—has some kind of fetish for certain pieces of apparel.

"What makes you say that?" Gooden asks. He figures Malarik's bra and boots and the Ferrell girl's coat were the best bets.

"The missing items were prominent," says Dr. Carter. "Very specific. Which speaks of fetishistic behavior. The footwear would be the most likely candidates. One of the traits of a person obsessed with shoe fetishism would be to masturbate and ejaculate into the shoe."

"He messed in her shoes?" Mozingo shakes his head and looks down at the table. The things people do nowadays.

Gooden, after hearing Blankenship's story of the man who liked to "rub furry things," had come to believe a fur fetish might be more likely than a footwear fetish.

"It's also possible," says another doctor, "that the perpetrator might, in fact, wear the missing articles."

"The coat could have been used to carry the heads," says a third doctor.

"About that," Gooden said, "do you think he cut off the heads because that's how he gets his kicks?"

The doctors all seem to dismiss this possibility. They think it more likely it was the result of a mentally handicapped person attempting to frustrate the police.

"To prevent ID?" Gooden asks. Yes, they all agree this is most likely. Gooden isn't as skeptical of academics as many of his WVSP colleagues, but the idea a mentally handicapped person removed the heads to prevent identification seems far-fetched. More likely, he thinks, the heads were removed to hide evidence—of bullets in the skulls or maybe strangulation, suffocation.

"And what about the method of burial?" Gooden asks the men.

"They weren't really buried, were they?" says Dr. Carter. "Superficially, on top of the ground. He couldn't think of a better way to bury them. Maybe he was in a hurry."

The other doctor from WVU disagrees. "Even buried like that, it would have taken a long time to gather all those sticks and debris. The rocks from the stream. No, it took a while. I think the superficial burial was to give himself a chance to return to the site periodically to view the bodies. Scene of the crime and all that."

"He lives in the area," Dr. Carter says, nodding. "Whoever it was, he's probably committed other, lesser crimes before."

"Obviously," the other WVU doctor says. "This man is emotionally flat. He does not react with aggressiveness in all situations. It's someone the family or pastor sees as a nice person. He's probably very good at blocking out his feelings."

"One of the suggestions we've heard," Mozingo says, "is that the murders were committed by a cult of some kind, possibly a hippie cult. Like that Manson thing last year. Is that possible?"

"Most anything's possible," Dr. Carter says. "But that's unlikely."

All the other doctors agree.

"Someone surely would have broken out of the cult," says one of the psychologists. The two psychologists are quieter, deferring to their psychiatrist brethren. "Something would have surfaced by now. A double murder is not easy to keep quiet about."

"That brings something up, though," the other psychologist says. "The way the letters are handled. Nothing should be done or said to the newspaper to indicate ridicule or contempt for the person who wrote them. This is very important. Ridicule could trigger further violent reactions."

"That's a good point," says Dr. Carter. "The letters, as such, and I'm speaking of the letters now specifically, the man who wrote them is in his later twenties. He's probably energetic and imaginative. He likes playing games."

"He reads detective stories. He's emotionally detached." Dr. Carter nods at the other WVU psychiatrist. "Like you said, he plays games. He's probably not married and gets his kicks from the use of symbols, like in the letters. He's aloof and thinks he's important."

"No question," says the third psychiatrist. "He's probably not a college graduate. He may have tried college, but he had to withdraw."

"Or flunked out." Dr. Carter steeples his fingers.

"He has a—" The WVU doctor hesitates, waving his hand in the air as if trying to think of the words. "A superior attitude. He thinks of himself as very clever, but he's not. This conflict of reality versus self-image causes problems, though. He gives very vague directions, but he might well think they are very specific and clear. He probably tells himself any trouble the police have following them is because they're not smart enough."

Everyone is silent for a few minutes after that, until one of the psychologists speaks up again. "The drawing. On the second letter. He might be a draftsman."

"Or thinks he has those skills," Dr. Carter corrects. "He has a strong fantasy life. That's where he lives. He probably works a day job, a routine job, and does a lot of daydreaming."

"He's a frustrated man," the second psychologist says. "His frustration might derive from failing in college. He probably also fails with women. He may hate them."

"Probably," the WVU psychiatrist says.

"For sure he hates women. All of them," Dr. Carter asserts.

Everyone is quiet again, and Gooden, sensing no one has anything else to add, asks the big question: "Would you say the man who wrote these letters killed the coeds?"

"Undoubtedly," Dr. Carter says, while every one of the psychiatrists and psychologists around the table simply nod agreement.

Gooden doesn't say anything. The consensus at the table is the same man who wrote the letters killed Mared and Karen. But Gooden's gut tells him otherwise.

11

"I HAVE SEEN HIM LOSE HIS TEMPER TO A VERY STRONG DEGREE."

As Mozingo sits at his desk in the back of the near-empty Morgantown WVSP barracks, he hears an announcement over the all-station com:

"There's a Mr. Estep up front," comes the voice from the front desk. "He says he has information that might pertain to the coed case."

Mozingo arrives in the lobby to see a young man, probably early twenties, wearing glasses with black wayfarer frames like Buddy Holly's. The man steps forward and extends his hand. "Sergeant Mozingo? Pleasure. I'm Leslie Estep."

Mozingo shakes his hand. "Is there something I can help you with, Mr. Estep?"

"Well." He looks around. "Is there someplace we could talk?"

"Sure, let's go to my office."

When they arrive, Mozingo motions to a chair and walks around his desk. "What can I do for you today, Mr. Estep?"

"I'm hoping to do something for you, sir. I'm a senior at WVU and there are some…" A nervous chortle. "Well, there are scary rumors going around that I—" His words seem to catch in his throat. "I guess I can't ignore in good conscience."

"You live on campus?" Mozingo picks up his pen. Slowly and deliberately, he drags a sheet of paper out while he stares at the student.

"Yes, sir. Summit Hall." Another nervous chuckle slips out. Estep sits stiffly with his hands clamped on the armrests. His grip tight, the knuckles show bright-white skin.

"What sort of rumors, son?"

"Last year, one of the engineering guys submitted a story about decapitation and religious cults for an assignment."

"All right." *This is a new one*, Mozingo thinks. "Can you be more specific to the time?"

"Oh, sure, December '69," Estep relays excitedly.

"Do you have a name?"

"William Gerkin. But that's not all. I heard he's been in and out of mental institutions."

"I see." It's not the first time Mozingo has heard a "mental patient" rumor. "Can you spell that last name for me?"

"Gerkin, with a G. G-E-R-K-I-N." Estep leans toward the desk, craning his neck to see if Mozingo jots it down correctly. Mozingo's no-nonsense eyes dart up. Estep flashes a sheepish grin and carefully slides back in his seat.

Estep waits until Mozingo's pen stops moving. "I heard he has a machete, er, *had* a machete. It's missing now."

This piques Mozingo's interest. "Missing from where? How do you mean?"

"His roommate had a machete, or it was like a house machete, but after those girls disappeared, well, he can't find it."

"All right, Mr. Estep. I thank you for your time. I'll have the investigators look into this." He stands and opens the door for the young man. "Do you have a phone number where you can be reached?"

Estep hops up quickly, nearly losing his balance, and gives him the number for a payphone on his floor. "Or you can just call the main information desk."

"Have a good day, Mr. Estep." Mozingo plops back into his chair. "You can leave the door open when you leave." He picks up his phone and dials the receptionist but hears the slow drone of the busy signal. He shrugs and puts his thumb and middle finger in opposite corners of his mouth. A loud whistle pierces the air. Seconds later, Gooden cautiously pops his head in the doorway.

"Right on time, Gooden," Mozingo holds out a sheet of paper with Gerkin's name on it. "Run a master check on that guy."

"Hope this is something. You know, Sergeant, I think this case might be going hinky. We don't have enough resources to—"

"We never have enough resources."

"I hear that, but we're running around like chickens. I've got a bad feeling, like we're spinning our wheels but not going anywhere. As soon as we hear of one guy, we hear about three more. We can't devote enough time to any one——"

"Just check this guy out."

Gooden sighs and steps into the room, accepts the paper. He peers at it, then tries to pronounce it with a hard G: "Gur-kin?"

"No, the G sounds like a J."

"Jer-kin?"

Mozingo nods, expressionless.

"Well, that's…unfortunate."

———◆———

WVSP troopers began to work their way through acquaintances of William Gerkin, one by one, most of them his fraternity brothers. In every case, the interviewing trooper created a pretense that required the interviewee to write something down. Each handwriting sample was shipped to Lieutenant Charlie West at CIB as he labored away in his lonely quest to match the anonymous handwriting of the Triangle Letters.

Trooper Rogers questioned Thomas "Tom" John Boyd. Boyd and Gerkin both belonged to the same fraternity, and Tom had known Gerkin for two years. He described Gerkin as six feet tall, around two hundred pounds, with "very dark black hair, worn straight and hanging fairly long." He also went on to characterize Gerkin's personality: "He appears to live in two different worlds. In one situation he will appear normal, and in another situation he will appear nervous and high strung." Gerkin's voice was unexpectedly high-pitched, "like a girl's," with an unnerving laugh.

When probed about Gerkin's violent tendencies, Boyd said, "I have never seen him strike anyone, but I have seen him throw shoes and yell at the top of his lungs." Boyd added that he heard about a spat between Gerkin and his ex-girlfriend outside her sorority house. Gerkin made advances she rejected, prompting him to carry her to the front porch and dump her on the floor. Boyd added, "I understand that during this time the girl was not fully clothed."

Rogers asked if Boyd knew of a short story Gerkin allegedly wrote concerning the use of a machete as a weapon. Boyd admitted he did not read the copy Gerkin gave him, but someone told him it involved a duel between Gerkin and another man: "The other person was using a machete and Gerkin was using his .22 pistol. From the way I understand it, the other person won and thereby cut Gerkin to pieces."

Trooper Rogers next interviewed David Gerald Sayre. Sayre had also known Gerkin for two years as a fraternity brother and confirmed Gerkin displayed symptoms of a mental illness. "He appeared very nervous at times and his words did not follow content. He would jump from one subject to another without finishing what he was saying."

Gerkin shared with Sayre the story he wrote about a machete attack. Sayre remembered it as, "Someone approached Bill either with a gun or a machete, and one of them was cut up. The other person then took the cut-up body and placed it in a plastic bag and put it in a garbage can." When asked, Sayre said, yes, he'd seen Gerkin with a machete; he'd used it to cut some Christmas trees. Other people had seen the machete in the trunk of Gerkin's car.

Rogers then asked about violent tendencies, and Sayre said Gerkin shared a story of getting upset and trying to set his trailer on fire, then stabbing the ground with a knife. Rush Week began the day after Mared and Karen disappeared, and Sayre saw Gerkin on that Wednesday or Thursday: "I remember that while we were singing he was banging on the piano, and as far as I know, he can't play the piano."

Dwane Randell "Randy" Ringer, recording secretary of the fraternity, told Trooper Rogers that Gerkin drove a blue Impala at the time. He saw Gerkin the night the girls went missing—remembered introducing him to a rushee—but couldn't recall seeing him during the cut session between 10:30 p.m. and midnight. He felt sure Gerkin left by 10:00 p.m. When asked if Gerkin had a firearm, Ringer replied, "Yes, he bought a .22 revolver, and I saw it in his bedroom at the house. He had it in a silver metal container that only he had a key for." Ringer went on, "I have seen him lose his temper to a very strong degree, but never to the point that he inflicted injury on anyone."

The Morgantown Detachment received from New Jersey State Police a report on an interview with Gerkin's ex-girlfriend Nancy Serfass, the girl he'd allegedly dumped at the sorority. In an attempt to ascertain Gerkin's predilections toward violence, troopers questioned Serfass regarding their four-month relationship. Serfass confirmed that he'd angrily dumped her half naked after she refused his advances. She'd never before seen any sign of violence, but he sometimes acted overly emotional and would "cry over his studies or past experiences." Twice she saw him swing at the wall in his depression.

Serfass said Gerkin married a girl from his hometown in 1968 after getting her pregnant. Three weeks into the marriage, she said Gerkin suffered a mental breakdown and sought psychiatric treatment at the University Hospital. She described Gerkin as six feet, one inch tall; two hundred pounds; brown hair and eyes; very emotional; and having a high-pitched voice. She provided his 1967 WVU yearbook photo: Gerkin in a gray suit and dark tie. In the photo, Gerkin's hair looked slicked into place with an extreme left part. His eyebrows were rounded and didn't arch sharply. It's unclear whether his hair was "dark black," as Boyd said, or brown, as Serfass reported.

———◆———

A picture of William R. Gerkin III began to emerge, and WVSP believed it had disturbing implications. Gerkin grew up in Grafton, about twenty-five miles south of Morgantown. He'd been a star high school student and was speeding along his road to success when he entered WVU. A bright, aspiring engineering student, he joined a fraternity and, by all accounts, looked forward to a promising career. However, the road quickly became rocky, his behavior increasingly unpredictable.

Gerkin reputedly disliked women. As the troopers continued interviewing several people regarding the subject, they found no one seemed extremely close with the man, and most described him as a "nervous type." Friends of his echoed Estep's testimony about the short story Gerkin wrote, but the contents of the story were never reported the same way twice: Two men killed and dismembered Gerkin, two men fought a duel and one ended up dismembered and beheaded, Gerkin killed and beheaded two women. Despite the various details, all reports of the story included a machete and at least one beheading. No one ever produced a copy of the story.

The troopers acquired a court order securing Gerkin's medical records, which chronicled his five admissions for psychiatric treatment after September 1968, the most recent being in April 1970. Three professionals agreed their patient appeared to suffer from an acute mental illness and, with his apparent lack of self-control, certainly seemed capable of the violence evident in the coed case. Further questioning revealed Gerkin's wife told doctors Gerkin often played with his gun in her presence.

In addition to his hospitalizations, the CIB background check also returned an auto accident on the evening before his withdrawal from school. He crashed his '68 Chevrolet Camaro about ten miles south of Morgantown on Route 119—near where the bodies were recovered. According to WVU records, an unspecified "illness" prompted his withdrawal on April 15, the day before Mared's and Karen's remains were discovered. Gerkin looked like a definite possibility.

Corporal Sparks served a warrant to the registrar's office and gathered samples of Gerkin's handwriting from records the school had on file. Those were sent to West for assessment. Despite all this somewhat incriminating evidence, still more persons of interest pushed Gerkin out of the limelight until late August.

12

"I THINK HE'S A GOOD SUSPECT."

On a hot and sunny spring afternoon, fifteen-year-old Regina Lou Miller is cutting through Constitution Park between Cumberland, Maryland, and Allegany Community College. Just past the baseball field, she's hit from behind by a car, scattering her schoolbooks. Fresh scrapes on her arms and knees sting when she opens her eyes, dazed. She hears the door of the car creak open and blinks to focus on the dark-haired white man who hustles out. He's gathering her books, mumbling apologies.

She lifts her head to see him pointing a penknife at her and feels his hands grasping her shoulders, trying to stand her up. He pushes, forcing her into his car. Frightened, Regina doesn't say anything as he drives a short distance then stops. She tumbles out of the car and runs, but she is still dazed and he catches her easily.

Now he's yelling at her to take off her clothes, and she starts to, but within a few seconds she again tries to run. He slams her head with something heavy, and she falls. He jumps on top of her and stabs, slashes her across the shoulders and throat and face until the knife breaks.

Regina blacks out.

———•———

Sergeant Mozingo is at his desk the first day of May when the phone rings.

"Mozingo."

"Sergeant, this is Corporal J.R. Potts of the Keyser Detachment. I have some information to relay that may be tied to your coed case." The corporal's voice sounds far away, the call crackling and clicking over the long-distance line.

"Go ahead, Corporal." Mozingo moves a stack of reports to the side to make room. He picks up a pen and cradles the receiver with his shoulder.

"We caught wind of a suspect picked up by Maryland State Police, a John Leroy Kroll. That's K-R-O-L-L. He sliced up a girl pretty bad. Near killed her. Almost cut her goddamn head off with a penknife."

"She survived?"

"Boy Scouts found her, saved her life, though *they'll* probably be scarred for life."

"Jesus, how old is she?"

"She's fifteen. Not his first, either. He attacked a thirteen-year-old last summer, same park. Stabbed her with a bayonet." Potts clears his throat. "She wasn't raped, Sergeant. Kroll feels intercourse is 'dirty.' After he attacked the older girl, he went to his bedroom and stuck a broomstick into his abdomen and ejaculated onto his bed."

Mozingo underlines *bayonet* on his notepad. "Thank you, Corporal. I appreciate the heads up."

Kroll was being held in Allegany County Jail in Cumberland. And until February, he had a white 1963 Chevy.

———— ♦ ————

The next day, Gooden and Mitchell sit at a table across from John Leroy Kroll in a tiny room in Cumberland, where the Triangle Letters were postmarked. The room is featureless, its gray cinder blocks painted over with a different color gray. The only break in the walls are two windows with horizontal blinds that stare out on the desks of the detention center's deputies.

Kroll is twenty-two, with short, dark hair. Looking at him, Gooden thinks his eyebrows look like the eyebrows of a jack-o-lantern. And *pudgy* is an understatement.

Mitchell instantly dislikes him. Kroll's chipmunk cheeks and dead eyes fill him with revulsion. There is nothing behind those eyes.

Kroll drinks stale jailhouse coffee from a paper cup. A little dribbles from the corner of his mouth, and he raises his thumb to wipe, smearing it in his stubble. He sucks audibly, smacks his lips.

"I think it was the eighteenth. A Sunday. I'd been to a funeral. Three that weekend." Kroll wipes his thumb on his shirt. "Them girls I picked up in Morgantown, they was going to Westminster, Maryland. To college. I gave 'em ten bucks 'cause they told me they were broke and didn't have no money to eat."

Mitchell scoffs. What a kind guy. "They said they were from Morgantown?"

"Yeah. Both had dresses on. I think. One had on a brown and white fur coat, plaid slacks. She had a shoulder pocketbook."

Gooden looks at Mitchell then back at Kroll. "Now, was it dresses or slacks?"

"Slacks. They both wore slacks." He takes another loud slurp of coffee. "I told my parents about them, and we went back out lookin' for 'em on the Baltimore Road."

"Why?" asks Gooden.

"Well, actually, we was already on the Baltimore Pike and I mentioned it. Daddy asked me why I took that road to just be taking a ride." He stares at the troopers, emotionless. His thin lips glisten with coffee.

Gooden pushes his coffee cup away from his direct vision, his fingertip tock-tock-tocking the table. "Had you heard about the coed girls missing from WVU?"

"Oh, yeah. I seen it in the papers."

Mitchell clears his throat. "I thought you couldn't read, John."

"My mother and daddy keep a big stack of papers at home. They read to me."

Gooden looks at Mitchell with raised brows.

MITCHELL AND GOODEN STAND outside the door while inside Kroll slurps at his cup. Mitchell rubs his eyes, then slides his hand into his curly hair and gently scratches his head. "Corporal Chabatt is going to hook Kroll up to the polygraph. He wants to ask about the Constitution Park attacks. Will you wait here to see what he says while I verify the funerals?" Gooden nods affirmatively, and Mitchell continues. "Also, Sergeant Hart wants to interview Kroll's mother, Doris, and I want to be there."

"You think this guy is good for it?"

"Sex deviant can't open his mouth without lying. I think he's a good suspect. He lives an hour and a half from Morgantown. But there's too many like him."

"Agreed."

Mitchell turns to leave. "Get a handwriting sample," he barks over his shoulder as he heads down the hall.

Two days later, Gooden and Mitchell drove back to Cumberland to speak with Kroll again, this time with Troopers Rogers and Cunningham. The polygraph was inconclusive, but they planned to investigate Kroll's past activities. Rogers was assigned to interview Kroll's employer and the fifteen-year-old victim; Cunningham was to go through the Cumberland newspapers for mentions of the Morgantown coeds. The Cumberland Detachment offered assistance as well.

Along with Detective Sergeant Melvin Boggs of the Cumberland Police Department, Rogers traveled to the hospital to interview Regina Lou Miller. It had been six days since she was admitted. She groggily told them what she could recall of the attack. She described how her attacker hit her with his car while she detoured through the park after school, how he brandished a penknife and forced her into his car.

When the troopers asked if she'd seen him before she said no, but she was sure she'd recognize him if she saw him again. As the troopers listened, they decided she wasn't a target but a victim of opportunity: She rarely walked home through the park.

Rogers was unhappy with her take on the attack. He'd hoped for more details. She'd been through a terrible ordeal: Her face and scalp had several deep lacerations, and Kroll had attempted to slit her throat ear to ear, only he hadn't cut deep enough to sever her carotid. She'd been seriously traumatized, both physically and mentally, but the police report read only, "Although Miss Miller is fifteen years of age, she appeared to be somewhat mentally incompetent, and was thereby unable to give a clear account of just what had happened in the park."

Rogers walked away noting the only similarities he could find between the two cases: the use of a "cutting type instrument" and the possession of a "light-colored vehicle."

Rogers and Boggs moved on to interview an administrator of the Cumberland Nursing Home and Convalescent Center, where Kroll was an orderly. According to him, there were no complaints about Kroll before that day and he was a "model employee up until the time he was arrested." He directed the troopers to Gretta Beeman, the night nursing supervisor over Kroll. She had a completely different take.

13

"PUT HIM DOWN."

Rogers set up a tape recorder while Boggs looked around the room. It seemed Mrs. Beeman had turned on all the lights in the house. She regularly worked the night shift, so this was probably morning for her. He could smell coffee brewing in the kitchen. She sat in an armchair across from the troopers, a coffee table between them. Nervously, she pushed her glasses up the bridge of her nose. When she and Boggs made eye contact, she tucked a strand of silver hair behind her ear.

Rogers looked at Boggs, nodded and pressed record: "May 4, 1970, 10:35, interviewing Gretta Beeman. Mrs. Beeman, please start from the time that you first met John Kroll up to and including the present date."

"John started to work for me at the nursing center approximately October 1969." Gretta sat with perfect posture a bit away from the back of her chair. "He seemed very quiet, withdrawn. From the very beginning I felt there was something wrong mentally. His duties were to take care of the male patients—specifically the male patients—but I would find him staring at the female patients. John was questioned about this and denied it, but then I started to watch him. I *did* find him staring at the female patients."

"Mrs. Beeman, you mentioned you'd often find John just staring into space. Could you go into this a little more, please?"

Gretta took a deep breath, slowly, exhaling before she continued. "I would find him in an empty room staring out the window, and if I would comment, 'John, is anything wrong?' He would say no, but just keep staring with a vacant look on his face. It was a frightening experience. I am not the only one. It's hard to describe. You felt afraid of him. The patients were afraid of him. They did not want him in their rooms at night, but still, when I wasn't around, he'd persist in going into their rooms."

She went on to describe how he resented direct orders and how she didn't like to ask him to do anything. "I felt that I would give him a fair chance." She sucked her teeth. "It's hard to get an orderly."

"Could you explain how he displayed his feelings toward you?"

She crossed her legs and laced her fingers. "He followed me around constantly. He was always at my side. I couldn't go down the hall unless he was there. He always wanted to come and get me, to take me to work and to bring me home."

"How many times did he either take you home or bring you to work?"

"Once or twice a week at least." She fidgeted with her wedding ring.

Boggs leaned forward, his mouth closer to the tape recorder. "Could you describe the incident where he failed to take you straight home?"

She uncrossed her legs, then shifted and crossed them the opposite way. "Weeks ago, I didn't have a ride home. I started to call a cab, and he saw me dialing, and he said, 'Mrs. Beeman, I'll take you home.' So rather than be rude, I let him take me."

Gretta's shifting made Rogers uncomfortable. He wondered if talking to the police made her nervous or if she was realizing she worked with a psycho and she should have trusted her instincts instead of being polite.

"We started out from the nursing home, and instead of turning left to go into town, he went out the Williams Road, and I said, 'John, you're going the wrong way,' so instantly he said, 'I'm going to kidnap you.' I said, 'John, I have to get home.' He said, 'You said you've never seen ACC College. I'm going to show you where it is.'"

Rogers tried to turn the conversation toward the coeds. "You mentioned before that John related to you a story concerning his picking up two girls on or around January 18, 1970."

"One night, several weeks after Christmas, we had commented that this particular weekend he had been to two funerals in one funeral home. Then he said that he was driving west of Frostburg and saw two girls. One was a blonde, one had brown hair. He commented at length about their faces, the fact that they had too much eye makeup on. He said he couldn't get a good look at her face—the one with dark hair—except her eyes, because her hair kept blowing down around her neck."

Rogers and Boggs exchanged a look.

"He made motions with his hands." She imitated his gestures by parting an invisible curtain of hair in front of her face as she spoke. "He said they didn't have money, and they were almost finished with college. He gave them each five dollars, and that was all."

"It was the girl with the brown hair whose face he couldn't see?" asked Boggs.

"He said he couldn't see her face right, but he did see her eyes. He said, 'I wish I could have seen *her* face better.' He said it in a rather nasty tone of voice."

"Mrs. Beeman," Boggs prodded, "you mentioned something about John becoming physically ill after the time that he was supposed to have picked up the girls?"

"He would come to work ill. He was nauseated, perspiring profusely. He commented that he had terrific abdominal pains, and he could not work." She leaned forward, speaking matter-of-factly, "Since he told me so many things, I asked him one night, 'John, is there anything I can do to help? Or do you want to go over to the hospital and get checked?' At the time he said no, but then he became violently ill. It was like there was something troubling him. He would get terribly upset."

———◆———

The next day, flanked by two Allegany County deputies, Trooper Rogers is ushered to John Kroll's cell in his civilian clothes, hands shackled and dangling in front of his hips. One deputy holds him by the arm while the other unlocks the cell door. Kroll, lying on his bunk, looks up from his worn *Life* magazine at his new roommate. Expressionless, but aware, Kroll's eyes stay on him. Rogers can't tell if he's curious or annoyed.

"In you go, Landis," barks the deputy with the keys. Rogers feels a shove from behind and hears the door slam shut. "Put your hands up to the bar." Rogers does as he's told and is roughly uncuffed. He slumps down on the bunk on the left. It's a worn-thin mattress, and he can feel the slats of the metal frame. He really hopes he doesn't have to do this more than a day.

Kroll stands up from his bunk and takes a couple labored steps over to a tiny sink. He slowly turns the knob until some water trickles out, puts his cupped hand under it, brings it to his mouth and slurps loudly. Rogers observes him without being obvious, but the man's sheer size gets in the way. Kroll has to be six-three or taller. Plus, he's chunky, making him look more like a tank. He looks older than twenty in Rogers's opinion.

Kroll speaks without looking at him. "You gotta drink. The air is dry in here. I think they pump some kind of gas through the vents. It dries me out." Kroll takes another slurp. Rogers looks at the magazine on Kroll's bed. There are children on the cover under bold white letters: "Sex Education for Little Children; Debate splits the nation's schools." He knows Kroll is barely literate.

"You aren't worried about them putting something in the water?" asks Rogers. "Saltpeter? My cousin in max says they put it in the food."

"You dry, you die. They want you weak so you confess whatever they want to hear. Don't let them hook you up to that machine." Another slurp.

"What machine?"

"Lie detector. They hook you up to that thing then hypnotize you. I told them I ain't doing no more of their tests. Huh uh. Not going down that road again." Kroll twists the knob back, shutting the water off. He wipes his mouth with the back of his hand, then wipes it front and back on his shirt. He shuffles to his bunk, this time sitting slouched and facing Rogers.

Rogers doesn't like looking into Kroll's eyes. There is something not right about them. No emotion when he talks. It's more than not smiling with his eyes, like people do when making small talk. Everything he's doing is false—like he just goes through the motions and tries to blend in with humans.

Rogers has been briefed on what was found in Kroll's bedroom. He knows about the dowels under his bed with women's names carved into them. He knows Kroll liked to push them into his belly for added pleasure. He feels sickened by Kroll's slow-blinking gaze, so he gets up and goes to the sink. "Gotta drink."

———◆———

Mozingo sternly flips through Rogers's report. Rogers can smell the rain through the propped window while he waits for his boss to finish.

"Okay, Rogers, looks thorough. You are of the opinion that John Leroy Kroll is no longer a lead suspect, is that correct?"

"No, sir. My time spent with Kroll wasn't fruitful. The man is insane. No matter what I said, I couldn't get him to talk about the girls."

"He confessed to you the crimes he committed in Constitution Park?"

"Not directly—he said the girls *attacked him*, sir. I don't think he's very smart. What's important is that he only attacks young girls he can control. Mared and Karen were teenagers, but I can't see him going after two full-grown teens like that."

Mozingo arches an eyebrow. "Would you suggest we rule him out completely?"

171

"Not completely, no, sir. But take him off the active list."

Mozingo laces his fingers and leans forward. "Off the record, Jim." He lets out a resigned sigh. "Am I to assume we have a violent pervert in custody, but not the *right* violent pervert?"

"I—I don't know what to say. He got rid of his car that fits the description—just said he didn't want to drive it anymore. Sounded like he associated something bad with it, but none of the samples came back with any ties to our bodies.

"Cunningham went through every article from Cumberland that mentioned the coed case. None of the details Kroll mentioned were in a single one, not to mention the buildings he described or the details he spouted about Grafton Road. Says he drove it one time with his parents, and he's had a photographic memory since he was nine.

"He refuses to take another polygraph. They got him on both the fifteen-year-old and the thirteen-year-old because they caught him in a lie and he just spilled out the whole thing. He admitted to everything, even jerking off with a section of broom handle still covered in that girl's blood, for chrissakes…" Rogers's voice trails off. He stops himself from getting too emotional. "Look, he's not going anywhere. He confessed to two assaults. We know exactly where to find him."

Mozingo's lips tighten into a line. "All right, Rogers. Good work."

"Thank you, sir." Rogers stands up and takes a step toward the door. He hesitates and turns toward his supervisor again. "If this guy ever gets out, he'll do it again. He's not right. I don't know what it is about him, but if he were a dog, I'd put him down."

14

"WE ARE RELIGIOUS PEOPLE HERE."

Since the April 8 Triangle Letter, Lieutenant Charles West of WVCIB was hard at work comparing the handwritten letters to the handwriting of everyone from whom investigators could get a sample. When the assignment hit his desk, he knew it would be an enormous task. He also knew his work was vital to the investigation; in fact, with a little luck, his efforts could actually break the case—*if* he could find the writer. The press still didn't have the letters, and Lieutenant West wanted to find the writer before they did.

First, West meticulously duplicated each letter by hand. He studied the stroke, loop and slant of each individual character. He wanted to know the handwriting so deeply he could actually feel what it was like to write those strange letters.

He had samples of the handwriting of all those closest to the case: Mared and Karen; Mared's boyfriends, Casazza and Mongiello; Karen's boyfriends, Hayes and Eye; dormmates such as DeYoung, Fitch, Burns and others; dorm supervisors like Spitznogle and McClure; and persons of interest like Eddie Thrasher. West well understood the stakes: The writer of the anonymous letters was the person of the most interest. Everything might be riding on his handwriting analysis.

Far from complete, the list of samples went on and on. Every time a trooper interviewed a WVU student, staff, witness or possible suspect, a handwriting sample would find its way to Charleston in care of Lieutenant West. He pored over the specimens. For weeks and weeks, those passing his office saw his wiry frame bent over a microscope, scanning each piece of handwriting that arrived with his name on it, looking for similarities. Sample by sample. Most of them he ruled out.

—————•—————

On July 10, West receives a visit from Superintendent Bonar, his large frame looming in the doorway of West's CIB office: "Well, Charlie, any ideas?"

The color drains from West's long, thin face, and he shakes his head.

"No?" Bonar stands taller, asserting his authority. "This is our guy, you know."

"I'm, um, not sure of that, sir. But we'll find him."

"We haven't yet. Mitchell thinks it's someone local. Says it had to be someone who knew the area. That dump site is too hard to find."

"He didn't need to find *that* site, sir. He needed to find *a* site."

Bonar snaps his fingers and points at West. "*Now* you're talking. It's not someone lives in town. Not a student, either." Bonar palms his mouth with his large right hand and swipes it away. "He comes to town to do his dirty work then—poof!—he's gone."

"Could be. Maybe we've already talked to him, though." West waved his hand over his desk, the handwriting samples.

"Here's something—I want you to take that microscope over to the Cumberland Detachment. Allegany County voter registration lists to start. If you don't score there, get on the Selective Service rolls."

An empty feeling starts in West's stomach. He feels dizzy, and his throat goes dry. At least eighty thousand signatures lurk in the voter registration list. Plus, signatures rarely if ever match body text; most will not even be legible.

Bonar continues. "If you still don't score, go back to Morgantown. Start all over in Mon County. This is our number one priority. Find that letter writer, West. Don't come home until you've scoured every record." He stares down at West for a few more seconds before breaking eye contact and leaving the doorway.

Inhaling deeply, West closes his eyes. He exhales long and slow and then picks up his phone. After a moment: "Hi, Sweetheart, can you put Mommy on the phone?"

—————•—————

The next Monday, West sets up a laboratory for himself at the LaVale barracks of the Maryland State Police and commences the arduous process of examining each registration signature. He works tirelessly, comparing each card to the letters. At this point, the Triangle Letters and the single hair on Mared's shoulder are the only clues WVSP has—and the thinking is that the hair is a pubic hair, maybe Mared's. Halfway through his third day, West finds himself struggling with the reality of 79,700 remaining signatures. West notices Lieutenant Sam Conrad and Sergeant Milton Hart of the MSP at the water cooler. He picks up a Triangle Letter and heads over.

"Lieutenant! You ever read one of my letters?" He tosses the letter at Conrad.

Conrad bends at the knees slightly to catch the folded letter in its spinning trajectory. Looking at West, he pulls his reading glasses out of his breast pocket and begins reading silently. He furrows his brow and glances in Hart's direction.

"Remember those three weirdos came in here? When we were working the Peugeot case? Do you still have those files?"

Hart blinks a couple times. "Yeah, hold on. I think I do." He returns to his desk and rifles through his filing cabinet. "Yeah, right here. Filed under P for *phantastic psychics*."

Hart plops a folder into West's hand. The folder brims with loose-leaf sheets of paper. Standing next to his desk, West purses his lips and flips through each one. He stops at a piece the size of a postcard.

Approx. from boat dock and bird house.
Ab't. ⅛ mile or less from steel bridge over the lake.
Near to bridge supports.

West holds the card up triumphantly. It makes little whooshing crackle sounds as he waves it quickly back and forth; a giant ear-to-ear grin gleams. "Whoever wrote this card wrote my letters!"

A long, exasperated moan comes from Conrad. His head tilts back. "Not the psychics again!"

West's grin fades. "You weren't kidding about the psychic part?"

"They call themselves the Students of Psychic Science," explains Conrad, "A religious cult. They came in to…*help* with the Peugeot case." His eyebrows raise as he tilts his head to the side. "Help's a strong word." He chooses his words carefully. "We never found Linda or Lori with the tips from outer space they brought us."

West plunks back into his chair, sour in his stomach. He remembers reading about the Peugeot woman kidnapped with her two-year-old baby. "Were those tips…were they instructions for finding their bodies?"

"Charlie, just sit tight, buddy," coos Conrad, "I'm going to make a call. You feel up to a short trip?"

West watches Conrad dial. They lock eyes as Conrad listens to the ring. West can see in Conrad's eyes when someone picks up.

"This is Detective Conrad. To whom am I speaking?…Yes. I'd like your permission to stop by and discuss the Peugeot case one more time….The other members will be there? Wonderful." He practically slams the receiver down as he stands up and grabs his coat. He appraises West and says, "Charlie, act like you're from Maryland."

An elderly man peers at the troopers through the crack in the door. Hesitantly, he snakes his fingers out around the edge and opens it wider. West notices a Freemason ring on his finger. The man inside steps forward, his hand rising to his chest, and lightly places his fingertips just under his collarbone.

"We are religious people here. Whatever we tell you is the truth." He waves for the officers to follow him. "This way. We're in the sitting room." He shuffles down the hallway and into a room where a young man and an older woman are seated.

West's eyes instantly land on the young man in the wingback chair, his legs crossed and to the side as he reads the newspaper. West watches the man slowly slide the paper down. His long, golden hair trickles to his jawline in puffy, wavy tufts. Curly bangs line his forehead. Something about him seems effeminate or asexual. The woman leans and whispers something to him, but he politely brushes her off.

Picture of the young R. Warren Hoover from *Fate* magazine, June 1978.

Lieutenant Conrad clears his throat. "Thank you for meeting with us. As you know, Hoss's instructions on where to find the Peugeot bodies have not been helpful, but there's a similar case in West Virginia."

"See?" the old woman hisses. "I told you they were here about the coeds!"

West jerks at the sound of her voice. He steps closer to the young man in the wingback chair and pulls out the card. "Is this your handwriting?!"

The man studies the card. He looks as though he wants to speak but sifts a long exhale instead.

West looks at the older man who met them at the door. "You said you'd tell us the truth." He looks back at the young man, his gaze boring into him like he is eyeing him through a sniper's scope.

"Yes. It is my handwriting," the man admits. He stands, his hands at his side, and lowers his head, more than a nod but less than a bow. "R. Warren Hoover."

15

"KILL THE PIGS!"

A few hours later, West is back at the Morgantown Detachment. The whole drive from Cumberland he's been considering how he's going to tell Mozingo, Herald and Gooden. He still feels drunk on his good fortune. It took examining over three thousand writing samples, but he'd finally hit paydirt. At the same time, he doubts that the man had anything to do with the crime. Bonar was so sure. If Hoover is the only suspect, Pres and the rest up in Morgantown are screwed.

In ten minutes, he's in front of Sergeant Mozingo, who raises a palm, "Wait, slow down, Charlie. You're telling me this cult consulted the spirits and took down an address they got from a ghost?"

"Herbert Spencer, a spiritual guide. He's a philosopher they claim they base their studies on. He started the concept of sociology."

"How does sociology turn into talking to the dead?"

"I can't tell you that. What I know is the old man, Fred Schanning, asked the cult leader to consult the spirits about what happened to those dead coeds. He's retired, lives in LaVale."

Mozingo lightly raps on his desk with his fist three times. "Tell me about this cult leader that speaks to the dead."

"His name is Richard Warren Hoover. Sorry, Reverend R. Warren Hoover. He's thirty years old, and he's from Somerset, Pennsylvania. He claims there's about thirty cult members in his psychic church, but we only met two others, Fred Schanning and Annabell Young. They're both in their sixties or older. When Schanning asked about the girls, the group held a séance. They recorded it, too. Young took down the instructions as Hoover let Spencer speak them through him."

"Whose idea was it to write the letters?"

"Schanning's, sir."

"And the triangle?"

"I think that's his, too, sir. He says it's the symbol of the holy trinity, but… he's also a Freemason. I saw the ring on his finger."

"Do you think they had anything to do with the murders?"

West's eyes narrowed. "I really doubt it, sir," he said. "They didn't really say anything they couldn't have gotten out of the papers. They could guess the bodies were in the woods. They certainly could have been more accurate about where they were buried."

"All right, Charlie. Really great policework." Mozingo rises and extends his hand.

West gets up to shake Mozingo's hand. "Thank you, sir. If you don't need anything else from me, I'd really like to see my wife and kid."

Mozingo smiles. "Get out of here already."

———————◆———————

A month later, at the end of August, the Associated Press also located R. Warren Hoover, the minister of Cumberland's Psychic Science Church: "The leader of a religious cult who wrote 'mystery' letters…insisted Monday that his letters helped in discovering the girls' decapitated bodies." The article said the "publicity-shy" Hoover claimed other members of his church were involved.

"Facts were revealed through [the minister's] voice during these reportedly 'emotional' séances," said a police spokesperson, "and later made up the content of the letters. It was determined that the man and his group were only interested in 'being helpful' in the case." The WVSP believed all information in the letters could have been found in newspaper accounts except "one or two items that were considered sheer speculation." To predict the bodies were in the woods near a stream was not a stretch in one of the most wooded and wet states in the country.

Prosecuting attorney Joe Laurita decided to release the letters and said, "It has been determined that the letter writer was not involved in the crime." He went on to explain authorities would not identify the man because he had nothing to do with killing Mared and Karen and had committed no crime when he sent the letters. "The man has absolutely been cleared of any involvement in the murders," said Laurita. "There is no reason to believe that he was in or near Morgantown or even in the state of West Virginia at the time of the crime."

Reverend Hoover and his "flock" claimed "they communicated with the world beyond in order to give police instructions for finding the bodies," said an AP article. Superintendent Bonar, however, disputed the claim, saying the letters "were of no help, sending searchers too far south."

According to the AP, one official in Cumberland said the members of the group, numbering between fifteen and thirty, cooperated with authorities "until they were refused a $3,500 reward." There was skepticism in some quarters about the actual size of the group. As the *Tuscaloosa News* said, "The trio has told authorities that there are about 30 in their cult, but police have never seen the other 27."

The press from all over the nation, fascinated by the mystic church group, hounded the members for specifics, but they refused any further discussions with police or reporters. When asked if his letters led authorities to the site, Hoover voiced his displeasure: "I wouldn't know how else it could have been done."

According to the article, the letters had been mailed on April 6, 10, and 21 from Cumberland to the Morgantown WVSP Detachment. Despite claims of the governor's office, no letters were sent directly to the governor. A fourth letter, dated April 25, was mailed to Mared's parents in New Jersey.

"Several items of particular coincidence were evident in the letters. All four letters were signed with a 'triangle,' a form in which branches covering the girls' bodies were allegedly found," read the article, citing Heis's claims during a press conference months earlier. "The man claimed the triangle was a religious symbol representative of 'the Father, Son and Holy Ghost.'"

———◆———

Hoover believed he was responsible for the massive search that eventually found the coeds' remains. And because of an error repeated over and over by the *Morgantown Post* and other newspapers, many people believed Hoover's claims. The paper said Hoover's letter was written on the sixth, two days earlier than the public learned that the purse was found south of Morgantown. Reverend Hoover continued to believe—at least as recently as 2008, when he was contacted by the authors.

In fact, for forty years after his letters, Hoover used his claim of leading the police to the coeds' remains to advertise his psychic services. It did not matter to him that the police had evidence that pointed south since the purse was found on March 1. It did not matter that the WVSP had ordered the air search of the Weirton Mine Section on April 4. He was simply positive the coeds were found because of his letters.

The idea that the Triangle Letters were based on séances performed by an "occult group" reminded people of Charles Manson and his "family." And one month after the coeds were decapitated, a family was murdered in Fort Bragg, North Carolina; an AP story in the *Fairmont Times* intoned, "Hippie-Type Band Stabs Mother, Two Children to Death." The only family member left after the massacre, Jeffrey MacDonald, described two men and a woman in a floppy hat who carried a candle and chanted, "Acid is groovy! Kill the pigs!" as they butchered the family.

"On the headboard of the MacDonalds' bed," said the article, "scrawled in blood, was the word 'pig'"—the same word that was found, in blood, in the Tate-LaBianca murders. Maybe the murders were all somehow connected.

16

"FORMER FAIRMONT MAN QUIZZED IN DECAPITATION."

Despite what WVSP uncovered about Gerkin, he all but disappeared from available reports. Sometime in the summer of 1970, he and his wife moved to Ohio, just across the river from Parkersburg, West Virginia. He was briefly interviewed in August and continued to deny knowledge of the murders. He finally agreed to come to Parkersburg to take a polygraph about his involvement. When he arrived, he was in such an agitated state that the troopers suggested he come back another time. He never did. No one looked closely at Gerkin again for almost forty years.

———————◆———————

The public heard little else about the case that autumn. WVSP released optimistic statements claiming they were no longer focused on the writer of the letters and were free to devote more time to the case. Despite this claim, the investigation withered. Fewer troopers worked the case, and the ones who did, chiefly Gooden and Herald, were also assigned other tasks. Colonel Bonar did not order anyone to reexamine all the persons of interest who were ruled out because of their handwriting. Lack of resources trumped public safety. WVSP's fading official interest was complemented by WVU's push to move on as if nothing had happened. Undergraduate enrollment for the fall semester was higher than ever.

Keeping the story alive, a *Charleston Gazette* reporter interviewed coeds on campus three weeks into the start of the new semester. He surveyed fifteen women and reported 60 percent expected another murder and over half believed police needed the killer to strike again in order to solve the case. Said one: "You never know if some idiot like this will strike again. I'd say most of the girls on campus, even the freshmen, are thinking about that." Added another: "The police around here don't seem to know what they're doing. They don't even seem to care."

Not much happened in the coed case throughout the fall. The rumors about the involvement of Hoover and his cult continued, but nothing of substance changed. In a long interview published in a Sunday *Dominion-Post*, Laurita said it was "an item found by a young man" that started the search south of Morgantown, not the letters. He couldn't go into detail because "the investigation is continuing," but he appeared to be referring to Mared's purse. When asked if he thought the killer was "still in the Morgantown area," he responded, "He may very well be."

Laurita also spoke about the bombing he survived. As with the coed murders, Laurita insisted the investigation was ongoing and the perpetrator or perpetrators would be brought to justice, but he spoke vaguely: "I think it wrong to say at this point my bombing was due to gambling or narcotics."

When photographer Rittenhouse was interviewed in 2016, he put it more pointedly: "They put the dynamite on the driver's side. Well, dynamite doesn't blow straight back. It blows to the left or to the right....[I]t blew out the right, passenger side of the car....That's why they figured it was amateurs, because pros wouldn't make a mistake like that."

Rittenhouse's observation dovetailed with the police rumor mill, then and now. Even though the case was never officially solved, authorities considered it resolved. The bomber wasn't a hired hit man, according to this notion, he was a vengeful husband, angry because of Laurita's affair with his wife.

But Rittenhouse had also heard an almost opposite theory: The explosion had actually been an attempt on the life of Zelda Laurita, Joe's wife. She usually rode to town with him, according to Rittenhouse, but for some reason had not done so that morning.

There's no telling if any particular rumor is informed speculation or empty talk. Throughout the fall, the public heard nothing more about the bombing or the coed murders. It would be Christmas before news emerged of another headless body covered with brush.

———◆———

On the Sunday after Christmas, Morgantown awoke to a front-page headline in the *Dominion-Post*: "Former Fairmont Man Quizzed in Decapitation."

A headless body had been found in Smoke Hole—in eastern West Virginia's Pendleton County—and identified as Herbert Cobun. The man who found the body, Carl Kimble, had seen a friend where the man shouldn't have been—coming out of a gate on Kimble's property on Christmas Eve. Suspicious, Kimble followed a trail of blood to a decapitated body buried under leaves and branches. He phoned the police, told them what he'd found and identified his friend, a man with the eerily on-point name of William Bernard Hacker.

Hacker was arrested by authorities in Baltimore County, Maryland, on Christmas Day. He had a room at the time in the home of Ida Novak and was arrested in long johns stained with Cobun's blood.

Hacker lived some of his life in Fairmont, near Morgantown, where he worked the mines as a foreman. He was convicted of a double murder in a bar near Fairmont in 1952. And, according to a WVSP report from 1952, Hacker's first wife came up missing in 1927, with his two small children telling police that "Daddy carried something out of the house this morning in a sheet." On the stand, Hacker countered he knew nothing about that, and besides, they'd long been legally divorced. While serving time for the double murder, due to his skills as a coal miner, he became a supervisor in Moundsville State Penitentiary's mine. There, he rescued a man in an accident, and his sentence was commuted in 1964.

Spurred by Hacker's history of violence and the fact that Cobun was decapitated, Mozingo, Humphreys and Rogers traveled to Baltimore. Hacker refused to talk. The three WVSP troopers, assisted by Maryland authorities, proceeded to the Novak residence to look for evidence. She allowed police to search her house, even presenting the officers with Hacker's personal effects. The officers took the items, only to return two days later to search again. This time, Novak pointed out Hacker's bed to the police. Under his pillow, they found a .32-caliber pistol. The chamber contained one empty shell and five unused, old, corroded bullets.

———•———

Hacker waived his extradition rights from Maryland, and he was moved to the Pendleton County jail in Franklin, West Virginia, where he was booked for murder. The case against him for Cobun's murder was solid, but WVSP very much wanted to see if he could be connected to the murders of Mared and Karen.

William Bernard Hacker escorted by police. *West Virginia Newspaper Publishing Company.*

Investigators came at Hacker again and still he refused to speak. Without cooperation from Hacker or any additional evidence, police began to have doubts. Could this man have kidnapped two coeds at the same time and killed them, cut their heads off and covered their corpses with heavy objects? Hacker was not a big man, but he was wiry and strong, having worked the mines most of his seventy-four years. But still, he was only five feet, seven inches tall and missing two fingers. What motive could he have for the murders? His crimes carried a pattern of spurned-lover fury, police thought, not the random murder of young women. Still, they tried to tie the two cases together by attempting to catch Hacker in a lie.

Hacker was convicted of Cobun's murder in 1971, and two stories have been told regarding a lie detector test used to question him. The first claims that after Hacker received his third life sentence, Sergeant Mitchell managed to convince him to submit to a polygraph. Road work interfered with the test—a jackhammer resonated through the walls, rendering the results of the test completely useless. But the second version tells of Gooden talking Hacker into the polygraph. The results of the test in this version were never made public, but Gooden said the "lead should be pursued." No documentation exists to support either story. Closer examination years later revealed that Gooden was right, and Hacker lived his life amid much more violence and murder than 1970 investigators imagined.

17

"WHATEVER HAPPENED
TO THE PROBE OF THE COED CASE?"

By the spring of 1971, less than a year after the murder investigation began, Preston Gooden fulfills his promise to Richard Werner and goes public with what he sees as the investigation's failures. When he last worked the case, he strongly believed several men should be looked at more closely, including Thrasher, Gerkin, Kroll and Hacker. None of them was—until 2006.

St. Patrick's Day, 1971. Superintendent Bonar read a summarized version of a letter to United Press International from an anonymous sender(s), signed "The West Virginia State Police for a Better West Virginia." The letter detailed morale problems and personal politics in the Department of Public Safety leadership that hindered investigations. The letter contended some people were afraid of a "strong and efficient police organization" and that a Fraternal Order of Police–type organization would benefit the rank and file. Ideally, this new organization would protect troopers by keeping politics out of investigations, enhancing job security, increasing the number of men on the job, providing training that was both broader and more specialized to fight corruption and crime and putting in place twenty-four-hour road patrols.

Bonar, incensed, responded with a three-page letter of his own. He considered the complaint letter a sabotage of the WVSP that lowered morale and tainted its image. He "seriously doubted that the letter was written by any member of the department." Calling into question the motives of UPI, he chastised the news agency for giving credence to an anonymous letter.

To take control over the situation and quell the talk of building a fraternal organization, Bonar announced fourteen new departmental transfers effective immediately, six of which directly affected the coed investigation: three inside the Morgantown Detachment (Mozingo, Sparks, C.L. Hall) and three attached to the case (Potts, Parsons and Rogers). These departmental shifts left Gooden and Herald the only remaining troopers in the Morgantown Detachment familiar with the still-unsolved Laurita bombing *and* the coed murders cases.

———•———

Gooden took his own complaints to the Combined Civics Club Committee (CCCC), begging them to push for an inquiry into DPS and the executive branch, knowing he faced the possibility of serious repercussions.

The CCCC was created in part as a response to the Laurita bombing. The organization served by "investigating social problems" in the community and liaising with the media about these problems. As the name implies, the CCCC was composed of representative members of service organizations, like the Rotary Club, Quota Club, Kennedy Youth Center and others. It wasn't uncommon for a member of law enforcement or a legal official to be asked to discuss issues such as funding problems, community concerns and crime prevention before the CCCC. In this capacity, Gooden addressed the CCCC on April 23, 1971. He intended to make the public aware of what went wrong with the investigation, but he also wanted to fulfill his promise to Richard Werner, Mared's brother-in-law.

———•———

"Thank you, Ann," says Mabel White to the committee's secretary after hearing the meeting minutes from the week before. "Does anyone have anything that needs brought before the group?" She looks up from the rickety lectern. Some twenty members share the space with a few newspaper reporters. No one speaks, so she continues. "If no one has anything else, Trooper Gooden will be speaking to us today about his concerns regarding the investigations into the Laurita bombing and the two missing WVU coeds."

She looks at her fellow CCCC chairs, Loulie Canady and Dr. Elias Costianes. Loulie speaks up first, "Well, I think Trooper Gooden has the floor."

"Agreed," confirms Dr. Costianes. "Thank you for coming, Trooper Gooden. We do appreciate your speaking to us."

Gooden takes the lectern. If it feels awkward for him to speak in front of a former suspect in the coed case, he doesn't show it. He helped search for the girls' heads on Mabel's farm, too. In the room, more people were involved with the case than not.

He sorts his handwritten notes and clacks them against the lectern. He has dark hair and a cleft chin, and while he isn't a terribly attractive man, he holds everyone's attention with his quiet intellect and stoic conviction. He isn't in uniform, but his posture and formality command respect.

"Thank you." He stands straight, shoulders back. "I'm here today to tell you the problems of the West Virginia State Police are rapidly becoming a crisis." He pauses to make eye contact with his audience.

"In 1971, this system still has serious manpower shortages. The promotional system is geared to who you hunt and fish with or who you know rather than on merit, a system that permits officers to be transferred for doing their job, and a system that still has not learned that professional police work and politics do not mix. It is a system that permits an officer to associate with known racketeers and still reach a rank of leadership." There is some mumbling, and Gooden pauses until he has their full attention.

"This is not a partisan thing with me. I couldn't care less about Democrats or Republicans. I'm concerned about the professionalism of the department." He is also doing this at the risk of his career.

"Throughout this past year, I have been ordered to lie to civilians, falsify dates and exaggerate facts. Our leaders advised officers to disregard students' civil rights and even suggested knocking them off chairs to get them to talk. And worst of all, I was commanded to overlook what I considered a terrible threat to young lives until the public forced the hand of the executive office.

"One would have to be a member of the families of those girls, or in my situation, *removing them from the grave*, to understand the real tragedy. Yet, this case is not receiving top priority." Gooden looks up again, letting his words sink in. "I am not concerned that the prosecutor's car is going to be bombed again, but it frightens me to think that a repeated coed crime may be a possibility.

"With the recent transfer of Sergeant Robert Mozingo and Corporal W.Z. Sparks, we lost firsthand knowledge in this case. Those transfers crippled the investigation. We could have had those cases solved today if we didn't have constant interference from the executive office in Charleston.

"Some of the things that have been said about the coed case disturb me. For example, I read in the papers where someone in Charleston said the case is receiving top priority and the investigation is going on round the clock.

I know better. I'm one of the investigators! Some of the times they said it received top priority, I was out removing junked cars or investigating wrecks. There's been times *nobody* investigated the cases.

"We will prove, and I have here documented proof—" He raises some papers, clutching them above his shoulder. "Proof the head of the Department of Public Safety and the executive administrator to Governor Moore lied about the department's activity in the coed investigation.

"I pledged to the Malarik family I would make public all facts in the case should the investigation ever cease. I'm here to tell you there are no current full-time investigators on the coed case, nor on the attempt on Joseph Laurita's life. As a police officer, I'm frustrated. I know it's unusual for a trooper to publicly criticize his superiors. I didn't want to do it. I put it off as long as I could, but I think it's something the public should know.

"I will probably lose my job, but I want those people in Charleston to know I will follow all legal avenues." He sets down his papers and scans the room. "I am prepared to carry this case to court if any action is taken against me, but I ask you to support an investigation of the Department of Public Safety." He pauses a beat. "Thank you, ladies and gentlemen."

Applause erupts from the seated audience. Gooden has just told them what they suspected all along. In that room there are faculty and parents of students who have seen firsthand how shaken up the WVU student body was. Now, with Gooden's testimony, they feel vindicated.

As Gooden scoops up his documents, Mabel stands beside the trooper. She lightly touches his arm. "Pres, you have the full support of this committee. You will not have to fight alone, if it comes to that."

Less than twenty-four hours later, Gooden is fired.

———◆———

A Trooper Gooden Fund initiated by the CCCC collected donations for Gooden's legal defense. Being a friend of the ex-trooper proved dangerous—several members of the CCCC began receiving menacing phone calls, even bomb threats. An undisclosed member left the group less than three days after Gooden's speech. Loulie Canady, one of three committee chairs, was told by a caller that the CCCC was "interfering with law officers." She was not deterred. She felt that "anybody that's going to try and change these things is in for something."

Bonar lobbied for Yost and Moore, but State Senator R.E. Barnett of Mercer County promised to talk to committees in the legislature to enact a probe of the WVSP. Delegates Terry T. Jones (former Morgantown mayor), Robert W. Dinsmore (successful Morgantown businessman) and Robert B. Stone (a prosecutor and future circuit court judge) pledged their support to Gooden and offered help with calling for inquiries. In late May, a preliminary legislative hearing was scheduled that highlighted the rift in the WVSP between mostly veteran officers supporting their colonel and a "hardcore group of dissidents" seen as stirring up controversy.

Bonar lashed out, boycotting the proceedings, protesting that troopers did not need to "voluntarily respond" to the Senate Joint Committee on Government and Finance subpoenas. Bonar's stress, coupled with his habit of two packs a day and daily consumption of twenty to twenty-five cups of coffee, took its toll; he suffered a major heart attack and was hospitalized the day of the hearing. His doctor insisted he lose weight and change his unhealthy lifestyle. Bonar's supporters blamed the rebellious "agitators" for his cardiac distress.

The hearing process was delayed twice, until Bonar felt well enough to attend, and resumed in mid-September. Mared's brother-in-law, Richard Werner, flew in to testify in support of Gooden. Unfortunately, his scheduled return flight forced him to leave before getting his chance to speak. In an improvised compromise, he voiced his opinion by addressing the press. Werner's frustrations lay with the stale condition of Mared's case compounded with his feelings that WVU "did little to exert pressure" early in the disappearance. There were "murderers loose who can still strike" since "the investigation ceased to be a full-time investigation," a decision he said came from either Moore or Bonar.

Bonar confirmed Werner's suspicions the next day when he announced the WVSP no longer treated the coed case as a full-time pursuit.

Gooden was eventually reinstated and received back pay and service credit, but not until April 1977, after a West Virginia Supreme Court judgment and a series of appeals—with Bonar fighting his reinstatement every step of the way. Even after Gooden was reinstated, he was assigned to the Beckley area, 275 miles southwest of where his family lived in Martinsburg. He did his job weekdays and went home every weekend. And in a demonstration that he was good police, he promptly solved four separate murder cases in the area that had languished, unsolved, for several years.

According to his oldest daughter, Terri, Gooden often said he would do it all over again. Right is right, and he felt compelled to speak up about wrongs within the WVSP. He felt vindicated after reinstatement but was still saddened by losing years at the height of his career.

In 2017, Dimas Reyes offered a coda to the tale of Gooden's odyssey. Ponch, as everyone called Reyes, was a WVSP trooper in 1970 and later went to law school and became an assistant prosecuting attorney for Monongalia County.

"I was working with Preston that night [April 24, 1971] they called him into the barracks. He had done the speech, and I guess it didn't go well with the administration." He snickered at his understatement.

"Preston's patrol car was a 1969 Pontiac. This particular night…I'm driving and we're on patrol up in the Cheat Lake area. We're getting ready to go across the old Cheat Lake bridge, and we get a call to come back to the barracks. And Preston says, he looks at me, he goes—" Ponch sucks his teeth. "—'Mmm, this is probably not good.'

"We drive back to the barracks. We had an office in the back room of the old barracks. Preston goes back with [a commanding officer] and they're back there for a while….Preston comes out, and his badge is off his uniform.

"Years later…I'm working the interstate and I'm coming up on, uh, what is now Route 68. It was called 48 back then. I clocked a car [going too fast and] pulled it over. It was Preston Gooden. He was on his way to Charleston to be reinstated. I was the last guy he saw when he got fired and I was the first guy when he got reinstated. Which I thought was kind of ironic, you know what I mean?"

After Preston Gooden's firing, politicians and police occasionally claimed the coed case was still open. "Still open" means department personnel are willing to look into the case if a lead falls in their laps, but realistically, no one actually cares if the case is ever mentioned again.

———◆———

In early October 1971, WVSP heard the first confession to the coed murders, although investigators were skeptical from the beginning. When Edward Lee Fielder confessed, he was serving a life sentence for a murder conviction in Mercer County at the southernmost tip of West Virginia. There, a man caught Fielder riffling his hotel room, and Fielder shot him. In May 1971, Fielder was taken from his cell to Roanoke, Virginia, to stand trial for the murder of a taxi driver the previous December. Fielder pleaded guilty to that crime, received a sentence of fifty years and was returned to West Virginia.

The more WVSP investigated Fielder's confession—which differed considerably from known facts of the case—and looked for corroborating evidence, the more skeptical they became. Fielder said he'd committed the crime with the help of another man but repeatedly refused to name his accomplice. He claimed he stashed his clothes in a building in Princeton, West Virginia, a small town in the southern part of the state. The building was located, but no clothes were found. Investigators found no proof Fielder had *ever* been in the northern part of the state. Two polygraph tests proved inconclusive: One suggested he was telling the truth and one said he was lying. After more investigation produced no corroborating evidence, the WVSP concluded Fielder made it all up.

Although people are often reluctant to believe it, false confessions occur with some frequency, for a variety of reasons. Suspects can be manipulated or coerced, whether or not investigators are aware of employing any coercive techniques. Confessions can also be offered voluntarily, and some of those are also false. For instance, in well publicized murders—and in West Virginia, the coed case qualified—people confess for the notoriety or, in the case of people already imprisoned, to boost their reputations in prison. The latter is especially common when a prisoner has already been convicted of other murders.

———————•———————

The termination of Preston Gooden and the transfers that gutted the investigation resulted in years of silence about the murders. Articles that recapped the investigation appeared, articles like "What Ever Happened to Probe of Coed Slayings?" and a four-part series written by Mike Connell, a *Dominion-News* staff writer. They looked back at Kroll as a suspect and Hacker as an untapped source of information, but such articles said more about the public's continued fascination than any official interest.

In February 1973, WVSP was looking into a series of murder-decapitations of University of California coeds in Santa Cruz to see if they tied to the murders of Mared and Karen. In May, a man named Edmund Kemper was indicted for the murders at UCSB, but no connection was ever found. The same year, a Florida deputy named Gerard John Schaefer was tried and convicted for the murders of two teenagers. Because of Schaefer's predilection for kidnapping two hitchhiking women at the same time, WVSP focused briefly on him as a suspect. No connection to the murders of Mared and Karen was found, nor any evidence he had ever hunted in West Virginia.

Over the years, fewer and fewer articles about the coed murders appeared. By 1975, silence reigned.

Then, two weeks into January 1976, near the sixth anniversary of the disappearance of Mared and Karen, a man incarcerated in Camden, New Jersey, claimed he killed and decapitated two girls, college students, years earlier.

III

SO MUCH SMOKE

1

"THE CONFESSION ITSELF SHOULD BE PUNISHED."

In the 1970s, people previously thought of as lust killers were increasingly being called serial killers, a term usually attributed to a 1974 speech by Robert Ressler, an FBI agent, though investigative circles in Germany have used it since 1930. In 1976, the public learned that a man incarcerated in New Jersey had confessed to the murders. The confession was so lurid it had to be true.

MORGANTOWN
OCTOBER 28, 1976

"Ladies and gentlemen of the jury, the defendant, Eugene Paul Clawson, was indicted by the April Term 1976 Grand Jury on two counts of murder. The first count is Eugene Paul Clawson on the 18th day of January, 1970, in Monongalia County did *feloniously* and *willfully* and *maliciously* and *deliberately* and premeditatedly *slay, kill* and *murder* one Karen Lynn Ferrell, and the second count charges him with the same murder of Mared Malarik."

Monongalia County prosecuting attorney David Solomon's words to the jury opened Clawson's trial.

"Now, ladies and gentlemen of the jury," he continued, "I will now open the *evil window of death* and relate to you what facts and circumstances the State of West Virginia will rely upon to prove, beyond a reasonable doubt, that Eugene Paul Clawson is guilty of the premeditated and willful murder of two young girls on Sunday night, January 18, 1970, in the lonely and silent woods of Monongalia County....The *evil window of death* will show that the defendant murdered these two coeds in cold blood, after *perpetrating upon their bodies every abuse and indignity* that could be perpetrated upon a human being."

Solomon took full advantage of the heinous nature of the case. The italicized phrases emphasize his overheated style, as marked on his own handwritten opening and performed in court. In his dark suit with his hair smoothed back against his skull, Solomon appealed to the jury's moral rectitude and highlighted the unquestionable horror of the crime as described by Clawson. As prosecutors do, Solomon falsely asserted his case contained overwhelming evidence of Clawson's guilt.

"The State of West Virginia will call approximately forty witnesses [from] the Morgantown City Police Department, the West Virginia State Police, and from the State of New Jersey. We have witnesses who will be experts in photography, fingerprints, hair analysis, blood..."

In his opening statement, Solomon denigrated Clawson's character, referring to him constantly as "immoral" and "depraved." Clawson didn't just kill two blameless young women, Solomon said, he "did deliberately and willfully murder these two beautiful coeds by decapitating them after subjecting them to sexual abuses and indignities beyond description and belief."

The phrasing of Solomon's opening statement projected confidence Clawson was the guilty man. Clawson's confession surprised the public, much of which had all but given up on ever discovering the real killer who had so shaken Morgantown six years earlier. Solomon used the first portion of his opening to summarize Clawson's criminal acts, hinting at the depravity:

"Several hours were consumed in these *preliminaries of death* to satisfy this defendant before *his final and ultimate act of the decapitation of these young ladies*, as even in his murder of these two ladies an *ignoble and humiliating means of death* was to be employed, that of decapitation."

But Solomon was just winding up. He then spent a great deal of time telling the jury what Clawson said he did:

> After driving what must have seemed an eternity to these young ladies, this defendant did in fact arrive at this remote area and his arena of death. He was now ready to inflict his savagery upon these poor ladies. And after parking in this lonely arena of death, this defendant got one of the girls up off the floor of the car, putting handcuffs upon her wrists and locking the other end of the handcuffs under the front seat of the car. Then, after being able to be sure that the handcuffed victim in the front seat

DNC, THANK, PAT

TO BE USED

YOUR HONOR, JUDGE KIGER, LADIES AND GENTLEMEN OF THE JURY,

IT IS NOW TIME TO CLOSE THE EVIL WINDOW OF DEATH.

AS I SAID TO YOU IN MY OPENING STATEMENT, I WOULD OPEN THE EVIL WINDOW OF DEATH TO ALLOW YOU TO WITNESS THE HORROR AND DEATH THAT OCCURRED TO TWO YOUNG CO-EDS ON JANUARY 18, 1970.

YOU MUST SURELY AGREE WITH ME THAT THIS WINDOW THAT WAS OPENED WAS A WINDOW THAT OPENED INTO HELL ITSELF.

WE ARE BOTH RELIEVED TO CLOSE THIS WINDOW AND GET THIS ALL BEHIND US, BECAUSE WE DID NOT LIKE WHAT WE SAW (PAUSE) THROUGH THE OPEN WINDOW.

I REALIZE THAT YOU / LIKE MYSELF / UNDOUBTEDLY FIND IT TOO DIFFICULT TO BELIEVE, BECAUSE YOU AND I ARE GOD-FEARING HUMAN BEINGS; AND SUCH ACTS ARE DIFFICULT, IF NOT IMPOSSIBLE FOR US TO BELIEVE; BUT AS UNBELIEVEABLE AS THESE ACTS OF RAPE AND MURDER ARE, WE MUST BELIEVE THAT THESE ATROCITIES OCCURRED!

TRUTH IS OFTEN TIMES DIFFICULT TO BELIEVE, AND SURELY TRUTH IS MANY TIMES STRONGER THAN FICTION.

Page of Prosecutor Solomon's notes for 1976 trial, from Monongalia County Circuit Court records. S. *James McLaughlin*.

could not escape, this defendant ordered the other girl to crawl over the top of the front seat into the back seat so that he could begin his night of terror and horror upon these young ladies.

With one of the victims now handcuffed in the front seat and the other victim in the back seat, he made the one in the back seat get undressed and then he also undressed, and then forcibly, with the gun upon her, perpetrated his sexual desires by having normal sex relations and then abnormal sexual relations in every conceivable fashion and perpetrating upon her every indecency that can be perpetrated upon a human being....

Solomon continued to describe "sexual depravities" that only ended when Clawson "got a machete, and while they were begging and whimpering, he chopped their heads off" and "took the heads and wrapped them in some dirty rags." He drove back toward Point Marion and "parked and got into the back seat of the car, naked with the heads and had sex with them and after getting dressed again, got out of his car...and threw the heads and rags and the gun into a hole or crevice."

Solomon's opening statement was effective, but it was also repeatedly argumentative and inflammatory and drew conclusions about the nature of the defendant's acts. A prosecutor's opening statement can describe the acts but not characterize them or "argue" that the acts are "immoral," "depraved" or "ignoble." The opening statement also cannot misstate the facts or refer to things as facts when that is for the jury to determine.

To say that Clawson "got a machete, and while they were begging and whimpering, he chopped their heads off" is to argue the facts. Technically, Solomon should have said, "According to Clawson's confession, they were begging and whimpering." But he didn't. He asserted that Clawson *did* certain things rather than saying that Clawson *said* he did those things. That may seem like a small point, but each time an argumentative or inflammatory statement is made, the defense can object. On the other hand, repeated defense objections can be viewed by jurors as annoying and can result in the jury disliking the defense from the trial's outset, which would not be a good way to begin.

After recounting the whole horrible night as if it actually did happen, Solomon shifted his focus to the activities of the police following the crime:

Apparently, some time on Monday, January the 19th, 1970, the day after the alleged [sic] murders, Chief Bennie Palmer, of

the Morgantown Police Department, received a Public Service
Call from the concerned individuals to the effect that two young
coeds were not in their dormitory rooms....

He spoke of Steve Trickett looking for pop bottles with his sister when
they found Mared's purse and of Fred Stewart finding Mared's glasses on
April 12. He described the large sweep that began and a few of the roads
searched. Very quickly he shifted to how "Steve Slavensky, a member of
the National Guard, came upon the grave site of the two coeds in that
he observed that parts of the girls' legs were visible." He lingered there
for thorough descriptions of the bodies, their placement, deterioration,
identification and autopsy.

Solomon said the trial would produce the evidence of the handcuffs, key
fob, hairs from the animal nest and the machete. He also read into the record
the taunting letter Clawson sent Colonel Richard Hall, in which Clawson
wrote that he's

> going to tell the guys if they want to commit the perfect murder
> all they have to do is go to West Virginia and kill someone.

Last, Solomon talked about the time window: "In other words, he had from
2:30 Sunday afternoon until 11:30 Sunday night to drive from Philadelphia
to the Morgantown area to commit this crime":

> You have now had a brief look into this evil window of death,
> and we will bring forth testimony and evidence to give you
> a detailed and exhaustive picture which you will be able to
> see through this evil window of horror and death as to what
> happened to these young ladies on Sunday, January the 18th,
> 1970, their last night on earth.
>   Thank you.

In the interviews for this book, the second chair for the defense, Michael
Tomasky, was characterized as a scholar and excellent lawyer, even one of
"the four pillars of the legal community," so he must have been aware that
Solomon's opening statement was often argumentative and inflammatory but
didn't object. He had his reasons. Still, Solomon's confident, morally superior
tone lent the case against Clawson an air of certainty that banished doubt
about Clawson's guilt in many people's minds. It set a momentum that would

carry the state's case successfully though two trials. His dwelling on the graphic details as if he would prove them—as if he *could* prove them—branded the images in the minds of many. The vividness of Solomon's dramatization, probably even more than the confession itself, cemented the story of the coed murders as a crime of drugs and sexual perversion.

Like his entire case, Solomon's opening lacked specifics but was long on moral certitude. Despite this, or maybe because of it, his opening statement may have gone a long way to convicting Clawson in the eyes of the jury.

Clawson's defense team consisted of lead Edward Friend and second chair Michael Tomasky. Friend gave the defense's opening statement, and he offered a distinct contrast to Solomon's overheated, dramatic style. He came across as, well, friendly. His courtroom demeanor exaggerated the folksy. He kept his opening short, one-third the length of Solomon's:

> Ladies and gentlemen of the jury, I'm Ed Friend and I want to, first, explain to you that I've been appointed by the judge to defend Mr. Clawson in this case. At counsel table, as Mr. Solomon explained, is Mike Tomasky, my partner. He's not been appointed in this case, but…my partner has agreed to assist me.

Eugene Paul Clawson (*left*), being taken from the prisoner entrance to the city jail. *West Virginia Publishing Company*.

Friend faced serious problems when it came to defending Clawson. The biggest hurdle, by far: his client's confession. In 1970, confessions set the gold standard in terms of evidence. Still today, it's difficult to imagine why anyone confesses to a crime they didn't commit, but people do it all the time. Current estimates are that somewhere between a quarter and a half of all confessions are false, and that's counting only the false confessions that actually lead to a conviction. Whether accurate or false, a confession goes a long way to "proving" a defendant's guilt. A confession differs from most evidence in that *it changes the way jurors look at all the other evidence.*

But as important as it was, the confession wasn't Friend's only problem. Clawson himself was a problem. He had a long arrest record, but perhaps even more important in a trial, he was an unpleasant man. Unsympathetic. He looked and acted oddly. His manner was furtive and his voice whiny. His affect was strange. He was not a likeable man and did not appear to be trustworthy. A number of jurors and court observers said as much, using terms like *creepy*, *pathetic* and *sniveling*. More than one person characterized him as someone "you would cross the street to avoid." People who encountered Clawson didn't like him. But Friend needed jurors to feel some sympathy for his client and chose to confront this problem head on:

> I really knew nothing about Mr. Clawson until May of this year when the judge made this appointment.…[W]e had in June 1976 a competency hearing or disclosure and we did not go to trial in June because Mr. Clawson was deemed to have been incompetent to stand trial, meaning he couldn't communicate with me and he didn't understand the seriousness of the charges. However, at a later time he was re-examined, found competent and here we are.…
>
> Mr. Clawson is not what we would consider, as you and I would consider, a completely adjusted person. He has a chromosomal defect. He during school developed large breasts.…So he's had problems. He's had problems since grade school in Point Marion, and I imagine at some time the prosecutor will bring out some of the problems he's been in.…It isn't the first time he's been sitting in jail.

Clawson's a mess, Friend said. He can't hold a job, never has been able to. He has severe mental and emotional issues. He's been suicidal many times. Friend went further than simply acknowledging Clawson's personal deficiencies to jurors, he emphasized them.

> I have read these confessions and I can state to you now that they are a terrible description of human brutality. They're horrible things to have to read; they're horrible to have to put before you all or anybody else. It's actually, I believe, almost so bad that the confession itself should be punished.…
>
> [Y]ou have to separate the confession and all its bizarre characteristics from what actually happened. I think this case comes down to, Did Eugene Paul Clawson commit this crime? Is this confession an accurate, believable story of what happened that night?

I also don't want you to think that Eugene Paul Clawson is the first person that confessed to this crime. We'll show you there have been…other people that the investigation has disclosed have confessed to this crime before Clawson was ever heard of. It's not unusual.

He implored the jury to separate the confession from the deed, to ask themselves if the confession provided a reasonable and believable account of events that night. Friend said Clawson's confession was drawn from an issue of a detective magazine dated December 1975. The article was read into the record during the trial.

In his confession, Friend said, Clawson made a serious mistake. He forgot that on Sunday, January 18, 1970, he was written up because he was an hour and a half late for work. He rode the train to work instead of driving, making it impossible to drive to Morgantown directly after getting off work.

Friend finished his opening statement with suggestions for the jury:

I ask you, without arguing the case, in closing, to listen to the evidence on behalf of my client. Listen to it. I ask you to be skeptical of evidence that violates your common sense and I, again, ask you, don't make up your mind until you've heard everything: both the prosecutor's case and the defense.

Thank you.

Two competing stories were presented to the jury. According to the prosecution, an immoral, depraved Clawson defiled two innocent young girls because he enjoyed doing so and admitted as much to authorities. The vividness of Clawson's confession was cemented in the minds of the jury, and Solomon claimed a mountain of evidence and experts would back up this claim. The defense insisted Clawson—an incredibly damaged and confused person—used a magazine article to concoct an absurd, improbable tale. Arguably, the greatest weakness in the prosecution case was that it offered little evidence beyond the confession. Perhaps the greatest weakness in the defense case, at least as presented in Friend's opening, was the lack of effort to explain *why* Clawson had confessed in the first place.

A West Virginia Homicide Riddle:
DID HE LIE ABOUT RAPING & BEHEADING TWO COEDS?

Headline from *True Detective* magazine, April 1977.

THE CONFESSIONS TURNED OUT to be enough to convict Clawson. The jury decided Clawson, and Clawson alone, kidnapped, murdered and decapitated Mared Malarik and Karen Ferrell. That verdict was overturned in 1980, when the West Virginia Supreme Court of Appeals ruled that pictures introduced at trial did nothing to demonstrate guilt and served only to prejudice the jury. The court ordered a new trial and a new venue, Elkins, West Virginia, in Randolph County.

Clawson was convicted again, this time sentenced to life with mercy. His confession did far more than incarcerate a man for the last twenty-eight years of his life. The lurid tales he told cemented the idea of Mared and Karen as victims of a drug-crazed sex maniac who humiliated and terrorized them before cutting off their heads and leaving their bodies to forest scavengers. The statements and confessions turned an unimaginable crime into an unforgivable one. But what if the confessions were completely false?

2

"I MET ONE EUGENE PAUL CLAWSON."

CAMDEN COUNTY JAIL, NEW JERSEY

January 13, 1976, nine months before the trial

Gene was having nightmares. At least, that's what Felton told the detectives. Felton Harpe and Eugene Paul Clawson shared the same cellblock, and Harpe said that several times in the early summer of 1975 he was awakened by Clawson's cries—terrible screams on the blackest of nights.

"During the month of June 1975, in the Camden County Jail I met one Eugene Paul Clawson, a resident inmate of the county jail." Harpe was laying it out for detectives of the Camden County Prosecutor's Office. "Somewhere between June and January of 1975 through '76, he recalled to me that he had in fact on or about March of 1972 picked up two female, two females near a movie house in the town of Morgantown and had subsequently taken them for a ride in his automobile, and that he had had some type of sexual relationships with the girls, after which he killed and beheaded both students."

Clawson confided in him because he wanted to come clean, Harpe said. Trembling something awful, Clawson whined he had done the unforgivable, many years ago, near where he'd grown up in Point Marion, Pennsylvania.

He raped two college girls and cut off their heads. The poor man just couldn't live with himself any longer. He told Harpe he was wracked with guilt and had to confess. Harpe, considered a "jailhouse lawyer," knew how to weave a vivid story.

A sergeant with the Camden County Prosecuting Attorney's Homicide Squad immediately notified the Morgantown Police Department he had an informant implicating a Eugene Paul Clawson in the murder of two hitchhikers. When told about the coed murders, the sergeant asked if one of the victims was named Karen and the other one was from New Jersey. According to the informant, Clawson was in Point Marion at the time of the murders, either visiting his sick mother or attending her funeral, and the car he'd used in commission of the crime had been stolen in Pittsburgh.

The call galvanized the investigative machinery of the WVSP. If the information turned out to be true, the case that had haunted West Virginia for years might finally be closed. WVSP's Criminal Investigation Bureau pulled Clawson's file to check his criminal record. Long and steady, the record revealed Clawson's history of convictions for a variety of offenses, starting when he was a teenager. Most importantly, he had not been incarcerated on January 18, 1970. The timeline fit.

By the end of the day, WVSP had determined Clawson's brothers lived in Point Marion and Cleveland, Ohio, both with good community reputations; verified the illnesses and deaths of both parents; and arranged for the investigation to be led by Trooper D.M. Shade and MPD detective J.A. McCabe. Other details emerged over the weekend, and Shade, McCabe and WVSP sergeant William H. Mitchell drove up to Camden on Tuesday. They wanted to talk with Clawson, but first they wanted to hear the informant's story for themselves.

———•———

Detective-Captain Frank Senatore, the officer in charge of the Camden County Prosecutor's Office, had Harpe brought up from his cell about 2:00 p.m. In the room were Senatore and a colleague, as well as Shade, McCabe and Mitchell. Harpe told the same story he'd related in previous conversations: Clawson's nightmares and desire to come clean, the two hitchhikers, the rape and murder and decapitation.

Harpe's story convinced Shade, McCabe and Mitchell to speak with Clawson directly, but first they wanted to begin the corroboration they would need if the case ever went to trial. Does the story match what authorities already know? Does the story reveal anything new? Does the story clear up known facts that can't otherwise be explained?

Harpe was asked if he would continue to cooperate with law enforcement, and he assured them he would. Before they talked with Clawson, investigators wanted to test Harpe and tasked him with gleaning three things from Clawson:

1. Did Clawson take any articles of clothing, jewelry or money from the coeds?
2. Where were the heads disposed of?
3. Where are the handcuffs and machete or bayonet now?

Harpe assured them Clawson was eager to talk and would be forthcoming and was sent back to his cellblock. A few hours later, Harpe called Detective Giletto. Clawson said he took a watch, a school ring and "some sort of necklace." This excited West Virginia investigators. Both Mared and Karen had been missing necklaces, and Karen's was reportedly a chain from which her high school class ring dangled. If it bothered investigators that neither girl was missing a watch or that Mared was found with no bra—Clawson hadn't mentioned that—their worries went unnoted in WVSP reports.

———— ◆ ————

Clawson was pulled from his cell about 9:15 p.m., his Miranda warnings witnessed by Senatore and two other New Jersey officers. At six feet, two inches tall, Clawson had unusually long legs and a short torso. Despite his height, he was curiously tentative, his demeanor almost timid. Based on their more complete knowledge, Shade, McCabe and Mitchell contributed written questions for Senatore to ask. The informant, Harpe, was also in the room. Though the reason for Harpe's presence is not clear, it is not uncommon for people not directly involved to be included by interviewers if they believe it will influence the suspect's statement.

The session got underway fifteen minutes before midnight. Senatore eased into it. Clawson was currently awaiting sentencing for another crime, and Senatore wanted to make sure he understood the interview had nothing to do with that crime. He also wanted to stress Clawson's right to legal counsel.

> Senatore: I'm only going to concern ourselves with the death of two young females….Now, you are represented by an attorney on your present charge. Is that correct?

Clawson: Yes.
Senatore: Would you tell the court stenographer what his name is?
Clawson: His name is—I don't know his first name. It's Mr.
        Weitzman. I can't spell it.
Senatore: And you got him through the public defender's office?
Clawson: Yes.
Senatore: Do you want Mr. Weitzman here with you tonight?
Clawson: He won't come this late at night. I don't have his
        phone number.
Senatore: Would you want him here tonight?
Clawson: I would like to have him, because I trust him very much.
Senatore: You would like to have him?
Clawson: It don't matter.
Senatore: Well, it matters, Gene. We want to take a statement
   from you.
Clawson: I don't want to cause no inconvenience.
Senatore: We're not talking about inconvenience. It's a matter of
        your rights....Do you want to give us this statement
        without your attorney here?
Clawson: I'll give it to you. I don't want to drag him down here,
        because I mean, it don't matter.

Clawson began to talk about his odyssey on January 18 and 19, 1970: "Well, I drove down there from Philly to visit my mother, and I had a '61 black-and-white Buick. I left that at my mother's house, and I hitchhiked to Pittsburgh."

Over the next few hours, Clawson detailed his activities. He drove down from Philadelphia to his mother's house in Point Marion, Pennsylvania, about ten miles north of Morgantown. He next hitchhiked to Pittsburgh and stole a car. Along the way, he said, he consumed LSD and smoked marijuana. He drove south to Morgantown, where he picked up two girls on a street he called Willey Avenue. He used the threat of a .38 to silence their protests and drove them to an area that was "remote" and "desolate." There, he forced them to undress and get back in the car.

Clawson launched into a seventy-plus-page confession of elaborate sexual abuse and rape. After this marathon, he had them get out of the car and shot them both in the head before decapitating them. He dragged them a ways into the woods, laid them side by side on their backs, covered them with logs and left, taking the heads with him. He found his way back toward Point Marion, where he parked the car, climbed into the backseat, had sex with the heads and then threw them and the .38 into a crevasse. He washed the blood off his thighs at his brother's house and put a necklace, a watch and a class ring under an old, abandoned house where he used to hide from his parents when he did something wrong. The confession was so lurid, the rapes and beheadings so degrading, that seven law enforcement professionals—and later the public and the jury—had no doubt this man committed the crime.

———◆———

The day after taking Clawson's confession, Mitchell, Shade and McCabe made the long drive home. Corroborating Clawson's confession had just become a top priority for law enforcement. There was so much smoke, the men felt there had to be a fire.

They decided to stop in Point Marion on the way back to Morgantown to look for the place Clawson said he had tossed the heads and the .38. They made several passes, looking for crevices, holes or pits that fit the description. They found nothing. The men called off the endeavor for the day and, defeated, finished their trip to Morgantown.

The next day, New Jersey authorities brought Clawson south and were met by the West Virginia troopers and Chief Bennie Palmer and Detective McCabe. Clawson led them to Conn Hill, located north of Stewartstown, West Virginia, near the West Virginia–Pennsylvania state line. The hill had a naturally occurring crevasse, but Clawson was not certain which hole he threw the heads into. Nevertheless, he indicated one particular hole was more likely than others.

———◆———

After searching the area with Clawson, Shade and Mitchell drove him into Morgantown. The WVSP reports say only that Clawson stayed the night and was taken back to New Jersey the next day, January 16. However, other documents conveyed a different picture. What follows is constructed from statements of the principals and from Clawson's own testimony. The statements overlap, to a degree, and differ only in what Clawson says he said—with one small difference.

The troopers wanted Clawson to point out a few things for further corroboration of his confession. The drive south on 119 from Conn Hill toward Morgantown cut through an undeveloped area covered with trees. On the way, according to Clawson, he complained he had to take a piss.

Mitchell, who was driving, stopped the car and said Clawson could go ahead. Clawson refused, saying there was no way he was going to do that. Shade would say he was trying to escape and shoot him. Shade and Mitchell later denied the incident ever happened, although others said it did happen and suggested Shade was capable of doing exactly what Clawson feared.

As they came into town via the Mileground and down to Willey Street, Mitchell said, "We want you to show us where you picked up the girls, Eugene."

They drove past the Vincent Pallotti Hospital, on the corner of Willey and Prospect; Clawson was born there. They eased around right to the section of Willey and Spruce, where the car stopped at the stoplight. Clawson looked at the street sign and saw he was on Willey.

"Right here," said Clawson. Neither trooper said anything.

When the light changed, the car proceeded toward Willey and High.

"This is it," Clawson said.

Shade turned, looked back at Clawson. "We want you to be sure."

The car rolled through the intersection and, in about 150 yards, curved right around the Mineral Industries building. They stopped at the stop sign there. No one spoke for a few seconds, and then Shade said, "Does this look familiar?"

"Yes," said Clawson. "This is where I picked them up."

"Very good, Eugene," Mitchell said. "Now, we want you to show us where you left the bodies."

"I still gotta piss. And I'm pretty tired. Can I take a nap before we go out there?"

It was late afternoon, but the officers figured they had time to head to the detachment and let their prisoner lie down for about an hour. As they entered the parking lot, they could see the press had been tipped off and were waiting for them. They hustled a handcuffed Clawson inside, but the press spotted them.

Inside, once Clawson was bunked up, the three of them discussed the situation.

"They're just going to follow us," Shade said. "We need to figure out a way to ditch them."

Mitchell thought about the situation.

"Let's go up to Waynesburg," he said, referring to a town a few miles north of the border, in Pennsylvania. "They'll think we're headed back to Camden. We can get a room, spend the night, and double back in the morning."

But the next morning, Camden authorities showed up to take Clawson back to New Jersey. Clawson was never again asked to show anyone where he left the bodies.

3

"CLAWSON REALLY, REALLY TRIED HARD TO CONVINCE PEOPLE HE DID IT."

Conn Hill had long been honeycombed with coal digs. A massive effort was mobilized to search Conn Hill's crevasses and ancient mining efforts. Shade and Mitchell and a group of state troopers were detailed to the search, which would last nearly a month.

For well over one hundred years, abundant coal had been often found on or near the surface in West Virginia. Families used it for heating and cooking and often had tiny coal operations on their land. Sometimes the "mines" were as small as a simple hole in the ground, but they could also be more extensive and comprise elaborate underground constructions, their ceilings shored up with timbers. Most were abandoned when the risk created by instability and depth outweighed the reward of plentiful coal close to the surface. Conn Hill had been a source of coal since around 1920. The makeshift nature of the construction meant no maps or descriptions of the underground work existed.

The search quickly produced a usable discovery: an animal nest with human hairs woven into it. The nest became a key piece of evidence in Clawson's first trial and told searchers the heads *must* be down there in one of those holes in the ground. Again—so much smoke there *had* to be a fire. Brave state troopers volunteered and were lowered into one hole after another, at least one to the depth of forty feet, but they found nothing of interest: no heads, no gun.

Searchers explored every surface inch of ground with metal detectors through the first half of the next week. Those efforts turned up only discarded refuse such as shovel blades, nails, horseshoes and other scrap metal. The search team continued to physically enter underground, where possible, and used video cameras where not. Some of the holes they worked were over one hundred feet deep but so unstable and hazardous that live searches were out of the question.

———— • ————

On Thursday, extreme weather conditions brought searchers a brief respite, and the search was suspended. However, the investigation continued to move forward. Detective Giletto, up in Trenton, was again in the prosecutor's Market Street office, this time to take a statement from David L. Glass, another cellmate of Clawson at Camden County Jail.

"I came to the Camden County Jail April the seventeenth, my first arrest in Camden. During the time I was there, I met Clawson," Glass said. "At the particular time, he was housing in Dorm 2, and I was housing in North C. He used to write us letters in the mess hall telling us he was homosexual and he would like to be moved to our block."

In some ways, Harpe's and Glass's statements were more like each other than Clawson's was like either one of them. For instance, both Harpe and Glass maintained, repeatedly, the car Clawson stole in Pittsburgh was light blue. Clawson said it was cream-colored, the same color of the car Paulette Burns and Clarence Lewis saw picking up Mared and Karen. In addition, both Harpe and Glass said Clawson picked the coeds up near a theater. Clawson was asked about this:

> Senatore: Are there any landmarks there, like any big stores or
> shopping areas or movies or anything else?
> Clawson: Not where they were hitchhiking wasn't no movie.

Because Clawson's confession agreed with eyewitness statements and because the Metropolitan Theater was actually more than a block and a half from where Mared and Karen got in the car, these differences could indicate Clawson knew more about the crime than Harpe and Glass. As he should, if he had been there, but if Clawson told the tale to Harpe and Glass, where had they gotten the idea he'd picked up Mared and Karen near a theater?

The search resumed on Saturday and continued for more than a week, but searchers found no new evidence. All told, after a month-long search,

Clawson's confession led only to the discovery of human hair in one animal nest found near the surface of Conn Hill and a few hairs woven into other nests.

———◆———

During January, however, still another arm of the investigation busily hunted for evidence to corroborate Clawson's confession. They contacted Eugene's brother James again. He agreed to turn over the machete Clawson said he used. When tested by CIB labs in Charleston, no blood or other evidence was found. Clarence Leppard gave Troopers a key fob and handcuffs he said he found in the spring of 1973, discarded along Route 119. Route 119 connects Point Marion to Morgantown to Grafton. Route 119 was the road Clawson would have driven to get to Morgantown, the road the killer had taken after going south from Morgantown with the two coeds. Most of Mared's and Karen's personal effects had been found near Route 119.

For the rest of January, all of February and into March, WVSP gathered the information they would present to Monongalia County's latest prosecutor, David L. Solomon. Solomon had held office since January 1973, having succeeded Joe Laurita. For Solomon, finding the hair on Conn Hill cinched the case. Solomon based his case on the confession, the testimony of the two jailhouse snitches, the hairs in the animal nests, some handcuffs Clawson said looked like the handcuffs he owned in 1970 and a boot-shaped rubber key fob that a witness claimed she had seen in Clawson's possession.

Many articles appeared in the *Dominion-Post*, by now Morgantown's only newspaper, formed by the 1973 merger of the *Dominion-News* and the *Morgantown Post*. Several times, Solomon publicly made such statements as, "He was giving us information that nobody but the killer could know.... He gave us enough to make us think this is the man we have been looking for." Observers sympathetic to Solomon said he was calming a nervous public with his claims of a strong case, but others said he was poisoning the jury pool.

In the months leading to the April term of the grand jury, Solomon spoke of Clawson's guilt like any prosecutor would: with absolute conviction. Some people believed—and continue to believe—Solomon did that because he faced a serious challenge in the rapidly approaching May Democratic primary. Solomon needed a high-profile trial, as the authors were told by more than one source, and a conviction of the coed killer would secure his reelection.

His opponent, Andrew G. Fusco, remembers a close election: "There was a margin of, what, a hundred votes," he told the authors in 2019. He had never heard the rumor that Solomon rushed the indictment in order to win the primary. "I started early and ran hard, and he sort of took me for granted, I think. Toward the end he realized he should have worked harder."

Whether or not Solomon acted so quickly because he feared losing the primary, he got his indictment of Clawson in April 1976. He lost the primary anyway.

———◆———

Eugene Paul Clawson's record painted the picture of a career criminal. In the twenty years before 1976, he was arrested for a couple of auto thefts, some burglary and larceny and vagrancy, the crime of having no money. Crimes such as these can hint the perpetrator commits them more often than he gets caught. They are essentially property crimes, even the ones that involved beating people up in order to rob them. Apparently, most of his life, Clawson didn't have any money, and he felt okay about simply taking what he needed.

If these were Clawson's only crimes, investigators might have hesitated to give his confession any credence at all. However, he had done worse. His most recent conviction, for which he was awaiting sentencing, was for "carnal abuse" of an underage girl, a term with a wide variety of meanings that usually encompasses sexual activity between an adult and a minor and often excludes penetration. This was the second time Clawson would be convicted of carnal abuse. Here, he details his crime:

> I drove way back into the woods with the girl, and she seen she was in the woods from down there on the floor, and she asked me if she could get up on the seat, and I told her yes. I was afraid she was going to run away and jump out and run while I was driving, so I told her I was sorry I picked her up, and as soon as I found a spot to turn around in, I was going to take her back where I picked her up at. Then when I got back in there, near a clearing, I rolled up and backed the car into the clearing.
>
> Before she could move, I put it in park and shut the key off and slid across the seat and had my arms around her. I told her I was going to fuck her, and when I got done with her nobody would want her because she was a slut

Neither that crime, nor his earlier "carnal abuse" of an underage boy, involved physical violence. He did not kill his victims or even beat them. This isn't to downplay his crimes but to illustrate the contrast between those crimes and the coed murders. Clawson attacked young people he could control but didn't penetrate them, and their gender was unimportant to him.

Clawson's arrest history didn't demonstrate he was likely to have killed the coeds but did suggest that was possible. People who commit sexual murder often start out committing lesser crimes: They begin as flashers or Peeping Toms and perhaps harm animals or younger people until they feel confident enough to…Clawson often described the "hot and tingly" feelings that overcame him, compelled him to force himself on someone.

If Clawson *did* kill Mared and Karen the way he said, his record revealed the expected escalation, a man growing bolder and more aggressive the more crimes he committed. If Clawson killed the coeds, he clearly "graduated" and was becoming a bigger threat to society. He had gone from attacking a single victim to taking two at once, from molesting young teenagers and letting them go to raping and decapitating adults. If this was the case, investigators had in their custody an extremely dangerous man driven by an uncommon rage. If Clawson perpetrated all the terrible acts he claimed and then killed and beheaded Mared and Karen, clearly he was a sex killer and would rape and kill again.

But if he did kill the coeds, got away with raping and killing two nearly adult women, his later arrest, again for "carnal abuse" of a young teenager, would argue he had gone back to being less violent and preying on weaker, easier-to-control victims.

Clawson did his best to appear guilty. As his 1981 defense lawyer Dan Ringer said in 2016, "Clawson really, really tried hard to convince people he did it. I counted a couple dozen statements that he made that were consistent with his confession and reiterating things about it."

Ringer never did say definitively whether he thought Clawson was guilty or not guilty, but toward the end of a 2016 interview, he had this to say:

> I didn't think he was capable of that kind of violence until the trial was over. He was really angry that he got convicted, and I went to visit him in the jail while he was aggressively angry.…I came away thinking, yeah, he probably was capable of doing that kind of violence to somebody. Exactly how or for what motivation, I don't know, but he was capable of

being violent. That was a question that we had had up to that point. Was he a violent person? Yeah, he coulda been.

In 1976, most law enforcement officials were certain Clawson was guilty. WVSP summarized the evidence against Clawson in a two-page document:

CONFESSIONS AND STATEMENT OF ACCUSED
1. Sworn statement of EPC, 74 pages, January 13, 1976, attached per copy.
2. January 16, 1976, 1330 hours, Clawson...showed officers where he placed skulls of victims and made incriminating statements of the murders.
3. January 16, 1976, 1550 hours. Clawson pointed out exact area...where he picked the victims up hitchhiking...
4. January 27, 1976, 1711 hours, Clawson admitted to Polygraph Operator Det. Gus Balanzo that he committed the murders.
5. February 11, 1976, 1145 hours, Statements made by Clawson....Transcript attached.
6. February 18, 1976, 1530 hours, Clawson's [says] that the key case in shape of a leather boot...was stolen by him....
7. February 22, 1976, Clawson wrote an incriminating letter...admitting the sexual acts and murders....
8. March 11, 1976, 1300 hours until 1800 hours, Clawson admitted of the sexual acts, murders, placing of the skulls at Conn Hill using a white '64 Cadillac convertible with stolen registration, selling the murder weapon and so forth....
9. March 11, 1976, 1845 hours at the Camden County Court House, Clawson admitted to the 1970 murders...
10. March 12, 1976, 0900 until 1300 hours, Clawson assisting...in the finding of the murder weapon....
11. Four hypnosis sessions of Clawson admitting to the murders....
12. The suspect Clawson from January 13, 1976, through to the writing of this report, on many occasions has admitted to the murders....

4

"TAKE YOUR TRASH."

Typically, females are born with two X chromosomes, and most males are born with one X and one Y. Clawson was born with one Y chromosome and two X chromosomes: Klinefelter Syndrome. Men born with Klinefelter are sometimes tall and often have abnormal body proportions—long legs and a short torso, with the shoulder and hips of equal size. They may have enlarged breasts and less body hair than XY men due to a shortage of testosterone. They often develop a small penis and small, firm testicles and have problems performing sexually.

Dr. S. Donald Babcock in New Jersey interviewed Clawson a number of times in the spring and summer of 1976. The interviews are referred to collectively as the Babcock interviews and ranged over a variety of topics. Clawson reputedly underwent hypnosis for each interview, but whether he truly entered an altered state is arguable. On March 1, Dr. Babcock asked about Clawson's childhood.

Babcock:	Are these happy years for you or not happy years?
Clawson:	Unhappy.
Babcock:	What makes them unhappy?
Clawson:	Kids pan me, kids teasing me.
Babcock:	What do they say about you?
Clawson:	They call me a sissy.
Babcock:	Why do they call you that?
Clawson:	Cause I look like a little girl.
Babcock:	What way do you look like a little girl?

Clawson:	I have breasts.
Babcock:	At eight years old?
Clawson:	Yes.

The Babcock interviews revealed a difficult childhood, filled with crippling rejection and no small amount of danger. One man who knew Clawson as a child said most people thought he was strange and a little creepy, even very early. In first grade, teachers made him sit in the far back of the classroom, separate from the other students. He was largely shunned during recess.

But he faced more than simple isolation. He had abusive parents, and—to hear him tell it—at least one abusive brother. He claimed he was regularly raped by his older brother; in fact, according to Clawson, he was raped often throughout his life: by neighborhood boys, by boys at school, by fellow soldiers when he was in the military and by inmates in jail and prison. None of Clawson's allegations was confirmed, but whether they happened or not, he may have *believed* they happened.

The Babcock interviews reveal only the smallest of pleasures—and those invariably turn dark. In one interview, Dr. Babcock regressed Clawson to the age of "nine or ten."

Babcock:	Let your mind drift back through the years—to the time when you were a child—and see yourself in a happy scene. What do you see, Eugene?
Clawson:	I see my mother. My mother taking me places.
Babcock:	Where do you see her taking you now?
Clawson:	To the movies.
Babcock:	Where do you see yourself in this scene?
Clawson:	Point Mary.

Throughout Clawson's confessions, statements to authorities and interviews under hypnosis, he referred to Point Marion as Point Mary.

Babcock:	Do you get along well with your mother?
Clawson:	Yes.
Babcock:	Okay, very good. Now, at the same time, try to see an unhappy scene when you're eight years old. What do you see?
Clawson:	My dad coming home drunk and beating me.

Babcock: What does he beat you for?
Clawson: Nothing.

Elsewhere, Dr. Babcock returned to the time Clawson spent with his mother.

Babcock: What kind of places did you like to go with your mom?
Clawson: I liked to go every place with her. In town, stores, shopping, movies, skating…
Babcock: Can you ever remember anything nice that happened to you?
Clawson: My mother bought me a rabbit.
Babcock: What did you name the rabbit?
Clawson: Bobby.
Babcock: What color is the rabbit?
Clawson: White.
Babcock: Can you see the rabbit now?
Clawson: Yes.
Babcock: Where do you keep it?
Clawson: In the house with me. It crawls all over me and follows me all around.
Babcock: What happened to the rabbit?

———— • ————

Her dripping hands hover over the sink full of dishes as Eugene's mother looks sharply back at him. "Gene! How many times do I have to tell you, no rabbits on the table!"

"Sorry, Mom." Gene scoops up his bunny and smashes Bobby into his lap. *Too hard! Dummy! You'll hurt him!* He holds Bobby tight against his belly. *Not too tight!* Bobby's fur tickles between his fingers, soothing and soft. He leaves his hand in Bobby's fur and finishes his cereal with his other hand. The spoon clanks against the bowl and—*Too loud! Dumbass!*—making sure his mother isn't looking, he lets Bobby lick the bottom of the bowl. He's had Bobby, like, forever. His best buddy, and never mean. Bobby's never mean, and Gene tries not to be mean to Bobby but sometimes he is mean, he doesn't want to be mean, but he is. Not too mean.

A sound in the house and Gene stiffens, listening intently. A thump from his father's bedroom? Maybe not. His feet shift, and he lifts his butt off his chair. He listens. Nothing more. He strokes Bobby's fur, soft fur—always tickles!—and enough silence passes he knows he won't have to grip Bobby too hard and jet out the door to the woods. Safe. He wants to keep Bobby safe.

"Gene, don't feed that rabbit milk! You'll give him diarrhea!"

"He just sniffed it! I swear!"

"The boy who cried wolf," his mom says. She always says weird stuff like that. "Don't lie, young man. I told you when I got the rabbit, you have thirty days to prove you can take care of him. If he gets sick, I'm not getting you another one."

"Okay, Mom." Gene slides out of the wooden kitchen chair. "I'm going see Johnny and Doc. I'll be back."

She answers without looking at him. "Don't get muddy!" but Gene is out the door. He sets Bobby down and motions. "Come on, Bobby!" He wants to teach Bobby to follow him, like the way dogs do. With other boys. He doesn't have a dog.

"Let's see if Johnny's home." He starts to leave and then looks back. Bobby is frozen except for his twitching nose, twitching and twitching like a little twitching thing. He laughs 'cause it's funny.

"Hey, Genie Paul!" a voice shouts.

It's his next-door neighbor, Jim, stacking firewood. He hates Jim for being older and bigger. Jim always calls him girl names, like the kids at school do. Gene zips his jacket so Jim won't say anything. Jim calls them titties.

"Don't call me that!"

"Then stop acting like such a faggot!"

Gene's father calls him that all the time. He motions for Bobby to follow him. "Come on, Bobby, let's go."

"Hey, I heard you sucked Phil and Ron's dicks behind the school. Did you learn that from your whore mother?"

Gene doesn't know why he snickers 'cause it's not funny. His hand goes into his pocket for his penknife. Running at Jim as fast as he can, he swishes his knife. Jim grabs his arm.

"What the hell? Did you just try to *kill me*!" He twists Gene's arm until the blade falls to the grass.

"STOP!" Jim let him drop to the damp ground, and Gene feels his eyes get hot. His mom will be mad at him for getting muddy again.

Bobby comes hopping over to the crying Gene. For a second, Gene feels relieved, but then Jim is bringing his axe down. Gene wails a high-pitched squeal as he hears the crunch of the axe on Bobby's skull. Bobby's leg twitches.

"Don't you ever come at me with a knife again, pussy." Jim shoulders his axe and kicks at the rabbit. "Take your trash."

Gene stumbles to his feet. He looks down at Bobby's head. It's shaped wrong, blood trickling out. He keeps looking. Red blood on white fur. Bright red.

He isn't thinking now, just running fast as he can until his lungs burn and he falls against a tree. Deep breaths become sobs. Gene clenches his fists until his nails cut into his palms.

He decides to hide in the woods until it's dark. He'll sneak back when Dad's at work. No, wait—Mom can't see his muddy pants. She'll get mad. What if she asks about Bobby?

———◆———

With Clawson's mother and father now deceased, and his brothers understandably reluctant to talk about Gene, the details couldn't be confirmed. However, the beatings by his father were reported by several sources who knew Clawson as a child and as an adult. His father, John W. Clawson, was a bartender in Point Marion and, according to rumor, a notorious drunk. In a chilling coincidence, John Clawson was known locally as John the Baptist, the messianic figure whose head was presented to Herod Antipas on a silver platter.

His mother was also abusive, although in her case it may have been more because of the brutality of the time and place than a particular brutality in her. For instance, after catching him "messing around" with a neighbor girl, his mother punished him by making him kneel on raw corncobs for hours. Everything from his genes to his childhood environment short-changed Clawson from day one.

———◆———

One of the factors police investigators look for in murder cases is a stressor in the life of the killer. If Clawson committed murder, what pushed him over the edge? Before people are driven to murder, they usually experience a setback of some kind—they've gotten fired or divorced or something else. The stressor can even be something mundane or positive, like a birthday, but it's experienced negatively. The birthday reminds him he is aging, life passing him by. The importance of the stressor is not what happened, but how it was perceived. Its importance is internal.

Clawson's confessions and statements can be read in many ways. From the outside, it sounds as if his life was always in turmoil and he was never far from the edge. But one stressor does stand out. In 1969, he fell in love. They were involved for months. Relationships had always eluded him; this time the attraction was mutual. The two even managed a sexual life of sorts, mostly oral. However, when he told her he had to force a partner before he could get hard and only anal sex would satisfy his desires, she broke it off, saying that was perverted and unacceptable. This was in December 1969. The failed relationship could have served as the stressor that resulted in his kidnapping, raping and decapitating the coeds. The stress would likely have been increased by the tick-tock of his birthday on January 13.

So, knowing about Eugene's miserable childhood and his recent breakup, one would have to say it's possible Clawson killed Mared and Karen. It could have happened just as he said.

5

"HE CANNOT STAND UP TO PUSHY, AUTHORITATIVE OR POWERFUL PEOPLE."

On February 6, Superintendent Bonar appointed a special task force, led by Colonel R.M. Hall, to further investigate Clawson's confession. This was Hall's first exposure to the coed case, which became an obsession that lasted until his death in the summer of 2016.

Colonel Hall first gained experience in law enforcement in the Marine Corps, and he was trained to conduct interrogations (now referred to by the less confrontational *interviews*). Superintendent Bonar, not yet convinced of Clawson's guilt, asked Hall to explore the confession's weaknesses. Hall read the confession several times and was skeptical of it before he even met Clawson in 1976.

Thirty years later, Lieutenant Colonel Hall, ret., said several characteristics of the confession made him suspicious immediately, chief among them the sex acts Clawson detailed. He doubted Clawson's ability to have that much sex or to control both women the whole time and said often there was "no way they could do all that in the back of a car." He also doubted the confession generally. Statements that gloss over details—or, conversely, provide excessive detail—often signal a lie.

On February 11, Colonel Hall, Sergeant B.E. Kirtley, Trooper Shade and Detective McCabe drove to Camden to see Clawson. Again they heard Clawson's story, this time with his attorney present. Hall then began to ask Clawson for further detail.

Which girl did you force to undress first?
Must have been pretty dark out there. How did you manage to see what you were doing?
How did you carry the heads?

Each time, Hall later recalled, Clawson would say he didn't remember, had smoked too much reefer, hadn't paid attention to this or that. Or he came up with something he hadn't previously mentioned, like a flashlight or a burlap bag. Even when Clawson appeared to be answering Hall's questions, his descriptions were uncertain and contradictory, difficult to pin down, as in this typical exchange:

Hall: Did the snow get heavy or was it light or what?
Clawson: It was snowing pretty good.
Hall: You say it was snowing pretty good?
Clawson: Yes.
Hall: Do you remember how good?
Clawson: Good.
Hall: The ground got covered with snow?
Clawson: Yes.
Hall: Did the woods get covered with snow when you were still back there with them?
Clawson: I don't know whether—whether I was still back there with them or when I was leaving, but I think it was snowing.
Hall: And it hadn't been snowing earlier that night?
Clawson: I don't remember. I think so. I think it was raining.
Hall: You think it was raining and then that turned to snow?
Clawson: I think so.
Hall: Well, are you sure?
Clawson: I'm not sure because it's been a long time.

Hall became more skeptical as the interview wore on. When he finally wrapped up the proceedings, Hall knew that even Clawson could tell Hall didn't believe him.

They drove back to West Virginia, Hall convinced they had the wrong man. The other officers—especially Shade—believed Clawson was the murderer. Hall and Shade couldn't even agree on small facts. Shade clocked the drive home, aware that timing might well become an issue at trial. His WVSP report cites the three-hundred-mile drive as taking five and a half hours, while Hall later said his own personal notes indicated it was a six-and-a-half-hour trip.

After Hall traveled back to South Charleston, he showed the confession to Larry Herald, a lead investigator on the case back in 1970, along with Preston Gooden. Herald later reported that Hall gave him the interview "to read and go over and give my ideas of what I thought about the confession. The thing that stuck out to me was—and I'm recalling this from years ago—when they asked him how the bodies were placed, he said they were side by side and face up. Well, that didn't square *at all*." The bodies were actually found crisscrossed and belly-down.

Herald commented only on Clawson's statements about the murder and the makeshift graves and did not address Clawson's ultimate guilt. His assessment: "I never felt comfortable with his confession. It made me doubt that he knew what he was talking about or knew anything about the murders, but he may have. I don't know all the facts."

In February 1976, Hall received a letter. Written in the oversized block letters of a man unused to writing, the letter read, in part:

I am going to tell the guys that if they want to commit the perfect murder all they have to do is go to West Virginia and kill someone and if they dispose of the evidence properly and if they have a buddy who works for the same place as him who he can get to punch his time card for him a couple of days so he can take a small vacation he can get away with it He can even confess to prove he is guilty and the West Virginia State Police won't even charge him with anything

P S I am smarter than the West Virginia State Police even when I am tripping on LSD Ha Ha Ha

Hall believed Clawson was taunting him. He badly wanted to stand trial for the murders, although Hall had no idea why. What he did know was Clawson was disciplined at Weyerhauser on January 18 for arriving ninety minutes late and the statements he gave Hall were full of holes:

- Clawson wrongly described the coats Mared and Karen wore;
- said he had quit Weyerhauser by January, but Weyerhauser records showed him working through January;

- said he stayed in Point Marion for several days after he killed the coeds, but Weyerhauser records show he punched in the next day;
- said his brother told him not to go to Morgantown because coeds had disappeared, but his brother was stationed in Cuba at the time;
- said he kept the pistol between the front seats of the car then later said the car had an armrest between the seats, back before armrests had compartments;
- said he sold the gun, then later said he threw it in a hole on Conn Hill;
- said he buried some things under a porch at his mother's house, but digging revealed nothing.
- Hall showed Clawson jewelry unconnected to the coeds, and Clawson said he recognized it as belonging to one of the girls.

None of these contradictions came out at trial. Clawson confessed, retelling his full story many times in bits and pieces. The specifics he related changed from confession to confession, but fundamental portions of the story remained constant.

On January 18, 1970, Clawson punched out of Weyerhauser at 2:20 p.m. and drove to his mother's home in Point Marion. He hitchhiked to Pittsburgh, where he located and stole a car to drive to Morgantown, where he saw Mared and Karen hitchhiking. He picked them up at the stop sign where Willey Street meets University Avenue. He immediately drew a gun and made them get in the backseat (or, in a couple of the confessions, "on the floor").

The girls were hysterical; he had to repeatedly order them to shut up. When he turned off 119, he followed a series of smaller roads. How many or what their names were, he couldn't say. Whether the roads were paved or gravel or hardpack, he couldn't remember. He was high on marijuana and LSD and hazy on the specifics.

Finally, he found a particularly tiny road and pulled over. He made the girls disrobe and handcuffed one to "something metal" under the front passenger seat. He took the other to the backseat and anally raped her. After that, he released the handcuffed one and had her get in the back, where he made her perform cunnilingus on the girl he had just raped. He ordered them to perform cunnilingus on each other, and while they were doing that, he anally raped the one on top. He's unclear about which girl he raped first and which second; in fact, rarely in the confessions is he clear about which girl he did what to. He claimed he didn't remember. Finally, he raped them both again and told them to get dressed.

At gunpoint, he marched them away from the car. He shot one in the head. He aimed his gun at the other girl to do the same, but her friend's body fell against her, causing his bullet to only wound her, which enraged him. He went and got the machete to cut off the wounded girl's head while she was still alive. He then chopped off the other one's head and dragged the bodies into the woods, where he laid them on their backs, side by side. He covered them with sticks, leaves and stones.

He found an old piece of burlap on the ground and wrapped up the heads to toss in the backseat. After that, he drove around and around, throwing their purses, coats and all their belongings out the car window. Somehow, he managed to find the road back north to Point Marion, but he stopped before he quite got home. He pulled over to have sex with both heads and then dropped them down a hole in the ground.

Clawson said he then drove home, burned his bloody clothes and stashed the machete and some papers under the stairs in the house. In one story, he stashed the material under steps in his mother's house; in another he took it to an abandoned house next door. After driving back to Pittsburgh, he ditched the stolen car and hitchhiked back to Point Marion, where he arrived home just when it was getting light.

By 10:30 that Monday evening, January 19, Clawson was on time for his next shift at Weyerhauser in Philadelphia.

———— ◆ ————

That essential confession was conveyed at both trials, despite all the various versions he gave between January and October. Initially, for instance, he drove his own car, which he said was a black and white Cadillac, from Philadelphia to Morgantown. Later, he changed that story to say he hitchhiked to Pittsburgh in order to steal a car. Clawson's claims often changed when detectives pointed out they didn't fit the facts. For instance, he said at first he wasn't at work on January 18. He insisted he quit Weyerhauser on January 5. He said he drove to Point Marion to visit his mother much earlier and stayed in the Point Marion area for several days after the crimes. When Hall obtained the Weyerhauser records that detailed Clawson's work record, Clawson finally settled on the version given here.

After the month-long search of Conn Hill turned up only some hairs in animal nests, but no heads or gun, his story changed again. He stated he was confused. He took the heads to Conn Hill, cut off some hair and threw it in the mine shafts. Later, he discarded the heads in some nearby coke ovens, where they burned up. But in 1970, the coke ovens had been closed for years.

His story also got increasingly lurid. He killed both coeds. No, he raped them first and had them urinate on him, then on each other. Wait, he also had sex with the heads. Hold on, he also ate the tongues. As he described it at trial, after he recanted his confession, he added in the sex scenes after he first wrote out his confession statement:

> I didn't have them scenes in the original confession.…[T]he other fellow that was named in the confession that the jury read, Harpe, well, he had two or three sessions with the West Virginia State Police, and each time…he came back over to the jail and told me there was no way I was going to fool them with the confession that I wrote because they were real sharp dudes.

Many people over the years have mentioned all the driving as the most unbelievable aspect of the essential confession. From Philadelphia to Point Marion to Pittsburgh to Morgantown is about 425 miles. Could he have traveled all that way in time to pick up the coeds?

The exact time he picked them up fluctuated a great deal, as reported by various sources. Clawson himself said in his confession, "It might have been 9:00 o'clock or 8:00 or 9:00. I don't know what it was. It wasn't too late. It wasn't real late." *Oliver!* began at 7:45 p.m. and let out about 10:30 p.m., as calculated by the start times of the show earlier that day. Solomon, the prosecutor in the first trail, said it was about 11:30 p.m. Paulette "Itsy" and Clarence "Skip" guessed it had to be after 9:30 p.m. but before 11:00 p.m.; bus service ended at 11:00 on Sunday.

Let's say Clawson picked them up at 11:00 p.m., the largest time window possible. That would give him eight hours and forty minutes to journey 425 miles. That would certainly be possible with straight driving; at 60 miles per hour a trip like that would take seven or seven and a half hours.

But Shade said the trip from New Jersey to Morgantown took five and a half hours; Hall said six and a half. And that's without a Point Marion to Pittsburgh to Morgantown trip, which would have taken three and a half to four hours in 1970.

And the journey would have been especially difficult on the roads that existed in 1970. Philadelphia to Point Marion was about 290 miles, but the last 40 miles or so would have been on two-lane roads well traveled by industrial trucks. Back then, the trip to Pittsburgh was mostly on two-lane roads—and half of that Clawson was hitchhiking. If he got a ride immediately—carrying, he said, a flashlight, handcuffs and a machete—in a car traveling very fast, it was possible, but unlikely.

Lastly, if Clawson did somehow hitchhike all that way in the time it would take someone to simply drive the route, he would have had to, almost instantly, find a car to steal—and already have the skills to commit the theft. Not impossible, but unlikely.

All in all, Clawson's route should have taken eight hours, at least, and could have taken as long as twelve hours. He had to travel it in *absolutely no more than* eight hours and forty minutes.

————◆————

Hall thought Clawson made up the entire tale, that it was just so much smoke. He wasn't sure why, but he believed one possibility, based on a rumor he had heard, was that Clawson was trying to get transferred out of the New Jersey system. Jails and prisons are not welcoming environments for pedophiles. They are not especially inviting for rapists either, but few criminals are treated as harshly by inmates and guards as child rapists.

Hall heard Clawson had a price on his head, put out by inmates, and wanted to get out of New Jersey as fast as he could. That explanation is plausible, but if true—or if Clawson *thought* it was true—he ended up staying in New Jersey anyway until his sentence for carnal abuse was served out.

Whether his confession was true or false, Clawson recanted and floated several "reasons" he made up the confession, but they were all less than satisfactory. At his 1976 trial, he testified, "If I could make the officials in West Virginia believe I was guilty and I could get indicted for it and brought down here...Jersey would drop the charges against me and then when I got down here I felt I could prove my innocence and then I wouldn't have more time. That's why I did it."

Informally, he told authorities additional components of this explanation. He had some muddled rationale about getting out of prison and then being able to help Harpe and Glass be granted parole. Another time, he said Glass's and Harpe's chances of parole would be improved if they "snitched" on another inmate, and he was okay with being that man.

None of these plans is realistic, of course. The legal system doesn't work that way. Which meant Clawson was lying, some said. Or maybe the police planted the lie. Either way, the objection overlooks a key factor: Clawson was not very bright. What mattered was not whether the strategies would work, but whether Clawson *believed* they would work.

Tests administered in the spring and summer of 1976 assessed his IQ between the high 70s and the low 80s, despite the fact that, as one observer later said, "I think he *thought* he was smart." His low IQ was not readily apparent. As one person who tested Clawson put it, "The general level of his vocabulary and verbal expressiveness seemed consistent with someone whose intelligence was 10 or 15 points higher." But Clawson said something that both made his mental challenges clear *and* demonstrated his confidence that he did not kill the coeds. He thought if he was convicted, he could profess his innocence to a polygraph, which would proclaim he was telling the truth, and he would be set free.

Clawson was initially found incapable of standing trial, an assessment made by Dr. Donald Carter of WVU, the same doctor who back in 1970 led the session that attempted to profile the writer of the Triangle Letters. Carter said Clawson neither appreciated the gravity of his situation nor understood the difference between right and wrong. He could not meaningfully assist in his defense. However, Drs. E.O. Fletcher and Robert Bell determined he could, and Carter reversed his opinion after meeting with Clawson for forty-five minutes in June. Carter has since passed, and no extant records explain what made him reverse himself.

But other findings about Clawson by two psychologists and at least two psychiatrists clarified the picture of Clawson as a damaged man. He was depressed and paranoid. He displayed inappropriate affect, meaning his expressed emotions were not what one would expect in given situations. His memory was "fairly good for remote events," according to Fletcher, but was "somewhat impoverished for recent ones." All four of the testers reported Clawson's social feeling, common sense and control were poor.

Perhaps most importantly, Carter wrote the following: "When faced with overpowering people…this man appears to have a history of being gullible, easily duped, doing other people's evil wishes to somehow please them… [and he] cannot stand up to pushy, authoritative or powerful people." Time after time, he showed himself to be susceptible to stronger wills around him and revealed his intense desire to be liked. He did whatever other people,

people he considered smarter or more powerful than him, insisted he should do. In lay terms, Clawson was a pleaser and attempted to please the most powerful people in his environment.

This directly speaks to the theory that Harpe, the jailhouse lawyer, thought he might benefit—either financially or by getting his parole reduced—if he could get Clawson to confess. Maybe Harpe, with the help of Glass, cooked up the whole story, and Clawson was a patsy. That's one of the things Clawson said happened. That would mean Clawson confessed because he was told to by people on his cellblock, people who wanted a reward, people Clawson wanted desperately to like him.

6

"IT WAS IN SOME WOODS, REMOTE."

In his closing arguments at Clawson's 1976 trial, Prosecuting Attorney David Solomon said, "They want to talk about a '73 *Detective Magazine* article.…The burden is on them to prove when this article was published. All they done is prove it was published in December '75.…If there is a '73 article, it would be here."

The article admitted into evidence in the 1976 trial was "The Case of the Headless Coeds," by Spencer Trent, and it appeared in the magazine *Detective Cases* dated December 1975. The article was read into the record at trial, but practical considerations, the time available, as well as a jury's anticipated intolerance of excessive detail, didn't allow close comparison of Clawson's confession—and the statements made by Harpe and Glass—to the details in the article.

But maybe the word *articles* is more precise, because in fact, there were two articles, just as Friend and Tomasky said. The 1973 article, the one Solomon implied didn't exist, was called, "Two Headless Coeds in a Wilderness Grave," by Scott Paulson. It had been published in *True Police Cases* and dated February 1973, the same year Clawson said it was published. The two articles were virtually identical. Solomon said this about Clawson in 1976: "All we have is a version out of that liar's mouth that it was published in '73. Are you going to believe that liar again?"

Solomon wouldn't ask the question that made more sense: Why believe "that liar" *at all*? Clawson hadn't just lied about portions of his confession—*his entire confession was a lie*.

The article contained *all* of the few details that were correct in Clawson's confession. In a few places, all three men's statements matched the article and the facts of the case. Far more often, though, the men's statements matched the article *but not* the facts of the case: what Mared and Karen were wearing, the direction the car went after picking up the coeds, how the bodies were placed and on and on.

More telling, sometimes their statements matched the article and the men drew misleading conclusions based on the article. For instance, the article opened with a dramatization:

> As the Sunday night crowd poured from the theater in Morgantown, West Virginia that January night, it was greeted by snowflakes drifting lazily against the glow of street lights. The crowd represented a cross-section of Morgantown citizenry—moms and pops who enjoyed the movie, young lovers who had enjoyed one another, and a liberal number of students from West Virginia University.

The article goes on to say that Mared and Karen walked a block up the street to hitchhike home. Both Harpe and Glass said the girls were picked up near a theater. Clawson himself said only, "Not where they were picked up weren't no movie."

Harpe said, "[H]e picked up two girls on a corner across from a movie house," and Glass's story was similar: "It was around outside of a theater... and like they were hitchhiking." In reality, the coeds were picked up two blocks north and one block west, completely out of sight of the theater. Harpe and Glass could only have gotten that idea from the article. Also significant was the use of language in the articles and the men's statements:

- The article refers to Willey Street but far more often to Willey *Avenue*. For the most part, like the article, Clawson refers to Willey Avenue. Actually, the name is Willey Street. Where had Clawson gotten the idea it was Willey Avenue?
- The article devotes several column inches to describing wild, wonderful West Virginia and contains this phrasing: "There are thick forests, some of them remote and desolate." When describing where he took the girls, Clawson said "It was in some woods, remote."

- When saying the coeds' names, Clawson said one was named Carol or Karen and the other had a name he couldn't pronounce. Of course, if he'd heard her name spoken, he could have pronounced it: "Mared" is not difficult to say. But if he had only seen it *written* and didn't want to *mispronounce* it…

Perhaps the most interesting comparison of the three men's statements, the two magazine articles and the facts of the case is in the material that was found discarded near where the bodies were found. The article mentions few things specifically: two purses, a pair of glasses, a bottle of medicine, a compact and "other personal effects." Clawson mentions only one purse and "some papers." He also said he stole a watch, a ring and a necklace. Harpe mentions both purses, "some items out of [a] purse which indicated that she had previously been a resident of the state of New Jersey," compacts and "probably lipstick and all that stuff." Harpe said Clawson didn't mention any jewelry. Glass alleged Clawson took a ring, a watch and a necklace and threw away a purse, some kind of identification and "something about a bottle."

In other words, except for the glasses, the three men between them specifically cited all of what was mentioned in the article and were only certain about what was specifically mentioned in the article. Searchers actually found plenty of other items: In addition to two purses, a necklace, Karen Ferrell's driver's license, a pill bottle and a pink compact broken into two pieces, searchers found a Ronson gas lighter and a book of paper matches, a ballpoint pen, two one-cent stamps, a small Manila envelope, three Anacin tablet packages, two tubes of lipstick, an eye shadow pencil, mascara, a black clothes brush, a second pair of glasses, a green headscarf and two men's jackets. Most of these items were linked to either Mared or Karen. Clawson could have "remembered" plenty but could only manage to "remember" the items mentioned in the article.

Searchers also found a carefully placed pile of papers in a sanitary landfill some eight miles south of the bodies: Mared Malarik's driver's license, social security card, student identification, personal identification card, checkbook, student receipt from WVU and a trial study card. At the same location lay Karen Ferrell's student identification and student receipt, one Greenbrier West football and basketball schedule (where Karen went to high school), a Westchester Hall card issued to Karen's roommate Sandra Fitch and a membership card for the Castle Club. Also at that location and with the other material that could be connected to Mared and Karen were a Dudley Lock Division card with combination, two snapshots of two different sailors, one

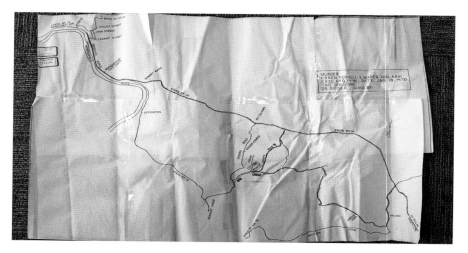

Law enforcement's hand-drawn map of the Weirton Mine Section south of Morgantown that was Exhibit 3 in Clawson's 1976 trial. From Monongalia County Circuit Court records. *S. James McLaughlin.*

partial snapshot of an unidentified person, a paper listing table tennis rules, one checkbook of blank deposit slips, a torn postcard and a Rogers Pharmacy calendar. Many more things Clawson could have remembered but didn't.

The placement of those items in a sanitary landfill argues for deliberate action, exercised with a care that should have made it memorable to whoever placed them there. They were piled seventy-five feet off the east side of 119; they were not simply thrown out a window, the way Clawson said.

———— • ————

Richard Hall said many times Clawson was a bad person who was right where he belonged. If he hadn't been in prison, he may well have hurt more people for a variety of reasons, in a variety of ways. Young teenagers of both sexes, Clawson's *actual* victims of choice, would definitely have been at risk if he was not in prison, as would have people who were in his way when he needed something.

But there was no physical evidence Clawson killed the coeds and no reason to believe him when he said he did—and many, many reasons not to believe him. As has been pointed out by a number of lawyers, without the confession, Clawson never would have been indicted, much less convicted. Clawson died of multiple illnesses in Mount Olive Correctional Facility for a crime he did not commit, and the person responsible still roams free.

7

"IT SEEMED LIKE A RITUALISTIC MURDER."

CHARLESTON, WEST VIRGINIA

George Castelle greeted Sarah McLaughlin and Kendall Perkinson, producers of the podcast *Mared and Karen: The WVU Coed Murders*, and Geoff Fuller. Castelle was a tall man of slight build, clean shaven and soft spoken with a hollow, gravelly voice. He very much looked like a lawyer in his standard office attire and frameless oval glasses.

Originally from Cumberland, Maryland, Castelle was chief public defender in Kanawha County, West Virginia, for twenty-five years before he had to step back for health reasons. He now worked part time as a public defender in the county. He knew about the murdered coeds from his undergraduate days and started law school at WVU in 1976, the year Clawson confessed to the murders. In 1979, he was employed as a law clerk by Justice Thomas B. Miller of the West Virginia Supreme Court of Appeals. After Clawson's 1976 conviction, the case was appealed to the Supreme Court and assigned to Justice Miller. Castelle was lead researcher and drafter assigned to examine the case. Generously, he agreed to record his thoughts about Clawson's initial conviction and why it was overturned.

"I'm really glad someone's taken an interest in this case." Castelle held the door for the three as they walked into the conference room. "I've always felt it needed to be reexamined."

Everything introduced in the trial, Castelle had seen. This included the trial transcripts, transcripts of pre- and post-trial proceedings and the physical evidence.

"It was a case I remember [well]," said Castelle as they settled around the table. To illustrate the level of access he had to the court's evidence, he added, "I remember opening up a folded paper towel…not knowing what was in it and having the victims' fingertips drop out on my desk."

Throughout the interview, Castelle spoke carefully, with many qualifiers, as lawyers generally do, and his demeanor was calm, his manner assured. He had been mulling over the case for thirty-seven years and had long ago come to his conclusions. He is *the* person most knowledgeable about the trials and conviction of Eugene Paul Clawson.

———◆———

"As I studied the case and studied the evidence entered into trial," Castelle said, "with almost a hundred percent certainty, Clawson was innocent. There have been studies over the years of wrongful convictions—and false confessions in particular—that…reaffirmed my conviction that Clawson's confession was almost certainly false."

Castelle continued, methodically, relentlessly, like someone determined to take every step of a very long journey:

> One of the concepts developed by social scientists and legal studies over the years is that in trying to determine whether a confession is false or not, one of the key questions is, Was the person confessing able to explain crime scene anomalies? Something that puzzles investigators, something that just doesn't make sense, and Clawson was unable to provide any of that….
>
> The things that Clawson added…about what he did personally, didn't match reality, didn't match his employment records. He just wasn't available at the time that he said he was. He talked about conversations he had with his brother at the time of the crime, and it turned out his brother was stationed in Guantanamo Bay, Cuba….
>
> I just had the sense that there was a pool of people—a fairly widespread pool of people—who believed he was guilty because the prosecution had made questionable statements

So Much Smoke

like "Clawson made statements that only the real killer would know" that struck me as totally misleading and irresponsible, and "the hair found in the mine shafts matched that of the victims," which were totally erroneous. A lot of what we would call today "false facts" circulated about the case.

It troubled me for two reasons: One, it looked like an innocent person was in prison, but equally troubling was that the person or persons responsible for the crime were still free... to commit more horrible crimes and there could be more victims....A very dangerous person was still in the community, possibly, or passing through to the next community, but someone had committed a hideous crime and gotten away with it and could commit future murders.

Not everyone was so firmly convinced of Clawson's innocence. For instance, Dan Ringer, one of Clawson's defense lawyers in his 1981 trial, was less certain. Clawson was tried twice, and as far as Ringer was concerned it was over. "I don't think anybody would say, 'I was convinced he was guilty,'" Ringer said when interviewed.

What you would typically get out of us was, Well, we certainly hope he was guilty. One, because he was convicted, and lawyers like to think that people who are guilty get convicted and people who are convicted are guilty, and two, if he didn't do it, then the person who did is still out there—or was at the time—running around, and that made us all feel very uncomfortable.

At the same time, Ringer didn't seem to think much of the state's case. When asked to summarize the physical evidence against Clawson, the hard facts that pointed to his guilt, Ringer laughed and said, "What physical evidence? There were things that were offered. A key chain was offered, and nobody could figure out what the relevance of it was...some hair that was found in an abandoned mine shaft."

"My memory is that everybody who reviewed the objective evidence," Castelle said, "either unanimously or almost unanimously believed that Clawson was almost certainly innocent."

Key issues in the appeal to the Supreme Court included the admissibility of the confessions, the issues surrounding change of venue, the hair analysis and, ultimately, the gruesome photographs introduced by the prosecution. After familiarizing himself with the record on the change-of-venue challenge, Castelle drafted his thoughts. He believed for a number of reasons the prosecutor and the press had tainted the jury pool in Monongalia County.

Reading from his draft, Castelle said,

> At the hearing for a change of venue, the defense introduced copies of 47 newspaper articles and transcripts of 41 radio news reports....[T]he news items announced that the defendant had confessed to the homicides and that he had pled guilty to numerous sex offenses in New Jersey and was a suspect in the rape and murder of a Pennsylvania child.

According to the media, Castelle continued, Clawson's statements also contained information "that police officers have stated...'could only be known by a person at the scene of the crime.'" All the aforementioned assertions were false, as was the prosecuting attorney's statement in a March 22 press interview that "that hair found on the body 'matches.'" The hair did not "match" the coeds' hair so much as *resemble* it, as the state's own hair expert witness testified in the 1976 trial.

In the same article, the prosecutor also said that "he feels Clawson should never be freed. 'A guy like that,' Solomon said, 'you just can't turn loose.'... Solomon said he is personally satisfied that Clawson is the murderer."

Castelle also wrote about conflicts between the confessions and the truth:

> [T]he defendant could have conceivably reached Morgantown in time to commit the offense, although not in the manner described in his confession. That is, driving to Point Marion, hitchhiking into Pittsburgh, stealing a 1970 Chevrolet, driving back to Morgantown....[T]here was no evidence of sexual molestation....[T]he three-person sex acts that the defendant described can't physically be performed in the space of the back seat of a car.

From Castelle's perspective, Clawson's assertion that he drew his confession from magazine articles about the case was vitally important:

> The defendant maintained that he had constructed his confession from several magazine articles detailing the

circumstances of the unsolved murders. The defense argued that this improbable explanation gains a measure of credence from an examination of the magazine article that the defense admitted into evidence.

For his analysis for the 1980 court, Castelle compared Clawson's statement to the article and to the facts of the case:

> The magazine article contained a number of errors in describing the details of the crime. The defendant's confession incorporated many of the same errors.…When I matched up that article with Clawson's supposed confession it was just crystal clear that Clawson was stating the contents of the article. Where the article was wrong, Clawson was wrong. And in not a single instance could Clawson say, "What the article said was A, but what really happened was B" and B then matched the actual physical evidence. Clawson only knew what was in the article.

Castelle also had reservations about the murder weapon. Investigators had speculated about how the heads had been cut off. Clawson said he used a machete and some investigators suggested either a machete or a bayonet, but the most common belief was they had been decapitated after death with a hatchet or axe. Castelle had come to the same conclusion:

> I could see the hatchet marks in the turtleneck part of the sweater. Multiple hatchet marks. They were identical-size slices. Each blow was identical. The turtleneck part of the sweater was wider than the blade of the weapon, so it contained entire blade marks—they showed the entire length of the blade. It was apparent with near 100 percent certainty that the murder weapon, at least the weapon that severed the heads, was a hatchet. It could not possibly have been a machete.…[T]he prosecutor had to have known just from looking at the physical evidence it was not a machete.

Ultimately, it was the gruesome photographs that proved to be a step too far for the Supreme Court. Ten photographs depicted the bodies of Mared and Karen laid out on the coroner's stainless steel tables. Quoting from the 1980 decision:

It is difficult to describe a scene as gruesome as that depicted in these photographs. For three months these human remains had lain in the forest decomposing....Exhibit 5A portrays the body as it appeared when delivered to the autopsy room, clothed in blood-soaked garments. The right leg contains remnants of flesh and tattered clothing....

The three photographs comprising Exhibit 6 portray a different, though equally gruesome condition....The three photographs portray only the unclothed upper torso, in color close-ups of the headless shoulders. Although the skin is blood-soaked and discolored, it is unbroken so that the body fluids have been retained....

It is apparent that the photographs in Exhibits 5 and 6 were not of essential evidentiary value. They depict nothing that was not otherwise thoroughly established by competent expert evidence....The only practical effect of the photographs was the shock value of their grisliness.

The court ordered that Clawson receive a new trial and ordered a change of venue for Clawson's 1981 trial.

"I know that those of us who were at the court...were startled that Clawson was convicted upon retrial," Castelle said in the conference room in the summer of 2016. "I can't speak for the justices, but I believe that everybody working on the case...believed that upon retrial a jury would not get it wrong a second time."

However, in the second trial, in November 1981, Clawson was again found guilty. But this time, Clawson was sentenced to life with mercy. According to Castelle, at the time life with mercy carried a sentence of ten years before a prisoner would be eligible for parole, and with two murder convictions and sentences imposed consecutively Clawson could apply for parole after twenty years.

"[A verdict with mercy] is generally a compromise," Castelle said. "This was not a crime that would warrant mercy. To me that's an indication that the jury had severe doubts about guilt but just couldn't bring themselves to say 'innocent' so they gave a recommendation of mercy....[T]hey just didn't believe in his guilt and should have had the courage to just find him innocent."

In appeals like this, the court not only rules on the verdict, but it can also rule on the strength of the state's case itself. The verdict can be overturned without prejudice, meaning that prosecutors are free to retry the defendant, or with prejudice, which means that, in the court's opinion, the evidence against the defendant is so weak the state cannot retry the defendant on the same charges. Castelle believed the case no. 8383 was so weak, it should have been dismissed with prejudice. If that had happened, Clawson would have been set free.

"The disappointment to me was that in the court's published opinion, there had to be some analysis of the strength of the evidence because there's a concept called 'harmless error,'" Castelle said.

> If the strength of the evidence is so strong that even without the error the defendant would have been convicted anyway. So, in deciding whether the error, the unnecessary admission of the gruesome photographs, was harmless or not, the court had to weigh the strength of the evidence.

> That's one of the reasons why in my notes I was so careful to point out the weaknesses in the evidence. It was disappointing to me that in the court's published opinion, they didn't recite those details. And of course I can't criticize the court for that because I was an employee. Justice Miller, in drafting the opinion, for his own reasons, felt that was unnecessary to the opinion, so he made some references to weaknesses in the case, but he didn't include the details that I stated. I wish he had, just to make it clearer to the public and to signal the prosecution and the defense for a possible retrial that there were severe doubts about Clawson's guilt. I was disappointed that the doubts did not make it into the published opinion. I tried.

For much of his career, Castelle has been trying to get someone to take up Clawson's case. He felt it needed to be reexamined, but he wasn't allowed to because of his role as a public defender: "I could have represented Clawson if a judge had appointed me."

But he strongly believed the refined forensic science available today might make a difference. For example, today the hair could be tested for mitochondrial DNA:

> [I]t would almost certainly not be the victim hair and would constitute newly discovered evidence that would meet the legal

criteria for overturning Clawson's conviction and reopening the case.

The case troubled me. I retained my notes from 1980, now thirty-seven years ago, for two reasons. One that it looked like, with almost certainty, an innocent person was in prison, but equally troubling was that whatever person or persons actually did commit the crime were still free. That was the Manson era and there was a fear that there was a Manson-like cult operating in this area.

There's something unusual about this case. There's something bizarre about it. There's something ritualistic about it. In every other case I've worked on that involved more than one murder, the violence was rushed and chaotic. One victim was shot in the front, for example, while the second victim was shot in the back while running away. But in this case, with two bodies buried together, clothed, dying in identical manner, both heads missing, no other apparent injuries? It seems organized—that there was either a ritual being performed or a script being followed, or both.

IV

HUNTING

Preface

"REMEMBER THAT HOUSE."

"Thirty-six years since the crime was committed. You listened to his first confession, but why are you now suddenly reinterested in this case?"
"Because there's a killer out there somewhere walking the streets, and Clawson's doing his time."
—*Hoppy Kercheval interviewing WVSP Lieutenant Colonel Richard Hall, ret., on statewide radio on October 5, 2006*

BREVARD COUNTY, FLORIDA, ONE THOUSAND MILES SOUTH OF MORGANTOWN

1985, four years after Clawson's final conviction and twenty-one years before Hall's investigation

In January, real estate investor Michael Roberts is scouting an underdeveloped part of Palm Bay, looking for the right location. Seventy-five miles southeast of Orlando, west of I-95 and east of the Intracoastal Waterway, he believes the area is well poised for more of the rapid development taking place in the county. It's a matter of finding the right lots for his plans. To that end, he's checking out a plot off Savery Road.

He's walking the edge of the plot when he sees a cloth with green and pink flowers beneath some overgrowth. The towel or blanket or whatever has become threadbare and has obviously been outdoors for weeks or months.

Roberts manages to wrestle it out from the concealing vegetation. He tugs the cloth, and human bones fall to the ground: a spinal column, a ribcage and parts of a leg. Despite clearing more than a tenth of an acre, investigators find more of the skeleton but fail to locate the head.

———◆———

Twelve days later and less than six miles south, teenagers Derrick Fisher and Steven Harrison are hunting turkey and find a large bone. They notify their parents, who call the Brevard County Sheriff's Office. For the next week, personnel at the office clear and search five acres of land surrounding the boys' find. They find two skeletonized bodies, almost complete. Tool marks mar the femurs of both bodies; neither skull is ever found.

In November, about ten months after the three headless skeletons are found in Brevard County, nineteen-year-old Laura Murphy is walking east on Malabar Road toward Route 1. She plans to buy a pack of cigarettes at the Jiffy Mart at the intersection there. She's staying with a friend while she's visiting from California, but he's not home and she doesn't have a car. When a light rain begins, she decides to gut it out—she *needs* those cigarettes.

Before long, a silver Nissan Stanza stops beside her. Inside, a man in a sport coat and dress slacks, wearing dark sunglasses, rolls down the window. She thinks he's in his late twenties or early thirties and slightly pale, which is strange in Florida. He reassures her with a smile.

"It's a bit wet today for a walk, isn't it? Can I give you a lift?"

Laura is a small woman, a few inches over five feet tall, weighing a little less than 110 pounds. She can't tell how tall he is, but he's thin and doesn't seem threatening.

"I'm on my way to Melbourne to meet some friends. You going anywhere near there?"

"Sure, I have to go that way. I'm a jewelry salesman. I just need to stop by my house real quick to pick up a notebook for work, but it'll only take a minute or two. Go ahead and hop in."

Getting in the car, she notices that he's driving barefoot, his loafers on the floor beside his feet. She gets in, and he pulls into traffic. Within a few minutes, he's easing onto a gravel driveway passing between tall rows of hedges back to a Colonial-style house with four pillars and a large carport. He jumps out of the car but pauses at the house's side door and shouts, "Hey, you want to come in for a drink?"

"Oh, no thanks. My friends are expecting me, and I don't want them to worry."

"Suit yourself." He goes into the house.

And he emerges shortly, empty handed, smiles broadly and admits that the notebook he's looking for is not in the house after all. It must be in the back of the car. She can hear him rummaging around for a few seconds before, suddenly, her seat shoots forward, her face smacking hard against the dashboard. Something slips over her forehead and down to her throat. The rope tightens.

———◆———

Thomas Harper can hardly believe what he sees this morning. Late November, he's just coming back from a quick trip to the hardware store, and now he is braking to a stop just past a naked girl, her hands shackled, her ankles tightly secured, painfully hopping along the side of the road. He idles for a few seconds and throws the truck into reverse. The truck stops beside her. He half expects this is a joke of some kind, but he can see how pale she is, how afraid. He opens the truck door and gets out.

"Do you really need help?" he asks, still not certain he isn't being pranked.

"I was held captive all night," Laura Murphy says, her voice weak and breathy. "I climbed through a bathroom window."

He goes over and helps her into the passenger side. "Come on, let's get you out of here and get you some help."

He climbs back in the driver's side. In seconds, she says, "Remember that house," gesturing to a house he can see through the trees. He does and later passes along the address to the sheriff's office.

1

"WE CALLED IT THE SHADE EFFECT."

West Virginia's official position is that Clawson killed Mared and Karen, case closed. But many people in West Virginia agreed with Castelle's assessment and kept hunting for fifty years, including the authors, Geoff Fuller and Sarah McLaughlin. Both of them grew up in Monongalia County, and Geoff and Sarah brought very different lives to their stories. Geoff was born about twenty-five years earlier than Sarah and remembered the crimes. Sarah was more of a digital native, comfortable exploring the web and accomplished as a researcher, with the eye for detail that can engender. Their diverse perspectives melded well, but their personal reactions—the ways they viewed the world of 1970, the murders of Mared and Karen and the possible culprits—are different enough that from here on their stories are individually narrated, with their names at the beginning of each of their chapters. Geoff narrates the first twelve chapters before the two join forces in "Broken dolls."

WEIRTON MINE SECTION SOUTH OF MORGANTOWN

Geoff

Bright sun, 11:00 a.m. Hall's 2001 Buick moved slowly, trees and greenery on both sides of the road. The unlined road was barely two lanes wide and wove through the Weirton Mine Section. For almost two months I'd been shadowing Hall's investigation. It was slowly taking over my life.

We'd driven up from Charleston, where we both lived, our first trip together. He had a short to-do list; my task was to shadow him, follow his lead. Hall pulled onto some gravel on the right. In the passenger seat, I was anxious, my heart beating fast. Hall eased his car onto the gravel and said, "Yes, this is it," his tone hushed. The woods glowed with midsummer's green riot.

Exiting the passenger side, I breathed the muggy summer air. Trees on all sides. The distant rush of I-79, about a half mile west.

Hall got out of the car and walked briskly to the back. A couple of inches over six feet, he was taller than me, more muscular. His bearing was erect and deliberate, the epitome of dignified authority. He opened the trunk, took out some plastic boots, slipped them over his shoes and said, "Mud."

To the right of the car, a tangle of underbrush covered a short downward slope to a broad, flat area, the flood plain of a small stream, about twenty-five yards from road to stream. Sun dappled the leaves, speckled the underbrush. A slurry pond had been there once, in 1970.

No car had yet passed.

The other side of the road was darker, shadowed. A horseshoe-shaped plain stretched over one hundred yards, the open end toward the road, bordered on three sides by small hills sloping upward, the closed end narrowing, less an upside-down U than a V. Few trees grew there. The stream crossed behind us under the road we'd come in on and ran along the base of the hill on the left. Pickup trucks had driven into the horseshoe in the recent past, and at least a few of them left trash: tires, a refrigerator, cans, piles of sales papers and envelopes, an overstuffed chair with the springs showing.

"It's over there, right?" I pointed across the road to the refuse among sparse trees. I couldn't help but feel as if we were doing something we shouldn't and might get caught. The clearing was hallowed ground, not a tourist site.

"I think so." Hall spoke as if he was uncertain but moved across the road like he knew exactly where he was going. As we stepped from the road to the muddy ground, a car passed behind us. I heard it slow, but neither of us turned to look. Everyone who lived in the Weirton Mine Section must know our car didn't belong there. I half expected the car to stop, but it did not.

I had familiarized myself with the WVSP report that detailed the position of the recovery site; Hall slid some photos from his jacket pocket and held them up with both hands, higher than his head, so he could glance from the photos to the land and back. They were pictures taken at the recovery site on April 16, 1970. Hall studied each photo for a few seconds before moving to the next. Twenty in all.

Hall lowered the photos and took a careful step forward. The ground was soft but not mushy. Small puddles dotted the clearing's floor, but most of it looked walkable. Hall stepped around tiny oblong puddles. He held up a photo and checked the lay of the land every few steps. About one hundred yards in, he stopped.

"This is pretty much it, I think."

I looked around—undergrowth, sticks, fragments of leaves from the previous fall, the dumped trash even more apparent than it had been from the road—and there: a fallen tree that looked like the prominent one in the photographs.

"Could that be the same tree?"

Hall sorted through the photos and chose the one with the fallen tree. The resemblance was marked. The fallen tree in front of us looked far mossier and more fragile but otherwise the same.

"Could be, I suppose," Hall said. "Been a long time, though." He looked around the clearing, squinting. "Three hundred feet from *that* telephone pole."

It looked right, and I kept glancing at that tree. Had to be the same one. Maybe. Do fallen trees last thirty-six years?

"It's kind of…" I searched for the right word and didn't find it. "*Strange*, standing here. Right on the spot. After thirty-six years, we still don't know who killed them."

"Yes. Well."

Neither of us moved or said anything for almost a minute and then Hall cleared his throat. "I guess we're done here. I just wanted to see the place again."

We began to walk back, quietly, gingerly, stepping around puddles. At the edge of the clearing, where the road's pavement started, we both looked back toward where the bodies were recovered in April 1970.

"You know I—" Hall looked away. "It's probably nothing, but when I think of this place, I have this image. From that night."

I waited, said nothing. Hall continued.

"Something I keep thinking about. Seeing. It's all dark. Winter. Some snow coming down. A man's standing right about here. He's breathing heavily, mist in and out. In his right hand he has a burlap sack stained with blood and bulging out around the two heads. He looks back toward the grave and then turns and walks down the road, and all you can hear is his boots on the wet pavement."

Richard M. Hall, retired lieutenant colonel of the West Virginia State Police, is the force that ensured that the wrongful conviction of Eugene Clawson was not the last word. He wasn't motivated by a desire to free Clawson, who he considered a dangerous career criminal. He believed Clawson belonged in prison—just not for killing Mared and Karen. In 1976, when he first talked with Clawson—or "Gene," as he called him—Hall was one of a small minority who did not believe Clawson was guilty.

Hall once told me a story in his kitchen about an argument he had with other officers during Clawson's 1981 trial. Near the beginning of the trial, Hall and other investigators were having dinner in his room and discussing the case.

"They knew I didn't believe him," Hall told me in the summer of 2006. "I was surprised they did."

This was the first time I'd heard the story, but during the years I shadowed Hall, I heard it a lot. I came to believe Hall's determination to find the real killer was based, at least partially, in his need to prove he was right in 1976.

"Let's see, there was Shade, McCabe, Kirtley." Troopers Shade and Kirtley and Detective McCabe. "And me. It got ugly."

"Ugly how."

"It almost come to blows."

"About what?"

"Whether Clawson did it. Three against one and we were standing, shouting." Hall shook his head ruefully. "I tell you, it was something."

"You were the only one who had any doubt Clawson did it?" I was proud to be working with Hall, who seemed to be the epitome of honorable law enforcement.

"I *knew* he didn't. I think they knew, too. They just didn't want to admit it."

"Do they all still maintain Clawson is guilty?"

Hall shook his head again. "Kirtley is dead, so I can't ask him."

"What about Shade and McCabe?"

"Starsky and Hutch?" Hall snorted derisively, as if he didn't much care what they thought. "Everybody called them that. Starsky and Hutch. Shade's dead."

"They acted like the TV characters?"

"They thought they were something." Hall tapped the tabletop twice with his index finger, a gesture that said, *Pay attention to this*. "You know, Shade would believe something and then just go after it, no matter what evidence came up said otherwise."

"That doesn't sound like how an investigator should act."

"Well, either way. Once he got his teeth in something, he never let go. One time he went after a guy for something or other. Took him years, but he finally cracked it. He was a good detective that way, unless when he was wrong about it. We called it the Shade Effect."

For years after that argument, Hall continued to casually look into the crime, to see if he could find the real murderer or murderers. Now he felt he was close to the solution.

———◆———

When I began shadowing Hall in June 2006, I saw him as a fit and alert seventy-seven-year-old retiree, a soft-spoken southern gentleman. But bit by bit, I learned more about his history. Hall was honorably discharged from the Marines in the early 1950s after being awarded a certificate in criminal investigation, focused on the Uniform Code of Military Justice. In 1976, he was sent by Superintendent R.L. Bonar to New Jersey to determine the truth in Clawson's confession. The more Clawson talked, the less Hall believed him.

I had the chance to see Hall's skillful interviews a few times while I was shadowing him. On the surface, he seemed like a friendly uncle who just liked to chat. But at certain times, while he was waiting for an answer to a question he'd just asked, he became still, watchful, like a hunter. Despite his casual demeanor, Hall was always prepared for an interview to go sideways, prepared for the quarry to bolt, prepared to pounce.

His statements often had a lilt, as if a question. Today that's referred to as upspeak, but it's long been common in West Virginia. Hall may have picked up the habit coming up in a southern West Virginia coal camp, or it may have been deliberately cultivated during his years of experience as an interrogator. A quiet voice and open manner invite people to speak.

At one point early in his career, Hall was the only trooper in Greenbrier County, in southeast West Virginia, the site of Karen Ferrell's Quinwood home.

"When you work in a place like that," Hall told me early on, "you get in everybody's business. We were required to have a listed phone number, and they'd call you or just come knock on your door."

He was on call 24/7, driving all over the large county, and people who needed his help often came to the home he shared with Betty, his wife. Sometimes she even helped. They kept a file of driver's license applications, criminal complaint forms and other commonly needed paperwork right in their living room, and Betty often found herself handing pages out to visitors.

"You ever been to Greenbrier County?" Hall asked me after he told me the story.

"Not since I was thirteen or fourteen."

"I want to take you over there when I go see Bess Ferrell. We'll go the old way? On 60?"

"Any time," I said. There I was, shadowing a WVSP lieutenant colonel as he sorted what remained of the murders that spooked me as a child, and now he wanted to introduce me to Karen Ferrell's adoptive mother. "One day's notice is all I need. You've already been to see her, right?"

"Yes. She's a tough lady. You'll see that right off. She thanked me a few times for looking at the case again. She never believed Clawson had anything to do with it. He used to write her letters, even sent her a Bible."

2

"I STILL THINK COSTANES DID IT."

POCA AND SCOTT DEPOT,
BOTH WEST OF CHARLESTON

Geoff

Investigation was a whole new world to me. Often, information is ambiguous and shows itself with various degrees of clarity. Take, for instance, Maxine Blankenship's encounter with the young man who offered her a ride. The man who liked to rub furry things. He *could* have been Eddie Thrasher, as Gooden and Herald suspected in 1970, but he might not have been. Eddie was a janitor at Westchester, and Blankenship tentatively picked Eddie's picture out of a photo lineup. Eddie also *might* have been the killer who took Mared's fur-lined boots and Karen's fur coat, but little suggested that other than Blankenship's story about a young man who liked fur. There needed to be far more solid evidence to demonstrate the connection. Investigators work as often with an accumulation of circumstantial evidence as they do with direct evidence.

Other times, information gathered made no sense at all: the copper plate with mystical symbols cited in WVSP reports? The stone circle with the burlap pouch full of stones? Such findings didn't seem to tie to anything, but I had to keep them all in mind in case they connected with something that turned up later. With all the random pieces of information, I became convinced the killer(s) would turn out to be a local man who either grew up here or was a semi-transient, like a WVU student. It was not a crime perpetrated by a man who just happened to be passing through. I had no reason to believe this, but it was a bias. Partly, this was based on the fact that, in 1970, without interstates, few people coincidentally "passed through" the Morgantown area. People were either visiting Morgantown specifically or they were on the way to someplace nearby.

Hall was convinced the dentist Elias Costianes killed Mared and Karen. That's where he seemed to be focused anyway.

"Where is Costianes now?" I asked him one day in late September 2006. "He still around?"

"I'm trying to track him down. Looks like he's in a nursing home, but they're moving him around. Four different nursing homes in four years. Probably he causes trouble. I'm betting he has a temper."

"That call he made to Westchester was what alerted you?" I was thinking of Costianes's call to the dorm, fielded by Donna DeYoung, the day after the disappearance.

"Yes. Costianes made the call to set up an alibi. *Why, no, officers, I didn't have anything to do with it. I even called the dorm looking for her.*"

I had no idea why Hall usually pronounced Costianes as a two-syllable name, but from what I'd seen in the WVSP reports, officers in 1970 were casual about precision when it came to names. Sometimes the same name was spelled two or three different ways in the same report. "I understand they call that alibiing behavior."

"Because that's what it is. Dentists don't call to check on missing patients, they just," he motioned as if checking off a piece of paper, "move on to the next patient."

"Okay, but if he did this, wouldn't there have been other crimes? Before or after? All we know—or think we know—is he probably sexually abused one person, Core."

Nancy Core called WVSP on April 24, 1970, to tell them she was molested by Elias Costianes in 1960. Hall talked with a dentist friend of his, a man who graduated in Costianes's class at WVU and had been in contact with Costianes since then. He told Hall that Costianes used to drive around town in his white Cadillac, day or night, whenever he had time, and try to pick up girls.

Hall shook his head. "I don't think he was too worried about his wife finding out. Don't know the timeline exactly, but in 1970 Robin Lynn Carney was either his secretary and he was fooling around with her, or she was his second wife by then. And apparently, he didn't mind if people in the community knew they fooled around. My friend said everyone knew."

"It's not enough." I wasn't convinced. A cheating husband is a long way from double murder.

"I talked to Nancy Core again a few days ago," he said. "He assaulted her when the secretary left the office. She didn't report it at the time, but she told her roommates, no one else. She left school and didn't go back until 1985, twenty-five years later. She gave me two numbers to call to confirm."

"Her roommates? She's still in touch with them?"

"I don't know about that, but they both confirmed Nancy told them about the assault back in 1960. You need to understand, back then no one talked about it. Not like now."

And actually, it was far worse than Hall remembered: Psychological trauma meant little or nothing in those days. A lack of physical trauma was taken to mean nothing serious happened.

"So how else you following up? You said Costianes's office was on Willey. I think I remember it."

"About a block from where Mared and Karen were picked up. And he was about forty at the time. Dark hair. They would have gotten in the car because Mared already knew him."

I briefly imagined them getting in the car, believing they were about to get a ride home and then finding out otherwise. It was something I did repeatedly: replay different stories to see what fit the facts.

"Maybe he made up some reason she had to get dental work done that night," Hall said. "He could have separated them that way, drugged Mared and then overcame Karen."

"That could explain why Mared's fur boots and Karen's coat were never found. I mean, if they were indoors—"

"I want to know what he did with the skulls. He probably would have had the chemicals to clean them right in his office."

I'd never thought about a black market for skulls. Would a dentist really have the chemicals to clean bone? "Could he have sold them?"

"Maybe he kept them. I'm going to find those heads. If they still exist."

"Probably in the river." The Monongahela River was just a few turns from the disposal site.

"Did I tell you, I talked with Larry Herald. He said he knew Costanes and interviewed him at the time. He ruled him out."

"So he's out?"

"Looking more like he didn't than he did at this point, but he didn't really look."

"Costianes?" I often had trouble with the shifting meanings of *him* when Hall talked.

"Larry. He talked to Costanes after he called the paper in March about Mared needing to see a dentist. Costanes was just trying to help, all that. He didn't rule him out. He just ignored him."

"Maybe we should do that. Focus on Cain." Cain was the WVU student who was photographed pointing at the spot the bodies were found.

"I should have a background check on Cain soon. I'm thinking about putting an ad in the paper."

"That says what?"

"I'm not sure yet. I want to put out a call for anyone molested in a dentist's chair between, oh, about 1958 and 1985, something like that. We need to find out if he made a habit of messing with his patients."

He didn't tell me where he was getting background checks done, and I didn't ask. I assumed an old buddy did them for him on the QT. Hall didn't telegraph his moves and often left me scrambling to keep up.

I'd been thinking of the investigation one-dimensionally, looking into Costanes to determine if he'd done it. In contrast, Hall was investigating the way real detectives operated: studying an entire field of possible persons of interest, all at the same time. Costanes headed that list, but he certainly was not the only person on it. I wondered how many people Hall was investigating. At first, I thought I was shadowing an investigation nearly finished but now saw the investigation was just beginning.

———◆———

As I settled into a chair at Hall's kitchen table in early October, he set down his briefcase and snapped the latches. We hadn't met in a couple of weeks.

"We've got something to talk about," he announced. He removed a folder. "I got the first call last Wednesday. From a Denise Bancroft. She was molested by a dentist name of Gerhard Rhine while she was in high school. I called the Dental Association, and there were no complaints filed against him."

I wasn't sure what Hall was on about. That morning, he called to see if I could drive out to the Scott Depot home he shared with Betty. It took me twenty minutes from Poca, where I lived. Scott Depot and Poca were two of the many small towns around Charleston. "How'd she know to call you?"

"Her mother just said Rhine is a good dentist and told her to forget about it." Hall pulled a folded newspaper and slid it across the table to me.

WVU Coeds
1955–1985
allegedly molested
in a Morgantown
dentist office you
are not alone.
Investigator needs
your assistance.
Info kept confidential.

Underneath was Hall's cell number.

"You put this in the *Dominion Post*," I said.

Hall nodded. "I'm going to run it for two weeks. Through Homecoming. People all over the state come into Morgantown. Better chance for more people to see it."

"Why would her mother—"

"I told you the other day, things were different back then. The first one called later that day. Carrie Walker. Claimed Costanes molested her when she was thirteen. She had big, you know, and he rested his dental instruments on them. She said her mother made her go back to him later. She kept her arms crossed over."

"Incredible. Any more?"

"Not Costanes, but three others so far."

"Maybe we should be investigating what the hell's wrong with Morgantown dentists."

"It's not just Morgantown. There was a show about it the other day. One of those daytime things. Women fondled in dentist chairs."

I shook my head.

"Five women so far," Hall said, "and the ad will be in for two more weeks." Hall slipped the paper back in the folder. "Another thing. Kay someone, from WJAR in Morgantown, called me. She wants me on Hoppy's show."

"Kay Murray. She's a honcho at WAJR and hosts a local show in Morgantown. When they want you on?"

"Thursday morning. A ten-minute segment."

"What do you think?"

I'd been wondering what would happen when Hall's police instinct to be secretive met the need to get help from the public. One of the first things I'd done back in June was start a thread on the unsolved crime site Websleuths to see if I could get any new information. Hall didn't know that; he wouldn't have approved.

"I think it's a good idea. Hoppy reaches a lot of people. I don't see a downside, as long as—" Hall said he didn't think WVSP should know he was investigating, although I didn't see why. "You know, you're not still concerned about the state police finding out what we're doing."

"I've talked with Colonel Lemon." Colonel D.L. Lemon was the superintendent of the WVSP. "He knows now. Guess I'll be on Thursday."

After I went home that day, I decided to draw up a formal summary of the information we had on Costianes for my own use and for Hall in case he needed it when he talked to Hoppy. The two-page summary began this way:

Profile of Elias Costianes, DDS

Timeline

DOB:	*1925*
Enters WWII at age of 17	*1942*
Serves two years, discharged toward end of war	*1944*
Attends university on GI Bill	*1946*
Receives bachelor's from WVU	*1951*

Nowhere in his life—education, children, divorces—could I find anything that indicated his bad temper had ever led to violence, much less double murder.

THURSDAY, OCTOBER 5

Over a jaunty rock sample, Hoppy's voice began the show: "Good morning. Welcome to *Talkline* on the Metronews Radio Network. We are underway."

Hoppy Kercheval hosts a statewide radio call-in show for two hours on weekday mornings. The show bills itself as The Voice of West Virginia and pretty much is in terms of coverage and profile. Everyone listens, from wage workers to politicians, company executives to civic leaders. West Virginia's politicos "go on Hoppy" when they want to speak to "the people."

"Hoppy Kercheval with you. Kay Murray, our producer, and a full agenda today. Lotta ground to cover. Got some politics interspersed here this morning, and also a story about one of the most notorious crimes ever in West Virginia, the decapitation slayings of two WVU coeds in 1970. Why is that back? Well, I'll tell you why, coming up a little bit later on, but first…"

After some talk about state politics, Hoppy introduced the third segment: "It was one of the most notorious crimes in the state's history." He summed up the coed murders case, up through Clawson's convictions, and made his dramatic turn:

"*But* there's a former West Virginia state trooper, a retired state trooper, Richard Hall, who worked on the case initially and who listened to Clawson's confession. He doesn't think that Clawson did it. And now, he's looking back into the case. Richard Hall joins us this morning. Richard, how are you?"

"Good morning. Fine, thank you."

"Thanks for coming on. Why do you think that Clawson did not commit this crime?"

"He was at work in a lumber company just north of Philadelphia the day of the crime and the day before the crime and the day after. He wasn't anywhere near Morgantown. And he confessed, and not one part of his confession could be corroborated. It was tried, and really, it was a social verdict."

"What do you mean, a 'social verdict'?"

"Well, the prosecution…The case was so heinous, and the crime was so heinous, really, the prosecution, if they'd gotten a not-guilty verdict, their political career would have taken a nosedive. And the defense attorneys the same way, their law practice would have been damaged if they'd gotten a not-guilty verdict. And those twelve jurors, I felt sorry for 'em. They didn't hear the story. They only heard Clawson's confession, which was uncorroborated. Their neighbors would have probably ostracized them for finding him not guilty."

"So you're saying that you don't think there was any physical evidence that conclusively linked Clawson to the murders, beyond the confession."

"There is *nothing*. Nothing was proven. He was convicted on his statement alone."

"Now, why are you interested in this again? This has been thirty-six years since the crime was committed. You listened to his first confession, but why are you now suddenly reinterested in this case?"

"Because there's a killer out there somewhere walking the streets, but Clawson remains in jail. He belongs there. He's a pedophile, a predator, and should remain in prison the rest of his life. He's a threat to society. And I'm not doing this to help Clawson. I just want to see the killer caught, and it would be a bonus if we could locate the heads and get 'em with the rest of their bodies. And also, the father of one of the coeds was a friend. Ferrell, Richard Ferrell."

"Richard Ferrell was a friend of yours."

"Yes."

Hoppy digs down, looking for details of Hall's latest investigation.

"What have you done over the last several months to try to find—if you don't think Clawson did it—who you think did do it?"

"In 1970, when the bodies were found, a lady came forward and told of being molested in a dentist office in Morgantown. And she gave the information to the authorities. And apparently, it fell through the cracks. There was no record of her being interviewed or the accused molester either.

"And, in 1979, the wife of the dentist told an attorney she believed her husband killed those coeds and she told him why. And that attorney told me. That's still in my mind, and it's just…it's bothered me all these years. It still does."

"Do you have—and I don't want you to give me any names because you're just poking around here. Do you think you know who did it if Clawson didn't?"

"We have two people of what you call *interest*—they used to call them suspects when I was a policeman—but two people of interest who show some signs, but yet, you have three things to a crime. You have to have motive, means and the opportunity to commit it. So these people have that."

"Clawson today is at Mount Olive, at the state prison. You went to see him a couple of weeks ago. Tell me about that meeting and what did you ask him and what did he tell you?"

"He still denies he didn't do it—"

"He denies he did it."

"Oh, yes. Yeah. And he's sixty-five years old now, walks with a cane, has a liver disease.…[He] has HIV AIDS, and he dreams of getting out of prison, and he wants to go and have a little place in the country with a dog. He would be a threat to society no matter where he is."

When Hoppy was done letting West Virginians know about the new look at an old case, he asked his closer: "How confident are you that in the months ahead you'll come up with the person that you think really did it and identify them to authorities? What are the odds?"

"The odds are not very good, really. But at least I'm going to try. And there's people out there.…There's somebody out there who can help me. If they just come forward, we can get it done."

3

"HE SET SOME FIRES."

SCOTT DEPOT AND MORGANTOWN

Geoff

Less than a half an hour after doing *Talkline* from his house, Hall receives calls from the *Dominion Post* in Morgantown and the *State Journal*; both want to set up an interview. He also gets a call from a woman in Morgantown who says she worked at a downtown restaurant, the Shake N Dog, in 1970. One of the regulars was a man named Jack Jackson. According to her, Jackson always dressed well. He stalked girls and groped them: "He did me that way."

But, she says, no one would make Jackson stop because his father was rich and powerful and popular. He ran United Mine Workers locals, emphasizing how powerful that was in coal country in 1970. She says the father knew Jackson did it because he; the father, had a white car that he got rid of after the girls disappeared.

"I swear to God Jack Jackson did it," she insists. "Clawson didn't do it."

He next receives a call from a Davis Appel, who lives on 119 at the edge of the Weirton Mine Section. Appel tells Hall he needs to take a closer look at Charlie Herron, who lived in the area back then. Appel calls Herron a cousin, but in West Virginia that can mean anything from first cousin to distant relative.

For ten days following the show, calls continue to pour in. On October 7, a woman calls to tell Hall she was molested by a dentist, a Dr. Rasmussen. "He unzipped his trousers and laid down on me in the dentist chair."

"When did this happen, Ms. Devore?"

"1974."

Two days later, a woman calls to say she worked with someone at Sterling Faucet in 1970. That woman's son was digging a ditch for a septic tank. After the ditch was finished, he went to Michigan and committed suicide. She believed the heads were in the ditch because it was near where Mared's driver's license was found.

On the tenth, another woman calls to say she was molested by Dr. Rasmussen. "He pushed sex to the breaking point. He did my girlfriend the same way."

The next day, Hall gets a call from John Zinn, the same man who in 1970 tipped the WVSP about a white Chevy Impala and a pair of fur-lined gloves. He had a music store in Grafton when the coeds were killed. He says that one day he heard two brothers tell some other boys they killed the coeds and buried the heads in a house they burned. Zinn also says both boys were on dope and that one of them is now dead.

However one evaluates the tips Hall received, it's clear to me that the case is still very much alive. WVSP sifted through dozens of supposed leads in 1970, and now, thirty-five years later, the tips keep coming. Everyone has their own theory, and much about the case still remains hidden, waiting to be found.

The same day, Mary Scott calls. Six months after the coeds were killed, she, her sister and her brother found a machete in a brown case in a storm drain on the Halleck Road, less than half a mile from where the bodies were found. She was twelve years old at the time and gave the machete to her mother. Her mother put it in the attic and should still have it. It had bothered Mary for years.

After none of these tips turned up new information about the dentist, Hall and I never discussed Costianes again. He just dropped from sight. I don't think Hall dismissed Costianes as a suspect but, like the WVSP in 1970, simply moved him to the inactive list.

——◆——

Hall finally decided to visit Bess Ferrell in mid-October. He picked me up, and we traveled south and east out of Charleston for almost two hours to her small house in Rainelle.

Bess Ferrell could best be characterized as proper and tightly contained. Her house was clean and neat, if not exactly welcoming—much like her. She sat stiffly in a straight-backed wooden chair at her dining room table. I couldn't tell if she was in pain, physically, and imagined she was holding back all the sorrow she'd experienced. Like many adult West Virginians, especially women, her face was set and sad but strong. Determined. Just like Hall said.

As a devout believer and a reverend, Bess attended church two or three times a week. She clearly knew about Hall's investigation and approved. She never believed Clawson was guilty and very much wanted to see whoever killed her daughter brought to justice. Bess said this with a mixture of sadness and hope, one of the only times in our short visit she seemed moved from her rigid dignity.

———•———

The day after Mary Scott called about the machete, Hall went to Morgantown to speak with her mother, Debbie Longstreet, who gave him the machete, a slightly curved blade about twenty-four inches long, with a plastic handle. It was in a worn leather case but not noticeably weather-beaten. If the machete was in the drain in 1970, it hadn't been there long. We were going back now to check the culvert underneath the Halleck.

"Spent a couple hours hooking up PVC last night," Hall said as we got in the car. "I made something I think will work."

"What's on tap?"

"Talk to Appel," Hall said, referring to the other solid lead he heard after Hoppy's show. "If we have time, I'd like to go see Kenny Cole." I recalled Cole from the WVSP reports, where he appeared again and again. The WVSP talked with him a few times just because they encountered him so frequently. Hall referred to him as the Mayor of Weirton Mine.

———•———

We pulled into Debbie's driveway two and a half hours later. There were only two houses in sight, Debbie's and one almost directly across the road, on the downhill side. Hall popped the trunk, pulled two lengths of PVC from the trunk and fastened them together. He anchored a wide board at the end of one to create a long-handled hoe. The plan was to dredge the pipe from the downhill side. Hall handed me a shovel.

Next he pulled from the trunk a pair of hip waders and some rubber boots. While he slipped everything on, I glanced at the perpetual white sky of late fall and thought I should wear more than a light coat to search a culvert in nippy October air.

Once suited up, Hall trudged the length of the field that stretched before the Longstreet house. Encumbered by the waders and boots, he walked like an astronaut on the moon. I followed, feeling in over my head. I had only a short shovel and a small notebook. Forty yards across the field from driveway to culvert, and the whole way I kept expecting someone to materialize and ask what the hell we were doing there.

"She said they were playing with a ball," Hall said, "and it rolled down this way." Hall stepped down from the field to the Halleck Road. The culvert started as a small opening in the ground, a natural spring, and ran into the roadside ditch and down into something shaped like the concrete drains on city streets, a large, flat rock as the top. Other flat rocks had been laid as a restraining wall.

Hall stepped into the road, headed across. On the other side of the road, he scrambled down the short embankment. I joined him. There was the large circle of an industrial pipe, maybe four feet across, where water ran out. Just in front of the drain, the stream was wide and not more than a foot deep. It narrowed to a little more than a foot wide as the water rushed over a three-foot drop down the hill.

"Here's what I'm thinking," Hall said. "I'll reach the pipe in as far as it will go and pull. That'll drag rocks and mess out, and you watch as it comes out. We're looking for bone, but it might be very small. If we get lucky, there'll be a curved piece, maybe, or something bigger. Maybe a tooth."

We were looking for pieces of skull.

Hall started raking PVC, and I sorted with the shovel and my hands. The air didn't stay cold for long, but the water felt like ice. Very few cars passed. Behind us sat the other house, a small doghouse beside it. A brown hound paced and sniffed but rarely barked. There was a pickup in the driveway, but I had the feeling no one was home.

More than an hour into it, Hall stopped to go back to the car. He lay his "hoe" on the bank across the road, and I dropped the shovel and stood on the shoulder. Hall brought the car down near where we were working. He was standing with the car between him and the road when a fire engine approached from the west. No lights on.

The fire engine stopped in the road next to Hall's car. Its side read Clinton Volunteer Fire Department, Kenny Cole's outfit in 1970. A man in the passenger seat yelled out his window, "Everything okay?"

Hall swept his right arm. "Our vehicle broke down, but it's okay now. Thanks."

"Good enough," said the man. The fire engine continued down the road.

Hall shook his head. "We're not supposed to be doing this, but they didn't ask who, what or where we were from. I don't think they even saw the tools. Or noticed my getup."

We got back to work. Hall raked and I sifted. After another hour of that, I asked for a chance at the raking. We switched places. Forty-five minutes of fruitless search, and we were both ready to call it a day.

"We need to get the highway department out here or something," Hall said.

"That's a wrap?"

"Let's go talk to Appel."

———◆———

Hall stopped in Davis Appel's driveway for what we both knew could be an important meeting. Appel mentioned a Charlie Herron, and on the surface, it sounded like a good lead.

"Just a little ways down there," I said, pointing, "the other way off the exit, is the 4-H Camp Road. Down where it crosses Goshen, a few miles, is right about where the bodies were found. If you keep going south from here, you'll get to the Halleck and if you turn right onto it, eventually you get to the same place from the other way."

I'd driven these roads all sorts of ways by this time. The roads were windy and convoluted, laced with smaller dirt roads, but I finally had a good visceral sense of the Weirton Mine Section.

We looked up to Appel's doublewide, which sat up the gentle slope from the driveway. The house looked well cared for and the yard well tended, with a few tasteful lawn ornaments. An orderly, hardworking man lived there.

At the front door, Hall knocked, taking the lead as he usually did in interviews and inspections. A middle-aged man with thinning hair answered.

"Mr. Appel?" Hall extended his right hand. "I'm Dick Hall. We spoke on the phone."

"Yes," Appel said, shaking hands. "Good to put a face to the name."

"This is Geoff Fuller. He's helping out on this."

Appel and I shook, and Appel stepped back, wordlessly inviting us in. The front door opened onto a tidy living room that mirrored what the house looked like on the outside. Appel led us through the living room to the kitchen. In West Virginia, kitchens—and kitchen tables—play an important role. When someone wants to maintain a distance from relative strangers, they're met on porches, weather permitting. Living rooms are reserved for more formal occasions and family get-togethers. Kitchens are for more intimate meetings.

"Can I get you anything?"

We both declined, Hall adding, "We shouldn't take up too much of your time, Mr. Appel."

Appel sat at the head of the rectangular table, his back to the front door, and Hall and I sat on either side. Hall spoke first.

"So what makes you think we should be looking at Charlie for this?"

"Like I told you on the phone, he was a bad person, dangerous. He used to follow girls all the time in high school, and I heard he forced some of them to 'do things.'" His lips tightened, and he seemed to be looking inward. "You know. When I was a kid, I used to go down there to buy eggs. My parents wouldn't let me go if they knew he was the only one around. They thought he might be crazy."

"He made them nervous, I guess," Hall said.

"He made everyone nervous. He was ten, fifteen years older than me. He got in lots of fights, drank a lot. The usual nonsense. But he was also known in the neighborhood for hurting small animals. I know he did that. I heard he set some fires, but I don't know if that's true. He was just a bad character."

"I can see why your folks didn't want you around him," Hall said. His words were noncommittal, and I noticed he was mirroring, roughly imitating Appel's posture and gestures. It's a technique that therapists—and apparently police—believe builds rapport. I wondered whether Hall knew he was doing it, or if, perhaps, like his patterns of speech and manner, it had become habit through years of police work.

I leaned forward. "When you say he used to hurt animals, what do you mean exactly? How badly?"

Hall looked at me, and I thought maybe I'd overstepped. But it was important to know exactly what Appel meant: Did Charlie just frighten animals, maybe throw rocks at them, or did he, say, skin them?

"By *hurt* I mean torture." Appel's eyebrows raised. "He used to pull the legs off cats."

4

"MAY BE."

MORGANTOWN

Geoff

"He used to pull the legs off cats." I glanced at Hall as Appel said that. The Macdonald triad, also called the homicidal triad, cites three characteristics shared by serial killers: As children, future serial killers wet the bed, set fires and abuse animals or smaller children. Belief in the Macdonald triad used to be widespread, but as Kenneth Lanning, one of the originators of the FBI's Behavioral Analysis Unit, pointed out to me in a 2014 interview, the Macdonald triad was more urban legend than proven truth.

For one thing, not everyone who exhibits these general behaviors grows into a serial killer. An investigator must take into account the severity of the behavior and, most importantly, the emotion surrounding the behavior. Burning an ant with a magnifying glass is qualitatively different than setting a neighbor's small dog on fire. And most important, excessive bed-wetting, fire-starting and animal abuse may not predict a future serial killer so much as indicate an abusive and violent childhood. But how ever one looked at it, pulling the legs off cats was extreme torture behavior.

Hall asked, "Whereabouts did you say he lived?"

"Now or then?"

"Then."

"Off the Halleck Road. Down in there, near where the bodies were found. He lived with his parents, Lloyd and Velma, and a couple of brothers, as I remember."

My breath caught in my throat: Lloyd and Velma were the grandparents of WVSP's first person of interest, Eddie Thrasher, who had perhaps been the young man with the fur fetish. In 1970, the WVSP never knew Charlie existed.

"Do you know what kind of car Charlie drove?" Hall asked.

"White sedan of some kind. I don't remember exactly."

"You said he was older than you. Do you remember how old he would have been in 1970?"

Appel thought for a minute. "About forty, maybe. Maybe younger."

"Do you know what's become of Charlie?" Hall asked.

"He lives in Morgantown somewhere. A nursing home, I think, or assisted living place." Appel stood and stepped over to a set of shelves, pulled out a phone book. "I ran into him at the store a couple of months ago. He's still creepy."

Appel looked up Nursing Homes in the Yellow Pages, scanned the listings.

"I can't remember the name," he said. "Mom would know."

As Appel reached for the phone, Hall asked. "Do you know a Charles Thrasher?"

"You mean Eddie. Sure. Scrawny guy. 'Bout my age." Appel poked out a phone number, held the receiver to his ear as he said, "Lloyd and Velma were his grandparents. His mother chased him off or something. Probably because of the drinking." He shifted and spoke into the phone, "Yeah, Mom? Do you know where Charlie Herron is these days? I need to talk to him about something."

Appel said nothing, the phone to his ear, then, "Thanks, Mom." He hung up. "He's down at Unity Manor."

————◆————

As Hall turned the car around in Appel's driveway, I said, "So Charlie Herron is Eddie's uncle."

"Looks that way. Let's go see the Mayor first. Look in my notebook. He's expecting us."

I riffled through the back pages, where Hall kept contact information.

"Give me the street number," Hall said as he started the car. "He likes to portray himself as the man who knows everything there is to know about Weirton Mine. We'll see what he has to say."

We drove down Grafton Road a few miles, slowing as we passed houses or mailboxes with numbers, driving south. A couple of minutes later we stopped in a driveway. One dark car and one red pickup, older models. A white outbuilding sat past the cars, and it looked as if there were at least two other cars on the other side. A steep hill stretched up to the left, and at the top of some steps sat a small, rundown house. Where Appel's house exuded order and care, Cole's was the opposite. On the porch sat a small, bald fireplug of a man in a T-shirt. Through the screen door, I could see the silhouette of a woman. That would be Alberta.

Cole waved, and Hall marched up the steps, trailing me behind him. "Kenny?"

Cole nodded. "You must be Dick Hall." He looked at me.

I nodded to the woman as we stepped up to the porch, where three chairs sat.

"Bert!" Cole shouted, even though she was right there. "Get you a chair and come on out here. These are the men I was telling you about. They want to talk about those coeds."

Hall sat down next to Cole, and I took the next chair over. Alberta Cole came out of the house and set her chair next to mine.

"You've got a hard place to find, Kenny," Hall said. "But not for you, I expect. You know this area pretty well."

Kenny seemed to find this funny. "Oh, yes. I've walked or drove pretty much every which way. Not so much anymore."

"I know you have," Hall said. "The way I hear it, you're pretty much king around here."

Kenny found this funny, too. "Don't know about that."

"We just wanted to talk to you, see if you might remember anything that would help us out."

"Been a long time." Kenny looked down and furrowed his brow, the face you're supposed to make when you're thinking; I thought he was making a show of remembering. "Everybody around here was talking about it. Troopers and National Guard tramping all over. We figured someone up in Morgantown did it."

When Kenny said *we* he didn't mean him and Bert, he meant folks in the Weirton Mine area.

"You don't know anyone around here might have done that?" Hall asked. When Kenny frowned and shook his head, Hall changed topics. "What'd you do back then?"

"I worked the Clinton Fire Hall. Did some other things. Worked on cars for people."

"You ever work on a white car or cream-colored car, with fins maybe?"

Another funny to Kenny. He laughed a lot.

"I had a couple like that. Worked on a lot of cars." He motioned to the cars on the gravel below and over beside the outbuilding.

"You ever know a man the name of Gerkin? William or Bill or Ray Gerkin."

That surprised me: yet another person Hall was investigating?

Kenny's eyes narrowed, and he shook his head. "Don't think so."

"He was from Grafton. Lived with his grandmother there."

"I don't know any Gerkins."

"You ever know a Charlie Herron? Lived around here."

"Now, him I know," Kenny said, laughing again. "He used to beat me up sometimes. Bounce me on my head."

"He did? You must not have liked him much."

"It didn't mean nothing." He waved his hand as if shooing mosquitoes. "He was okay. Kinda wild is all."

"I knew him when we were kids," Bert said. All three of us looked at her, waiting. "He was pretty wild later on, but when he was a kid, he went to church probably three days a week." That was a surprise. Bert looked at Kenny. "He did beat you up a lot. He beat up everyone."

"Kenny," Hall said, "did you know Eddie Thrasher?"

Kenny nodded. "Charlie's nephew. They were about ten years apart, but they were like brothers. Eddie moved in with his grandparents and Charlie and his brother Linn at some point. I forget why he stopped living with his mother. She was Charlie's older sister is all I know. Liked her liquor."

"Ruth," Bert said. "She was older than me. I didn't know her too well."

"She still around?" Hall asked.

Kenny looked at Bert, who shrugged. "I heard she died a few years ago. She hadn't been doing too well for a long time before that, though. Seems like I heard she was really mourning her boy."

"Eddie's dead then?" Hall glanced down at the cars parked beside the outbuilding.

"Over in Ohio," Kenny said. "He moved away around the time those girls were found. He died there."

———◦———

Hall said, "Just tell me where to turn," as we cruised down Woodburn Hill toward downtown Morgantown. I pointed out Unity Manor, a multistory building on the edge of downtown, where Charlie Herron lived.

"Let's see if we can talk to him," Hall said. "They probably won't let us in, but let's try anyway."

"Turn down there." The last thing I wanted to do was talk to a dangerous killer.

Hall found a parking space, and we walked into the building. Hall walked up to the front desk wearing his unassuming, aging-uncle act.

"We're, um, we want to see a Charlie Herron."

"Go on up," the woman at the desk said. "He's in 312."

Hall turned his back on her, toward me, his eyebrows raised to signify surprise. We walked to the elevator and Hall punched 3. "Let's meet the bogeyman."

Out of the elevator, we walked down to room 312 to find the door slightly ajar. Hall knocked. No answer, but we could hear someone talking inside. Hall knocked again, harder this time. Again, no answer. I thought the man inside might be hard of hearing. Hall pushed the door softly.

The door swung open. A man in a wheelchair faced a desk, his back to us. He was talking loudly into the phone, apparently to someone he knew well about a machine part he needed. Herron was a big man, thick neck, broad shoulders. When Hall and I talked later, we both figured him for about six feet, five inches tall. He was obviously still a powerful man, even though he had the body fat of an athlete gone soft.

Hall knocked louder on the open door.

Herron turned and motioned us in. His eyes were wide, bulging. He was dark haired and clean cut, like the dark-haired and clean-cut man Skip and Itsy saw driving the car that picked up Mared and Karen. Itsy said the driver was in his mid-twenties, while Skip said he was "about forty." Herron was between their estimates, thirty-two years old in 1970.

"What can I do for you?" Charlie said after he hung up the phone. His eyes darted back and forth between Hall and me. He was plainly wondering who had come to visit. And why.

"Richard Hall." Hall held out his badge for Herron to see. The badge was one issued to retired state troopers, but Hall had his thumb over the word "retired."

I simply said my first name and stood, feet at shoulder width.

"Now what could you want from me?" Herron said.

"We're looking into a very old case," Hall said in his best avuncular voice. "Old and dusty. We're wondering if you could help us with it. Back in 1970."

"The coed murders?" he said right away. "I don't know nothing about that." He looked from Hall to me and back. He had latched onto the case awfully fast.

"We're talking to people who used to live in the area, trying to figure out who might have done it."

"I don't know nothing about it," Herron said again. The repetition triggered alarm bells in me and probably in Hall. People who are lying often repeat themselves or repeat questions to stall for time. Herron seemed to pick up on our unease and added, "Just what I read in the papers. But I didn't read the papers much."

The idea he wouldn't know anything when he lived less than a few miles from where two decapitated bodies were found stretched credulity. People talk—Kenny had said so. If Charlie wasn't plugged into the neighborhood rumor mill, he must have been seriously scary. Or he was lying.

Hall said, "We're just trying to find out if anyone from that time might know something. Someone we might look at maybe. Someone who might have done it."

He hesitated, but then a torrent of names followed: Daft, Hearly, Shaffer, Wilson, name after name after name. We had talked to many people over the last few months, and everyone had a theory or "knew" someone specific who did it, but this was the first time anyone listed that many names at once. And unlike every other informant we talked to, Charlie offered no reasons for giving a particular name. I got the impression he was trying awfully hard to get us to look at anyone but him.

"And there was them hippies," Charlie said at one point. "They had a little house down there. Don't know what *they* were up to."

Hall thanked him for the information and said we'd follow up, then asked about a couple of pictures Charlie had on his bookshelf, the only pictures in his small room. They were of his sister Ruth and his nephew Eddie, both of whom were dead. He seemed to have a special fondness for Eddie, talked as if he was protective of him and said how well he'd been doing in Ohio and what a nice family he had. "Everybody loved him," according to Charlie.

Hall asked a few more general questions, trying to get the measure of this man. Throughout the interview, I was silent, my arms crossed, but I was obviously on Charlie's mind—his eyes flickered toward me often. He was trying to figure out who I was. Still, he was relaxing. Hall had apparently succeeded in lulling him with the aw-shucks approach. That is, until Hall asked this: "We were wondering what kind of car you drove back then."

Herron's demeanor instantly turned steely and cold, as if the air had been sucked out of the room.

"Why do you want to know *that*?" Herron asked, his voice low, threatening.

"Just nosy, I guess," Hall said casually.

"That nose of yours is going to get you hurt," Herron said. "We're done."

"Okay," Hall said after a second. He looked at me. "I guess we should go now. I didn't mean to offend you, Charlie."

"You didn't offend me. Just sticking your nose in where it don't belong."

We left Herron's apartment, and on the way down the hall, I murmured, "That's our boy."

Hall muttered only, "May be."

5

"SKULL'S THE HARDEST PART."

Scott Depot

Geoff

The kitchen phone is ringing as Hall gets home, and he tosses his keys on the counter as he answers.

"Yes?"

The speaker at the other end hesitates a moment before her soft, aged voice comes over the phone.

"Mr. Hall?"

"Who is this?" Hall never identifies himself before the caller does.

"Bess Ferrell."

"Yes, Mrs. Ferrell," Halls says, his voice transforming into welcoming. "How are you doing?"

"I just want to know if you have found anything new."

"Too soon to tell, but we are pursuing some things." He wants to tell her of his upcoming meeting with Colonel Lemon about having the case being reopened but feels maybe he shouldn't just yet.

"You probably could not tell me if you had," she says. "I know you are doing all you can to find the real killer and locate the heads. I could help pay some of your expenses. Just say so."

"We're fine. It's not that expensive to go talk to some people. We're working on this every day."

"I know you are. The reason I thought to call you is I had a dream last night. I dreamed I was in a strange place. There were six beds. They were clean. Eugene Clawson was in one bed. He raised up and showed me his hands. They were clean, like they had just been washed. I do not believe Clawson had anything to do with killing the girls."

Bess's dreams are meaningful and important to her, her visions when she's awake even more so.

"I don't either, Mrs. Ferrell."

"I need closure before I die. I pray for that every day."

Hall hopes she won't be disappointed.

HALLECK ROAD, MORGANTOWN

Hall and I met with WVSP sergeant Daniel Swiger and another state trooper. Four men from the West Virginia Department of Transportation were also there in a WVDOT van. Hall told me he had been successful in getting Colonel Lemon to reopen the coed case the week before; CIB was testing the machete for blood residue. WVSP's resources were also available to better search the Halleck Road culvert, and WVDOT was there to provide the hose and water pressure.

As the WVSP's cold case man, Swiger's purview included "twenty or thirty" cases. A tall man with a ginger crewcut, solid and strong, Swiger exuded the stoic demeanor common among state troopers. The goal that morning was to dredge the drain for a decisive search for the missing skulls. WVDOT would run a powerful hose through the north end of the drain and flush the contents out the other side, where Swiger would stand in chest-high waders with a sifter he'd built of wood and screen.

The weather was relatively mild for late November, but Hall and I wore light jackets. Swiger was the one who would get wet this time. As he donned his boots and rubber wading outfit, close to his car and out of hearing of the WVDOT men, he let Hall and me know where he stood on the case: Clawson's confessions didn't sound credible, he thought, but he didn't yet totally buy into the idea Clawson was not guilty.

Swiger reached inside the north end of the drain, feeling around but not finding anything. He motioned, and the WVDOT men brought the hose around. Swiger hauled his sifter, three feet square and built of 2x4s, across the road and clambered down the small embankment. The WVDOT turned on the hose.

In seconds, water came out the south side, water and dirt and rocks and bits of debris. Standing in the small creek, Swiger caught everything through his sifter as it passed, trying to tell rocks from plastic from bone.

"I learned a lot from a guy I worked with," Swiger said once the process was underway. "He was FBI. Used to be an archaeologist. We worked on an excavation up in Moundsville. He was about the most meticulous guy I've ever seen."

Not much traffic on Halleck Road at 7:45 a.m., but I wondered what the people in the passing cars made of two state police cars and a WVDOT van clustered around a drain.

"Would the skulls even have survived, Danny?" I asked. "Thirty-six years is a long time. A lot of water would have washed over them."

"Skull's the hardest part of the body, top of the skull," Swiger replied as he sifted.

Several times, Swiger motioned for the highway guys to cut off the water. Some piece of debris had piqued his interest.

"That look like bone to you?" He'd hand the piece to Hall or me. We looked at it, pinched it, scraped it to hear what it sounded like, and then said, "Plastic" or "rock."

Periodically, Swiger or Hall or I would work around to where one of us could shine a light into the drain to see how much detritus was still left. The stuff that came out showed how many years the drain had been in a long, slow clog: some plastic bags from local stores, product labels that looked by the graphics to have been there twenty years, a few odd and unidentifiable plastic things. And dirt and rocks of all colors and sizes. Throughout the morning, Swiger's methodical intelligence and reservoir of patience became clear.

I commented on his patience at one point and he shrugged. "You gotta be somewhere."

Swiger may have been nonchalant, but Hall and I were increasingly disappointed.

"I think that's the last of it," Swiger said a little before 10:00 a.m. He signaled for the highway men to cut the power.

"Sorry to have wasted your time," I said as Hall and Danny shook hands. Swiger shrugged again. "You don't know until you look."

6

"ONE OF AMERICA'S FIRST SERIAL KILLERS."

PRESTON COUNTY STATE POLICE DETACHMENT

"I'm working off the theory that whoever did this, it wasn't the first time," Swiger said to me. "And it wasn't the last."

I'd rendezvoused with Swiger at his post in Preston County, the county east of Monongalia. Where the Morgantown Detachment felt all steel and concrete—very institutional—the Preston Detachment was much smaller, with lots of woodwork that matched the more rural setting. I was a little nervous about the meeting, but Swiger had seemed to be an agreeable man a month earlier when we worked the culvert.

In December, I had wanted another session with the exhibits from Clawson's 1981 Elkins trial. I called Elkins to arrange to come up there again to take a look, only to find Swiger had been there a few days earlier and took all the exhibits with him.

"In December of the same year the coeds were killed," Swiger said, "there was a case down in Pendleton County. It was dumb luck he was caught. A Mr. Herbert Cobun was killed, apparently around Petersburg. His body was discovered on a farm located on the Grant-Pendleton line. The head was found eight miles south of there. William Bernard Hacker was indicted in February of 1971 and convicted by the end of March."

"Why did he do it?"

"Love triangle. He killed the guy, and then he tried to talk the woman—apparently a woman he was seeing at the same time Cobun was—into coming down to his place, where he and Cobun had been drinking all day. She wanted to talk to Cobun, but he told her Herb couldn't come to the phone. He was passed out drunk. But she wouldn't come down. He would have killed her, too."

"So what makes you think he might have killed the coeds?"

Swiger shrugged. "Some people thought the heads were severed in the same way, same vertebrae. More than that, Hacker's wife disappeared in 1927. She was never seen again, but some years later, a man living in the house found a shoe when he broke up the cement porch. I don't know. Doesn't mean much, but in 1952, Hacker was convicted of a double murder. He shot his girlfriend and a man she'd been carrying on with. He served until 1964, when he was pardoned by the governor. Seems he was the foreman of the prison's mining operation—they did that at the time—and there was an explosion and Hacker rescued a man. The governor pardoned him because of his heroics."

"So he's killed before? That's why you're interested?"

"No one else checks all the boxes. Whoever did this, it wasn't the only time."

POCA

I brooded about Swiger's Hacker theory all week before I got a chance to do any work. Swiger was focused on him, despite the fact that I thought he should be looking at Herron and Thrasher. Who knew how many men Hall was considering, but as far as I was concerned, Herron and Thrasher were our best suspects. We had little to call evidence, but I couldn't get past how cold the room had gotten when Herron said, "Why do you want to know *that*?" I'd heard about that sudden, drastic change before, but I never believed such a thing was real—until I experienced it. I had chills, as if sensing immediate evil. If nothing else, Herron had something very dark inside.

But *Hacker*? I looked at him a little before, when I was reading newspaper accounts, but I hadn't researched him at all. I'd assumed the police had their own reasons to ignore him back in 1970. I'd talked it over with Hall briefly, but Hall was dismissive. There was nothing to tie Hacker to the coeds except the beheading; his actual victims were completely unlike Mared and Karen, as were the settings and circumstances of his other murders.

The only connection seemed to be the similarity of the beheadings. Swiger thought that, anyway, but similar how? Just the fact of decapitation? Other than that general similarity, I couldn't see it. The coeds were both decapitated at different vertebrae, one at the fourth vertebrae and one at the sixth, and Hacker's victim, Cobun, had his head cut off between the second and third vertebrae. Maybe the similarity Swiger was referring to was that they all appeared to have been decapitated after death, rather than before.

Hacker was arrested on December 25, 1970. Swiger believed a crime like the coed murders was not a one-off thing—whoever had done it had done similar things before or after he murdered the coeds. Hacker had a spot-on name, but other than that—I wondered what I was missing.

In 1970, Hacker was seventy-four, an advanced age, especially in those days, but Hacker was fit enough to kill and behead a man twenty years his junior. Hacker was convicted of previous murders in 1952. And his wife disappeared in 1927. He also worked in the Weirton Mine in the 1950s, which connected to the coed murders; at least he had known the area ten or twenty years before the coeds were killed.

Hacker grew up in Monongah, within five miles of Fairmont. He worked the mines there as a child. In the early 1900s, child labor was common in the mines because they boosted a miner's load, which meant more pay. Monongah stood near the southern edge of the Pittsburgh Seam, one of the richest mineral deposits in the world. On December 6, 1907, most of the men in Monongah were killed when the mine exploded. Probably over five hundred miners died, many when their heads were blown off by the force of the explosion. One man was reportedly found with a sandwich raised to where his mouth had been. As a ten-year-old working coal miner, Hacker may have been part of the clean-up crew after the disaster; the explosion left hardly any men in town alive. If he helped retrieve dozens of headless corpses, he could have developed a fixation on decapitation, especially if his father died in the explosion.

The next day, I learned that wasn't the only reason to suspect Hacker. I assembled my notes on Hacker so I could see what gaps needed to be filled in.

Profile of William Bernard Hacker

Date of Birth: 1897
Place of Birth: Brooklyn, New York

Father moved the family to Monongah when the mining boom began, around the turn of the century. Hacker began to work in the mines as a child.

Hacker served in World War I, shipping out in 1917 at the approximate age of 20.

I included what I knew of his life: his wife disappearing, the murders in 1952, his rescue of a fellow miner and subsequent commuted sentence. My mind kept coming back to what Swiger said about the coed murders not being a one-time thing.

I began searching for unsolved cases of beheadings. Maybe there were others for which Hacker had been responsible but not caught. I worked all night and hit paydirt, over and over. By the time morning rolled around, I found a troubling pattern of unsolved beheadings, all of them occurring either within walking or riding distance of Monongah, within a half day's journey by rail. At the time, the railway system from Monongah up through Fairmont and Morgantown, up through Uniontown and Connellsville and on to Pittsburgh, was one of the most sophisticated transportation systems in the world, allowing swift and easy travel along that corridor.

The first reported unsolved beheading was in 1921, southwest of Pittsburgh, a year or two after young Hacker returned from World War I.

- 1921, a woman beheaded on the porch of her house just south of Pittsburgh, her throat slit ear to ear.
- 1925, a man found decapitated south of Morgantown, near the future site of the Weirton Mine.
- 1927, a man found headless along the railroad tracks outside of Sabraton, about halfway between Morgantown and the Weirton Mine.
- 1931, 1937 and 1938, the "boxcar murders" around the railroad lines of southern Pittsburgh, usually tied to the Torso Murders in Cleveland.
- 1942, outside of Uniontown, between Morgantown and Pittsburgh, a man found in a railroad yard with his head sitting next to him.
- 1944, a man found along the tracks north of Point Marion— Eugene Paul Clawson would have been a child in Point Marion at the time. The man's head was never found.
- 1948, another man found with his throat slit near the Weirton Mine Section.
- 1950, a man found outside of Fairmont, between Morgantown and Monongah.

In 1952, Hacker was arrested and convicted for murder. The unsolved beheadings stopped. He was released in 1965. Reports of unsolved beheadings started up again in 1965. One in 1966, two in 1967, one in 1969, the coeds in January and Cobun in December 1970. Hacker was a suspect only in the Cobun murder, and the beheadings stopped again after his conviction. Prison released him to a Cleveland hospital, and he died in Cleveland in 1979.

Eighteen beheadings near where Hacker lived or worked over a period of nearly sixty years. I could find nothing that tied Hacker to these killings, but the implications seemed unmistakable. Hacker had just moved into the second spot on my list, behind Herron and Thrasher. If true, Hacker may not have just killed the coeds. He may have been one of America's first identified serial killers.

7

"GETTING THEIR DRINK ON."

POCA AND SCOTT DEPOT

Geoff

"I tell you, Hacker didn't do it," Hall said, his scorn palpable over the phone. I wondered where the scorn came from. When I first shadowed Hall, he didn't make blanket assertions of guilt or innocence, which made his initial insistence that Costianes was responsible all the more plausible. Now, it seemed like he was making more black-and-white statements.

"I'm inclined to believe that," I said. "We have zero that ties Hacker to any of these beheadings, plus seeing them as a series just doesn't *sound* right for some reason. But this is a lot of beheadings. And the way they stop when he went to pri—"

"He killed because of romantic triangles. Both of his convictions."

"That's not entirely clear, and Danny thinks—"

"I don't care what Danny thinks. I'm not even sure he's working the case. He's focused on that nun thing in Wheeling."

In June 1977, Roberta Elam, known as Sister Robin, hiked up a hill overlooking her convent in Wheeling. She wanted some meditation time before lunch. Less than four hours later, the groundskeeper and his wife found her partially clothed body. She had been raped and murdered. Swiger thought he found a viable suspect.

"But if it wasn't Hacker, where does that leave us?"

"Same place it did before you talked to Danny."

I cupped my hand over the phone and sighed. There was an unbridgeable gap between me as a civilian and Hall and Swiger as cops. Cops know things civilians don't; they see the world differently. The grounding in experience of the grittier sides of life lends their views an undeniable weight.

"Okay, where are we?" I asked, more to stall than anything. "We thought Costianes did it, and then it turned out he didn't. Pretty much. We can't say he didn't, but we can say there's no reason to think he did."

Hall didn't say anything, so I went on.

"We've decided to rule out Cain and the guy that wrote the letters. And Kroll and Lantz."

"Casazza and Munch, too. Don't forget them. Remember, I found Munch. I talked to him. He didn't kill his girlfriend."

"So that leaves Herron and Thrasher."

"And Gerkin. He's the one that did it."

"The engineering student?" There it was again, another blanket assertion. And I was surprised to hear Gerkin's name again. I'd thought he was off the table. Hall had mentioned him a few times, and the 1970 investigation probably stopped looking at him prematurely, but I just didn't see it. Where Hall saw violent and criminal acts, I saw behavior propelled by booze and bipolar disorder.

"Take my word for it," Hall said. "I'm going to call his frat brothers again. I haven't talked to them all yet."

"I'll draw together why I think it was Herron." I wondered for the first time if Hall was suffering from the Shade Effect. It was as if he had forgotten his own interview with a neighbor of Herron's, Lillian Brown. He characterized her as a domestic worker, now in her nineties. He said she walked with a cane but was "spry" with a "good memory." She recounted a time that a group of men, including Charlie Herron and Eddie Thrasher—as well as two members of the Daft family, several of whom had turned up repeatedly in the police reports—beat her husband severely. They stole guns, tools, furniture and many other things. She said she'd kill Charlie if she could find him. Hall gave her his address and noted in all caps, "WHERE WERE THE LAW ENFORCEMENT AGENCIES WHEN THESE PEOPLE WERE ROBBING THE COMMUNITY."

He now seemed to either forget this interview or discount the relation of assault and theft to murder.

"I'll put together one on Gerkin, too," was all I said. "You can help me fill it in."

"I talked with Herron again last week. Third time."

"You did?" Maybe Hall wasn't lost in the Shade Effect.

"I'm still not sure about him. I went up there, and he was sitting outside. He was with some friend, probably some guy at the nursing home. I wasn't going to say much at first, but he said it was okay. At one point I just told him, 'I've got the machete in the car. You want to see it?'"

"How'd he react?"

"He said, 'I don't want to see them girls.'"

Hearing this, I thought of other stories from the police reports that would make sense if Herron and Thrasher had done it. Thrasher could have been the young man who tried to pick up Maxine Blankenship. He might also have been the man two parkers had reported near where the coeds' remains were found; they saw a man in camo spying on them through binoculars. Another man said he saw two men at dawn in January carrying a stretcher covered by a sheet; when the informant offered to help carry the obviously heavy load, the bigger man growled at him to mind his own business.

Two other suggestive facts might relate to Mared and Karen:

- Karen's driver's license was found at the base of a driveway on April 15, 1970, down the hill from a pile of the coeds' identification off the east side of Route 119. The paper license could have blown down the hill, but it also could have been thrown out at the last minute. The driveway was right next to the turnoff to the Herron farm.
- Graduate student John Rowe saw the backs of three girls standing beside a light green car with the passenger door open. The one with shoulder-length blondish hair had gotten in back. Thrasher had shoulder-length blondish hair; from behind, Rowe might have mistaken him for a girl.

Now it turned out Hall had been back to see Herron, who he called Charlie, twice. He'd just told me about the second time. In the first visit, Herron had been more forthcoming. He was in a mood to talk. It seemed his "little girl" had just been killed by a hit-and-run driver while she was waiting for the school bus. If he ever found that driver, Herron said, he would kill the man. No question.

This happened in Maryland, and his precise relationship to her wasn't clear. He called her his "little girl," but Hall believed she wasn't his biological daughter but a girl he'd taken a paternal interest in. This happened, Hall learned, during the twenty-five years Herron lived with the Amish in Maryland.

Herron had not only left town but also gone off the grid completely, and he did it in the summer of 1970. He disappeared into Amish country. One couldn't pick a better place—as *devout* a place—to hide while remaining geographically close to his biological family. To most of the United States, the Amish were quaint people who dressed oddly, built furniture and rode around in horse-drawn wagons. Their lives were entirely devoted to God and family. What better way to atone for one's sins? Herron had said to Hall, "It's good there. People don't get drunk and do stupid shit they later regret."

Herron the drunken hellraiser, known around his neighborhood for beating people up, setting fires and torturing animals, reverted to the Charlie of his youth, the one Alberta Cole described, who attended church regularly to get right with Jesus. The way the bodies were positioned when they were found—headless, stomach down—could be symbolic. One belief about homicide was that bodies positioned face-down or with their faces covered (or missing?) signaled an offender feeling guilty about what he had done.

The missing fur coat and fur-lined boots made sense with that theory, too. The coat and boots were good candidates for trophies: items often taken by killers to remember their kills by. And Thrasher may have had a fur fetish. But if Thrasher and Herron killed Mared and Karen, why? And how? Wondering how it could have happened, I imagined that it might have been an accident, at least partially.

———— ◆ ————

Charlie and Eddie are out cruising, getting their drink on. They're heading north to Morgantown in search of a party. Sunnyside might be best. Lotta students drink in Sunnyside—as do country people and other out-of-towners when they want some action: booze, beer, sex, fights. They could find some chicks there. College chicks are always freaky. Charlie and Eddie are up for whatever they find.

The way to Sunnyside from the Weirton Mine Section goes through downtown, especially if one wants to scope out the action a little on the way. The students are back in town. Time to party. So Charlie and Eddie drive through downtown, make the loop up Spruce Street, across on Willey and down High Street a couple of times. They see Mared and Karen coming out of the theater, and Eddie recognizes them. He knows they're likely headed back to the dorm. He convinces Charlie to cruise around, try to pick them up.

By the time Charlie and Eddie come around the block and slide down Willey Street, they're in luck. The girls have their thumbs out. Practically an invitation! This'll be easy. They stop, and Eddie opens the car door. They recognize him as a Westchester janitor, even though they don't know his name, and as he gets out of the car, he sneaks a peek at the fur coats both girls wear. He invites them to get in and slips into the back.

Charlie convinces them there's still plenty of time to make it back before curfew, and the four go to Sunnyside for a quick beer. Or maybe they park and go to Mared and Karen's hangout, the Castle Club, just a block away.

At some point, everyone a little drunk, someone mentions having some pot. *Come on! So what if you're late? Nothing really happens*, Charlie says, and it sounds like no big deal after a couple of quick beers. Charlie and Eddie know the perfect spot, out near where they live, somewhere no one will bother them. If the 4-H camp has partiers, they can go nearby, over next to Owl Creek. They can get high there.

What happens next is probably a terrible accident. They're talking, laughing, getting high. Until Eddie, drawn to Mared because of her outgoing personality, tries to make a move on the pretty freshman. Maybe he tries to kiss her or maybe he's just getting strange again, talking about liking her boots, and he tries to touch her. Mared, by all accounts a fighter, tells him to back off, maybe even slaps him. They struggle briefly, and she falls and hits her head on a rock. Or maybe he rages when she rebukes him and hits her with a large stone.

Either way, Mared is knocked unconscious, maybe dead. Karen's eyes are wide, caught in the headlights; her deepest fear, that she will be raped and killed before the age of twenty, is coming true. She freezes. Maybe Charlie, feeling guilty over innumerable petty crimes and believing this will not work out, decides both women have to die to cover it up. Or maybe Eddie does. Both men are known to possess and carry guns. Either one of them might have done it, but Herron seems the most likely. One of them shoots Karen once, in the head, before she has time to do anything.

Now they've done it. They have to do what they can to hide their identities and the way they died. Mared has blunt force trauma to the head, and Karen has been shot. Charlie's brother has a Marine-issue machete at home, three minutes away by car. Eddie goes to get it while Charlie, a large and powerful man, carries rocks from the stream to where they will put the bodies. Eddie returns with the machete, and together they string Mared and Karen up like deer. Both men are hunters and can do that with their eyes closed.

By the time they're done, they're not drunk any more. They drive away, down Goshen Road to Route 76 to the Monongahela River. Drop the heads in the river. Then back south and east on Halleck Road, along the way stopping to hide the machete in a hard-to-see storm drain one of them knows of. They stay on Halleck as it turns north and begin to get rid of Mared and Karen's things, stopping several times to distribute items far off the road.

At the section of Halleck Road and 119, they turn south toward home. They get rid of most everything else as they travel south. When they get clear down almost to Grafton, they take all the stuff they've dumped out of the purses about seventy-five feet off the eastern side of Route 119 and pile it in the middle of a garbage dump. No one will find it there. They head home, less than a half mile away. Just before they turn up their long driveway, Eddie finds Karen's license on the floor and tosses it out of the car.

8

"BILL WAS AS CRAZY AS THEY GET."

Scott Depot

Geoff

I watched Hall read the summaries I prepared. He didn't seem too interested in my thoughts about Thrasher and Herron; I couldn't tell if he still considered them persons of interest. He was drawing a veil between us. As closely as we'd worked for a few years, the differences between how we saw the world, how we saw the case, were getting more profound.

Draft Profile of William Ray Gerkin III

DOB: December 23, 1946
Description: Six feet, 200 lbs
Home Address: Lived with grandmother in Grafton until he started WVU in 1967.

Mother and father divorced when he was young.

Meets Suzanne Williams in the summer of 1967.

Dates Nancy Serfass in 1969. He parks near her dorm, tries to disrobe her. She resists. He becomes angry and drops her onto the sorority porch partially naked.

Marries Williams in 1969. After they move to Morgantown, he continued to live in the fraternity house.

Several people report seeing a violent story written by Gerkin in the fall of 1969. Reports of its contents vary. It's a story or essay

- *on religious cults dealing with decapitation OR*
- *in which someone approaches Gerkin with either a gun or a machete and one of them was cut up; the other person then took the cut-up body and placed it in a plastic bag and put it in a garbage can OR*
- *in which another person has a machete and Gerkin has a .22, and the other person cuts Gerkin to pieces OR*
- *in which two women decapitate and cut up Gerkin OR*
- *in which Gerkin decapitates and cuts up two women.*

Everyone reports different specifics, and no one can provide a copy.

January 14, 1970: Gerkin wrecks his light blue Chevrolet Camaro on the Halleck Road and transfers his insurance to a new car.

April 15: Gerkin drops out of school, citing illness as the cause.

April 23: WVSP and the prosecuting attorney meet with psychiatrists and psychologists from WVU medical school and Kennedy Youth Center. They feel burial could have been superficial to allow the killer to periodically view the bodies. This could indicate the killer lives close; Gerkin traveled frequently between Morgantown and Grafton, where he grew up, taking him periodically near the disposal site.

April 28: WVSP and Prosecutor Heiskel meet with doctors to discuss Gerkin's medical background. Gerkin was admitted to WVU Medical Center five times for psychiatric treatment between 1968 and 1970. They say he was suffering from an acute mental illness but will not elaborate. They believe it possible he killed the coeds because at times he would have no control over himself. Suzanne told the doctors Gerkin had a pistol and had played with it in her presence a number of times.

April 30: WVSP contacts Father John W. Doane at the WVU Catholic Church, which sits at the section of Willey and University, where the coeds disappeared. Father Doane had contact with a man in the chapel. Doane asked the man if he could help, and the man went into his office and sat at his desk and stared for a half hour. Doane didn't know whether he was going to break down or attack. The man would often "mumble and talk incoherently." Finally, the man says, "Guess you know why I'm here. I have done something for which you cannot help me. I have already taken steps to correct the situation." Subject later identified by Doane from thirty-five photos as either a man named Robert Richmond or William Ray Gerkin.

May 14: WVSP troopers go to Belpre, Ohio, to interview Suzanne. Gerkin is there. They invite him to come to the Parkersburg WVSP Detachment across the river. Four hours later Gerkin shows up alone. They ask a few questions. He is very nervous and they stop the interview. He never makes himself available for a follow-up, and WVSP records show no evidence of any attempts to contact him again.

Hall set the papers down and looked across the table.

"Been talking to people about Gerkin," Hall said. "He's been trying hard not to be found. For twenty years now."

"How do you know that?" We both had cups of coffee from the bottomless pot of coffee the Halls always seemed to have warming in their kitchen.

"Background checks. Fifteen years ago—more like twenty, 1988, 1989—he used two false addresses in Charleston. From 1998 to 2000, he used three false addresses. In the fifteen years from 1985 to 2000, he used a total of thirty-three addresses in Ohio, North Carolina, and West Virginia."

"That's a lot of moving around. How do you know they were false addresses?"

"Some of them don't exist. Never did. I want to talk to Suzanne again, Gerkin's ex-wife. They divorced in 1985. He was living with Carol Marks at the time, so their marriage must have really ended before that, maybe long before."

"So that's what you've been up to."

"I've also been talking with his fraternity brothers. They were scared of him."

"That reads more like a running joke to me." In the reports, several fraternity brothers reported they said—or heard said—things like, "Get the hell out of here! Here comes Bill with the machete!"

"No," Hall said. "They were *really* scared. One of them said Gerkin came into his room one night toward the beginning of the semester about 2:30,

3:00 in the morning. With the two girls. They woke him. No one turned the lights on, and the girls sat on the edge of the bed. Gerkin was talking real fast, excited, and tried to get him to go with them. He wouldn't, and Gerkin said in that high voice, 'Let's get out of here, girls.'"

"You sure it was them?" I said, and Hall waved his hand dismissively.

"You missed something here." Hall tapped the summary. "Suzanne was a telephone operator in Morgantown. Transferred there from Parkersburg on February 5. The day the bodies were found, before that was in the news, she got a call and the man said, 'They found the bodies. What do you think about that?'"

"Someone spreading gossip?" I was also thinking that the recovery of the remains had already been published.

"It was her husband. Gerkin."

I didn't say anything. Hall was certain that the "two girls" were the coeds and that Gerkin called his wife on the day the bodies were found, but he offered nothing to back up either assertion. Still, I didn't want to object. The distance I'd sensed the last few months was increasing. My counterarguments now made Hall shut down. "I think Ma Bell was on Chestnut Street back then. Across from the Castle."

"That so?"

"So what else did you hear from the fraternity brothers?"

Hall flipped through his notebook.

"One thought several times over the years that Gerkin could have been involved. He thought maybe Gerkin was bipolar. That was why he did wild stuff. He would lift weights like crazy when he was manic. Some of the guys saw the machete in his trunk."

"Why wasn't this in the reports?"

"Another thing—Gerkin was gone a lot at night. Some people figured he was studying someplace because he had good grades. One guy also said the last time he saw Bill was during rush week. He said they were singing and Bill was banging on the piano, even though he can't play. Let's see…" He flipped a couple of pages. "Get this. This is a quote: 'Gerkin lives in two different worlds. I've seen him mad, throw shoes and yell at the top of his voice…' and, mmm, 'I heard he had a machete. It was two feet long with a black plastic handle.' That's the one I found."

"That it?" As soon as I said it, I knew it sounded too skeptical.

"He said Gerkin, quote, believed an all-knowing power existed and reincarnation and the human mind could control a person's destiny, unquote." Hall looked up from his notebook. "Bill was crazy as they get."

Once again, the chasm between our worlds: Hall may not have heard that New Age belief before, but growing up in a university town I'd heard stoned people say such things about ten thousand times since the 1970s.

"I talked with a woman who worked the reference desk in Wise Library back in 1970," Hall continued. "I showed her some pictures and asked her if she could recognize anyone who spent a fair amount of time there. She picked out Bill's picture and said he came in a lot. He always wore black and was interested in Wicca. That's witchcraft."

"I know." He obviously thought that was more of an indictment than I did.

"She said sometimes he had knives and she was scared of him." Hall flipped pages. "Last guy here. He didn't want his name used either, but he was one of those guys who exercised with Gerkin in the mid-70s. One day when they were lifting weights, Gerkin told all four of them that his wife had caught him trying to rape the babysitter. Then later on, he said Gerkin called and threatened to kill him. He recognized the voice, high-pitched and like a girl's."

"Yeah, we keep hearing that, too. He—"

"One more thing," he said, flipping pages again, "he had, um…A couple of years ago—2005—he had five vehicles in seven months. He did this to avoid identification. Had to be. Start getting your stuff together, I think we might be about done. I've got some more calls to make, but I want to interview Gerkin. He's in Ohio. I talked with police up there, and the sergeant I was talking to got quiet when I mentioned his name. He wouldn't say anything specific, but the word *pedophilia* came up a couple of times. His word."

9

WHOEVER FIGHTS MONSTERS

POCA AND SCOTT DEPOT

Geoff

I just didn't buy Gerkin as a suspect. The man sounded too… out of control to fit what we did know about the crime. I'd known bipolar people, both medicated and unmedicated, and without their meds, they could get awfully wound up. I'd heard lots of stories about nonstop talking jags and thousand-dollar credit-card charges, but none involved violence—at least not beyond throwing shoes and dropping half-naked coeds on porches. Everything about Gerkin indicated melodrama as much as violence. Cleaning his gun in front of his wife? Stabbing the ground in front of the trailer that he tried—and failed—to set on fire? Only the rape allegation spoke of real violence, and who knew if that actually happened. Maybe it didn't, and Gerkin said it in a twisted effort to impress his buddies.

But then, Hall was an experienced officer and knew how to spot suspects, how to rank them. He was one of the rare officers of his generation who could not only grapple with drunken bar fights but also handle the finer points of investigation.

Over time, Hall kept coming back to means, motive and opportunity as the three pillars of criminal investigation. Herron and Thrasher had the first one, certainly. They had the second one, maybe, in that they could have tried to get with the girls and something had gone wrong. Looking for action on a Sunday night seemed far-fetched, but Herron clearly had the potential for violence. He pulled the legs off cats and often body-slammed Kenny Cole. And they had the third one—sort of—in that Thrasher worked in the coeds' building and may have known them. But that was the closest tie they had to Mared and Karen.

Gerkin had the means, certainly, the machete and a gun. Opportunity was clear; he was on campus and left the rush party about 10:00 p.m., up the street from where the coeds were picked up. Motive wasn't really evident except for his generalized hatred of women. Means, yes; opportunity, yes; motive—none that I could see.

———•———

When I got home, I couldn't focus on my editing work. I turned to my collection of crime books and pulled out the first one I'd ever bought on the subject: *Whoever Fights Monsters: My Twenty Years Tracking Serial Killers for the FBI* by Robert Ressler. I'd bought it after attending a Ressler speech at WVU in the early 1990s.

The book recounted early attempts to apply psychological understandings to criminals and their crimes—serial killers, specifically—and includes descriptions of various crimes Ressler worked over the years. I idly flipped through, stopping to reread passages. The chapter on organized and disorganized murders caught my eye. In 1970, no effort had been made to look at the murders as organized or disorganized; the terms hadn't been invented yet.

An organized offender plans the crime, tends to bring with him the means of murder, likely knows the victim, however tenuously, and attempts to conceal incriminating evidence. An organized offender usually follows some internal script that has been part of his fantasy life since adolescence. A disorganized offender strikes impulsively at stranger-victims, uses whatever is at hand and makes no effort to conceal his crime.

Few crimes perfectly fit the categories; organized versus disorganized was not a hard-and-fast "rule" so much as a guideline. Here, I found something useful: Disorganized offenders leave bodies out, exposed, with no evident concern about getting caught. In the coed case, the bodies were hidden, suggesting a more organized offender.

And very quickly after that, this: "The organized offender often takes personal items belonging to his victims as trophies, or to deny the police the opportunity to identify the victim." Boots and coat. Crucifix on a chain and a necklace with a class ring. Trophies. Organized.

But most of what I read couldn't be correlated to our suspects at all: There was no way of knowing, fifty years after the fact, if the offender kept track of the investigation. No reports that any of them ever felt themselves "to be the smartest, most successful people to come down the pike," although Gerkin might have felt superior before his illness began to manifest, when he was a high-achieving student.

What Ressler had to say about identification of the bodies did strike me, though: "It may seem a very large step from wiping away fingerprints on the knife to *decapitating a body and burying the head in a different place from the torso*, but all these actions are in service of preventing identification of the victim and of the killer" (emphasis added). Hacker did this at least once. Herron, Thrasher and Gerkin were possibly capable of it but had never done anything like that—as far as we knew.

On balance, though, Hacker, Gerkin, Herron and Thrasher seemed more likely to be disorganized—caught up in the moment, impulsive— than organized. All four of them partially fit, or may have fit, the organized category, but only Hacker was known to have committed other, similar crimes. Nothing uncovered so far about Hacker, Gerkin or Herron and Thrasher indicated the crime was premeditated—except *maybe* Hacker— and what little information there was indicated the opposite.

The realization disappointed me. I wondered for the first time if Hall's investigation would ever bring resolution to the case. Maybe it was just too late, and too much time had passed to determine who killed Mared and Karen.

But Ressler's *Monsters* held one more revelation: the story of a man born in Pittsburgh, twenty-four years old in 1970, and tied to several murders with the bodies disposed in the woods. When he was arrested in 1985, investigators confiscated a cache of over twenty women's necklaces.

10

"THE INVESTIGATION'S OVER."

SCOTT DEPOT

Geoff

When I arrive at Hall's Scott Depot home, through the screen door I can see Hall at the dining room table, papers spread before him. He looks up and beckoned me in. He starts to rise, saying, "Coffee?"

"I'll get it." I set my satchel on the table and step over to the kitchen, take a mug from the cupboard. "I think I've stumbled across something."

"You listen to the interview?"

> *"The following is going to be an interview with William Ray Gerkin,"* the CD began.
>
> *I recognized Swiger's voice immediately. Hall was also there, as was Mark Rohrer, a BCI investigator in Ohio. The interview was in an assisted-living facility near Cleveland. After some rustling and footsteps, I could hear seven rapid knocks and, seconds later, a door opening.*
>
> *Swiger's voice again, polite, deferential: "Hello, there. Mr. Gerkin?"*
>
> *"Yes." The voice was higher pitched than I expected.*

"Several times." I join Hall in the dining room area.

"What did you think?"

"He's squirrelly, that's for sure. But that showed in the reports from 1970. Medication could be holding his bipolar in check, but it still shows. And he's probably paranoid. Maybe not clinically, but—"

"You sure you listened? He lied at least six times. His story kept changing."

"His thinking was disordered," I say. "He thought he was in school '65–'69. He was there '67–'71. It was forty years ago."

"He didn't want to admit that he was there when the girls were killed," Hall counters. "What about seeing Mared when he was bouncing? In Parkersburg."

> *"No. I was never a bouncer in Morgantown. I used to do it sometimes around Parkersburg. To help out, mostly, not so much as a regular thing."*
>
> *Hall: "So you were never a bouncer at the Castle in Morgantown?"*
>
> *"I remember the Castle. A lot of students went to the Castle. It was very popular. But I was never a bouncer there." Gerkin paused. "But you know, I do remember that one girl, the dark-haired one, coming to a club in Parkersburg when I was working. She used to come there a lot, I think."*

"Yeah. No way he saw her in a club in Parkersburg." Mared would never have driven three hours to drink some beer. I'm not sure what the misstatements mean, though: confusion or lies? My guess Gerkin probably *was* a bouncer at the Castle, but over the years all the bars and bouncing blended together in one big blur. Especially if he'd been self-medicating.

"He didn't want to tell us he lived in Morgantown. And that was before we said we were there to talk about the coeds. He knew it, though. He just didn't want to say. He knew how they died, too. Just didn't want to say."

> *"So you never knew these girls, had never heard of them?"*
>
> *"Never at all."*
>
> *"Do you remember how they were killed?"*
>
> *"I heard they were decapitated, but I don't know how they were killed."*

I lean forward: What had I missed?

"I wanted to see if you'd catch that," Hall says.

"He said the coeds were decapitated, but he didn't know how they died?"

"He knew they were decapitated after they died. How did he know that?"

I don't see how Hall can conclude that. To me, the most significant part of the interview is where he addresses the story he was alleged to have written.

Swiger began a new line of questioning. "Do you remember writing a term paper about people dueling?"

"No, I never wrote a paper about it."

"Did you ever write one about decapitation?"

"No."

"Don't remember writing that paper?"

"Never wrote anything about that."

"Okay. 'Cause we read in the reports there that somebody mentioned a paper you'd written that talked about people dueling and one of them got their heads cut off."

"That's ridiculous." Gerkin's laugh was a burst, not a signal of amusement but contempt. "I never wrote anything like that. In fact, I think all the time I was in college I only wrote one term paper and that was on John Locke and the American Way in political science—in English—yeah, in English 1."

"But I don't know," I say. "I don't think there was anything definitive."

"I do." He sighs and takes a drink of coffee. "But I don't think Danny does. I want to lay it all out for Marcia. She's the prosecuting attorney in Mon County."

"I know who she is. Listen, I'd be happy to pull together what we've got. You can look it over and correct it however you want. Before you send it, though, I should tell you what I found. A suspect we've never even looked at. Nobody's looked at him."

I tell Hall I stumbled across him in *Whoever Fights Monsters*.

"I've got that book," he says.

"He talks about a John Brennan Crutchley. In Florida. He picked up a hitchhiker and kept her captive for days. He was convicted for raping her and drinking her blood. Investigators tied him to several other victims, women found buried in the woods. He might have killed as many as thirty women."

"What's that got to do with this case?"

"He was born in Pittsburgh and was twenty-four in 1970. There's a lot about him on the web. They call him the Vampire Rapist. Apparently, some of his victims were found in the woods in southwestern Pennsylvania. A few miles north of Morgantown. Buried under sticks and leaves."

"That has nothing to do with us."

"Maybe, maybe not. It's worth a look. We should take the time to get this right."

"We've got our man."

"Probably we do, but... this Crutchley guy needs to be looked at. You don't know until you look."

I'm echoing what Swiger said to me when we searched that culvert, but I also know by now that one doesn't always know even when one *does* look.

"If you want to waste your time. This—" He taps the papers in front of him. "Gerkin's the guy."

Case closed.

———◆———

Based on Hall's corrections and additions, I prepared a Gerkin summary to send to Monongalia County's Prosecuting Attorney Marcia Ashdown. Some of what Hall wanted it to say conflicted with my memory and notes, but it went in anyway. I sent the resulting material to Hall for his approval.

But I also tried several times to persuade him that Crutchley needed to be a part of any investigation, but Hall would have none of it.

"I'm just saying we need to look," I said. "Nothing concrete, nothing proven. But we have to consider it."

"The investigation's over! I found the one who did it." Hall's mind was made up, and now he was shouting over the phone, dead set against it. His shout hung in the air. He *knew* who had killed Mared and Karen; the Shade Effect had prevailed after all.

"I can't do a book like that," I said after a moment.

"And you call yourself a writer. I made you a writer!"

Was he serious? We actually met when he took my writing course. I didn't know what to say, but I didn't get a chance to say anything. Hall clicked off abruptly, and that was our last conversation.

We exchanged a few short emails over the next year but never spoke again. I'm sure it was by email we made it official we were not working together anymore, and it was by email that I learned Prosecutor Ashdown declined to file on Gerkin. Apparently, she didn't think it was enough to bring charges, either.

Ashdown's refusal to prosecute ended Hall's hunt. As far as I was concerned, my work on the case was also over. I'd been shadowing Hall off and on for several years; I'd organized my life around the case but had little enthusiasm for the work anymore. I felt sour about how it had all gone south. It seemed sudden, at first, but the more I thought about it, the more I realized it had been a long time coming. I wasn't sure whether I was sorrier for Hall, who had not solved a case he considered so vital, or for me, the mystery of a lifetime left unresolved.

For the next couple of years, I found myself traveling to Morgantown more often. My stepmother's Alzheimer's was getting worse, and my parents could clearly use the help. As a writer-editor, I could work from anywhere, so in mid-July 2012, I moved up to Morgantown. My folks had a small carriage house over a detached garage. I could live there for a while, see how much help my parents actually needed.

The same month I moved to Morgantown, a local high school girl, Skylar Neese, was stabbed to death by her two best friends. I approached a local author about investigating the case with me. That effort turned into a book that came out in the summer of 2014. The project exhausted me. The emotional and physical toll of such a tragic event convinced me that I was finished with writing about crime.

THE VAMPIRE NEXT DOOR

Morgantown

I believed I was done searching for who had killed Mared and Karen. But in the downtime that followed the book on Skylar's murder, I found myself wondering again about the coed murders. How much of my preliminary information on Crutchley was accurate? Had I actually come close to accidentally finding their killer? I found myself searching the web casually, sometimes over morning coffee, out of a desire to move from Internet "information" to true information.

Crutchley received a sentence longer than recommended for the rape because Ressler testified passionately to what a dangerous man he was. As Ressler wrote in *Whoever Fights Monsters*, "John Crutchley was convicted only of kidnapping and rape, but I believed his actions to be extremely similar to those of an organized serial killer."

Crutchley was certainly capable of killing Mared and Karen—he had motive and, probably, means—but I had to find out more. On Websleuths, personal blogs and murder sites, I found suspected kills in Pennsylvania, Maryland and Virginia, bodies always found in the woods. Such entries were intriguing, but not reliable.

I did find a couple of things that, if true, tied Crutchley more closely to West Virginia: His father, William Frederick, was an executive at Consolidated Coal, a large company with widespread holdings. I'd heard about Consol all my life; in 1970, Consol owned Weirton Mine and much of the rural area south of Morgantown.

And I discovered an odd, anecdotal bit of information: According to one site, Crutchley claimed he learned to drink blood from a nurse in West Virginia in 1970. Again, interesting, but not reliable because it was from the web. I'd have to start with determining what—if anything—I'd read was true.

By the spring of 2015, without ever noticing it was happening, I had been fully drawn back into looking for who killed Mared and Karen. I again became obsessed. I sent a FOIA—Freedom of Information Act—request to the FBI, for all information they had about John Brennan Crutchley. Within a few weeks, I received a CD in the mail.

The key document was a letter from Sheriff Claude W. Miller of Brevard County, Florida—one page in the middle of almost 250. At that point, I knew—or *thought* I knew—a few specific things that made Crutchley a likely suspect:

- John Brennan Crutchley was a Pittsburgh native.
- He got his undergraduate degree in Ohio in 1970 or 1971 and his master's at George Washington in D.C.
- His marriage was falling apart in 1970.
- He was suspected of killing four women in Pennsylvania, one in Ohio, three in Maryland, a couple in Illinois and at least four in Florida.
- Many of the women he was suspected of killing he picked up hitchhiking.
- He may have dismembered several of his victims.
- He drank blood as part of an erotic ceremony.
- His mother was from Bridgeport, forty miles south of Morgantown.

Because of tight deadlines, newspaper articles often contain errors that are repeated over and over until they are accepted as facts. I learned this when I was shadowing Hall. Almost all articles reported that both Mared and Karen were nineteen years old, but when I checked their birthdates, I found that Mared was nineteen and Karen only eighteen. And the Internet made it worse, the reflection of errors infinitely bouncing back and forth, turning a small misstatement into something said so often it had to be true.

The reports I read about Crutchley were most likely a mix of the accurate and inaccurate. He was convicted of crimes against a single woman, but according to the web, he killed dozens of women in several states. Had the horror of what he had actually done encouraged overwrought speculation about what he *could have* done?

The geography of the case tugged at my intuition. Morgantown was at the center of a cross formed by Pittsburgh to the north, Bridgeport to the south, Maryland to the east and Ohio to the west. One didn't *have* to travel through Morgantown going from Ohio to Maryland, but one could, and to get to Bridgeport from any of the three states in 1970, one almost had to go through Morgantown.

When I started through the FOIA material, I was surprised that the FBI's interest was not murder, but espionage. Crutchley had been working as a computer programmer for several defense contractors since the 1970s and had even helped create the missile defense capability of the U.S. submarine fleet. Computer floppies found at Crutchley's home and office were forwarded to the FBI. Page after page, most heavily redacted, showed FBI attempts to decode and search the floppies.

The parts of the FOIA material that weren't redacted had paragraphs and paragraphs like this: "The subject is a sophisticated computer engineer… who hoarded a massive amount of material…most of which he had access to through his employment, or possibly developed through contact with friends, associates, and co-employees."

Despite the FBI's focus, there were occasional references to Crutchley's behavior and criminal activities. Crutchley was "a most bizarre individual," the FBI CD said, and "likely responsible for the deaths of several young women." But such statements were a tiny percentage of the material.

The Tampa office of the FBI noted that the "available evidence strongly supports a belief that the subject is in fact guilty of other crimes, and may be a serial killer, and with renewed interest by the local SAO, he may soon be indicted on additional murder charges in calendar year 1989." It further stated that "the primary thrust of the local inquiry regarding the captioned individual is still directed toward making a determination as to whether the subject was in fact a serial killer." So Crutchley had possibly murdered many times, as Swiger insisted Mared and Karen's killer must have done: "Whoever did this," as one report said of one murder that Crutchley was suspected of, "it wasn't the only time." Just like Danny said to me about this case.

I came across the letter from Sheriff Miller about halfway through the FOIA response. Centered at the top was a five-pointed star, the badge of the Florida Sheriff's Association: CLAUDE W. MILLER, with BREVARD COUNTY and 700 Park Avenue, Titusville, FL 32780 under it. The letter was to the FBI's research documents section:

> *Attention:* [redacted].
> *Re: John B. Crutchley.*

"Pursuant to our conversation of 12 June 1987," the letter began, going on to say that "this writer has forwarded under separate covers four sealed boxes via two separate submissions of documentary evidence." The sentence that jumped out was in the second paragraph: "John Crutchley has intimated killing numerous women by decapitation."

Damn. I had something.

Crutchley appeared to be the sort of man I was looking for, but then, so were Ted Bundy, Gerard Schaefer and maybe a dozen others. His connection to Morgantown was tenuous—his mother from nearby Bridgeport and he from Pittsburgh. I didn't have a clue where he was in January 1970.

This was where Hall's contacts had come in handy. He could probably have found out more just by calling the state police in the states Crutchley lived. I was just a meddling civilian; police don't think much of people like me. After a few more web searches, I found myself at a dead end, Crutchley just one more possible suspect in the parade of horribles.

That was when a web search turned up a book that came out in 2014: *The Vampire Next Door: The True Story of the Vampire Rapist* by someone named J.T. Hunter.

———◆———

My copy arrived in two days. I *hoped* the book would conclusively demonstrate that Crutchley was a viable suspect but suspected it would rule him out completely.

The book opened with prose that was long on atmosphere but entirely speculative, pages of Crutchley's supposed interior monologue about the all-consuming nature of his appetite. It was clearly meant to be atmospheric more than substantive. When the book did get down to specifics, I found more concrete information. The first story was about a woman the book called "Christina Almah." I'd already seen her referred to on the Web as "Laura Murphy." This was the case Crutchley was eventually prosecuted for.

Crutchley kidnapped Christina/Laura—a nineteen-year-old hitchhiker, similar to Mared and Karen—in late November 1985 and held her captive, repeatedly draining her blood and raping her. After the second night of her ordeal, he had a work meeting he couldn't miss and warned her not to try to escape because his brother, who was still in the house, would catch her and kill her. That rang a bell. According to Ressler in *Monsters*, Jerome Brudos, a serial killer in Oregon in 1968 and 1969, posed as an imaginary brother, "Ed," to convince a victim not to tell anyone what he had done ("Jerry's been in therapy.…This is going to set him back a lot. Please don't tell my parents or anyone about this."). I wondered if Crutchley knew about the case.

Despite having lost nearly half her blood, Christina/Laura escaped. She staggered down the street, bleeding from the abrasions she'd sustained crawling out the impossibly tiny bathroom window. As author Hunter unspooled the grim story of Christina's torture and heroic escape, he also revealed skeletons the Brevard County Sheriff's Office believed were Crutchley's Florida victims: four of them, two of those found next to each other and headless. Crutchley had not only killed before but also killed and decapitated two victims and put them in the same "grave." That stopped me: not just a crime similar to Mared and Karen, *the exact same crime*.

Step by step, the details of Crutchley's life firmed my hunch into a belief:

- He was born on October 1, 1946;
- He wasn't born in Pittsburgh, but in Clarksburg, West Virginia, forty minutes from Morgantown;
- His father, William Frederick, though originally British, moved to Clarksburg before he was married;
- His mother, Mildred Burnside, was from nearby Bridgeport;
- He was very bright, with an IQ of 168, according to *Vampire* (that sounded like an exaggeration to me—IQs as high as 168 are *extremely* rare—but he was smart enough to be a computer programmer in the early 1970s);
- His oldest sister, Donna June, was born in 1931 but died under mysterious circumstances in 1944, two years before John Brennan was born ("Mildred's desire for another daughter so consumed her that she raised JB as a girl for the first five years of his life," dressing him primarily in girls' clothes; I suspected that the reasons Mildred dressed Crutchley as a girl were more complex than simply her "desire for another daughter," but I didn't doubt that "Mildred's insistence on treating him like a girl caused JB considerable confusion during the years most influencing the formation of his identity");

- His brother, William "Sunny," was twelve years older and became a physician, graduating from WVU medical school in 1967;
- His sister Carolynn Adele was five years younger and eventually became a forensic psychiatrist—further illustrating Crutchley's pathologies was the author's assertion that John Brennan had an affair with her that began on the night of his graduation from college;
- His father was a vice president in 1969, and he and his wife traveled the country, looking for a place to build a house—did they have a house in Upper St. Clair that was occupied in 1970, or did they already have a place in Clarksburg, where both parents lived after traveling?

I wasn't even seventy pages into the book, and I was already thinking JBC apparently had the means and motive—did he have the opportunity? What was he doing in January 1970?

ONE EVENING IN DOWNTOWN Morgantown, I ran into Danny Swiger. He wasn't detailed to Cold Case any longer, but I told him what I'd found to see what he thought. My speculations made sense to him. Crutchley was worth looking into. I told him I planned to delve deeper into the book and confirm whatever I could using local records. He wanted me to let him know what I found.

12

"SOMEONE WAS WRITING *MY* BOOK."

Morgantown

Geoff

Fri, Sep 25, 2015, 10:01 AM

Lt. Swiger,

When we spoke, I mentioned that I had some interest in John Brennan Crutchley....You asked me to send you a note to tell what I learned.

Most of the following information comes from TVND, *email exchanges with Hunter, FOIA requests to the FBI, documents on file at Defiance College, land books in the Harrison County Courthouse, Polk's directories in the Clarksburg library, and newspaper morgues (specifically* Clarksburg Telegram *and the Morgantown papers in 1970) and other media reports I could find.*

TVND did not mention the coeds at all, and when I reached out to the author, he was unaware of the murders. I did what I could to verify information in the book and find more. By September 25, I had a detailed summary for Swiger.

> *He attended grad school in the DC area and afterwards worked for a variety of defense contractors, with high level government clearance....*

> *JBC had an active sex life with many, many partners over the years. He was alleged to have participated in swingers' parties, group sex, bondage, S&M, etc. There is some indication that he was linked to a sex club that met in southcentral PA throughout the '70s. He was married three times, his first marriage ending in early 1971, though his divorce wasn't final until 1973. His first wife, Maude Moats, alleged that he flew into rages and was abusive, but that seems to have changed after 1971; none of his later partners said he was abusive.*

In my note to Swiger, I wanted to make sure to highlight key details, including the decapitations, the similarity of victim disposal, the report by his cellmate that Crutchley had said he killed "prostitutes and hitchhikers" and that he favored nondescript white cars—like the one the coeds were seen getting into.

Most importantly, I found that in addition to means and motive Crutchley *did* have the opportunity. From the online records of Defiance College, which had only 1,100 students when Crutchley attended from 1967 to 1971, I found the college ran on a 4-1-4 calendar. The 1 referred to a one-month "special project period" in January, during which students were free to remain on campus or live elsewhere:

> *Students either pursue a special interest or do nothing for that month. The school yearbook lists the students and their special projects individually. JBC had special projects listed for each year* except 1970; *he was apparently not attending school the month the coeds were murdered. I think it's possible he went to his folks' house in Upper St. Clair, PA,* [forty minutes north of Morgantown] *while his folks were traveling the country searching for a place to settle and may have stayed there throughout January.*

In other words, Crutchley had the opportunity to kill the coeds. He didn't do a project for school, but he may have had his own "special project," one that he couldn't do at school.

I mentioned two facts I wanted Swiger to note: Crutchley fit the description of the dark-haired man who picked up Mared and Karen, and when he was arrested, police found over twenty women's necklaces, like the two Mared and Karen were missing.

Lastly, I told Swiger that in 1986, Crutchley and his lawyer attempted to strike a deal. He would plead guilty to murders in Florida, Ohio, North Carolina, Virginia and *West Virginia*. According to *TVND*, turf squabbles among Florida investigators led to Crutchley calling off the deal. I closed the long email with these words:

> *I know you're not working cold cases any more, Lt. Swiger, and you more than have your hands full. But if there's any way you—or some other trooper—could find time for this, I'd appreciate it. Obviously, you have access to many records I don't....*

> *If you don't have the time...please let me know, and I will try to figure out another route....*

> *In any event, thanks for your time,*

> *Geoff*

John Crutchley

John Brennan Crutchley in 1970.

> *Attached, please find a photo of JBC, taken in 1970.*

Swiger wrote back, quickly this time:

> *Mon, Sep 28, 2015, 10:30 AM*
> *Hi Geoff,*
> *Thank you for the information. I have to say that John Crutchley seems like a good suspect. He has connections to WV and committed similar crimes. As we discussed, I am covered up with my current position, but I will try to make some time to see if I have a contact in Brevard County.*

I was elated, as much for the validation as for the half-committal promise of help. It was encouraging that an actual professional investigator, trained police, believed that Crutchley was worth looking into.

———◆———

But six months later, the fire in my belly was going out again. Crutchley had the means, motive and opportunity, but despite more searching I hadn't

312

been able to find definitive proof. There were still some claims to follow up on, but it was clear that I needed help from the inside, from the police. But Swiger had not gotten back to me beyond a few polite responses.

In June, a friend tagged me in Facebook, as she always did when she saw a thread about the coed murders. The post laid out the whole story of the original crime, and the poster seemed to believe that Clawson's confession was fraudulent. The poster knew a whole lot more than most people. There was even information that appeared to come from sources I had seen but thought no one else had.

Shit. Someone was writing *my* book. I had to find out who and where they were located. If they were local, I wanted to meet and find out what they knew. And what they intended to do with their information.

I responded immediately, which is how I met Sarah James McLaughlin.

13

"BROKEN DOLLS."

Sarah dove into the story of the coed murders when she discovered the macabre tale while her fiancé was out of town. She devoured everything she could find about the crime and eventually posted the story as she knew it on Reddit. She showed the post to Kendall Perkinson, an experienced journalist and podcaster. The Reddit post also led to her meeting Geoff, whose own postings in the aughts informed her writeup. Sarah wasn't convinced by the theory that John Brennan Crutchley killed Mared and Karen, but the closer she looked at the new material Geoff provided the more appalled she became at how traumatic the 1970s were—especially for women.

A SPORTS BAR NEAR THE McLAUGHLIN HOME IN FAIRMONT

Sarah

A few weeks after our first dinner with Geoff, my fiancé Eric and I were sitting on tall chairs around a small table to escape a dreary, rainy evening. I still wasn't entirely sure I was going to help with this project. Research and write a book *and* help create a podcast?

"Geoff sent me some photos of the evidence." I swirled the ginger beer to mix it with my hard cider. Geoff had been trickling case materials to me in no apparent order.

Eric set down his IPA. "What kind of photos?"

I closed my eyes to recall the set of images: Mared's purse, a magazine cover, something blurry that looks like hair stuck to a rock, a bloody fur coat, a machete, two pair of striped pants and a ratty leather woman's shoe with a buckle. "The fur coat looks…its fur is matted in streaks on the back." I stopped abruptly. "Are you sick of hearing about this stuff? We can talk about something else."

Geoff and I brought different experience to our mutual obsession with the savage coed murders. A product of "urban" Morgantown, Geoff was eight years old and dimly aware when Mared and Karen were murdered. The coed murders became Morgantown's own cult mayhem, and for the first time, home was no longer a safe space. But for me, growing up in rural parts of the county, the monsters did not come from movies and books; the murders exemplified a constant threat of violence I'd grown up with.

In the rural parts of the county, we worried about mine explosions because we all had family working underground. We worried about car accidents where cell service was nonexistent. About drunken hunters shooting on properties they didn't have permission to be on. I remembered '92, when my friend told kids at school that she found an arm in her backyard after a mine explosion. In the city—which is how Morgantown and the more urban parts of the county looked to us—you get a quick response after you dial 9-1-1, but in the country, there are no city cops. You have to wait on the sheriff's department or state police to send a car. Sometimes it takes an hour, sometimes longer.

When I was ten, there was a rash of armed robberies around the county. I remember people talking in fearful tones about con artists knocking on doors, asking to use the phone for an emergency, then strong-arming their way in and robbing homeowners at gunpoint.

One night that winter my mother rushed into my bedroom, tugging my brother by the arm and carrying the .310 shotgun. There was a truck driver at the door asking to use the phone, and I needed to watch my four-year-old brother and stay very quiet. My mother placed the shotgun on my bed.

"If you hear anything bad outside this door, you aim that gun at whoever tries to get in here. Take care of your brother and stay quiet."

As Mom left and the door closed, I looked over at the gun. I looked down at my brother. A man's voice came from the living room, talking to my father. A fear rose up inside me, and I knew for the first time that if I had to defend my family, I'd absolutely kill another human being.

We were lucky that night—the trucker really had broken down and needed to use the phone. After the shotgun was no longer on my bed, the impression it left in the fabric of my comforter remained. While I stared at the embossed shape of a .310, I tried to come to terms with the idea that I had been prepared to end someone. This was deeper than the fear of outside predators preying on the weak, mingled as it was with the uneasiness of knowing I could be faced with that same situation again. As the kids say, shit got real.

Years later, while Eric left for two weeks to attend a wedding in Spain, I found myself with a lot of time on my hands. When I'm alone with no distractions, I tend to hyperfocus, this time on a vague memory of two girls whose heads were never found. I remember my parents telling me about this when I was young, but I also remembered them telling me about a man found decapitated in Cameron, in West Virginia's northern panhandle. I wanted to know if the two cases were related, so I became immersed in everything I could find online.

"No!" Eric said when I told him I could stop talking about the case. "I'm interested, too. Can you tell what kind of weapon was used? Were there cuts in the coat?"

"There are cuts, but it's not easy to tell in the pictures if the cuts are from a weapon or just being in the elements for four months. Geoff said that it's most likely a hatchet that was used on their necks, but it's not obvious to me from looking at the coat. At least not the pictures I saw."

"Was there a lot of blood on the coat?"

It felt so good to talk about the case. Even though I hadn't decided for sure, I couldn't hide how passionate I felt. If I wanted to know what happened so badly, countless others did, too. And I wanted to know.

I was riveted when Geoff sent me pictures of the disposal site. Already, my perspective changed. Newspaper descriptions had led me to believe the killer laid the bodies out ritualistically inside a tomb, but it wasn't a tomb, it was a brush pile. The bodies weren't carefully arranged in some weird funeral tribute; they were thrown away like broken dolls.

"There's not enough blood on the coat," I said in answer to Eric's question. "Were they already dead? I'm obviously not a forensics expert, but come on—shouldn't that thing be drenched?"

"So you think they were drained? Or they were cleaned up? What made the blood loss that minimal?"

"I don't know. Maybe I'm seeing something skewed in those pictures. I really want to see a copy of the autopsy report, too. I'm just speculating as one does after a beer or nine."

"Geoff was pretty steadfast on their clothes being…neat? Is that the right word? Mared had a pack of cigarettes still tucked in her waistband. Doesn't sound like someone put their clothes back on them."

"Maybe they were redressed, maybe not. That's the thing—what kind of person kills two girls, cuts their heads off and isn't interested in sexually assaulting them?"

Our waitress was walking toward us but suddenly changed her mind mid-stride and turned to another table. I shook my head and took a deep breath.

"What about Geoff's theory?" Eric asked. "You think he figured out the real killer?"

"He knows a lot. What do you think?"

"Such a non-answer!"

The reports Geoff had sent so far made me wonder about other people, other leads.

"I'm not so sure."

Geoff gave me his vampire theory the first night we met: John Brennen Crutchley, a possible serial killer born in West Virginia who had sex with his sister. Great. Just what West Virginia needed—more incest press. I didn't want the killer to be homegrown, but that's not the only reason I didn't like him for the crimes. Something about the possibility felt off. Two victims at the same time. It felt audacious, hinted at a confidence that comes from experience.

Some of the information Geoff used came from a book that made it hard to sort facts from claims made for shock value. If Geoff only looked for evidence that tied the case to a single suspect, he risked discounting everything that didn't fit. That was dangerous. I felt the only way to move the case in an additional direction was to move it myself. I had to get back to basics.

More than anything, I wanted to get to the bottom of the story. It was going to upset some, inconvenience others and keep my status as a party favorite, but I had to try. I had a feeling I was right where I was supposed to be—meeting Kendall and Geoff at almost the exact same time after obsessing about the case for months.

"I think you should tell him you'll do it," Eric said. "You won't be happy unless you take this as far as you possibly can."

What had my new obsession gotten me into?

14

"WOMEN IN MORGANTOWN WERE STILL VULNERABLE."

FAIRMONT

Sarah

I went into this project looking for answers: not just who killed Mared and Karen, but how and why they died. In a case as cold as the coed murders, I couldn't count on stumbling across new evidence. There was nothing new to test, no confession waiting to be corroborated. I could track people down, talk to them, maybe find out what secrets they'd been keeping for fifty years. Sometimes, we keep secrets only as long as someone we fear is alive. I'd have to draw on every resource and database I had access to, including microfilm in local libraries, digital news archives, campus-accessible data banks, genealogy sites and the Freedom of Information Act. Anything new, I'd have to suss out.

I had to dig and couldn't rule anything out. I needed to look at every single suspect, then and now, and work backward by collecting as much personal information as possible. I saw it all with fresh eyes. I might tie up the many loose ends that still wove through the case. If nothing else, I could sharpen the picture, clarify a blurry fifty-year-old snapshot. I was all in.

———•———

I collected last known addresses and phone numbers and, in some cases, dates of death. As I expected, my list of dormmates, witnesses, friends, family members and even suspects grew and grew. Each time I confirmed a person's death, a fleeting but sharp discouragement hit me. Nancy Best's death hit especially hard. I would never get clarification about Karen's cryptic demand she not be left alone. I felt an urgency to reach out to the remaining key players.

At first, I kept coming back to the disposal site. The graves were constructed with large stones, logs and brush. It could have been the work of a single strong man, but it would have taken hours. Dragging dead weight, placing the bodies under the fallen tree, dragging or flipping rocks over to the bodies, lifting the rocks to place them on top—it had to be exhausting. And all this after killing two women and removing their heads, late in the night after maybe being awake all day. It would certainly be faster to have a partner. The cops always disagreed whether it was one perpetrator or two. Was it two men making light work out of heavy lifting? Or was it one man taking a huge risk and getting away with it?

And there were a million ways to interpret every bit of evidence: The girls were found in a rural area only known to locals. The killer must be a local, right? How else would he have known about that spot? However, it was just as likely that he *wasn't* a local and he drove around until he found a pull-off area. He didn't need *that* place; he needed *a* place.

I was familiar with what the public knew from newspapers and local talk, but the closer I looked, the more of the inside story I learned, the more horror I felt. The Morgantown we civilians see is not like the one revealed in police reports. I imagined the murders shook the community into safeguarding its young women by working to prevent further victims. I wanted to believe that some good grew out of something so awful. I wanted to feel safer, but the truth was, this story was bigger than just one tragedy.

Morgantown is a sleepy college town with an underside that is deliberately hidden, but in 1970, it was much worse than I had ever imagined. Police records indicated a regular assortment of harassment, stalking and assaults: Coeds were threatened with near-abductions and deadly weapons—*weekly*. Young women fighting off stranger danger, trying not to get pulled into cars, trucks, and vans. It wasn't just public streets exposing them to danger. Young women endured humiliation at the hands of exhibitionists, break-ins occurred regularly: in their own apartments, inside campus buildings like the Mountainlair and Wise Library. Where was the outrage? Where was the criticism? Certainly not in the *Morgantown Post* or the *Dominion-News*.

And as if the environment wasn't bad enough, the authorities lied about the case taking priority. From the very start, Morgantown police wrote off the disappearance. When it looked like the state police were finally giving the murders the proper attention, WVSP brass kicked the legs out from under the troopers. Not only were Mared and Karen denied justice, but the coeds coming forward to tell their own stories of victimization were left behind as well. State police identified a man who was exposing himself to hitchhiking students, but even after getting his description from several coeds and uncovering his violent past, they did not arrest him. Eradicating abandoned cars became priority number one.

Trooper Preston Gooden blew the whistle on his superiors for lying to victims' parents and hamstringing the investigation, and Superintendent Bonar put more effort into shutting Gooden up than he expended on solving the case. He ranted about Gooden's blow to morale but never addressed the blows dished out to all the young women who were neither served nor protected.

As for the community, even after Mared's and Karen's bodies proved they weren't runaways, the city blustered at civic meetings and nothing changed. Women still dealt with men grabbing at them in the street—in fact, it escalated. As reports of assault and battery rose, WVU pushed enrollment numbers higher than ever.

Newspapers never detailed the full cycle of arrest, arraignment and conviction of suspects they covered, and arrests trumpeted on the front page became quiet exonerations on page 7b. Three years after Mared and Karen's unresolved case lingered, a man pleaded guilty to twelve molestings. He was convicted in five cases out of the twelve, and in response, the system discarded a proposed five-year sentence in favor of fifteen days in jail and his pinkie promise to undergo psychiatric treatment. Less than a year later, the same man pleaded guilty to exposing himself to two high school girls.

Property was better protected by the law than women. The punishment for physical violation of a woman was less severe than one for graffiti. West Virginia University didn't care enough to keep lurking predators away from its students, and when students went missing, few alarms sounded. The coeds' education came at the cost of their freedom and safety. And most terrifying, no one seemed to take issue with that. Maybe it was only shocking that more women didn't turn up dead, and every interview reminded me of that.

Tracking people down after five decades proved difficult. Women were hardest, since each marriage changed their last names. And reaching out took its toll when a person *was* finally found. Some thought it distasteful to discuss and wanted the girls left in peace. Other messages were condescending, deeming our efforts inadequate and demanding more action. Often I sensed that people either regarded me as too nosy or not nosy enough, with little in between. The entire process became a series of emotional ups and downs.

After the first episodes of the podcast gained traction, we began to contact people we wanted to interview. We reached out to Ron Rittenhouse, the main photographer at the *Dominion-News* in 1970. We also began to exchange emails with a number of people who either worked on or were familiar with the background of the story. Valeena Beety, an assistant professor in WVU's law school, brought us up to speed on the West Virginia Innocence Project's deep dive into the 1981 conviction of Eugene Paul Clawson. We interviewed Kelly Ayers, a crime scene expert who taught in WVU's forensics program. Kelly also became personally interested in the case, and she hooked us up with a number of forensics experts, many of whom provided suggestions and still more connections.

We also started getting tips via our Mared and Karen Facebook page. For me, it highlighted what law enforcement must go through every time they set up a hotline for a case. So many people had something they wanted to share, whether it was when they found out or who they genuinely believed was the killer. They wanted to point us in the right direction.

It didn't stop with Facebook; people kept coming forward with tidbits of information in emails, phone calls and in person. I even got texts from friends: "[My mom] thinks her and my grandma saw them at Jimmy's Sunoco. The guy had 2 girls in the backseat and asked for directions to Weirton Mine Road." Many of those tips were helpful to the podcast and this book as we continued our research, but like investigators in 1970, most tips required effort and led nowhere.

Of course, I preferred when people came forward on their own. Hearing the community come together to work on solving a fifty-year-old murder case was exhilarating, but the flip side was hearing heartbreaking personal testimony. There was a lot of the latter. Women unloaded horrific anecdotes of sexual trauma, physical abuse and terrifying memories. As a picture of 1970s Morgantown came into focus, it seemed to be one of endless predators.

The anxiety drained me, emotionally. Speaking of the unspeakable. Making cold calls to strangers about morbid, heinous things that involved their family or friends: *I need to talk to you about the bodies found near your property* or *Do you think your brother is capable of murder?* A police officer, a licensed private investigator or even a reporter could make those calls with an air of legitimacy. I was none of those things and felt zero entitlement to information. What right did I have to request anything?

It got to the point where the apprehension of what might happen bothered me so much I saved the phone calls for high-anxiety days. One particular time driving home from work, I had a close call with black ice that almost sent me over a steep embankment. I kept the brake pedal to the floor for several minutes while I waited for a neighbor to return with a chain to tow me to safety. My front tires were precariously close to the edge. If I went over, there was no coming back. After the ordeal, in the safety of my own home, I downed shot after shot of rum until my hands stopped shaking from the adrenaline.

"Well," I thought, "might as well follow up that lead. This shit day can't possibly get any worse."

I picked up the phone and dialed the number, cracking my neck as it rang. "Hi, my name is Sarah James McLaughlin and I'm doing research for a book on the decapitation murders of Mared Malarik and Karen Ferrell that happened in Morgantown, 1970. Your number was passed on to me. Do you have a few minutes to talk with me about it?"

———— • ————

"Yes, That's him! Creepy…" Stephanie Aucremanne replied by email. I sent her a picture of Thomas Wesley Lantz from a 1962 newspaper, and she identified him as the one who picked up her and her friend Jeanne Claro in 1970.

At the time, she was a sophomore. Lantz asked if they were afraid he would rape them. "When he unzipped his jacket and then he started to, uh, unzip his fly, I grabbed Jeanne." She trailed off.

Stephanie and I had talked a couple of times before, and she was certain: "The state police never came to see me. It was straight FBI. Two FBI agents." After reporting the incident to her RA, she guessed it was a week to ten days before the FBI showed up to question her and Jeanne. "They wanted a description of the man, a description of the van. They wanted to know where we were picked up and where we ended up."

"Did they have you work with a sketch artist?"

"No."

"Where did they interview you?"

"There's an alley between…" She paused a moment, trying to remember the names. "It used to be women's and the one above it was Terrace Hall. And there was an alley for, like, service vehicles, and when you came to school you could bring your car in and drop your junk off and pull your car out and the next car came in. They came in two cars, and they interviewed us in separate cars."

"Do you remember their names?"

Stephanie laughed. "No, no! I am the world's worst when it comes to names anyway, so there's not a snowball's chance that I would ever remember their names." She never heard from the agents again. The FBI may not have been working the case, but if Stephanie's memory is accurate, they were monitoring it closely.

"That was the one and only time I ever hitchhiked."

"That was the only time?" I couldn't believe Stephanie's bad luck.

"It was the first time, and it was the last time." Lots of her friends hitched, but she was always too afraid. The only reason she hitched that time was to keep from missing an evening class. She doesn't remember how she made it to class after that ordeal.

"He had locked the doors," she continued. "Somehow, some way, I got that door open and I yanked [Jeanne]—back then there were no seatbelts—but I yanked her so hard, and we ran like hell. So whatever happened to him? Did he go to prison?"

"He did twenty-five days for assaulting a coed in '72. Twenty-five whole days."

"Well, hey, that stuff still happens today."

I described Lantz's notorious criminal career, from attacks in Morgantown to catfishing men in Ohio to getting out of prison in Texas. "He's seventy-nine, he'll be eighty this year and he's still living."

"Well, it's scary that we did get into a car with somebody that was so dangerous."

I couldn't agree more. It's one thing when police can't find a suspect, it's a completely different kind of wrong when they know exactly who he is, what a threat he poses, and yet leave him free to prey on young women.

It didn't end in 1970 for Stephanie. She returned to WVU in 1985 to complete her degree. "I was walking to the Creative Arts Center from the PRT, and a guy exposed himself in a car. So I told campus police." She even got the man's license plate. "I don't think they ever did anything to him. So it's the same old, same old. You've got sexual predators out there, and nobody's stopping them."

She made a point to tell all the women in her class, to warn them of the predator. "It was well known on campus. They all knew 'cause they lived there, but I commuted. They said, 'Oh, they'll never do anything. They never do anything.'"

Each time Stephanie was enrolled at WVU, she fell victim to a sexual predator. And each time she told authorities, nothing came of it. Even in 1985, fifteen years after a gruesome double murder, women in Morgantown were still vulnerable.

15

"THESE GUYS WERE VIOLENT AND ABUSIVE."

FAIRMONT

Sarah

One day a new message turned up on the Facebook page, yet again naming the Dafts. Members of the Daft family turned up often in WVSP's 1970 after-action reports. They first appeared when Trooper Preston Gooden took a call from a man who told Gooden he "took down a road in the Weirton Mine area" recently and stopped his car to clear some debris from the road. As he picked up beer bottles and other trash, a man of about fifty came by in a pickup. He got out to help clear the garbage and struck up a conversation.

The older man had a friend in the area who rented a cabin to some hippies. He said they had cleared out right after the bodies turned up and left in such a hurry they abandoned a practically new motorcycle in the garage. This friend wanted to sell the motorcycle for a profit, so he kept the details from the police.

Gooden thought he knew exactly the house the "hippies" had lived in—a half mile from the disposal site. Police referred to it as the "hippie cabin," and it sat on property owned by the Daft family in 1970.

Officers spoke to Virginia Daft about the filthy conditions left by the hippie squatters before she and her husband, Ivan, moved in. She showed them bullet holes in her cabinets and refrigerator and gave them several items the hippies left.

On one visit to the "hippie cabin," Gooden and Sheriff Joseph C. Janco questioned thirty-six-year-old Ivan Daft about the motorcycle. The cabin owner had assured Ivan no one lived there when Ivan agreed to rent the place, not long after he'd gotten out of prison in Ohio. Ivan cleared the house of wine bottles, pictures, books and pots and pans before moving in. He believed the hippies held several parties in the cabin while they squatted there and also abandoned the motorcycle in the garage.

Not long after, a woman stopped by and asked Ivan if she could take the motorcycle. He told her he didn't want to do anything with it until he checked with the sheriff's department. She told Ivan she planned to return for it later. One week later, he came home to find the motorcycle missing from the garage.

After Ivan admitted he "turned his family and friends loose and they had helped themselves" to whatever items they wanted, Gooden and Janco asked if his family could have taken the motorcycle. Ivan said they might have borrowed it, but no one had asked him permission to take it, so he assumed it was stolen.

The Daft family included Ivan's brother Kenneth James "Jimmy" Daft, age twenty-seven, and his cousin Dale Ralph Daft, age twenty-six, as well as several other brothers. The Dafts were a large family, and most grew up in the Weirton Mine area. When the officers probed Ivan about his brother and cousin, he admitted Jimmy "is capable of committing a crime of this type, but [I do] not think that he did," and Dale and Jimmy had "picked up hitchhikers in the Morgantown area previously." Jimmy hadn't owned a car since he got out of prison for breaking and entering and forgery, but Dale owned a light-colored Pontiac GTO with Maine tags. He'd lived in Maine until about three months earlier. He often lent his car to Jimmy.

Dale offered to let officers search his car, which they did. Police collected a small paperclip, a white comb, a bobby pin, hair and some Winston cigarette butts—which happened to match Mared's brand—to send to the CIB for blood and other forensic analysis.

———◆———

The Facebook message about the Dafts stated that the writer knew Dale and Jimmy, and she'd been a victim of theirs. She really believed they picked up and killed Mared and Karen. Amma was not her actual name, but that is what I'll call her.

I emailed Geoff to ask if he cared if I was the one to contact Amma to check out what she had to say. I felt it would be easier for her to talk to a woman when discussing personal sexual abuse. He advised me to double-check the incarceration dates of Ivan, Jimmy and Dale before talking to her. He wanted to make sure we knew the facts of what could have been possible. At this point, we weren't sure what was accurate memory, what was gossip and what fifty years had distorted.

Ivan and Jimmy were brothers, but Jimmy and Dale were double-first cousins. Ivan's release from prison in London, Ohio, took place in January 1970, but police reports indicated that he wasn't back in the Morgantown area until February. But both Jimmy and Dale roamed free after serving time for forgery and for breaking and entering.

Amma called me the same day I posted a note to her. It was clear she knew the entire Daft family pretty well. I furiously took notes when she detailed the abuse she endured from the Daft cousins. And the abuse of several other women. She described an incident between Dale and a young girl he picked up in his GTO. The girl said she told Dale's wife, "Your husband raped me," and that he'd slammed her face into the windshield before leaving her alone in the woods to walk home. Amma also described Jimmy and his wife, Judy, sitting in the living room of a fourteen-year-old girl's home, Judy pregnant and pleading with the girl and her parents that "it wasn't like him" to beat up a young girl like that. Judy asked if they could "give him another chance" and convinced them to drop the charges.

Her first encounter with Dale stood out. Dale, about twenty-nine at the time, picked up sixteen-year-old Amma in his GTO after seeing her walking down the road. In what she characterized as his MO, Dale was "accused many times of molesting young girls he picked up walking" and stressed that both Dafts "were violent and abusive to young women." She also said she "did post some concerns on the West Virginia state police website" but really did not think "anyone took it seriously."

Dale often drove her by the spot Mared and Karen were found, saying, "That's where it happened." He told her that's where he and his cousin Jimmy used to "park" with other girls they picked up. She said Jimmy's sister, Sheila, confessed to her that the night Mared and Karen disappeared, Jimmy and another Daft, either Ivan or Dale, showed up at Sheila's doorstep, covered in blood. They later burned their clothes "outside in a barrel just down the road from where the bodies were found." (Ivan, Jimmy and Dale were notorious for burning stolen copper wires in barrels.) She reckons that in this case, in addition to their bloody clothes, they burned the girls' heads.

Jimmy died in prison after a conviction of sexual abuse of a minor. Dale slowly died of diabetes after losing some appendages to the disease. There would be no contacting either of them. Sheila and Judy had passed away as well. Dale married three times that I could find, leaving the possibility of three living ex-wives. Both Jimmy and Dale had living siblings. I started gathering more possible contacts, adding them to the list, and tried reaching out to the family for comment, but no one would confirm or deny the rumors.

———◆———

Not all the Dafts were serial abusers of women and small-time criminals. I told one that I was writing about the coed murders, and he agreed to speak with me. He certainly didn't sound like a man in his seventies. He started off by telling me that the first thing the press got wrong was that Owl Creek Road was completely passable in 1970.

"You could take a car out there no problem?" I asked.

"Oh yeah. From one end to the other," he continued, pleasantly. "Where they found them girls—it used to be a house on that land." He described Consol Coal Company buying the lot and tearing down the house, which reminded me of something I'd learned that I had to share with Geoff. Mr. Daft went on to say that the house's porch was all that was left then and that the bodies were found in the field behind it.

"Were you ever afraid while living there?"

"No, but it was a heinous crime."

"Jimmy was a suspect at one point in time. Did you ever think that was a possibility?"

He was neither offended, nor did he shy away. "I don't think he could have or would have done that," he said, but admitted he was biased because Jimmy was his brother.

I asked him about the press referring to the area as a lover's lane. He explained that there was a dirt road to the left of Owl Creek that "parkers" would use for privacy. "Parkers was what we called 'em," he said. I asked if the parkers were just locals or if college kids wandered that far for a little secrecy. Locals only, he said, but there was a bad Peeping Tom problem in the area then, which dried up most of the risqué traffic. "Guys would go up there and spy on the parkers with binoculars."

I made notes about the binoculars, my writing splattered around the page, fast and sloppy. "Do you think the Peeping Toms had something to do with the murders?"

"There were rumors."

Speaking slowly, I asked, "Did anyone know who the Peeping Toms were?"

"Oh yes." He didn't pause for a second before rattling off names. We can't repeat all the names, but they were recognizable from my research and the police reports. One of the peepers used to wear camo and army clothes and hide in the woods. "Sometimes he'd jump out and scare me. He was good at hiding. He was the only thing that really scared me about those woods."

One of the pieces of the entire puzzle clicked into place and was later confirmed by another informant. In a WVSP report, one of the peepers was described by two people necking in a car as an unknown figure wearing camo, carrying binoculars and driving a green Jeep parked by the road: the "Mayor" of the Weirton Mine Section, Kenny Cole.

———◆———

Back in 1970, Ivan, Dale and Jimmy all agreed to take a polygraph regarding their testimony. Mitchell, one of the primary investigators, examined each man and deemed him truthful. They were moved from the active to the inactive suspects list. Geoff and I had no reason to conclude otherwise, but things I'd heard still nagged at me, suggested they had done the murders.

One source told me Jimmy thought the exam was a joke. Another deemed the results of a polygraph irrelevant when the subjects were notoriously comfortable with lying to police. This source said members of the Daft family were themselves convinced Jimmy and Dale killed the coeds.

16

"SOME KIND OF FOREST COVEN?"

Morgantown

Geoff

I always got there early to secure our usual table so I could nurse an ice tea until Sarah arrived. We met weekly to discuss progress, share discoveries and plan next steps. From the beginning, Sarah came across as capable and confident, far more methodical and organized than I was. One of Sarah's first contributions—made the first time we met—was her discovery that Carolynn, John Brennan's sister, was a freshman at WVU in 1970. I don't know how I missed that; it was right there in the newspaper caption. Originally, I brought Sarah on board impulsively, but her involvement forced me to up my game. All good.

After Sarah and I met, I'd begun corroborating the information I had on Crutchley. *The Vampire Next Door* was suggestive but needed to be verified. Plus, the book didn't tie Crutchley to any murders before 1978. Could he have been in Morgantown in January 1970? Could I find proof? I wondered if Mared or Karen knew his sister Carolynn. Karen wanted to be a psychiatrist, which Carolynn later became. Was there a connection? I wanted to interview all two thousand 1970 freshmen. Also, since I'd lived in Morgantown a long time, I knew a lot of people, and those people knew people. I started asking around to see what I could find out about the Crutchleys.

Sarah arrived right on time. She worked for one of WVU's nearby research organizations. Her days had a fair amount of flex but were much more regulated and constrained than mine. Our meetings happened around her schedule.

"Hey," she said, putting her satchel on a chair opposite me. She looked around, spotted our waitress on her way over. Sarah ordered an IPA and sat, while I pulled some papers out of my satchel.

"For you," I said and slid a stack of clipped papers over. An agenda for our meeting was on top, with miscellaneous other reports. Her habit of copying, scanning and uploading everything to a web folder was invaluable; as a podcast producer, Kendall could also check the folder, as could anyone else who might help out in the future.

"Another after-action report," I said, "but the best part is a bunch of interviews with Richard Werner and several people from the fourth floor. Like that. Donna June's death certificate's there, too."

Donna June Crutchley, John Brennan's older sister, died under mysterious circumstances at age thirteen, before he was born. Her death certificate cites the cause of death as being something she was given to prepare her for surgery to remove a foreign object from her bladder. Her older brother Sunny later said, "She went into convulsions. She was frightened to death for some reason or other." *TVND* claimed John Brennan believed she "died as the result of injuries inflicted while masturbating with the glass tube."

"I know your money's on Crutchley," Sarah said, "but I think it could be someone they ruled out in 1970 for whatever reason. I'll keep reaching out to people whose names are in the files. Maybe they were counted out because their handwriting didn't match the Triangle Letters. Maybe they passed a polygraph. The interviewing officer just 'didn't think' they had anything to do with it." She made quote marks in the air sarcastically.

I nodded. I wasn't as skeptical of the police as Sarah was, but that wasn't a reason not to be thorough. "Anything useful lately?"

Sarah, Kendall and I responded to the messages the podcast brought in. Sarah and I handled content questions or tips; Kendall fielded the comments that praised or criticized the podcast in general—mostly the former because the first four or five episodes had been well received so far.

"That Daft tip worked out well," she said. "But I found something else interesting. You know that cross or crucifix that you thought Mared had?"

I swigged my ice tea and peeked around for the waitress. "Yeah."

"It's more a religious medallion. Not a cross so much. That's from Shade's 1976 report. I've been finding out a lot of stuff. The '70s were even scarier than I thought."

"More tales of hitchhiking terror?"

"Endless. I don't know how the women who survived the '70s didn't all get PTSD. I suspect more did but just don't know it." She looked down, considering something. "Hey, did you say you were going to upload the autopsies to the folder?"

"I don't think I have them, just those summaries you've seen. Maybe Judge Clawges has them." Judge Clawges was a circuit court judge, and I'd known his law clerk, Kathie Foreman, since we were kids. She'd told me they had a stash of the materials that had been in the Clawson trials, and Judge Clawges gave us permission to search it.

"Maybe the autopsies will be in there," Sarah said. "Listen, there's something I keep forgetting to tell you. Crutchley's father didn't work for who you thought. I checked. Consolidated Natural Gas is not the same company as Consol Coal."

"Are you sure? I've heard about Consol Coal and Natural Gas all my life. They were the biggest thing going around here."

"That's Consolida*tion* Coal and Natural Gas. Consolida*ted* Natural Gas is a different company. Not nearly as big."

I assumed the bodies were found on land owned by the company Crutchley's father worked for. I'd been toying with the idea that leaving the bodies on Consol land was the ultimate "Fuck you!" to Daddy.

But Sarah was shaking her head. "It was just somewhere in the woods. A dark place in the woods. Would have been to Crutchley, that is. If it was someone else, who knows?"

"You still don't think it was him?"

"Maybe," she said, but shook her head at the same time.

"Why not?"

"He was all about the sex, and neither Mared nor Karen showed any signs of sex. Or sexual assault. At this point, I think there are others who are just as likely as Crutchley."

I stalled while I finished chewing. There could be someone we didn't know about, but I didn't think any of the ones we knew were near as likely. Serial killers have fantasies that they carry around for years. Not all the crimes fit their fantasies. It's like they keep trying until they get it right. To my thinking, the fact that they weren't raped only meant he didn't yet have experience making his crime fit the movie he played in his head. "Like who?"

"I'm thinking Hacker. He——"

"His murders were all rooted in love triangles."

"Maybe. The cops thought that at the time, but maybe they didn't look close enough." She drained her beer and looked around for the waitress, who seemed to have disappeared. "Here's the thing, besides that, I've been thinking about that copper plate."

"What about it?"

"What the hell is it? From some kind of forest coven or something?"

"Police never figured out what it was." Truth was, I thought it was irrelevant. It looked like it meant something, but it didn't. There is all kinds of junk in the woods, and the copper plate, while definitely a mystery, probably had nothing to do with the women's deaths. "There were a lot of people doing quasi-religious stuff in the '70s. I just assumed the copper plate was like that."

The plate looked like the mysticism common at the time: planetary and zodiac symbols, magic squares, Greek letters. And so on. The FBI were unable to translate or explain it, but again, it never hurt to be thorough. Maybe a real translation would turn up something I didn't see.

"Could be," she said. "Find any local connections to the Crutchleys?"

"A friend of mine is living with a woman whose best friend's father knew the Crutchleys. I hope to talk with him soon, but it's difficult. He's not well."

"Hear from Swiger?" She looked up as our waitress approached us.

"Not yet." I'd been reaching out to Danny for a while but still hadn't received a response other than a polite *not now*.

The waitress reappeared out of nowhere, ready to take our order. Sarah always got a lunch-sized gluten-free pizza. I always looked for something new and never found it. I began scanning the menu. "Go ahead and order. Talk slow."

———◆———

We went on like that for the next few months and worked on the podcast at the same time. The podcast story was tentatively broken into six or eight segments, the specifics of which were determined as various parties were interviewed. Sarah was knowledgeable about the local music scene and proposed most of the musical selections. As the experienced journalist, Kendall did the engineering and final edit of all the material.

For both the podcast and book, Sarah made cold calls and I talked to as many people as I could: podcast listeners with tips or memories, 1970 students I knew or found and all those they could refer me to. I listed all the relevant names we came across and kept it handy to ask people: *And did you know an April Morgan? Patricia Marchio—you might have known her as Patty or Trish.* I had photographs of some people and could email them when necessary.

When I sent yet another note to Danny and still didn't hear from him, I decided to look for James Wilt. Wilt was a private detective in 1978 when he was hired by the grandparents of Debbie Fitzjohn, a woman who was thought to be Crutchley's first victim. According to *The Vampire Next Door*, Wilt was originally from West Virginia, and he felt Crutchley responded well to that. Wilt had been working in law enforcement for twenty-eight years, some of that time with the Fairfax County Police Department. He'd tracked Crutchley for six years, trying to find direct evidence linking him to Debbie's disappearance, which eventually was confirmed as a murder when her remains were found. *TVND* said Wilt believed Crutchley committed the murder but could never find definitive proof.

Luckily, on Facebook only one James Wilt had visible data and was from West Virginia. And I found an interesting coincidence: He was born in Rainelle, near the tiny town of Quinwood, where Karen Ferrell was born. I messaged him—*I'd love to talk with you a little at your earliest convenience*—and told him briefly who I was and what I was doing, with care to mention where Karen was from.

Then I sat to reread the parts of *TVND* about Wilt, finding things I'd missed: He received training at the FBI Academy; he believed Fairfax County Police should have searched Crutchley's trailer, but they did not; he believed the investigation was not well run and that the commonwealth attorney should have indicted Crutchley after Debbie's Bible was found at his Malabar, Florida, home in 1985.

I was eager to speak to Wilt; an experienced investigator might be able to tell me if we were on the right track. Even though Crutchley's father worked for Consolidated Natural Gas rather than Consolidation Coal and Natural Gas, the investigation just might be on the right track.

17

"THEY SHOULD KNOW."

FAIRMONT

Sarah

I tracked him down after seeing his mother's name in a 1976 WVSP after-action report. The call made me more anxious than usual, because I assumed he'd disapprove of my invading his privacy.

"Hi, Tyrone. My name is Sarah James McLaughlin, and I'm doing some research for a book. I was wondering if you had a few minutes to talk."

"Research for a book for what?" He sounded mildly irritated that he had to ask.

"I'm looking into the murder of a girl in 1970 in West Virginia." There was a chance the abrupt invasion of privacy might burn the bridge before it was even built.

"I don't— I don't know if I really want to discuss that or not. I know who you're about to talk about."

I was taken aback and started to say, "You knew her?" but he cut me off.

"It's Karen Ferrell, isn't it?"

And just like that, it clicked into place: Tyrone knew about Karen. Tyrone knew about his *sister*.

"Yes, sir."

His tone went from mildly irritated to upset; I could hear anger and notes of deep hurt. "Are you sure you're writing a book?"

I thought he didn't trust me and expected him to hang up in the next ten seconds.

"Yes, sir," I promised, hoping he'd just hear me out. I heard him tell his wife, Edna, that she needed to hear the conversation because it was important to both of them. "Okay, would you mind talking to me about it?"

He put me on speaker and his voice blasted through the phone, sharp and stern: "Well, it's going to depend on what you're going to ask."

I told him again that a police report mentioned his mother. "Um…so… Karen was your sister?"

Another expectant pause. A far-away voice sounded like "Yeah." I couldn't tell if Edna was encouraging him to tell the truth or not, but he finally answered, almost reluctantly: "Yes."

"And she never knew?"

"Yes, she did know."

———◆———

Karen's story, already tragic as a life cut short, seemed more so if she died never knowing her brother, Tyrone Trujillo. Everything about the coed murders portrayed Karen as an only child. Tyrone learned of Karen from his mother in his teens. She couldn't afford to keep Karen; at times, she couldn't keep him either. Tyrone explained that his father wanted nothing to do with him or his sister and that while the Ferrells adopted Karen into a good home, he bounced from home to home until he was at least ten. He dismissed the difficulty as practicality: "Hard times, no money." Despite the way things ended with Karen, he still thought she had a better shot with the Ferrells than if she'd stayed with him, citing her college education and the love and stability she found with Bess and Richard.

His mother kept in contact with Bess Ferrell. Sometimes she and Tyrone or, later, Tyrone and Edna, visited Karen in Quinwood. He believed that if Karen were still alive, they'd have continued to build a better and stronger relationship. For reasons he was unsure of, Bess and his mother kept Tyrone and Karen's relationship a secret and allowed no one to know of Karen's parentage.

"No one else knew about me except her and her mother," Tyrone said, and told me he was surprised I'd found out about him.

Since Tyrone was never considered a part of Karen's family, he'd been left out of the loop with those in a position to know actual information. He'd only heard false rumors over the years. "I was told that the man who did this was put on parole and I was never notified—I would have gone against it."

I reassured him that Clawson died in prison, never granted parole. Tyrone's voice broke while he thanked me for letting him know; my heart sank because I also had to be honest about my feelings on Clawson's guilt. The real killer had gotten away with it.

Tyrone lived in pain and doubt for almost fifty years. He attended Karen's funeral without telling anyone who he was, and while there, he was misinformed that the person who killed her "was studying to be a doctor and that's why he did the procedure on her." He went on to describe the Mad Butcher of Oak Hill, West Virginia. A stranger conflating two stories mistakenly told Tyrone that the person who terrorized Fayette County in the early 1960s killed his sister. Tyrone had lived fifty years believing Clawson was the Mad Butcher—who was never actually caught—and that he'd been set free.

I wanted to somehow correct the heartbreaking rumors, and it all came tumbling out: the improbability the Mad Butcher had killed his sister, the facts surrounding Clawson's confession, the reasons we thought the confession was false. He didn't ask many questions.

"One thing I wanted to say about Karen that I know, she was a professional piano player," Tyrone told me. "She could play about anything." (According to Bess, Karen began playing before she was ten.)

Something Tyrone and Karen shared: They were both born in Quinwood. Their mother moved often, and by the time he and Karen met for the first time, he was traveling from Ohio. "She was always excited when I came down to see her. I could tell she was really happy to see me, I could tell that."

The first time the siblings met, he guessed Karen to be seven or eight years old, and the last time he saw her she was sixteen or seventeen.

"Did she talk about what she wanted to do after college?"

"I knew she was pursuing a career of being a psychologist, I do know that. She never did really say why, just that she wanted to do that."

"Did she ever meet her mother?"

"Oh yeah. When I first seen her, my mother was with me."

"Did she seem to get along with her? Did they seem to have a good time?"

"She seemed to. Seemed that way, anyhow, to me."

I thought about several people telling police that Karen hated her mother. That may or may not have been true, but it must have been so hard for her to accept that she was given away while Tyrone was not. Karen may not have hated Roberta but possibly believed she'd been thrown away.

Some pieces of Karen's story may forever remain a mystery, like how her biological mother met Bess and arranged Karen's adoption. Tyrone and Edna speculated that the families knew each other, and I believe that's a good guess about two families in a tiny town, but we don't really know for sure. Bess and Tyrone's mother kept in touch over the years. Bess knew where Karen's biological mother lived in 1976, because she told Trooper Don Shade and he put it in his report.

"My mom always liked the Ferrells," Tyrone said. "She said they were very good and religious people....Me and [Karen] always wandered off together and went walking, and we would talk about things, about her being a psychologist—just about different things. But we always—even when my wife went down with me—we always took off and went somewhere together."

At some point in the conversation, Tyrone stopped and asked, "You don't know who her father is, do you?"

I admitted I didn't, but ventured a guess. "Was it your dad—was it Mario?"

"That's it."

"So she was your full sister."

"Yes."

Tyrone's father abandoned him and his mother, and soon after, Roberta found herself pregnant with Karen. "I had a kind of rough life growing up. Karen didn't, Karen had a real good life." He was told Bess couldn't afford to keep him, too. He felt that though it was a shame they couldn't grow up together, Karen becoming a Ferrell opened up more opportunity for her.

As for keeping Tyrone a secret, he told me, "Mrs. Ferrell, she kept that between us and her." None of the people who knew Karen had any idea Tyrone existed, though some had heard rumors. "She kept that between my family and her family, so people would not know anything about it."

"Well, I think," I said cautiously, "I think we don't have to worry about that anymore."

"No, no, there's no reason to anymore. Right! I agree, 100 percent! They should know that I am her brother, and what my name is—she needs to be recognized with that—that she had a brother with that name."

As apprehensive as Tyrone was at the beginning of the phone call, he requested that I keep him posted on the book and left me with, "I'm glad you're telling the whole story...because she really deserved it, as far as I'm concerned."

18

"PROTECTION FROM ANYTHING."

CHICAGO AND FAIRMONT

Sarah

The week my now-husband, Eric, and I spent in Chicago started out in the upper seventies, but by Friday it was pelting down the sleet. We trudged from the L train to the Occult Bookstore. Neither of us packed for winter conditions, and it was a long slog through the ice and snow. We reached the store only thirty minutes before it closed.

We stamped on the brown rug just inside the door to knock the slush off. My soaked tennis shoes squished on the dark hardwood floor with each numb step. It was a small, narrow store. I gazed at the bookshelves lining the left wall with books, religious statues of deities, symbols, talismans, candles and altar pieces. Small benches displayed even more books on various rituals, love magic and dream interpretation. On the right sat a large blue counter with a cash register, and there stood an attractive woman, pale, with long, wavy red hair. To her left, a man was organizing books behind a glass display case. Aside from the four of us, the shop was empty.

I tried to take it all in for a minute to give the store's heat a little longer to ease the aching burn of my legs, plastered with wet denim. The woman behind the counter asked if we needed any help.

"I'm not sure if my hands work yet, but I was hoping to show you something on my phone and get your advice." I explained that I was researching a 1970 double murder and a copper plate with symbols that turned up in evidence. My fingers began to cooperate, but my cell signal did not.

"This is a very old building with lots of spiritual activity," the woman told me. "Most people have trouble using their phones in here."

"Is copper a common material for sigils?" I asked.

"In 1970? Oh yeah. Wouldn't you agree?" She was directing the question to the man organizing books.

He stepped closer to the counter. "Yeah. Copper, silver or gold, depending on what you're asking for. Copper is conductive, Venusian. Sometimes it's used in place of gold and silver because it works with most spells. Where was this plate found?"

Eric answered, "Morgantown, in northern West Virginia. About an hour and a half south of Pittsburgh."

"Was it buried?"

I shifted on my numb feet. "We don't know much about it, actually."

"Usually, something like that, you bury it after you burn it. Ashes to ashes. Sometimes you bury it at the base of a large tree to bind it."

Finally, the image fully loaded and I passed my phone to the woman. She and her coworker examined the image. They commented back and forth: *Could be a sigil, or an amulet…Looks like Buddha's eyes…Maybe Solomanic or Kabbalic gridwork…*

She handed the phone over and swept back a strand of red hair. "Could also be a Martial talisman."

I tucked the phone back into my hoodie pocket. "Martial?"

"Drawing on the strength of Mars—it's a twenty-five-square grid, so it draws power from the god of Mars. It's a magic square, maybe. Like the one on our door." She pointed. In the shape of a shield, a nine-square grid was painted in red under a crown. "All the numbers in the rows and columns add up to fifteen. It's for protection."

I turned around, my brow furrowed. "What's your opinion of this plate? Does it seem like this person knew what they were doing?"

"Oh yeah," she answered. "He knew what he was doing. Guess I shouldn't say he. *They*."

"There's something about it that strikes you as masculine?"

"I think so. Feels like it to me, anyway. Mars is a masculine god."

"Mmm…" Her coworker pursed his lips and his face scrunched in disagreement. "It could be female. I knew several women that used that type of scribing back then."

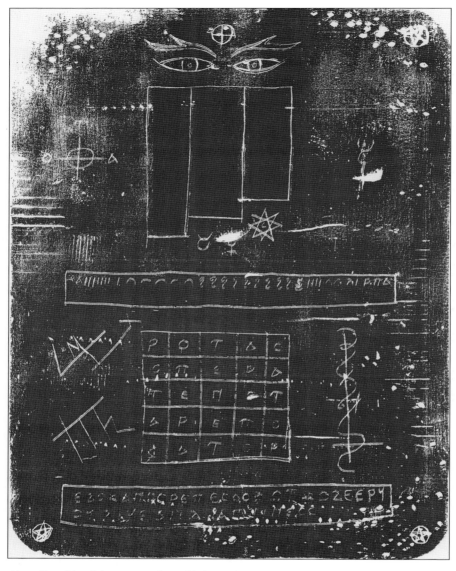

Above: One side of the copper plate with letters in three vertical rectangles redacted to maintain the anonymity of the person for whom the plate was made. *WVSP.*

Opposite, top: Sator Square, or Rotas Square. The earliest depiction was found in the Pompeii ruins. *Public domain.*

Opposite, middle: Closeup of Sator Square on copper plate. *Public domain.*

Opposite, bottom: Sator Square in Coptic. *Public domain.*

Back in West Virginia, determined to learn more about the plate, I began looking into sigils and amulets. The grid looked like a magic square but with letters instead of numerals. The only row that looked like a word

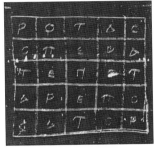

was *tenet*. Looking for magic squares with tenet added in the Boolean search brought up something a little more familiar. It had many names: the *sator-rotas square*, *sator square*, the *sator charm*.

Suddenly, I felt like an idiot. *Tenet* is a palindrome. It was used vertically and horizontally. How the hell did I miss that before? Taking a closer look, I realized the other rows and columns were anadromes.

But the acrostic wasn't in Latin like the sator square, it looked more like Greek. Turns out, it was actually Greek-Coptic.

However, the translation and origin of the sator square are debated. No one can say conclusively what it means or where it came from, but available sources agree that as a charm, it is most commonly used for protection. Protection from anything: fire, heartache, sickness, theft or even witchcraft.

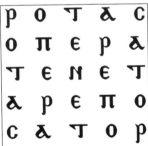

As for the rest of the plate, I reached out to the Julius Maximilian University of Würzburg's *The Coptic Magical Papyri: Vernacular Religion in Late Antique and Early Islamic Egypt* team to see if they would take a look at the plate and offer any insight. I hoped to get better results than the FBI did in 1970. I sent a quick message and crossed my fingers someone on the team would reply. The reply came more quickly than I expected:

> *Many thanks for your interesting message about the Coptic sator square found in 1970. I cannot guarantee if I can help, but if you send me the photo and further information about the context I may be able to give you some tentative answers, or pass you onto someone able to better help you.*

Boom! The message came from Dr. Raymond Korshi Dosoo, the junior team leader of the project. He had an impressive vita that included lecturing at the University of Strasbourg in France. I was excited. For the first time in fifty years, finally an expert could evaluate the mystical talisman found in the woods. From his résumé it appeared that if anyone could make sense of the plate, it was Dr. Dosoo. I sent a Xeroxed copy of the plate and waited for his reply.

19

"THE FERRELL GIRL PROBABLY WOULD HAVE FROZE."

Morgantown

Geoff

I didn't hear from Wilt right away. Pretty sure the James Wilt on Facebook was the right man, I told myself he rarely used Facebook or maybe he "wasn't around" anymore. Facebook was pretty lax about removing pages after people passed. Since Sarah and Eric were out of town, there wasn't much else I could do.

Then abruptly and to my surprise, I heard from Swiger. He supplied an email address of a man who retired from the Brevard County Sheriff's Department, the man I had read much about in *TVND*, Robert Leatherow, the lead investigator from the Crutchley case.

January 10, 2018

Mr. Leatherow,

Danny Swiger emailed me this morning that you would be willing to speak about the possible connection of J.B. Crutchley to the 1970 decapitation-murders of two West Virginia University coeds here in Morgantown. I have attached a summary of the circumstantial case so far so you can familiarize yourself.

First, I outlined the coed murders and told him where I'd gathered my information, ending with a list of the most significant findings so far; I still had twelve main reasons to believe John Brennan Crutchley had killed them:

- William Frederick Crutchley Jr., JBC's older brother, graduated from WVU med school in 1967.
- Carolynn Crutchley, JBC's younger sister, was a freshman at WVU in 1970.
- JBC began to attend Defiance College in northern Ohio in 1967. DC has a 4-1-4 calendar, the 1 referring to a month-long special project period in January. JBC had special projects listed every year *except* 1970—the month the coeds were murdered.
- JBC claimed he chose victims of opportunity, ones that wouldn't connect to him, like prostitutes and hitchhikers—like the coeds.
- When he was arrested in 1985, JBC had a small white car from which he had removed all exterior decals and labels. The car fit the description of the car the coeds were kidnapped in, and JBC said he used "nondescript" white cars to pick up his victims.
- By the '80s, JBC had bleached his hair blond, but earlier in life he had dark hair, as witnesses Lewis and Burns reported of the driver who picked up Malarik and Ferrell.
- JBC said that corpses should be disposed of in more than one place. He often decapitated his victims—like the coeds—and sometimes dismembered them.
- JBC said victims' belongings should be scattered to confuse attempts to identify them or build a case—which is what happened in the coed case. Sixteen items were found in seven different places over four square miles, not including items found at the disposal site, and twelve more items found about ten miles south of that—all the items with clear ID indication.
- Patrick Dontell, JBC's cellmate, and Joe Mitchell, JBC's lawyer, separately said JBC told them his first kill was in 1969 while he was at Defiance. Official investigators and our own search have found no evidence of anyone being killed or "helped to die" in or near Defiance in 1969.
- JBC said he was introduced to consuming human blood by a nurse from West Virginia. One notable element of M&K's disposal site is the lack of blood on the clothes or around the site.

- Karen's high school class ring hung from a chain, and Mared wore a necklace with a religious medallion of some kind; neither necklace was found in either girl's room or at the disposal site. JBC had over twenty women's necklaces when he was arrested.
- Dontell and Mitchell said Crutchley told them about murders in Ohio, Pennsylvania, Virginia and *West Virginia*. JBC was never tied to a murder in West Virginia, but he said he'd killed there.

When I sent the summary to Leatherow, I could not—yet—offer any direct evidence. Everything was circumstantial. I knew that circumstantial evidence is nothing to dismiss offhand, as people often do; even with modern forensic science, indictments and convictions often rely on circumstantial evidence alone. Especially in crimes of murder.

Still, we didn't yet have enough to be sure.

The next day, I was surprised when I heard back from Wilt. After some email correspondence, I sent him the same summary of the coed case I'd sent to Bob Leatherow. He doubted he would be much help, but I couldn't yet tell if that was because he wasn't forthcoming or he genuinely didn't have much to tell.

I knew the general outline of Wilt's career in law enforcement. I also knew he was a polygrapher, but I didn't realize how extensive his experience was. Based in the Washington, D.C. area, he worked, as he said, many, many "big cases," like the polygraph on Paula Jones during the Bill Clinton investigation, on the U.S. attorney general and so on. "Once you do a big case," he said, "they all want you and they're willing to pay."

Jim Wilt was clearly the real deal.

He talked to Crutchley a number of times in 1978 and after, and was convinced Crutchley was a "killer." That was the word he used. Wilt was hired by Milda Fitzjohn, Debbie's grandmother, and the police were following him because he had determined Crutchley was the last person to see Fitzjohn. He told me the police "were already on the outs with the grandmother because they told her, 'Don't worry about it. She's an adult. She can go when she wants to.'" That didn't sit right with Milda. She went to the bar Debbie visited the night she disappeared, and "there was the girl's car, still sitting there." Milda didn't believe the Fairfax police were doing a thorough job.

Wilt and I got on well, and our conversation wandered from the 1978 Fitzjohn case to the coed case to life in West Virginia. He was eighty-three and having some minor health problems, but he was sharp and focused.

He said it sounded like there was a strong argument for Crutchley having killed the coeds. "I think you're right on target. Of course, the deal is how do you prove it?"

"We'd like to see the necklaces Crutchley had when he was arrested."

"I'll bet you that sucker...that was part of his deal was to get those necklaces as remembrances."

I also asked if he thought Crutchley would have any trouble controlling two victims at once. He first spoke of how smart Crutchley was. "He could have easily handled them, especially if he had a gun." Besides, Wilt felt that people in West Virginia were easily frightened, especially girls. "The Ferrell girl probably would have froze."

We didn't set up a definite time to speak again because he wanted to get his notes from the attic and go over them before we talked again. He left me with, "I think you're well on the right track on this case. Keep in touch with me and keep me informed."

20

"I CAN'T BELIEVE IT LEADS TO SOMEONE."

FAIRMONT

Sarah

I didn't expect a reply for a week, maybe two, but Dr. Dosoo responded right away:

> *This is a very strange case. I'm on holiday right now…but I'll try to follow it up over the next few weeks. In the meantime, I've made a few preliminary observations which I give below.*
>
> *As you observe, the sator-square is upside down, compared to its classical form—in an ancient text this would not necessarily be significant, but since this is clearly modern, it may be. I am not sure whether the writing is best characterised as Greek or Coptic.*

He went on in the detailed letter about the design of the plate, its materials ("Metal tablets in ancient magic are best known from curse tablets, in which the name of people to be cursed are written on lead and buried") and its contents. His analysis, though as yet incomplete, did reach a few conclusions: "This could indicate that the ritual was carried out when Venus was in Taurus, which does not seem to have occurred until Friday 3rd April in 1970; this in turn would indicate that the plaque was created several months after the murders."

We were still unclear about why the copper plate was in the case file and speculated that the plate was found in the woods near the bodies. Dr. Dosoo suggested it was created *after* the murders. The copper plate may not have anything directly to do with the murders, but it could be a key piece in a larger puzzle. He discussed at length whether the letters on the plate might be—most likely—Greek or Coptic. As he translated, he came to believe that the plate was inscribed by a person who did not know either language: "My impression is that the person who wrote out this object had never formally studied Coptic or Greek, but were working from a printed alphabet, leading to strange letterforms and transliteration choices." He "used the alphabets to transliterate English phrases." And that was Dr. Dosoo's most important finding:

> *I cannot give you a definitive solution for now, but I suspect that the tablet is a love spell either created by, or targeting, a woman whose name might be Deborah Cramer.*

Finally! Immediately, I began searching for Deborah Cramer, which yielded several results in West Virginia alone. But each time a West Virginian Deborah Cramer popped up in the vital records, her age put her at twenty to thirty years older than Mared or Karen. It wasn't impossible, but it seemed unlikely that a middle-aged married woman would be targeted for a love spell found in the woods. Just when I was about to call it a day, another email arrived in my inbox right after dinner.

> *I've just realised that* [this specific sequence] *is almost certainly…*
> *Millicent. The full name now seems to be Deborah Millicent Cramer.*
> *All the best,*
> *Korshi*

I felt the excitement rising again. It was hard not to scream with the rush of different emotions. I searched the name in Ancestry's database first.

At the first sign of results, a mantra popped into my head: *Holy fucking shit. Holy fucking shit. Holy fucking shit.* A Deborah Cramer was a high school senior in Monongalia County in 1969. The same year as Mared and Karen.

For the next few hours, the task of tracking down Debbie Cramer consumed me. I needed to know if she had ties to WVU or the Weirton Mine area. Finally, a break came through when a Debbie Kelley, living in

Tennessee, showed ties to the surname Cramer. She even maintained a current Facebook account, which said she was originally from Clarksburg. It also listed WVU as her education.

Holy fucking shit. Holy fucking shit. Holy fucking shit. I was absolutely sweating from the piling coincidences. Geoff hadn't seemed too enthusiastic when I told him what I'd first learned from Korshi, so I called Kendall and unloaded in a babbling diatribe how I contacted Korshi and what he'd translated and determined from the astrological symbols. "She's a real person. She graduated in nineteen-sixty-fucking-nine! She went to WVU!"

"What? There's too many coincidences here to rule his translations out. This is incredible!" It took a lot to blow Kendall's mind, and he seemed pretty mind blown.

"I tracked her name to a business with a phone number. I'm going to call her. I just never in a million years thought anything would translate from that plate into a full name. I'm reeling."

"Well, let me know what you find out. I can't believe it leads to someone who fits the bill so well. I hope it leads to something."

"Me too." I paused. "She might have no knowledge whatsoever about the plate."

21

"DANNY RAN THE JACKETS FOR DNA."

MORGANTOWN

Geoff

"You might actually succeed where the FBI couldn't," I said to Sarah during our first meeting in a few weeks. Sarah and I were now trying the Varsity Club, a small bar that served food near Sarah's office. Sarah had just told me about her initial success with the copper plate—or half of it. In the report, only one side of the plate was reproduced, and she wanted to get a look at the back side.

"We'll see what she says. *If* she says anything. I think I found her but maybe not. She might even have passed."

"Maybe," I said, finishing a bite of my cheesesteak. "So you're still not convinced Crutchley did it?"

"Turned out the Dafts weren't likely, but I just think something's off about your Crutchley theory." She picked at her salmon salad before going on. "It doesn't feel like a first. It took a long time to do that—decapitating them, carrying rocks from the stream, all that. That was a lot of work. Especially for one person."

"So you think there *were* two?"

"Maybe. A couple of things here. If it was his first, why would he risk doing something so elaborate and only a hundred yards from the road. Why wasn't he seen?"

"In that murder I covered a couple of years ago, the Skylar Neese murder, when we first went to see where they killed her, I had the same thought. It couldn't have happened here. It was too visible. The body was only a few feet off the road.

"Then one night I was out there with a film crew. They were doing a piece on the murder. My car was just like the one the murderers used, and they were filming b-roll, so they filmed me backing in, taking off. Over and over. We were out there three hours, and *not one car* passed. After that, I got why they weren't seen. Later, we heard from people who walked right past the spot for months and never knew her remains were there."

"Still…Dumping them. Carrying stones from the stream. All that. Why would he make it so complicated?"

"Maybe it wasn't just him."

"Now *you're* saying there were two. Like Herron and Thrasher? Or Crutchley and his sister?"

I shrugged. "Maybe Herron and Thrasher. Or maybe Carolynn was the third girl seen by the witness in Mineral Industries. But I'm not saying that necessarily. I was talking with Larry Herald—the other lead trooper back in the day, along with Gooden—and he wondered if Gerkin and Crutchley knew each other."

Sarah looked skeptical.

"That's what I thought, too. At first. But I started thinking. They were the same age and grew up twenty minutes down Route 50 from each other. They were both very smart, Gerkin aerospace engineering and Crutchley computer programming. They might have met at some event in Clarksburg or something."

"Is there any evidence they knew each other?"

"Not that I know of."

I didn't say anything more because I was wondering if Deborah Cramer and Carolynn Crutchley, who were about the same age, could have known each other.

———◆———

About then, I heard from Corporal Chris Berry of the WVSP. Berry was one of the lead investigators in the Skylar Neese case, and we'd spent quite a bit of time together. Now he asked if I wanted to meet him for beers to discuss the coed case: "I listened to the podcast, the episodes you all have out. I want to hear more about what you're doing."

Berry and I met over dinner and beers a week later. He told me the case had nagged him for years: "My dad told me about it, and you know, I heard more after I went to the Academy."

Berry grew up around here, mostly over in the western part of the county, the area Sarah was from, and the case was still talked about when he joined the WVSP. He always wondered if the case was solvable and wanted to hear what Sarah and I had learned, what we suspected. By the time I laid out why I suspected Crutchley, which hadn't yet really been in the podcast, he was clearly excited and began offering investigation directions.

"You say the sister's alive?" he said, the beer mug at his lips. "She needs to be questioned." He drained his beer.

"She's in Pennsylvania. Sarah and I talked about going up to see her."

"She won't be happy to see you." He seemed pleased by the prospect. I remembered his eagerness back in 2014 when he described the urge to "shake the trees, see what falls out" back when he and his partner were trying to find out what happened to Skylar.

"Listen," he said, "can you spend an afternoon at my house? I'll pull the files at the Morgantown Detachment, see what else we have. You can look at those while you bring me up to speed."

That was what I wanted to hear. "Name the day."

On the Sunday I drove out to his place, Chris guided me into the large living room/dining room/kitchen. He had the perfect counter on which to lay out case materials, a long stretch he had obviously cleared in preparation. He'd also set up a couple of whiteboards and markers. He waved at two banker's boxes filled with files.

"I brought the case files from the detachment. Been reading up. You definitely got something."

"So you think Crutchley could have killed the coeds?" I asked as we settled into the room.

"I don't know enough yet, but it would help if we could put him here, though."

"That's what we were thinking."

"We'll dig into those in a few," Chris said. "Why don't you talk me through it first?" He moved in front of the largest white board, uncapped a blue dry erase marker and drew a line straight down. He scrawled High St. beside it, crossed the line with another blue line to make a capital T with the words Willey St. "Now they were picked up where?"

For the next forty-five minutes, I talked him through the events of January 18, 1970. He asked questions, and I answered them. He might have felt it was all routine, but I felt like we were finally getting help from real investigators; maybe they could close the gap we'd been unable to bridge.

I went over the whole crime, step by step, and ended up with what was probably the last of what the killer had scattered.

"They found a pile of papers and stuff behind those storage sheds north of Grafton," I said. "The pile was seventy-five feet off the east side of 119. Kind of smooth and scooped out. Some scraggly trees. I guess it was an actual dump back in the day. I want to go down there with a metal detector. I think that stash might be, like, a memorial. Skulls might be there."

"Cadaver dogs might work better."

"They'd still hit fifty years later?" The possibility excited me. Dogs would obviously be better than a metal detector.

Chris shrugged. "Depends. Maybe try ground-pounding radar." He turned toward the evidence boxes he'd brought. "Looks like Danny ran the jackets for DNA. One came up positive."

That was news to me. "Those two jackets they found near Mared's glasses?"

He nodded. "The DNA was unidentified. There would have been a blood card when Crutchley was autopsied. I want to get that."

"Blood card?"

"At an autopsy, medical makes a blood sample. It's routine. We should be able to get DNA from that." Chris turned toward the evidence boxes, obviously thinking of something else. "Didn't visitors have to sign in at the Towers? A guest book or something."

"Used to. I don't know if they still do."

Chris waved his hand as if that didn't matter, and I realized it didn't.

"You said his sister lived in Towers 3, right? Maybe Brother came to visit. We should check if those sign-in sheets are still around."

I was used to kicking things around with Sarah, how we'd get to this as soon as possible, find out about that eventually. I was taken by surprise when Chris immediately poked out a number on his phone. "Here we go," he said.

He held the phone away from his face, on speaker. "Towers information desk." He thumbed speaker off and pulled the phone to his mouth. "Yeah, this is Corporal Chris Berry, with the West Virginia State Police."

He raised his eyebrows in a what-the-hell expression. I was thinking it really paid to be a trooper. I'd still be trying to explain who I was and why I was calling.

"Those sheets visitors sign in at," Chris said at last. "We're looking for some old copies."

He paused again, then said, "Nineteen-seventy." Pause. "Give me his number, please."

When the call was over, Chris handed me a piece of paper with a name and a phone number: "This guy's in charge of records. He'll be in the office tomorrow and might know where to look. I'm on duty tomorrow."

"I'll call," I said because that's what he wanted me to do.

Berry eventually went back to talking about rousting Carolynn Crutchley, maybe pressing her about what she knew about the murders of Mared and Karen. She was the only living person in Crutchley's orbit who might know something. If talking to her didn't turn up enough for a search warrant, maybe we could search her trash. "I'll talk to some PA guys, see what they know about her and her brother."

The case was no longer stalled, and we now—finally—had some input from actual law enforcement. A couple of days later, Chris called to tell me about Nick DeMedici, a childhood friend who had also long been fascinated by the case. Berry had nothing but praise for Nick's investigative skills. Nick was a Monongalia County deputy sheriff for nine years, first in patrol then investigation, where he spent three years as a detective. He was then selected by the WVSP to attend the first class of a new program designed for experienced law enforcement and spent three years with the WVSP. Maybe with the help of Chris and Nick, Leatherow and Wilt, we might finally break this case.

22

"SHE REACHED UP AND SHE GRABBED JOHN BY THE THROAT."

Morgantown

Geoff

Bob Leatherow and I had the first of several meandering conversations soon afterward. It lasted over an hour and a half; nothing new came up, but Bob was clearly interested, and his knowledge of the case against Crutchley was second to none. In an effort to establish rapport—and rein in my nerves—I spoke of Daniel Swiger, Danny, and how he had helped with the case off and on.

"He's got the connection with our chief of detectives," Leatherow said. "They went to the academy together. Dan and I talked, and he mentioned you, and I said, 'Well, have him call me.' Did you read that book we put out?"

"Of course, yeah. *The Vampire Next Door*. That's where I first came across your name. I first saw Crutchley's name in Ressler's book a few years before yours came out. I just didn't realize what I was reading."

"Bob Ressler was my mentor from the FBI Academy. I met him at Quantico when I was there for my training, and he came down here and we talked to John a couple times in prison."

I told Leatherow that the more specific details I learned about Crutchley, the more I thought he might have killed the coeds. Everything I'd found on the net showed me he was the kind of man who might have done it, but the book seemed a little sensationalized, possibly exaggerated in some parts. Maybe he could help me clear a few things up.

"You seem to be the main source for the book."

"Yeah, we collaborated. I got my attorney involved in it, and we put the book together."

"What you learned at the FBI Academy was helpful to the case?"

"I'd made supervisor up [in New Jersey] and put in for the academy. I met the chief deputy from the sheriff's department here, and they told me come on down, we need new people in homicide. I was here three or four months, and I walked into the Crutchley case."

He began to recount the events of that night, how he'd already been at the "big hospital down here" when a uniformed officer told him about a woman coming in who had been raped and drained of her blood. Leatherow began to interview her, and within "fifteen minutes all the bells started going off. I knew right away. I stopped my notes and had her moved into a private room. I called my supervisors."

He recommended the department obtain warrants to search Crutchley's house. "We sent our guys down [and] surrounded the house. In the woods, because it's a very wooded area where he was. The whole town [of Malabar] might have had a thousand people. It was all dirt roads."

Leatherow said Crutchley was affable at the beginning, insisting that the victim—who he called a "Manson girl"—consented. "He said she wanted it, sexual, rough and everything. Showed me the beaker that he drained the blood into, where he kept her, like that."

Crutchley went to jail, but he wasn't there long: "He got back out because he owned property and was an engineer, and he had a family."

Brevard County's investigation was much more thorough than WVSP's had been. Of course, it was 1985 instead of 1970. Leatherow knew who they were looking into and had resources; WVSP had neither.

"We had our dive teams go through all the ponds. I even got the U.S. Air Force involved, scanning the whole town. There was so much we did, it was unbelievable. I spent two and a half years on the case. We did the whole Crutchley case in 1988 again. To see if we missed anything. John threw his bodies along the bicycle path near the power lines. One Harris plant was out in the woods, and he worked in the main one downtown, but he had an office in the other place there, and that's where we found two bodies."

"Were the bodies always dismembered?"

"Basically, it was hard to tell because of the high animal activity. You know, down here, gators, hogs and everything." Florida law enforcement usually clears at least an acre when they find a body. "We clear out all the brush because we have to. Working homicide in New Jersey, a body would be in the woods for a few days before there was any bug activity. Down here, within two or three days, everything is in shambles."

The thorough searches of Crutchley's house and grounds followed every lead. They heard from his cellmate that "John had buried [one victim's] head out in his barn. And in '88 we redid the case, and I dug the whole property up. We got permission to tear the barn down, and the concrete floor, there was a hole dug out where there was fresh concrete. Just big enough to put a head in. And that's not only my assumption, we all thought that. We smashed the concrete up to look, we found nothing."

Leatherow has one main regret about the initial operation. "We made a mistake. One of the crime scene guys found his computer. [John] was an engineer at Harris, a computer whiz kid already. This is 1985, now. November 23. One of the crime scene guys mentioned that we should take that computer. They told me; I told my boss. I was willing to go back and write an addendum on the search warrant, but they said no, and that was our mistake. We got the computer about seven days later," a few days after Crutchley made bond. He had ample time to erase incriminating information and the skills to wipe it thoroughly.

"Did you ever go up to Fairfax?" I wanted to determine how far-reaching the investigation was.

"I called up there and asked for homicide. How many times you call someone, and you can't get 'em for a couple days? [A detective] answered the phone and I started talking, 'Hey, you know John Crutchley?' 'Oh yeah, he's a suspect in a murder up here.'"

"That would be Fitzjohn?"

"Yeah, yeah. So they flew down here and spent a couple days with us going over our case, and I flew up there, spent a couple days with them, and the strange thing that I found, as soon as I got out to the scene where Fitzjohn was found? It was right along the power lines. The only thing different was the foliage."

"You spent time in West Virginia, didn't you?"

Investigators received word that Crutchley "had mailed some stuff up to his mother in West Virginia. I flew up there [with Steve Donnally from the state attorney's office] and spent three weeks with the troopers up there. It was good to go up there and see where he came from. I found out about his sister that died, you know, at the hospital there before John was born. I found out when he was born his mother treated him like, uh, as a female until the other sister was born later on.

"We were hearing rumors. That the mother used to…There was a lot of sexual abuse at the house. We heard a lot of stories. Bob [Ressler] did a lot of that amplification for us."

The local post office told investigators when the package arrived, and Leatherow and the WVSP troopers tried to intercept it at William and Mildred Crutchley's house. Mildred tried to escape out the back with the package; two WVSP were there to intercept her.

Leatherow hadn't expected her to take off like that. "I expected a West Virginian, like a grandma, and at that time the old man didn't talk much. He was very sick, and his sister, the psychiatrist, she tried to sue me."

"She did?"

Carolynn Crutchley sued several parties, including Leatherow, over publicizing the revelation that she and her brother were having an affair that began on the night of his first wedding. (*TVND* says the affair began on the night of his graduation from Defiance College, but Leatherow said the affair began the night of John Brennan's first marriage.) Leatherow was well known for his thorough and extensive documentation, and his notes became part of the case and, therefore, public record. The *Miami Herald*, the *Centennial*, *Florida Today*—"all the big newspapers down there," as Leatherow described them—all published articles that cited the brother-sister relationship.

"And it started on his wedding night? Wow."

He laughed. "Bob Ressler was with me when we got that. Bob interviewed the sister. What she told [him] was that John and her, the sister, went to bed. Then we interviewed the wife and the reason they got divorced real quick was…he used to choke her out all the time. During sexual activity? And the one time, she reached up and she grabbed John by the throat and started choking him and John freaked out. They got divorced right after that."

I remembered one of the questions I wanted to ask: "The necklaces that were pictured in the book, do you all still have those?"

"Yes. I was going to mention that to you. They're in our evidence lockers. All the necklaces were there and that was about three years ago. We found a whole string of them in his walk-in bedroom closet. And that's another thing. He was going to run for council, and one of the crime scene guys went in there, and they called us in and said, 'Look at this. There's all kinds of phone wires.' So we called the phone company, they came in and found out that he was listening to all the people that were going to run for council. They were kinda shocked he could do all that."

"So he was a pretty smart guy."

"Oh, yeah, yeah, yeah." He paused. "His IQ was about 146, 148, something. He was a bright guy." That sounded more believable to me than an IQ of 168.

"So you think we might be on the mark? Crutchley might have killed the coeds?"

"When I read your thing, that was really impressive. I like the sister was going to West Virginia University. Dan said the crime scene was only about twenty miles away from the university, if I got that correct."

"About half that—ten miles."

"That's even better. Everything you sent me I like. I just wish I'd heard about this when I was up there."

"Yeah, but they thought they had the guy at the time you were here. No one would have thought to mention it. Now, as I understand it, Crutchley told some people his first victim was in Defiance. He said she wanted to die, and he just 'helped her' realize her dreams. We can't find anything, though. Sarah's pretty good at this, and she can't find any mention of unknown or unsolved cases there in the late '60s."

Leatherow had also come up negative on that: "We talked to Defiance but could never find anything."

I was glad to hear that. I was working off the theory that Crutchley lied in many ways to be able to brag without giving anything that would incriminate him. By all accounts, Crutchley savored manipulating people. Maybe his first victim was not *in* Defiance, but in West Virginia while he lived in Defiance, and she didn't *want* to die so much as *fear* she would die before she was twenty.

"One last thing," I said, remembering what Betty Jo Hypes said about the young man who looked "goofy" stalking her the day before Easter in 1970. "Did John have a goofy grin?"

"I thought he was a goofy-looking guy."

When I hung up it hit me: Maybe his first victim "wanted to die" the same way his hitchhiking Florida victim "wanted it."

23

"VERY SINISTER AND VERY DARK."

Fairmont

Sarah

The numbers I found for Ms. Cramer were no longer accurate. I decided to take it as a sign that I needed to learn more about the plate before we spoke. Korshi had limited time to focus on this new side project but sent me a PDF of Fred Gettings's *Dictionary of Occult, Hermetic, and Alchemic Sigils* to look through to identify the various glyphs on the plate. It was 406 pages.

Four unidentified symbols remained: the eyes and eyebrows/horns at the top and three symbols scratched into the plate on either side of the sator square. To me, the symbols on the left looked like rigid, connected initials—something high school students might scratch into a desk with a knife. Korshi agreed but urged me to look further. He sent the Xerox to some colleagues and came back with notes. These notes were usually just what the symbols *weren't*: They weren't Austin Osman Spare's sigils, and they didn't belong to Aleister Crowley, either, according to members of Ordo Templi Orientis, a group founded by Crowley and still in existence.

But sigils exist for everything from the planets to metals, even egg yolks and demons. It wasn't until page 169 that the first symbol fell into place, 𝘍𝘩 the sigil for Mephistophiel, according to Johann Scheible in 1848.

A quick search of "Mephistophiel" brought up an image of the demon in his friar form, surrounded by the three sigils flanking the sator square on the plate.

Illustration of the demon Mephistopheles in his friar form surrounded by his sigils, depicted in the 1849 grimoire by Johann Scheible. *Public domain.*

Why would a nineteen-year-old girl have her name scribed in metal with that of a Grand Duke of Hell? It was seriously time to track down Deborah Cramer.

———◆———

I sat on my porch, enjoying the calm, warm weather. Sometimes the traffic buzzed by too loudly to hear the conversation on the other end, but there was no better place to talk in the house and sustain a steady signal.

"I still can't hear you. Are you on mobile?" Debbie, however, came in crystal clear, even though her connection was last on the phone line in the middle of a 209-acre farm inside a five-thousand-acre game land.

"Yeah, I'm on mobile." I took a breath. "I'm asking if the police ever talked to you."

"The state police did, yeah."

"Did they take a plate from you?"

She sounded confused. "Did they take a *what* from me?"

"A plate? A copper plate?"

"No, that was given to me by a Michael Oscar McKee, and he had—he was into numerology and had made that. My dad confiscated it and turned it over to the police."

Michael Oscar McKee? Was this the Black Michael we'd heard owned an occult store and was questioned in 1970? I'd find out later, but right now, I needed to know if Debbie knew her name was on a plate with a powerful demon's: "Did you ever know what was on it?"

"No, I did not."

I explained how I found her, how Korshi found her name on the charm. Debbie didn't even know her name was scribed onto the thing. I asked if McKee designed the plate at her request.

"I was a very naïve, ignorant freshman, and I never went past freshman stage at WVU. And that's where I met him....He was trying to absorb me into his..." Debbie searched for the words. "He had a coven and he considered himself a warlock. And he lived with several other people and he would hold séances in the cemetery. The one cemetery that he frequented was about a block from where I lived with my parents. He would meet me at the [student] union center and try to talk me into coming over to his apartment where he would have coven meetings, satanic rituals, and I just didn't—it was too dark for me." The disgust carried in her voice. "It was sick."

The public often conflates witchcraft, Kabbalah, alchemy and Satanism, but they are four distinct schools of thought. The Christian tradition sees Mephistopheles as a devil, a minion of evil Lucifer, but others see Mephistopheles as more akin to a force in nature, neutral but present. But there was no need to go into that with Debbie.

"So he made up that copper plate, uh, and put in all the numerology because it actually had some of my future in it. But he never got to actually explain any of it to me because my dad confiscated it. And once Dad turned that plate over to the police, they came and interviewed me. And that was the end of that! There was no more contact with Mr. McKee."

I offered to show Debbie the plate and go through the translations with her. I emailed the Xerox to her and battled the poor connection to explain each identified portion. The line dropped, so I called again.

"Are you familiar with the demon Mephistopheles?"

"No. How is that spelled?"

I spelled the name out.

"Wow," came her response. Her voice sounded far away, and the silence that followed resonated like she was deep in thought as she processed the new information. After each detail was revealed about the demon, Debbie would answer in the same flat "wow" and get quiet again. Sometimes she would repeat it. "Wow."

"Did he ever mention that demo—"

"No."

"Because it's pretty hardcore."

"So was he!" Debbie let out a loud chuckle. "The common thread there, the opinion was, he was very sinister and dark."

Debbie and I discussed the different symbols, what each could mean when they had several meanings across religions and languages. The eyes at the top though, Debbie felt sure, were under antlers. She said McKee had "protrusions above his eyes that he thought were horns." She also believed that the sator square is backward to reverse it to "the dark side."

One of the things that came out during the discussion was where Debbie's mom worked: the geology department.

"Was that in the Mineral Industries Building?"

"It was, and so was the Geological Survey. It was on the fourth floor. That's where my dad worked. He worked one floor up from my mom."

The coincidences were stacking up. Debbie was a freshman at WVU, like Mared and Karen, and both her parents worked in the building beside where they got picked up. How many times did she cross paths with the victims without ever knowing it?

When Debbie left home, she hitchhiked her way to another state to start anew.

"Weren't you scared?"

"I had a companion with me, and he was armed."

Before the conversation ended, Debbie encouraged me to explore for further connections to the coed case. "Keep digging. Keep digging."

I located contact details for Michael Oscar McGee, and Geoff, Kendall and I all reached out to him for his side of the story but did not hear back by publication time.

———◆———

Geoff emailed me a copy of the notes about William Bernard Hacker he made after talking with Danny Swiger back in 2007. Geoff listed the dates and locations of unsolved beheadings that peppered the railroad tracks from 1921 up until 1952, when Hacker was imprisoned for murder. Like Geoff, I wondered if Hacker could have been one of America's first serial killers. WVSP investigators were suspicious of him back in 1970, but they never knew about this unsolved list of beheadings. I wondered what else could be found about this man.

Expanding on Geoff's list, I quickly found even more dismemberments and decapitations. The list grew to twenty-one murders—nineteen involved headless victims—between 1921 and 1952, plus the four after 1966. And still no similar murders between 1952 and 1965, when Hacker was incarcerated, or after 1978, when he was again incarcerated. Like Preston Gooden and Danny Swiger, I thought Hacker was well worth another look; I needed first to talk with witnesses at his 1971 trial.

24

"THE MURDERS LOOKED RITUALISTIC, SCRIPTED."

MORGANTOWN

Geoff

After the first conversation with Bob Leatherow, I sent him links to the podcast episodes we'd finished so far. The podcast had become a kind of calling card, proof that we were legitimate and serious. It wasn't as useful that way as Chris's WVSP corporal rank, but the thorough and well-produced podcast automatically garnered credibility. I also asked Bob if he would consider being interviewed for the podcast. He thought that would be fine, but he had to check with his lawyer first.

I met with Morgantown's Chief of Police Ed Preston about the possibility that old police records still existed, perhaps somewhere in the basement of the Public Safety Building. I hoped for an accounting of arrests, like those published in the newspapers. I wanted to see if John Brennan was ever arrested—or even questioned or ticketed—in Morgantown. Chief Preston was skeptical; he was certain such records no longer existed. Maybe somewhere in a retired officer's attic…

First Sergeant P.J. Scott checked AFIS and other law enforcement databases for us but had no luck. I again checked microfiches of the Morgantown, Clarksburg and Fairmont newspapers—yet one more time—to see if there was any mention of John Brennan or his sister Carolynn between December 1969 and April 15, 1970. Just like Gooden and Spitznogle suspected back in April 1970, I thought it possible that Crutchley, seeing that the remains of

Mared and Karen had not yet been found, decided to hunt at WVU again. Maybe he committed one or more of the attacks on women in March 1970. Maybe he was the "goofy-looking guy" who'd harassed Betty Jo Hypes on Easter weekend—she'd said the picture of Crutchley looked familiar.

I doubted the newspapers would pan out, though, and they didn't.

In the meantime, Chris was checking out a possible lead on Crutchley in Indiana. Chris and I had been talking about how Crutchley had taken a job in Indiana in 1973, and we realized that an internship Carolynn secured in the summer of 1973 was also in Indiana, about fifty miles from where he worked. At that time, Indiana authorities were working on two unsolved murders in the region, and those murders were still open cases. We realized we needed to learn more about them, on the unlikely chance that John Brennan or Carolynn could be linked to the murders.

It took a few days, but Chris was able to reach the detective in Indiana who was the lead on the case. After verifying that Chris was with the WVSP, the detective sent incident reports; unfortunately, reading the material convinced Chris and Nick, as well as me, that the murders showed no sign of being connected to Crutchley. Yet another dead end. But it cleared up the Indiana murders that had been attributed to Crutchley on the net.

Nick was required by his job as a regional manager for Defense in Depth, a commercial self-defense and shooting range, to travel regularly to Pittsburgh and other nearby branches. He took the opportunity to find the old Crutchley home in Upper St. Clair, just south of Pittsburgh, just to take a look. He found it easily. It was nestled in an upscale neighborhood, a low ranch-style house, unremarkable except for a single detail that surprised him. It was the kind of detail one only discovers by visiting a site.

"You gotta be shitting me," he muttered as he pulled out his cell and snapped a few pictures. Right behind the house was a stretch of high-tension powerlines—like the ones along which bodies tied to Crutchley were discovered in Florida and Virginia. Power lines were perfect: Crutchley could be assured that no excavations for new homes, no construction of factories or strip malls, would ever lead to the accidental unearthing of victims. Brilliant.

Crutchley moved there when he was about eleven, and his parents had the house until he was around twenty-five. Maybe those were the years he first thought that along powerlines would be a good place to dispose of bodies. After sending the pics to Chris, Sarah, Kendall and Geoff, Nick texted a suggestion: "Maybe the heads are here? I'll check a place that has cadaver dogs."

Since I read *The Vampire Next Door*, I'd been struck by an odd fact that Hunter reported. In 1985, Crutchley had several times referred to his victim as a "Manson girl." That seemed oddly out of place. In 1985, Manson had been in prison for a decade and a half. Why would John think of calling his victim a "Manson girl"?

When Crutchley was arrested, sheriff's deputies confiscated a book about John Wayne Gacy, a serial killer. I also knew that Crutchley secured his last victim by telling her not to try to escape because his brother was home and would surely catch her. This was similar to a tactic that Ressler reported having been employed by Jerome Brudos, a serial killer active in the late 1960s.

Crutchley may have made a habit of studying other serial killers. Articles about the Manson family began to appear in December 1969, about a month before Mared and Karen were killed, and dominated the news for months. Everyone was talking about Charlie Manson, his "Manson girls" and the murders. Charlie became a celebrity. If Ressler was right, if Leatherow and the Florida investigators were right, Crutchley had been fantasizing about killing since his early teens. Maybe all the press and attention that Charlie was getting pushed Crutchley into doing what he'd long imagined doing. Maybe that was why the term *Manson girl* was stuck so firmly in his mind that he still used it a decade and a half later.

George Castelle, the lawyer who examined the coed murders case for the West Virginia Supreme Court, said there was something ritualistic, something scripted. Since the time of Ressler and Douglas, law enforcement often said the same thing about serial murders. Serial murderers were propelled by fantasies they carry from the time they were very young. The murders often looked ritualistic, scripted.

It also occurred to me that because Karen's remains were so decayed—her tattered clothes "falling away"—was it truly possible to rule out rape or other sexual abuse? The belief that the coeds were "relatively unmolested" was based in the fact that Mared's body was dressed, her hose were neatly on her legs, her cigarettes tucked into the waistband of her skirt. But Karen was on top, her remains severely deteriorated. Was there even enough left to rule out sexual molestation?

I passed the question on to Nick, who had experience investigating death scenes where the victim was in an advanced state of decomposition. After looking again at the photographs from both the disposal site and those taken in the morgue, he had this assessment: "Based on these photographs I am very comfortable saying there is absolutely no definitive way to say

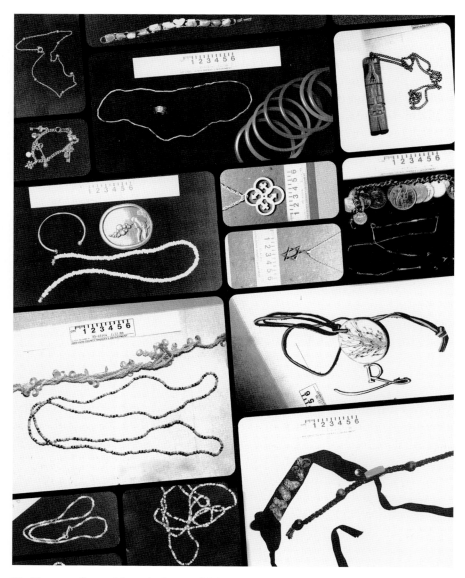

Necklaces confiscated from the home of John Brennan Crutchey during his 1985 arrest.
Photos courtesy of Brevard County, Florida, Sheriff's Department; collage by S. James McLaughlin.

that the human remains were, or were not, the victims of a sexual assault." Investigators Gooden and Herald reported in 1970 that Mared's stocking seams were straight, and Nick called this "the most telling piece of evidence to me. Even if they had been sexually assaulted at another location and told to dress themselves by the suspect, most likely her stocking seams wouldn't be straight. The cigarettes in the waistband could go either way for me, but straight stocking seams are pretty telling." He was saying that he didn't think Mared was sexually abused, but there was no way of telling if Karen was or not.

There was no reason to believe that both women suffered the same fate. Mared was a "fighter," as reported by many people who knew her. Many witnesses reported that Crutchley reacted intensely when events did not go his way; he was confident and had a hair-trigger temper in the early '70s. What if he proposed a three-way to them, and Mared objected, loudly. I imagined Crutchley slamming her face into the dashboard, as he did with the "Manson girl" he took captive in 1985.

Maybe a more or less "accidental" murder was followed by the rape of a petrified girl who most feared that she would be raped and killed before she turned twenty. And just like James Wilt suggested, she "froze."

———◆———

The wait for the photographs of the necklaces was longer than I expected; Leatherow had hinted that it might be. He still had some pull in the department, primarily through people he knew who were still active, but he had retired years earlier. He couldn't move too fast, and I certainly didn't want to push.

When the package finally arrived, the photographs exceeded my hopes: 8"x11" glossy photographs, high quality and crystal clear. Twenty-three in all.

But none of the necklaces belonged to Mared or Karen, as far as we could tell. One WVSP report spoke of Mared missing a "religious medallion." Since Mared was Catholic, we assumed it was a cross or crucifix. Crutchley's collection included many religious medallions, but none were Catholic.

25

"HE EITHER KILLED SOMEONE OR ROBBED A BANK."

FAIRMONT

Sarah

I knew tracking down Carl Kimble was optimistic at best. At ninety-five, Kimble might not even possess the faculties to talk, just like Hoover, who Kendall tracked to a Florida hospice, only to be told he was very ill, largely unresponsive. Even if Kimble enjoyed good health, he might just hang up. But if I didn't try, the story stayed hidden, possibly forever.

I tapped out his number. With my pen and pad ready, I closed my eyes and took a slow, deep breath. On the exhale, I hit send. No going back now. The ring told me the line was active. A young woman's voice greeted me after a few rings.

"My name is Sarah James McLaughlin, and I'm researching a crime that occurred in Morgantown in 1970. I'm trying to track down Carl Kimble to talk to him about it." I had written out the line so I didn't stumble or say something morbid like "decapitation" or "heads cut off."

"He's here. Just a minute." I guessed her voice belonged to a caretaker. Either that or a great-grandchild. The garbled sounds on the other end made me picture a woman holding the phone out as she explained loudly, "Something about researching a crime in Morgantown in 1970." I found out later Carl didn't want to take my call. He figured it was either another prank or just someone being nosy. He got it half right. The woman pushed the phone at him until he took it. He listened to my spiel before prodding, deadpan: "You mean those girls that got their heads cut off?"

I felt a surge of optimism. "Yes, sir."

He let out a small chuckle. I pushed on. "Do you remember Herbert Cobun?"

"Who?"

I spoke a little louder. "Herbert Cobun? He was murdered in December 1970—"

"Oh, that guy whose head was cut off?" I grinned in spite of the subject matter. *What bizarre thoughts were going through his companion's head right now?*

"Yes, sir. As I understand it, you knew Hacker, the man who did it."

Carl chuckled again. "Yeah, I knew Bill."

I struggled to keep up in my notes as Carl rattled off the tale of Bill Hacker as he knew it. He spoke fast. Faster than anyone I'd interviewed.

At age seventy-four, Hacker was a father, stepfather, great-grandfather, husband, lover and killer. He liked to drink, and he liked to travel. Driving from Baltimore, he bounced between Fairmont, where his wife lived; Moundsville, where his love interest lived; and Smoke Hole, where he liked to hunt and fish with his close friends.

Hacker lived in several places in West Virginia for most of his life but was born in Brooklyn, New York, sometime between 1890 and 1897—he never settled on the same year when filing paperwork—but most likely in 1896 or

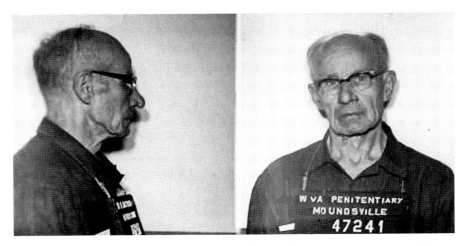

Mug shot of William Bernard Hacker, 1970. *West Virginia Division of Corrections and Rehabilitation.*

'97. He quit school after the first grade, and by the time he was ten years old, he was working in the mines in Monongah, West Virginia, to supplement the family income. When Hacker was about eleven, in 1907, he witnessed the aftermath of the massive Monongah Mines explosion, which left as many as five hundred men and boys dead.

He tried to avoid the draft in World War I by claiming he was the sole source of income for his family, but young Hacker found himself stationed on a submarine, although it's unknown whether he saw action. He came back from the war and rejoined the miners, eventually working his way up to foreman at Bethlehem No. 41, despite his violent temper. In 1925, yet another horror visited Hacker in the form of the Barrackville Mine Disaster, where he co-captained the mining rescue squad, pulling friends and coworkers out of the rubble.

The first clear account of Hacker's violent life resulting in murder happened in Wright's Tavern, known locally as the Bucket of Blood. There, Hacker found his girlfriend, forty-three-year-old divorcée Verna Nelson, on November 1, 1952.

———◆———

Verna sits in the booth by the jukebox. Her bony hands straighten the rumples in her skirt and blouse before patting her graying dark hair. Her face is pale as she stares vacantly at a beer bottle on the table. She's just gotten off her shift here at Wright's Tavern. Instead of heading home on this All Saints' Day, she plopped herself in the empty booth to sip a cold Schlitz to pass the time.

"He's gone, Verna." Owner Red West, standing next to her table, cranes his head toward the door. He turns back to her, his eyes lingering slightly on her powdered black eye. "Why don't you stay a while? You don't have to go home to that."

"He'll be back. He wants me to fix his supper." She slides her finger down the bottle between the edges of the label, leaving a glassy, brown trail in the condensation. "I told him to get his wife to do it and leave me the hell alone."

"He shoved you hard. You okay?"

Vera lightly massages her smarting arm. She's sure that by the next day, a deep purple bruise would blossom. "I'm fine. Henry pulled him off me." She gives a half smirk, glancing at the drunken garbage collector who's resumed drinking at the bar. "Good thing you opted not to let the cops take him outta here or Bill would have drug me out that door by my hair."

Red lets out a resigned whistle. "He gave ol' Bill a sweet smooch on the face, didn't he?"

"He'll be back. You know it, I know it." Verna slumps lower in her seat.

"Well, he oughta be too embarrassed. Betty and I'll make sure you get home safe."

The next hour goes by slowly. By the time the yellow cab pulls up outside, the bar is louder and busier and no one notices Bill peering through the glass of the door. In the booth across from Verna, Red and Betty now sit, listening to Henry as he stands, slightly swaying, between their table and Verna's. All four of them turn their heads when they hear a bellow.

"Who was the son of a bitch that hit me?" yells Hacker.

"I was," Henry says over the new quiet. "What are you going to do about it?" He squashes his cigarette in the ashtray on Red's table and straightens his shoulders. "I'll hit you again."

"Oh, no, you won't!" Bill edges closer until he's a few feet from Henry. His gnarled hand jerks out of his gray topcoat; patrons gasp and mutter as they spot his pistol. A young waitress ducks under the counter. Verna presses herself against the wall of the booth.

Bill points the Walther P38 at Henry, his arthritic finger on the trigger. It almost looks like a toy gun, the kind that shoots a "Bang!" flag.

"You won't hit anybody again!"

The loud pop from the gun is not toy-like and sends the entire room into a panic. Screams and scuffles erupt as Henry falls to the floor.

Verna's hands protectively fly out as though she's trying to push him away. "Please!" she screams. "Please, Bill! Don't shoot me!"

He regards her angrily, squeezes the trigger once more. The bullet zips between her fingers, jerking her head back as it cracks a hole above the center of her left eye, bursts out just above her left ear and lodges in the wall with a wet stamp of warm spray. Her head bounces off the booth, falls face-first onto the table. A quarter-sized hole oozes chunky red blood as the door swings closed behind Bill Hacker.

———◆———

Hacker was fifty-seven years old when he pleaded guilty to the murders and received two concurrent life sentences for his crimes. His incarceration in Moundsville prison lasted almost twelve years, until 1964, when Governor William Wallace Barron pardoned him right before Christmas for acts of bravery during a prison mining accident.

He was arrested again in Baltimore on Christmas Day 1970 at the residence of Ida Novak, where he rented a room, based on a tip from Carl Kimble's brother, who'd spotted Hacker on his land unexpectedly and called authorities. Ida had been a pen pal of Hacker's when he was in prison for the killings in the bar. Novak's brother, Brice Edward Warren, died trying to save others in a mine accident. She claimed Hacker "pulled her brother's broken body from a mine at Farmington" when the two worked together in mine rescue. In her gratitude, she offered him permanent shelter in her home.

———◆———

When Carl Kimble and Ricky, a teenage neighbor of his, came upon one of the gates on his brother's property on Christmas Eve 1970, someone had cut a small tree down to get past the chain. He saw Hacker in his car, sweating in the below-freezing weather. Hacker apologized about the chain, said he'd pay for it later, then took off. Carl went home and phoned his brother, Harlan, because Harlan knew Hacker much better than he did. Harlan and his wife had Hacker over to dinner a week earlier. Carl told Harlan how he saw Hacker by the busted gate and Harlan needed to check it out because the way he was sweating "he either killed someone or robbed a bank."

Harlan didn't believe anything was wrong. "You know Bill wouldn't do that," he told his brother, trying to get out of searching the property. Carl convinced him to go anyway, and after Harlan got past the downed tree, he noticed blood in the road. He still wasn't worried; in fact, he thought Hacker probably killed a deer. He followed the blood trail to a pile of brush. The pile was out of place, and he pulled some branches off to see what Hacker had been up to. He froze suddenly when he revealed a naked human leg. Shaking, Harlan tore back down the road toward his truck. He needed to find Carl.

"That was the only time I ever saw my brother scared," Carl told Sarah over the phone. "I asked him later what he'd have done if he'd seen Hacker on the mountain. He told me he'd have run him over with his car." Carl chuckled.

Harlan thought he uncovered a woman's leg. It wasn't until later that the police told them it was a naked man under all that brush. Hacker removed Cobun's clothes. "He cut them all down the side," Carl explained, even the shoes. He later realized that Cobun's head and clothes were in the car when Hacker talked to him earlier.

At ninety-five, the impression the entire ordeal left on Carl was seared into his memory. He blamed Bill Hacker for the untimely death of his first wife, Ellowene. He told Sarah that Hacker's "kin" made threats against his family around town; two men even attacked his brother at his service station. He said his brother "knocked 'em both down" and they left without bothering them again, but not before the rumors got to Ellowene that Bill Hacker had been released from the jail. Carl called the sheriff's department and asked if Hacker was still in custody, and a deputy confirmed that he was, but Ellowene was terrified until he took her down to the jail so she could see Hacker for herself. Ellowene's health deteriorated after the mutilated body turned up on the farm, and Carl said she never got over it. In January 1972, she died.

Once I had heard what Carl had to say, I decided to see if Geoff and Kendall were up for a trip to Pendleton County.

26

"A WHITE CAR AND A BOOT."

PENDLETON COUNTY, WEST VIRGINIA

Sarah

When the WVSP arrived to investigate the body hidden on the Kimbles' farm in 1970, the brush was taken off piece by piece to reveal a nude male, over the age of fifty. Not only was the body hidden in a shallow grave, but it also was cleanly decapitated, reminiscent of the coed case that took place 130 miles north of this new grave site.

That night, Carl told the cops he bet he knew where to find the heads and the clothes, but they coolly dismissed his offer. When the police couldn't find anything after two days, Carl and his son, John, started their own search to prove Carl knew what he was talking about. Hacker liked to camp at Eagle Rock, and they both knew exactly where. They searched the riverbanks of the South Branch of the Potomac for anything that washed up. Carl found a belt, a boot and a dollar bill. He kept looking. A hatchet lay on the shore, and pants—split up the sides—lay in the water. Convinced he found all the bank offered, he headed back to town with the evidence. He informed WVSP he planned to get a boat to search the other side, but they stopped him, told him they'd get the boat to search.

The next day, Corporal A.F. Humphrey of the state police, John Holloway of the Petersburg Volunteer Fire Department and John Kimble searched the opposite bank of the South Branch. John remembers being told to lift up a flat rock and thinking, "There's no way something fits under there," but he did as he was told and flipped it with a hoe. To his surprise, a patch of hair stuck out from the sand and gravel. Holloway leaned down and dug away with his gloved hands, pulling piles of silt from the hair. He reached into the hole and pulled Cobun's head out of the ground by its ears. John stared at the head in Holloway's hands. It didn't look real to him. The bullet hole was clean; there was no blood that he could see.

"We found it! We found the head!" Holloway called out.

Humphreys swirled around and saw the fireman handling the evidence. He pointed at the young man and roared, "You put that damned head back in the ground where you found it!"

Though the police and the prosecution built a strong case against Hacker, Carl's problems intensified. Hacker put the word out that he didn't want Carl testifying. Prosecuting Attorney George Sponaugle told Carl he couldn't force him to testify, but if he chose not to, there was a good chance Hacker walked away a free man. For the safety of his family, and the safety of anyone who ever landed the misfortune of crossing Hacker, Carl agreed to take the stand.

———◆———

About a week after meeting with Carl and the Kimbles, I received the transcript of *Hacker v. West Virginia* in the mail. Carl's account filled in most of the pieces, but the transcript added the gritty details of Hacker's downfall.

Betty Snyder testified first. She told the court she and Cobun dated for over two years. She described their last night together up until he dropped her off at her home. He told her, "I'll be back," but she never saw him again.

Hacker's defense tried to drag her through the mud, reminding the jury that she dated Cobun, a married man, and that she tried to incite rivalry between Cobun and Hacker. She explained that Cobun and his wife separated years ago and calmly denied anything beyond friendship with the accused.

Hacker's lawyers called her reputation into question, trying to prod her into admitting a relationship as far back as 1967. She countered that Hacker acted possessive of her and her teenage daughter, Bonnie. He showered them with gifts, even though neither she nor her daughter welcomed his gestures.

"Didn't he take you to your husband's grave site?" Attorney James E. Ansel challenged her during cross-examination.

"He took me to the grave site against my wishes. I didn't know where we were going. My children didn't even know where I was at." No matter how hard she fought, nobody, not even reporters, believed she was afraid of Hacker. She testified that he wanted to move into her home, take control of her life, but sadly, her testimony was given little credence. Even today, people don't remember her name but refer to her as "Hacker's girlfriend."

Carl told me that he spoke to Snyder in a witness room during the trial. He'd told Snyder that he worried he and Ricky might compel Hacker to get rid of them because they were witnesses. Snyder said that Hacker confided he considered killing both of them when they'd approached him at the gate. Up until that moment, Carl never really knew how close he'd come to becoming a murder victim himself.

During the remainder of the trial, the experts painted a picture of a seventy-four-year-old man getting into a scuffle with a man twenty-two years his junior. Hacker shot him in the head, then cut off his clothes before lopping his head off with an old hatchet and burying the body under leaves and brush. And Hacker did all this while wearing a dapper pinstripe suit.

In his own defense, Hacker took the stand. He casually described Snyder as an alcoholic with loose morals who barely kept a roof over her daughter's head. His gifts, he told the court, went toward taking care of Bonnie, because they lived in poverty and he felt compelled to help them. The day of the murder, he'd been awake for over thirty hours, binge-drinking whiskey and vodka the entire time. He fought with Cobun after the man disparaged Bonnie but blacked out and remembered nothing after the fight.

———◆———

John Kimble was twenty-three when Herbert Cobun's body was found. Geoff, Kendall and I talked with him when we visited Pendleton County to speak with all the Kimbles. And just like Carl, he was there when the dollar bill and the clothes were found. But unlike Carl, John was never questioned or asked to testify in court. John described how he helped search the sandy ground of the Potomac River bank.

"But also, the [night before]," John said, "when I was leaving Keyser and going back to my home in Smoke Hole, directly above where they found [Cobun's] head, I remember, very distinctly, I saw eyes—two eyes up there on that hill, exactly straight down from where the head was. It was dark, but I saw two eyes. I'm not making this up. The head was like [exactly] where I saw eyes that night. The head was buried under a rock, but I didn't know it at the time—that was the night before. The next day they found the head."

"Did you think that it was Hacker?" I prodded.

"No, it was like…"

Kendall clarified for him as he trailed off, "You think it was a disembodied head?"

"Right. Yeah. Or something like that. Somebody trying to tell me something. Intuition…something was trying to tell me [where] the head was."

"So, like an omen?" I asked.

"Yeah, like an omen. Mm-hmm…I got to thinking, after we found this head under a flat rock…but I'm thinking, who's going to look under a flat rock?"

I pointed out to him that Mared and Karen were found under rocks that had been dragged from a creek.

———◆———

A year after Cobun's death, reporters Ron Roat and Jon Hall traveled to the Moundsville Prison to see Hacker. Roat's name was up next on the waiting list—he submitted his request twenty weeks before—but once they arrived, it quickly became apparent that something had changed. Officials still denied their entry.

Citing a no-reporters policy, prison officials told Roat that Hacker was off-limits. Roat and Hall knew of Gooden's unfulfilled interest in Hacker and the similarity between the coed murders and Herbert Cobun's untimely demise. Roat hoped Hacker might confide to him what he refused to divulge to the police since Hacker himself got Roat on the waiting list. Now he found himself writing, in editorial form, a report of his failed attempts to sway the prison warden, the director of corrections or the governor to allow his interview to proceed. Federal policy only recently changed to allow reporters to correspond with inmates, but the state stood fast with the idea that Hacker's motivations leaned more toward drawing attention to himself than helping a newsman solve a cold case.

Roat fought the policy. He truly believed Hacker when he told him he knew something about the coed murders and would talk to only Roat or Hall about what he knew. He railed against officials, claiming the setback reeked of hypocrisy. Prosecuting Attorney Laurita previously discounted Hacker's knowledge of the coed murders, saying he questioned the inmate at length and felt that Hacker only wanted attention, but the *Dominion-Post* argued that their newsmen faced a unique type of discrimination and that they only wanted to question Hacker on the behalf of law enforcement to propel the case forward.

Whatever Hacker knew, or compelled him to pretend to know, died with him.

———◆———

The transcript of *Hacker v. West Virginia* highlighted mistaken beliefs I picked up from the newspaper articles chronicling the case. Both Hacker and Snyder testified that they had not dated each other. The love triangle motive was what the papers tried to push—and what the police remembered—to portray a crime that made sense. But what if Hacker's motivation had less to do with lust and more to do with his need to coerce and control women?

Hacker came from a different time. Until 1935, couples dealt with divorces from "bed and board," rather than absolute divorces, for acts of "cruelty" that today we consider domestic violence. A divorce from bed and board meant a legal separation only. The result left women trapped in abusive relationships with no legal recourse or financial way out. Women suffering abuse in dead-end relationships were—and still are—common in Appalachia. It wasn't until 1969 that West Virginia finally decreed that "a reasonable apprehension of bodily harm" was grounds for an absolute divorce. Until Hacker entered his forties, the courts didn't consider beatings to be grounds for dissolving a marriage, no matter how frequent or savage.

If the courts didn't value women's safety, or promote their agency, why would anyone treat them better than the legal standard? Women lost the right to their own property the second they married. Without courts recognizing property ownership, women lacked any real power in the eyes of authorities.

It was easy to imagine Hacker taking Cobun out of the picture to ensure that Snyder remained in his debt. He'd also tried to coax her out of her home at 4:00 a.m. the night he killed Cobun. What if she'd gone outside to help Hacker? Did he plan to murder her as well? The timeline suggests that Cobun was already dead. What could he possibly gain from Snyder coming outside, other than to let her know what he had done before killing her?

If Hacker was capable of killing Cobun and considered killing Snyder and any witnesses who stood in his way, certainly he possessed the ability to kill two coeds for reasons we may never understand.

If Hacker did kill the coeds, did that mean he stashed their heads near the Potomac? Carl's son John Kimble thinks so: "Come back in the spring or summer. I'll take you down there; I think we should look for those heads," he told me with conviction in front of the rest of the Kimble family, who nodded in agreement.

Carl added, "I know where he used to camp. I found a boot up there once when I was pulling lumber. This was before anything happened, so I didn't think anything of it at the time." A boot. Was it a woman's boot? Carl said he couldn't remember if he even examined it that well. But now he wishes he'd paid more attention to it.

Before the day was over, Carl mentioned one more thing that I had not heard before: Hacker used to drive a white car. Ressie Kimble, Harlan's widow, also said, "Bill used to come down here from Fairmont in his big, white car." A white car and a boot. Incredibly coincidental.

I later discovered another connection of Hacker's to the world of the coed murders: He was listed in the 1971 Monticola as a "patron parent," a contributor to WVU, where perhaps some member of his family attended school or, if he had killed the coeds, he was trying to atone for his crimes.

27

"I WAS CONVINCED."

MORGANTOWN

Geoff

Sarah's digging spotlighted the insufficiency of the earlier investigations into Hacker. There was no reason to view the string of unsolved beheadings throughout the twentieth century as necessarily related, but the timing—the lack of unsolved beheadings each time Hacker was in prison—bothered me. It may never be known if Hacker had anything to do with the unsolved murders, but the fact that Hacker hid Cobun's head far from his body and scattered his clothing had some similarity to the murders of Mared and Karen. The boot Carl found on the bank of the Potomac, which could have been one of Mared's missing boots, and Hacker's white Cadillac were suggestive, although we didn't know *when* he had that Cadillac. And there was the contribution to WVU—assuaging his guilt?

Soon after our visit to Pendleton County, we wrapped up the podcast—with the proviso that we were still looking into the crime and new episodes would follow when there were further developments. For months, most of our subsequent discoveries were negative—that is, clues that turned out to be red herrings or dead ends.

For instance, I followed up on dorm sign-in sheets from 1970. Over the last fifty years WVU had expanded, building heavily as the student population doubled. By 2019, WVU had many buildings that were not classrooms or offices but storage areas for the huge amount of paper records that accumulated. But if the 1970 Towers sign-in sheets still existed, we never managed to find them.

Betty Jo Hypes, the retired English instructor who was stalked in 1970 by the young guy who looked goofy, owned a house in Morgantown but now lived in retirement in southern West Virginia. For her whole career, Betty Jo maintained records of her classes and promised to let me look through them next time she was in town. Since all WVU freshmen were required to take Freshman Composition, I hoped to find that either Mared or Karen shared a class with Carolynn Crutchley. Unfortunately, Betty passed, and I never got to check those records.

Nick heard through former colleagues at the Monongalia County Sheriff's Office that detectives there were alerted to a human skull that was part of the estate of a prominent Morgantown veterinarian. Stymied in their efforts to identify the skull, the sheriff's office forwarded it to the FBI labs in Quantico. Pretty much anyone over a certain age in Mon County might think any unidentified human skull *could* be Mared's or Karen's, but as of this writing, the FBI has not identified the skull.

Nick also had come to believe that Herron and Thrasher, working together, might have killed the coeds. I was glad to hear of his suspicions, because I considered them second on my list. Herron and Thrasher lived in the Weirton Mine Section; two perpetrators would have made the "burial" far easier; and they were both experienced hunters, for whom the beheadings would have been simple. Thrasher was not at his job at Sterling Faucet on January 18, 1970, and his car—though probably not burned in the Sterling parking lot—was missing. Thrasher also had several injuries in April 1970, possibly inflicted by the older, cannier Herron to coerce Thrasher's silence. Both men moved away from the area soon after the bodies were found. Nick decided to look more into the possibility that it had been Herron and Thrasher.

Nick also learned from a former law enforcement colleague, a retired Morgantown detective, that the MPD *did* have a file on the coed investigation. This, despite that I was told they did not exist and Sarah's FOIA resulted in claims that there was no such file. Nick was determined to find out if the file did, in fact, exist.

Bob and I continued to speak often, and I kept both him and Jim Wilt apprised of our progress—or lack of it. We—meaning Bob, Chris, Nick, Sarah and I—talked the case over on a few conference calls and tried a few angles, but we still hadn't produced any connection between Mared/Karen and either Carolynn or John Brennan.

One afternoon, I received an unsolicited phone call from a man who'd just seen an article about the podcast. He said he'd known Carolynn well, fifteen years earlier. He told me his name but asked that it be kept confidential.

I was skeptical at first, but the more we talked, with him doing most of the talking, the more convinced I became. He brought up incidents and assessments that he wouldn't have known if he didn't hear about them either from Carolynn or from someone close to either Carolynn or John Brennan. He knew, for instance, that there was a great deal of abuse in the Crutchley family, and, he said, "Mom was the source." The caller cited other facts he shouldn't have known, one based on a Pennsylvania investigation in the 1980s. He also volunteered, without my bringing it up, that Donna June, the sister who had died under mysterious circumstances, had in fact severed her urethra with the glass tube she was masturbating with and bled out on the operating table. That was new information and possibly true.

The most telling information he passed along was that Mildred Crutchley was a nurse. It seems that a member of the extended Crutchley family was diagnosed with porphyria, a blood disorder to which some people are genetically predisposed. One treatment is to drain some blood from the body periodically to reduce toxic buildup. To save medical costs (or maintain a family secret), Mildred may have performed the required blood draws, and John may have witnessed this. He may have learned to draw blood from watching his mother—*a nurse in West Virginia*.

Porphyria has been believed by some ethnographers since the 1960s to be the root of legends about werewolves and vampires and could be the source of the nicknames John and Carolynn sometimes called each other as children: *vampire* and *werewolf*. Crutchley's favorite movie was *Cat People*, in which a brother and sister who are part of an incestuous family transform into black jungle cats to kill.

All of this was interesting, but in the end, the caller's assertions were about the Crutchley family and had nothing to do with John Brennan's possible culpability for killing Mared and Karen.

Around this time, we received a brief Facebook message from someone I met when I was about eleven, when my family lived in the small community of Stewartstown, just north of Morgantown. Apryl and I had lost touch, but she'd recently listened to the podcast because she vividly remembered the murders. She was shaken to hear the name of one of the men she'd worked with in the mid-1980s: John Brennan Crutchley. They both worked for Harris Corporation when John Brennan was arrested in 1985. I was obviously interested in talking with her, and within a few days, we made it happen.

After Apryl and I caught up on our lives and families, we got down to the business of the call. She was often assigned to work teams led by JB, as he was known. JB didn't "cheer up a room" when he entered it, but he always "raised the energy level, made it electric." She described him as "skinny" and "maybe 5'10", maybe a little more," and thought of him as a "toe-walker," because he was so high energy and hyperactive that instead of walking flatfooted he practically sprang forward and would "jump out of his chair" to greet you. She remembered him wearing out-of-style light-blue leisure suits. He rarely got angry, she said, and even when someone on the team messed up, JB would frame it as nonconfrontationally as possible.

JB was generally appreciated for his programming abilities, although not for his managerial "skills." He was often referred to sarcastically by other employees as "our fearless leader." She thought he saw himself as "everybody's buddy" but "other people didn't see it that way." Despite his upbeat manner, he made other people uncomfortable and they kept him at a distance.

She didn't remember ever talking with JB about both of them being from West Virginia, but everybody at work knew it. Some even teased her with it: *Oh, she's from West Virginia, just like JB.*

Around the office, he would come and go unexpectedly. She rarely saw him for long. She remembered one particular night when she was working late and he "came be-bopping in," asking *What are you doing here? Going to be here a while?* She said she was just leaving, actually, and quickly did. She didn't so much feel threatened as she felt a sort of distaste about being alone with him.

In one odd conversation she remembered, she was nearby as JB talked to a couple of coworkers. He was bragging about how his car could not be identified. He'd removed all the identifying tags and seemed to be proud of the fact that people could never pinpoint his specific car. His white car.

What Apryl told me corresponded with what many others had said, from his disconcerting manner to the arrogance and overconfidence, but though we'd found much that implicated Crutchley—he definitely had means, motive and opportunity—we couldn't place him in Morgantown on January 18, 1970, or any other time, really. I'd addressed Sarah's objections—controlling two at once, disposal site too exposed, too much work "burying" them and no evidence of sexual abuse. I no longer believed the murders were too elaborate for a first: If Crutchley carried an elaborate death fantasy inside him since early adolescence, his repeatedly exhibited intelligence, arrogance and, yes, brazenness made the elaborate killings possible.

———————◆———————

We planned to use metal detectors, cadaver dogs or ground-penetrating radar to search the area behind the storage sheds on Route 119 and decided it might be time to try one of those methods. First, though, I drove thirty minutes down Route 119 to check it out once again.

I arrived to see the area behind the sheds, formerly a neatly scooped bowl covered in grasslands and scraggly trees, now stretched flat. Someone had covered the landfill with about fifty feet of fill dirt.

I had a sense of the frustration that must have filled both Wilt and Leatherow: so many murders and a great deal of circumstantial evidence, but no proof. We might keep looking for another twenty years without directly connecting John Brennan Crutchley to Mared and Karen. Crutchley had once told his cellmate that he hadn't killed anyone, but if he had, he was too smart to leave evidence. Criminals often say this, but maybe, in Crutchley's case, it was true.

When the pandemic hit the United States in January 2020 and spread wildly, especially after March, Sarah and I decided there wasn't much more we could do and began to wrap the investigation up.

Until further notice.

But while we were all to some degree locked down, some surprise help came our way. A friend, Lily Mentgen, listened to the podcast and on her own found several useful leads. One she found among the Amazon reviews for *TVND*. She must have read all of them, because deep among them was a review by a woman named Barbara Thayer. Thayer worked with Crutchley at a radio station in Defiance around 1970, and she proved helpful.

"Crutchley was a very strange person with a strange sense of humor," she told me when I reached her by phone. "You know, he would make offhand remarks and sexual remarks…and so, there was, yeah, I felt very uncomfortable around him at times, because he was…strange."

Much of what she said about Crutchley mirrored what Apryl had told me. Both women characterized him as smart and good at what he did, but Barbara did more than confirm what we already knew.

"Do you know if John ever went to visit his sister at WVU?" I asked her at one point.

"Not specifically, but he took a lot of little trips, like day and weekend trips."

So Crutchley *did* travel frequently at the time he lived in Defiance, at the time of the coed murders. "Do you remember what kind of car he drove?"

"My memory bank says it was a little white car....It seems like that's what he drove. That's the first thing that came to my mind."

Bingo. Another white car, this time in 1970. At the time of the coed murders, Crutchley's car matched the description given by Skip and Itsy. We hadn't been able to find a record of the car Crutchley owned, but now we had a witness.

So we didn't have enough to *prove* John Brennan Crutchley killed Mared and Karen, but we had enough circumstantial evidence for a strong case against him. I kept thinking about a conversation with Andrew G. Fusco in the summer of 2019. Fusco was the attorney who defeated David Solomon in his run for Monongalia County prosecutor in 1976, after Solomon's initial conviction of Eugene Paul Clawson.

We talked some about the election, but once that was covered, I turned the conversation toward Crutchley's possible involvement in the murders. I sent Fusco a couple pages summarizing what we had.

"I found the evidence you put in your letter was persuasive," Fusco said. "I was impressed with your research. And in retrospect—and I only know about the Clawson case from what I read in the newspapers—it seems like there's a better case against this guy you point out than there was against Clawson."

"Do you think there would be enough for an indictment of Crutchley? If it happened today."

"You sure got a hell of a circumstantial case. There were a couple of things that you put in your report that were very persuasive. Yes, probably enough for an indictment. Keeping in mind that an indictment is nothing but a formal accusation. After reading [what you sent me], I was convinced."

He then gathered his thoughts and put it to me this way: "Given what has turned up now in regard to Crutchley, it would appear there certainly would have been enough to indict him."

Epilogue

"IT'S NEVER TOO LATE TO UNCOVER THE TRUTH."

THE DISPOSAL SITE IN THE WEIRTON MINE SECTION

December 6, 2020
Sarah and Geoff

Nick is on the other end of a measuring tape reel as Sarah holds the hook end in the middle of Owl Creek Road. Nine months into the pandemic now and it's been a long, gray time for everyone. We have begun to acknowledge that we might never find the ties that bind Mared and Karen to John Brennan Crutchley, or William Bernard Hacker, or Charlie Herron and Eddie Thrasher.

It's just before 8:00 a.m. on a Sunday, the day before the first day of fall hunting season. Nick has secured permission to search the land, but we need to be both thorough and fast. We don't want to be out here when hunting season begins.

Nick's plan is to drop a three-foot rod into the ground as a permanent marker that can be found by a metal detector in the future. We measure from the center of the road, then the distance to the foundation of an old house that stood here until it burned down sometime in the 1960s, and set the pin in the ground beyond it. Sometimes the brush is so thick, we have to hand off the tape toward the middle, reaching under thorns and branches.

"I think I'm a little bit rusty," Nick says. It's been a few years since he was law enforcement, but he still relishes the opportunity to scrutinize a scene again.

Soon, the entire gang assembles at the site: Geoff pulls in, followed by Kendall, followed by Anthony Bohna, yet another volunteer with law enforcement experience who has come forward to work on the case. Anthony steps out of his truck in hunter's orange head-to-toe. Kendall is completely in black, his Nikon hanging from his neck. He takes stock of everyone wearing orange and shrugs: "I guess I'm the only one who wants to get shot. *Please, fucking please*, someone shoot me."

He's half serious. His aspirations include being murdered as a journalist who's uncovering a conspiracy.

Anthony and Nick both bring metal detectors for this venture. To be perfectly clear, none of us are expecting a miracle. It's a semi-secluded spot in the wilderness—we expect false alarms for each spent shotgun shell, bullet casing and beer can left in this section of the woods. But maybe, just maybe, we'll find a hatchet, a gold chain, a class ring, earrings or even a gold filling.

Dry leaves shuffle and metal detectors beep as Anthony starts where both Richard Hall and Dave Campbell—a local man who lived nearby, originally interviewed by Sarah—indicated that the bodies were located. Anthony has a high-powered Whites DFX. The first thing he finds is the casing for a 30-

Nick DeMedici and Kendall Perkinson digging at spot that set off Nick's Garrett AT Pro metal detector. *S. James McLaughlin.*

30. And another. And another. After he finds broken mason jars with lids, it's clear that he's stumbled into the remains of some target practice.

Nick takes his Garrett AT Pro about one hundred feet beyond the area Anthony searches and strings neon orange ribbon between two trees, then ties another small section to it as a sliding indicator to gauge which ground he's covered. Sarah follows Nick out and marks the straight line with the reel tape.

Almost immediately, Nick's machine starts beeping. He turns the sensitivity down, checks it again. He keeps repeating the process to get a feel for how deep the metal object lies. When he's satisfied, he starts shoveling until he uncovers something sinewy. He tugs at it with the shovel's blade. Sarah reaches down and tugs the tendrils until it's coming out of the ground. It looks like a rug.

"You think maybe someone wrapped something in a rug and buried it?"

"Could be a rug, could be the ultimate pickup truck seat cover."

Shoveling again, he uncovers enough that Sarah can pull the fabric out. She holds her breath as the rest of it unfurls from the dirt. No skulls tumble out, no necklaces. Just shards of a broken mirror and the lid of an old Comet cleaner can.

"What kind of asshole throws away a mirror?" Nick jokes.

"The same kind of asshole that throws away a rug, I guess," answers Kendall.

"This is the main theme of the case," Sarah says. "Where we find so much it's slowing us down and we're not any closer to what we're looking for."

Sadly, that's the legacy of this case. We've tracked so much, every viable suspect and red herring the police found in 1970, a couple we've uncovered, and the beeps of metal detectors that promise a class ring or a medallion—or pull tabs, light bulbs, beer cans and rusted fenders.

Kendall leans into the optimism of the situation. "With all this old stuff we're finding close to the surface, it seems like maybe the ground wasn't moved all that much." If the land had been logged and bulldozed, any evidence would have been displaced, maybe even buried on the other side of the plot.

Anthony is used to trolling beaches with his Whites DFX. He says the most common thing he uncovered was bottle caps. "When I used to go hunting when I was growing up, it would always worry me if I was walking in the woods and I saw a piece of garbage bag sticking out of the ground." He lets out a nervous laugh. "It was like, I don't know what's in there!"

"I get it," Sarah tells him. "I feel like I have a responsibility now we're doing this—if there's barrels, I have to look in them, if there's a garbage bag, I have to check it out. I've listened to too many podcasts where bodies were found in the woods."

Sarah has a nagging feeling any time she's in the woods these days. When walking her dog at a local nature preserve, she has intrepidly looked inside barrels that have obviously been discarded. She once saw an episode of *Rescue 911* where a baby was found, still alive in a trash bag, by an older couple. The baby's brother later said to the camera with zero guile, "My mom says thank God for nosy people," and that always stuck with her.

———•———

The biggest issues we face in knowing without a doubt where the bodies were found lay in not only changing topography but also the missing landmarks WVSP cited to triangulate a position: "396 feet due west of the east side of Secondary Route 76/2…34 feet and 6 inches from a creek lane running North of the bodies, and approximately 702 feet from a telephone pole East of Secondary 76/2. The pole is marked 804/4."

Pole 804/4 no longer exists. Dave Campbell and his brother cut it down decades earlier and used it in the construction of a garage. The road felt like the only consistent marker, as the creek could have meandered a few feet in fifty years. What we have is Geoff's recollection of Richard Hall pointing it out and Dave Campbell pointing to the same spot for Nick and Sarah. But two people pointing to the same area didn't make it the *right* area. And the initial spot we'd been directed to felt so vulnerable to passing cars—one of Sarah's objections to Geoff's Crutchley theory.

We look at the color photo taken of the crime scene before the "tomb" was dismantled. The shot came from a higher vantage point than ground level, just a standard lens, not a wide angle, and you could see the creek flowing in the background. There was a large tree about half that distance from the creek that looked sixteen to twenty inches wide with some officers standing near it.

Nick is especially interested in the fence post near the fallen tree that covered the bodies. He climbs the hillside and searches for the vantage point in the photo. Covered in burs but excited, he shows off the picture he's taken; it is very similar to the 1970 photographs, but the thickness of the brush makes it difficult to see the creek on the other side.

Above: WVSP troopers standing near "tomb" in 1970. *WVSP*.

Opposite, top: Were these part of 1970's fallen tree? *WVSP*.

Opposite, bottom: A 1970 flyover photo of the disposal site. *West Virginia Publishing Company*.

Facing north, Geoff looks at the copse between Nick's vantage and the creek. It feels odd, being here, on the spot first introduced to him by Richard Hall in 2006. The topography doesn't quite match his memory, and the tree in the picture has either been logged or fallen due to age. "This all could have been moved around," Geoff says. "A lot of this stuff—we're just making guesses."

And that's exactly how it feels in that moment, still missing important pieces of the whole picture. A strip of land with obvious equipment traffic indentations stretches out, following the curve of the creek, and tucks into the hillside, away from the main road. *Close enough to the creek to drag out the heavy slabs of rock, and less vulnerable to passing traffic, but still a long haul to drag dead weight, unless he marched them out there while they were still alive.*

But the 1970 photos showed an undeveloped dirt logging road that branched off Owl Creek Road and followed Owl Creek upstream. The little road was on the other side of the stream from where the gang searches and measures, and the old road is essentially gone now. In 1970, it was in much better shape. If the killer(s) used that road, he wouldn't have had to

travel far, but he would have had to cross the creek—carrying the bodies. As Nick said one time when he and Geoff were discussing the theory, "That is absolutely what I would do for two reasons. My car would be concealed from main route traffic, and if I am moving bodies, I'm doing it downhill."

Nick is energized with the potential of the new location and sets about with his metal detector. "Look at that! It's barbed wire! I think we found a former fence post." We need to establish a fence line, otherwise the post and barbed wire could have been discarded in a pile. He takes another look at the photo and asks Sarah where she thinks the second post in the picture would be in relation to where we stand.

Sarah points northeast. "It looks like it crosses the creek at an angle."

Picking up where he left off, Nick aims the detector toward the northeast side of the last find. We watch in silence as the beeps set off. A plane flies overhead, the only sign of life outside our little group in the woods. Nick sifts through the leaves and into the dirt, pulling out nail after nail and more barbs from the rusted remains of barbed wire.

———— ♦ ————

We stand in the middle of the road and weigh our options. Sarah gestures at the brand-new culvert. Nick takes out his notebook and looks at his diagram, then back at the scene. We can hear hunters shooting their guns in the distance, maybe a few hills over, sighting them in, preparing for the first day of hunting season. We don't have much time.

"In the photos," Anthony points to the center of the property facing us, "it looks like there's a lot more saplings now than there was. I'm wondering if they didn't just go straight on through. I mean even if you—if you're going in at the right on the road, are you off by twenty feet? Well, more than that."

It is Nick's turn to shake his head. "Yeah, well, I always go back to the fact that there were only six autopsy photos taken. That's unheard of."

Sarah speaks up. "Well, that's what we have because they were exhibits, right?"

"There should be like sixty."

"There probably are."

"I would say, with a high degree of certainty, that there's not. That's what I wanted to see, and the only ones that were physically present were the ones you guys already had." He is talking about the WVSP case materials Chris Berry borrowed from the Morgantown Detachment. "'Cause I think you guys would have gotten those from the FOIA request, right?"

Sarah shakes her head. "No, uh, the reports that we have are the ones Richard had. We FOIA'd MPD, the sheriff's office, and the FBI."

"The sheriff's department wouldn't have had anything—I know for a fact. Morgantown, I don't know, but Richard would have had everything. As a lieutenant colonel, if he didn't have what he wanted, he could have got it."

Nick walks off toward the 296-foot mark, leaving Anthony and Sarah to decide for themselves. Geoff first visited the site with Richard Hall, who insisted that the disposal site was 296 feet from the telephone pole, but the WVSP report said it was 396 feet. Anthony purses his lips and decides to charge through. "Let's just measure from here, then I'll measure from the right entrance and we'll see where we end up at 296 feet and 396 feet."

"Let's do it!"

The first 296 feet puts them exactly at the spot pointed out by Richard Hall and Dave Campbell, the area that has already been searched. Kendall and Sarah take the reel tape and go 100 feet more. Sarah takes some vantage points from a ledge that hovers over the 396-foot view and goes slightly farther and takes another on the section close to the creek at over 400 feet. She walks back to the party and shows Kendall and Nick the shots.

Nick takes the phone. "This is at 396 feet?"

Kendall interjects about the original crime scene photo. "The camera wasn't using a wide angle."

Sarah swipes the photo to the next shot without the wide angle. The photo from 1970 made the depth of field look different than the photos the gang is taking, making a close comparison difficult. Kendall shields the phone screen and lets out an exasperated sigh. "Hard to say."

If he was 396 feet from the road, or really, even 296 feet, one man would have enough privacy to take his time. And with the creek so much closer at those ranges, he could have pulled rocks out and not had to drag them 100 feet before he lifted them up over the bodies.

"It looks clear enough to detect though. You want to start sweeping?" Kendall offers the metal detector to Sarah.

"Sure." Sarah lifts the machine and tests the land in small sweeps. She's never had good luck using one before and is concerned that she is going to have issues with it. It isn't long before the device beeps at a section of the ground. She digs, testing after each swipe. Still beeping. The detector says there is something made of iron about six inches into the ground. She keeps going until she finds it: another nail.

The next time the detector goes off just over a foot away from the first hole. Pulling out the dirt, shovel full by shovel full, Sarah uncovers a couple

2020: A last look at the site where Mared and Karen were found in 1970. *S. James McLaughlin.*

of pieces of cloth. One red, one blue. Maybe another rug? A piece of white comes to the surface. She pulls on it with her rubber-gripped gloves. It feels flexible, like a piece of vinyl. Maybe a car mat. A white car mat. From a Cadillac? She digs deeper and wider, avoiding the rocks and dirt with the detector.

Kendall comes around, and together, they dig the hole wider, trying to find the edge of the mat. They uncover more cloth, this time a gray color, and the detector keeps indicating that there is something metal still under the dirt.

Nick pulls out a mass and takes a trowel to it. "This is too heavy. It's got to be metal."

Sarah takes the other detector and hovers it over. It beeps. It's a hunk of metal for sure.

"Take it down to the creek, rinse it off."

As soon as the ball hits the water, the dirt plumes out. Sarah submerges the mass and rubs off as much mud as she can, then moves to a clearer spot in the creek and rinses it over again until teeth emerge from the mud. It looks like a small wheel with bulldozer tread. It's hefty, too, like a large caster wheel.

The rest of the day pans out exactly the same, more digging, hopes rising with each beep, but no hatchets, no fillings, no necklaces, no earrings and no class rings. Just garbage and spent shell casings scattered with more barbed wire. Even through all the ups and downs from the search, it feels good to get answers, even if they are "no."

———◆———

We call it a little after 3:00 p.m. Sarah goes home and calls Kelly Ayers, the regional forensics specialist and certified crime scene specialist who has been a part of the investigation since the early days of the podcast. She and Kelly stayed in touch, and Sarah wants to pass along the latest news—or lack of it.

"You know, I still think you guys should try ground-penetrating radar," Kelly says.

"Nick said that when he was a cop, they had to get a group of professionals from Arizona out here to do that. Even if we could rent the equipment, we'd need to be trained on how to use it."

"Oh, that's too bad. Just imagine what that might find! You know, I've still been thinking about how the cuts are made so close to the shoulders might indicate that a Vietnam vet was the killer. The investigator that looked at the files you guys compiled—that was his first thought. They were trained to cut close to the shoulders when they decapitated Viet Cong."

"I've been thinking about the lack of blood, too. We know they were killed the night they were taken because the food in their stomachs was what was served on campus, but what if the killer let them freeze in the cold weather before he severed their heads? It might explain the lack of blood."

"That's true. And if they were already dead, there wouldn't be blood squirting all over when he cut into them. I recently looked at a case where a girl was decapitated by a guy wire when she stuck her head out the car window. Her body was still in the car, seat belt still on, but there was blood everywhere. The cupholders were full of blood—it was massive. She wasn't even driving that fast."

———◆———

We don't want to give up, but there isn't much within our power left to do. We still want more definitive answers and will continue to look for them, but there comes a time when you know you've mostly run out of options. The best you can do is hope that you've collected enough evidence, gathered enough facts and looked hard enough at what's left that you can at least act as a steward of the case to hand it off to someone with more time, money and resources. And more people keep coming forward. That's all we can hope for: that we've done the hundreds of hours and called out loud enough that someone down the line might pick up where we left off, determine some new trail and follow it to its conclusion. It's never too late to uncover the truth.

INTERVIEWEES

Thanks to all of you who made yourselves available and, in doing so, helped us make this book as accurate and thorough as we could make it. You helped bring fifty years of investigations to life. We tried to list everyone but have undoubtedly left some out. You might be one of them. If you are, we apologize profusely.

Amma*
Davis Appel*
Kelly Ayers
Valeena Beety
Chris Berry
George Bradshaw
Nancy Burkheimer
Vic Burkheimer
Patrick Buzzini
Dave Campbell
George Castelle
Russell Clawges
Derek Clawson
Kenneth Cole
Debbie Cramer*
Mary Lucille DeBerry
Nick DeMedici

Korshi Dosoo
Jim Elkins
Ray Evans
Bess Ferrell
John Francis
Chapman Hood Frazier
Andrew G. Fusco
Barb Gooden
Preston Gooden
Jan Graber
Richard M. Hall
Larry Herald
Charlie Herron
R. Warren Hoover
Betty Jo Hypes
Hoppy Kercheval
Carl Kimble

John Kimble

Ressie Kimble

Bob Leatherow

Trish Marchio

Mike Mays

Doug McCarty

Debbie Miller

Margie Miller

Freda Moore

Sally Musick

Terri Nahari

Charlie Nash

Holly Naylor

Ed Preston

Mary Beth Taylor Renner

Ponch Reyes

Dan Ringer

Ron Rittenhouse

Hugh Rogers

Evelyn Ryan

Jim Shriver

Philip Shuman

Tom Sloane

John Spraggins

Grant Stewart

Danny Swiger

Cathy Teets

Barbara Thayer

Tyrone Trujillo

Sam Webster

Jim Wilt

Tom Wojcik

Ray Yackel

*indicates pseudonym

And to the numerous others who did not think they should be mentioned or wished to remain anonymous: We are forever in your debt.

We were assisted by several volunteer beta readers. You all read early versions of parts of this book, and we appreciated all of your suggestions, quibbles and corrections. You helped smooth our rough manuscript, and for that, we salute you.

Kathleen Cash

George Castelle

Peggy Curtis

Jim Elkins

Paul Fetty

Kathie Forman

Winston Fuller

Candace Jordan

George Lies

Lucia Lies

Scott Marsh

Karen McLaughlin

Phyllis Moore

Mark Pellegrin

J. Kendall Perkinson

David Schles

Therese Vanzo

Finally, we want to thank the following for the images that appear in the book:

The West Virginia Newspaper Publishing Company
1251 Earl L. Core Road
Morgantown, WV 26505
Publishers of the *Morgantown Post*, the *Dominion-News* and the *Dominion-Post*

Private photographers:
        Mark Crabtree
        S. James McLaughlin
        Holly Naylor

INDEX

A

Apollo 13 124–125
Associated Press (AP) 127, 130, 143, 179–181
Aucremanne, Stephanie 138, 322–323
Ayers, Kelly 321, 397–398

B

Bailes, Candace "Candy" 76–78, 133–135
Berry, Cpl. Chris 351–354, 394
Best, Nancy Elizabeth 50–51
Blankenship, Maxine 38–41, 88–90, 103–105, 256, 287
bombing(s) 36, 43–44, 66–67, 70, 72, 76, 82, 183, 188
Bonar, Col. Robert L. 85, 87, 130, 152, 174, 180, 182, 187–188, 190–191, 224, 254, 320

Bowers, William A. 115–116, 133–135, 152
Brevard County, Florida 247–249, 305–308, 312, 343, 356
Burns, Paulette "Itsy" 55–56, 58, 83, 173, 213, 344
busing on campus 34, 53, 56, 66, 75, 125–126, 229

C

Cain, Glen Franklin 119, 120–122, 125, 259
Camp Muffly 105, 143
campus life 66, 72, 75, 127, 150
Carter, Dr. Donald 154–157, 231
Casazza, Lawrence "Larry" 48, 83
Castelle, George 237–243, 267
Charleston Gazette 119, 182
city council 44, 66, 72, 73, 126, 148–149
Claro, Jeanne 322

Clawson, Eugene Paul 197–243, 250, 253–255, 262–263, 278, 283, 313, 336

Cobun, Herbert 184–185, 280–282, 371–374, 377–380

Cole, Kenneth "Kenny" 92, 96–97, 150–152, 266, 272–273, 297, 328

Combined Civics Club Committee (CCCC) 188–190

Committee of Evaluation of Student Safety and Welfare 148

confession(s) 192–193, 197–205, 209–210, 213, 214, 216–217, 219, 222, 225–230, 233–236, 238–243, 247, 262, 278

copper plate 144–146, 152, 256, 332, 338–342, 348–349, 362–364

corroborating evidence 7, 192–193, 207, 210, 214, 262

Costianes, Dr. Elias 49, 64, 72, 79–80, 142, 188, 256–261, 263

crimes against women 76–78, 81, 137–139, 141

Criminal Investigation Bureau (CIB) 86, 122, 160, 173–174, 207

Crutchley, Carolynn Adele 309, 329, 344, 351, 354, 358, 365–366

Crutchley, John Brennan 249, 298, 301–302, 305, 308–310, 313, 314, 317, 331, 343–346, 351, 355–359, 365–369, 383, 387

cult involvement 109, 146, 156, 159, 181, 243, 315

Cumberland, Maryland 94, 101, 105, 110, 132, 164–165, 167, 178–180

D

Dafts, the 68, 275, 286, 324–328

Daily Athenaeum 63, 127, 133, 153

DeMedici, Nick 354, 366, 367, 369, 383, 388–395

DeYoung, Donna 53, 57–58, 61, 64, 68–69, 72, 75, 79, 81, 82–85, 97–98, 99, 110

Dominion-News 42, 43–45, 70–73, 130–131, 133, 148, 214

Dosoo, Dr. R. Korshi 342, 347–349

E

Evans, Ray 43, 44, 133–134

F

Fairmont Times 130, 181

fear on campus 34, 76, 82–85, 94, 127, 132–133, 136–139, 148–149, 158–160

Federal Bureau of Investigation (FBI) 60, 61–62, 64–65, 67–69, 71, 75–76, 92, 93, 131, 142, 144–146, 154, 198, 270, 297, 305–307, 322–323

Ferrell, Bess 24–25, 60, 66, 71, 74–78, 83, 88, 93, 127, 265–266, 335

Ferrell, Richard 24–25, 66, 74, 84, 263, 335

Ferrell's dream, Bess 277–278

feud, newspapers v. police 131, 143, 152–153

Friend, Edward 202–204

fright calls 127

Fusco, Andrew G. 215, 387

G

Gerkin III, William Ray 158–163, 182, 187, 273, 286–287, 291–302, 302, 351

Glass, David L. 213, 230, 232, 233–235

Gooden, Trooper Preston "P.B." "Pres" 82–90, 92, 95–96, 97–98, 101–104, 109–114, 117–122, 129, 138–139, 141, 143–146, 147, 154–157, 159–160, 165–167, 188–192, 320, 324–325, 379

Goshen Road 97, 102, 105, 111, 268, 290

H

Hacker, William Bernard 184–186, 187, 193, 280–285, 298, 364, 374–382

Halleck Road 102–104, 265–268, 271, 278–279, 290

Hall, Lt. Col. Richard Mansfield 129, 142, 201, 224–227, 228–230, 236, 247, 250–255, 257–288, 291–303

Harpe, Felton 206–208, 213, 229, 230, 231–232, 233–235

Hayes, Steve 47, 67, 87–88

Heis, Sgt. Det. John 59, 71, 74–75, 86–88, 93, 99, 102, 146, 152

Herald, Sgt. Lawrence "Larry" 88–90, 93, 95, 97–98, 101, 102–104, 109–114, 117–118, 119–122, 128–130, 136–137, 142–144, 147, 226, 351

Herron, Charles "Charlie" 129, 264, 268, 271, 273–276, 286–288, 296–298, 351, 383

High Street 37, 53, 54, 55, 56, 59, 80, 81, 211

Hoover, Rev. Richard Warren 177, 178–181

Huntington Herald-Dispatch 129–130

Hypes, Betty Jo 81–82, 359, 366

I

investigation, criminal 33, 82, 91, 109, 128–130, 256–257, 259, 296

J

Johnson, Richard 133–135

K

Kimble, Carl 184, 370–371, 374–375, 381

Klinefelter Syndrome 218

Kroll, John Leroy 164, 165–167, 170–172

L

Lantz, Thomas "Tom" 139–140, 322–323
Laurita, Joseph "Joe" A. 42–45, 67, 72, 179–180, 183, 190, 379, 380
Leatherow, Robert "Bob" 343–346, 355–359, 367, 386
letter, DeYoung's to J. Edgar Hoover 68–69
letters, anonymous 187
Letters, Triangle 95, 100, 101, 129, 131, 152, 154–157, 160, 165, 175, 181, 231, 330

M

Malarik, Dr. Edward 24, 48, 62, 64–65, 74, 83, 93, 115, 117–118
Malarik, Margaret 24, 48, 60, 71, 74, 83, 93, 127
Manson, Charles "Charlie" 37, 115, 156, 181, 356, 367
Marshall University 26, 99
McClure, Gwen 57, 59, 61, 67, 83
Mephistopheles 360–361, 363
Metropolitan Theater 53, 55, 213
Mitchell, Sgt. William H. 82–85, 88, 91, 95, 165–167, 185, 207–208, 210–211, 328
Mongiello, John A. "Munch" or "Munchy" 47–50, 53, 79, 84, 97, 142
Moore, Freda 23–24, 25
Moore Jr., Arch A. 43, 76, 93, 190
Morgantown Post 44, 45, 63, 73, 214
motor pool 125–126

Mozingo, Sgt. Robert "Bob" 119–120, 122, 130, 146, 154–157, 158–160, 164–165, 171–172, 178–179, 184, 188, 189

P

Palmer, MPD Chief Bennie F. 59, 64–65, 93, 139
Personal Rapid Transit (PRT) 35, 149–150, 323
petitions, student 66, 72, 75–76, 148–149
polygraph 98, 166–167, 182, 185–186, 193, 231, 328
profiling, criminal 154–157
protests, student 148–149

R

Ressler, Robert 197, 297–298, 304, 355, 358, 367
reward money 44, 45, 65, 66, 72, 73, 81, 99, 127, 180, 232
Ringer, Dan 109, 216, 239
Rittenhouse, Ron 42–43, 111–112, 130, 183, 321
Rogers, Trooper James "Jim" 94, 160–161, 170–172
Route 119 71, 88, 92, 95, 101, 102, 115, 150, 162, 214, 230, 264, 287, 386
rumors surrounding the case 34, 45, 53, 61, 82, 89, 109, 126, 127, 144, 152, 158–159, 183, 215, 222, 230, 275, 327, 336, 337, 358, 375

S

sator square 340–342, 347–349, 360–362
Shade Effect, the 253–254, 286, 287, 302
Shade, Trooper Donald 207, 208, 210–211, 224–225, 229, 253–254, 330, 337
Smith, Cindi 76–78, 133–135
Solomon, David 133, 197–202, 204, 214–215, 229, 233, 240
Sparks, Cpl. William "Bill" 59, 111, 163, 188
Spitznogle, Mary Kathryn "Kathy" 58, 60–61, 83–84, 97–98, 105, 110, 125, 133–134
stressor 222–223
Students of Psychic Science 175–177, 181, 183
Swiger, Sgt./Lt. Daniel "Danny" 278–283, 285–286, 299–301, 306, 309, 310–313, 343

T

Thrasher, Charles Edward "Eddie" 102–105, 128–129, 256, 271, 273, 281, 284, 286–288, 296–297, 298, 383
Towers dormitories 126–127, 148, 353
Townes, William A. 44–45, 67, 70, 133–135
transportation on campus 53, 56, 66, 72, 75, 125–126, 148–150
triangles, case linked to 152, 179, 180

Tritchler, Gene Edward 76–78, 133–135
Trujillo, Tyrone 334–337

U

United Press International (UPI) 37, 187
University Avenue 48, 52–53, 56, 76–78, 94, 227, 292

W

Weirton Mine Section 68, 92, 102, 103, 111, 125, 150, 181, 236, 250–252, 264, 266, 268, 271, 272, 282, 283, 288, 305, 321
Werner, Richard 25, 64, 66, 75, 79, 117–118, 187–192, 191
Westchester Hall 40, 50, 55–56, 57, 59, 60, 66, 72, 76, 82–84, 88, 90, 94, 97, 103, 109, 125–126, 142, 235
West, Lt. Charles "Charlie" 160, 163, 173–179
West Virginia Newspaper Publishing Company 135
West Virginia State Police for a Better West Virginia, The 187–188
whistleblower speech 188–192
Willey Avenue 209, 234
Willey Street 48, 54, 56, 72, 79, 80, 211, 227, 234, 258, 288–289
Wilt, James "Jim" 333, 335–336, 354, 369, 383, 386

Y

Yost, Norman 93, 190

Z

Zinn, John 143, 151, 265

ABOUT THE AUTHORS

An editor and writer for over thirty years, GEOFFREY C. FULLER has edited dozens of books, mostly nonfiction, and written articles for many literary and commercial magazines, from *Appalachian Heritage* to *Dirt Bike*. He has also contributed short stories and chapters to twenty-five fiction and nonfiction books and authored a novel, *Full Bone Moon*. In 2014, he co-wrote the e-book *The Savage Murder of Skylar Neese* (no. 12 on the *New York Times* list) and the more comprehensive *Pretty Little Killers*, both about the 2012 murder of Skylar Neese. Along the way, he was the only person in West Virginia ever awarded prestigious writing fellowships by the West Virginia Commission on the Arts in all three prose categories: fiction, nonfiction and memoir. He lives in Morgantown.

S. JAMES MCLAUGHLIN is a podcast producer of *Appalachian Mysteria*. Written and produced in West Virginia, the series covers unresolved cases in Appalachia, including the murders of WVU freshmen Mared Malarik and Karen Ferrell in 1970.

The interest started with conversations about the murders with her parents at a young age, then meeting a fellow WVU freshman whose father served in the National Guard and searched for the coeds. Now, an investigative podcast and a true crime book later, the interest changed into a mission to give an in-depth view of the crime and those affected. McLaughlin attended both West Virginia and Fairmont State Universities, studying journalism and earning a degree in graphic design/engineering. She lives in Fairmont with her husband and dog.

Visit us at
www.historypress.com